BV
3773
.C35

Carwardine, Richard.
  Transatlantic revivalism : popular
evangelicalism in Britain and America,
1790-1865 / Richard Carwardine.
Westport, Conn. : Greenwood Press,
1978.
  xviii, 249 p. : ill. ; 25 cm.
(Contributions in America history ; no.
75 ISSN 0084-9219)
  Bibliography: p. [231]-236.
  Includes index.
  1. Revivals--United States--History.
2. Revivals--Great Britain--History.
3. Evangelicalism--Great Britain--
History. 4. Evangelicalism--United
States--History. 5. United States--
Church histor   y. 6. Great Britain--
Church histor   y. I. Title

05 JUL 79   4037176   OMMMxc   77-94740

Transatlantic Revivalism

Recent Titles in Contributions in American History
Series Editor: Jon L. Wakelyn

Essays on American Music
Garry E. Clarke

Culture and Diplomacy: The American Experience
Morrell Heald and Lawrence S. Kaplan

Voting in Provincial America: A Study of Elections in the Thirteen Colonies,
1689-1776
Robert J. Dinkin

The French Forces in America, 1780-1783
Lee Kennett

Cold War Political Justice: The Smith Act, the Communist Party, and
American Civil Liberties
Michal R. Belknap

The Many-Faceted Jacksonian Era: New Interpretations
Edward Pessen, editor

Manning the New Navy: The Development of a Modern Naval Enlisted
Force, 1899-1940
Frederick S. Harrod

Riot, Rout, and Tumult: Readings in American Social and Political Violence
Roger Lane and John J. Turner, Jr., editors

The Long Shadow: Reflections on the Second World War Era
Lisle A. Rose

The Politics of Wartime Aid: American Economic Assistance to France and
French Northwest Africa, 1940-1946
James J. Dougherty

The Oil Cartel Case: A Documentary Study of Antitrust Activity in the
Cold War Era
Burton I. Kaufman

The Social Bases of City Politics: Atlanta, 1865-1903
Eugene J. Watts

Two Nations Over Time: Spain and the United States, 1776-1977
James W. Cortada

Trans-atlantic Revivalism

POPULAR EVANGELICALISM IN BRITAIN AND AMERICA, 1790-1865

Richard Carwardine

Contributions in American History, Number 75

GREENWOOD PRESS
WESTPORT, CONNECTICUT • LONDON, ENGLAND

Library of Congress Cataloging in Publication Data

Carwardine, Richard.
    Transatlantic revivalism.

    (Contributions in America history ; no. 75 ISSN
0084-9219)
    Bibliography: p.
    Includes index.
    1. Revivals—United States—History.
2. Revivals—Great Britain—History.
3. Evangelicalism—Great Britain—History.
4. Evangelicalism—United States—History.
5. United States—Church history. 6. Great
Britain—Church history. I. Title.
BV3773.C35   269'.2'0973   77-94740
ISBN 0-313-20308-3

Library of Congress Catalog Card Number: 77-94740
ISBN: 0-313-20308-3
ISSN: 0084-9219

First published in 1978

Greenwood Press, Inc.
51 Riverside Avenue, Westport, Connecticut 06880

Printed in the United States of America

10 9 8 7 6 5 4 3 2 1

FOR MY PARENTS

Contents

Figures   *ix*

Tables   *xi*

Preface   *xiii*

Key to Manuscript Collections   *xvii*

Part One   "The American Short Cut to Heaven"

1. The New-Measure Revivalism in the United States   3

Part Two   Voices from America

2. English Calvinists and the New Revivalism   59

3. The New Revivalism in Wales and Scotland   85

4. James Caughey and Methodist Revivalism   102

5. "A Great National Mercy": Charles Finney's Itinerancy
   in Britain, 1849-51   134

Part Three   "Transatlantic Marvels"

6. Transatlantic Revival   159

   Conclusion   198

   Notes   *201*

   Bibliography   *231*

   Index   *237*

Figures

Figure 1.   MEC Membership in New York City and in the Rest of New York State As a Percentage of Their Respective Populations, 1810-65   30

Figure 2.   MEC Membership in Boston and in the Rest of New England As a Percentage of Their Respective Populations, 1810-65   31

Figure 3.   American and British Methodist Membership As a Percentage of the Population, 1801-70   48

Figure 4.   Baptist Growth Rates, 1834-55 (England) and Combined Methodist Growth Rates, 1830-55 (England and Wales)   81

Figure 5.   Wesleyan Methodist Growth Rates in Seven Towns and Cities Visited by James Caughey, 1842-46   114

Figure 6.   MEC and MECS Growth Rates, 1846-60   161

Figure 7.   Selected British Nonconformist Growth Rates, 1855-65   194

Tables

Table 1. Percentage of Methodists in the Total Population of
Baltimore, Cincinnati, and New York City, 1820-60   28

Table 2. Country of Birth of Men Entering the MEC Itinerancy,
1771-1865   33

Table 3. British-born Methodists Entering the MEC Itinerancy,
1771-1865   35

Table 4. Birthplace of British-born Ministers of the MEC,
1771-1865   36

Table 5. Place of Conversion and First Preaching of British-born
Ministers of the MEC, 1771-1865   38

Table 6. Annual Growth Rates of American and British Methodists,
1791-1865   46

Table 7. Wesleyan Methodist Membership and Growth Rates
in Seven Towns and Cities Visited by James Caughey,
1842-46   112

Table 8. James Caughey's Sheffield Campaign, 12 May to
8 September 1844   123

Preface

One manifestation of what has been described as "the recovery of American religious history" since the 1930s is a substantial corpus of literature on revivalism.[1] The works in question vary in aim and emphasis but share a common premise: revivalism, far from being an aberration in American life, has played a central role in the shaping of this society and culture. In the first half of the nineteenth century, as Perry Miller has argued, the pulse of revivals was for Americans "the one clearly given truth of their society"; it was "a central mode of this culture's search for national identity."[2] Americans saw their voluntarist, revivalist religious society as distinctive and separate from the church life of Europe. But in fact the umbilical cord had never been completely broken. The experience of evangelicals in the eighteenth century—when Methodism made its impact on America and when the literature of the colonial Awakening was hungrily read by British audiences—attests to the transatlantic character of the First Great Awakening. This closely related British and American evangelical Protestant community did not perish with the Revolution.

This book focuses on that community during the early and mid-nineteenth century. It aims, first, to examine American revivalism at a crucial stage of its development. During the Second Great Awakening, from the 1790s to the 1830s and 1840s, the less traditionalist, more aggressive American evangelicals came to review their approach to "means"—the methods that might legitimately be used to produce conversions. By the 1850s in most evangelical churches a more calculated, more obviously "worked-up" revivalism had replaced what traditionalists regarded as "waiting for God's good time."

This study seeks, secondly, to show the significant effect of these changes on British evangelical society.[3] It would be a mistake to suppose that American influence was limited to the brief appearance of a few secondary figures who failed to touch the mainstream of British evangelical life. From the time

of Crazy Dow's stimulus to camp meetings and his role in the emergence of
the earthy evangelism of Primitive Methodism to the more reputable, better-
organized American contribution to the British revival movement of 1859-
63, there was a continuing American presence. Writers and revivalists of the
status of Asahel Nettleton, Calvin Colton, William Buell Sprague, Edward
Norris Kirk, Edward Payson Hammond, and Walter and Phoebe Palmer
considerably affected the shape of British evangelical thinking and practice.
Even more dramatic was the impact of James Caughey and Charles G. Finney.
Exact measures of their influence are not easily fashioned, but the sale of
over eighty thousand copies of a single edition of Finney's *Lectures on
Revivals of Religion* by 1850 and the twenty thousand conversions claimed
by Caughey during his first visit alone give some indication of the dimensions of their appeal. In midcentury-Britain Finney and Caughey were
household names in the extensive subculture of Dissent.

Thirdly, an investigation of these American influences in Britain throws
light on the revivalism of that subculture during a period recognized as
enormously significant in the history of British popular religion. Revivalism
never held as religiously prominent or socially acceptable a place in Britain
as in North America, but it was deemed a primary distinguishing characteristic
of all properly evangelical churches. During the period under consideration
hundreds of thousands, many of whom dated their conversions to a time of
revival, joined these churches. Yet later denominational and local church
historians often under emphasized or deliberately ignored a side of evangelical
life whose emotionalism, disorder, and impropriety were an embarrassment
to them. More recent historical scholarship has recognized the importance
of revivals in the last century, but the historians in question have been more
interested in tracing their secular implications, their impact on church growth,
or their role in church schism than in tackling the subject directly.

Finally, a study of American evangelicals at work in a different, though
not wholly alien, culture offers opportunities for comparison and contrast.
There was much that united British and American revival communities in
the period under consideration: a common attachment to the saving of the
individual's soul, a common desire for church growth, and a common concern over the standing of evangelicalism in an era of "infidel" threats and
urban challenge. But there were also critical dissimilarities. The dramatic
contrast between the attention afforded revivalism by American historians
and its comparative neglect in British historical circles is more than accidental.
It reflects the fact that revivalism was at the center of American social and
religious life during this period but stood at the periphery of the British. In
one country, under a voluntaristic church system, revivals became an orthodoxy; in the other, under the critical eye of a church establishment, they
never achieved total respectability. This contrast needs to be explored.

The present study does not begin to examine the host of minor sects that contributed to the rich texture of transatlantic life, although fortunately the more fascinating of these—the Mormons, the Millerites, and the Campbellites—already have their historians.[4] This is an unrepentantly revival-focused study of those major evangelical denominations, particularly the Methodists, which in both countries provided the primary expression of evangelicalism and which gave it its cutting edge.

Finally, a word about usage. Contemporaries used the term "revival" to describe two phenomena. Frequently it referred to a period of unusually intense "religious interest" in a single church, a time when penitents sought counsel and salvation in above-average numbers. It was entirely possible for the revival to be restricted to that church, leaving the denomination as a whole and the wider community unaffected. The term could also mean what might be more accurately called a revival movement, or the multiplication of local revivals over a broad geographical area for a prolonged period of perhaps several years. Such was the revival of 1857-58 in the United States. To avoid pedantry I have not distinguished between the two concepts in every case, but the particular meaning involved will be clear from the context.

Though I have incurred many debts in researching this book, it is easy to know whom to thank first. Anyone who has had the good fortune to have been taught by John Walsh will realize just how much his students owe him. As my undergraduate tutor and graduate supervisor, he both kindled my interest in American history and showed me that transatlantic revivalism was a subject rich in possibilities. His advice, encouragement, and tactful but telling criticism have been a constant stimulus. If the book does not fall too far short of his own standards I shall be well pleased. Richard Dupuis's infectious enthusiasm for Finney and Finneyana was matched by his generosity in lending me quantities of contemporary materials and in offering considerable bibliographic help; he also scrutinized the manuscript and saved me from many errors. So too did Clyde Binfield; I have been fortunate in having as a colleague someone so deeply knowledgeable about British Nonconformity. Charles Sellers and Roger Sharp gave the American sections a close reading; Donald Dayton, M. E. Dieter, William Gienapp, Brian Harrison, Steven Maizlish, Richard Mullen and J. E. B. Munson provided references; Bruce Ortwine helped with the research into American Methodist ministers; Caroline Davies contributed the translations from Welsh. My wife, Linda Kirk, does not type or compile indexes; instead she has proved an unwearying and most exacting critic of the manuscript. She, Michael Bentley, Mark Greengrass, and R. I. Moore helped with proofreading. To all these, and others unmentioned here, I am deeply grateful.

Amongst the many librarians who have provided help I should like to thank in particular the staff of the Bodleian Library, Oxford; Martha Slotten of Dickinson College; Kenneth Rowe and Louise Capron of Rose Memorial Library, Drew University; the staff of the Graduate Theological Union Library, Berkeley; Dr. John Bowmer and his staff at the Methodist Church Archives (when at City Road, London); Ruth Wells and the staff of the Inter-Library Loans Department of Sheffield University Library; Edward Lyons and others of the George Arents Research Room, Syracuse University Library; and Evelyn Sutton of the United Methodist Church Commission on Archives and History, Lake Junaluska.

The research for this book was begun while I was the Ochs-Oakes Senior Scholar at The Queen's College, Oxford, and at the University of California at Berkeley. I am obliged to the late George W. Oakes and his brother John B. Oakes, who founded the scholarship, and to Queen's, the University of California, and the Social Science Research Council, who financed my studies for three years. Since then I have gratefully received financial assistance from the University of Sheffield Research Fund and from the United States-United Kingdom Educational Commission, which awarded me a Fulbright Travel Grant in 1974.

The following institutions kindly gave me permission to use extracts from items in their manuscript collections: the Special Collections Library at Dickinson College, Drew University Library, the Archives and Library at Oberlin College, and the George Arents Research Library for Special Collections at Syracuse University. Parts of chapters one, three and six first appeared in the *Journal of American History*, vol. 59 (1972), in the *Journal of Ecclesiastical History*, vol. 29 (1978), and in Derek Baker, ed., *Studies in Church History*, vol. 15; I am grateful to the editors concerned for giving permission to reprint here sections of the original articles.

Sheffield
January 1978   Richard Carwardine

Key to Manuscript Collections

B-WL   John Blackburn Papers, Dr. Williams's Library, London.

B-DC   Thomas E. Bond Papers, Dickinson College, Carlisle, Pennsylvania.

C-OC   Henry Cowles Papers, Oberlin College, Oberlin, Ohio.

F-OC   Charles G. Finney Papers, Oberlin College, Oberlin, Ohio.

G-T   Goodman Papers, in the possession of Mrs. P. Tebbutt, Hartford, Huntingdonshire.

K-OC   John Keep Papers, transcriptions in Oberlin College, Oberlin, Ohio.

MC-BPL   Manuscript Collection, Boston Public Library, Boston, Massachusetts.

MC-DU   Manuscript Collection, Rose Memorial Library, Drew University, Madison, New Jersey.

MC-MCA   Manuscript Collection, Methodist Church Archives, John Rylands Library, Manchester.

N-HS   Asahel Nettleton Papers, Hartford Seminary, Hartford, Connecticut.

NR-SCL   Nonconformist Records, Sheffield City Library, Sheffield, South Yorkshire.

NYC-NYPL   Methodist Church Records, New York Conference, New York Public Library, New York, New York.

OC-OC   Official Correspondence, Oberlin College, Oberlin, Ohio.

PC-NYPL   Walter and Phoebe Palmer Papers, Methodist Episcopal Church Records, New York Public Library, New York, New York.

P-SU   George Peck Papers, George Arents Research Library, Syracuse University, Syracuse, New York.

R-NLWA   Thomas Rees Papers, National Library of Wales, Aberystwth.

S-SU   Gerrit Smith Miller Papers, George Arents Research Library, Syracuse University, Syracuse, New York.

SNEC-BU   Southern New England Conference (Methodist Episcopal Church) Archives, Boston University, Boston, Massachusetts.

T-LC   Lewis Tappan Papers, Library of Congress, Washington, D.C.

W-WL   Thomas Wilson Papers, Dr. Williams's Library, London.

part one

"THE AMERICAN SHORT CUT TO HEAVEN"

one

The New-Measure Revivalism in the United States

In 1826, on the fiftieth anniversary of the Declaration of Independence, a confident Methodist enthused over the "cheering prospects . . . the future splendid scene before us. . . . Blessed with a healthy climate, a moral people, a free government, our situation is without parallel on the earth."[1] Evangelicals shared in the optimism and burgeoning self-confidence of American society in the Age of Jackson. The Panic of 1819 had not shattered the belief that the young republic, with her growing population, vast territories, natural wealth, and developing commerce, had a special destiny that set her apart from the corrupt Old World. The evangelical believed that America—blessed with a Puritan heritage, voluntarist church structure and a vast engine of benevolent societies—had been charged by the Lord with the task of regenerating both itself and the whole world. "Our object," Francis Wayland announced confidently to his Boston audience, "is to effect an entire moral revolution in the whole human race."[2]

The wave of religious revivals of the 1820s and early 1830s, which brought to the boil once more the simmering evangelicalism of the Second Great Awakening and saw unprecedented additions to the churches, justified and reinforced this optimism. At the same time the revival outburst reflected in much of its practice and theology another central characteristic of Jacksonian society—a democratic egalitarianism resting on a faith in the common man. This practice and theology—the "New Measures" and the "New Divinity"—represented a watering down and liberalizing of an older Calvinism that had emphasized both the exclusiveness of the elect and man's helplessness and inability to act in securing his own conversion. Here was a religious parallel to secular developments. Just as the Jacksonian period saw a political and social challenge to the liberal aristocracy of the early nineteenth century, so new-measure revivalism represented a challenge to an older ecclesiastical authority "laced and stayed by rule";[3] just as the Jacksonian movement symbolized a turning toward political democracy, so the new measures indicated a swing toward greater spiritual autonomy for the individual.[4]

We do not lack scholarly examination of the newer, more calculated revivalism that became so widespread in the generation before the Civil War.[5] But much remains unexplored. How did denominations influence and compete with each other in this field? How did revivalism have to adjust to the changing conditions of city life? Given the transatlantic dimension of so many movements related to revivals—particularly moral reform, antislavery, and temperance[6]—how did Britain influence America in this area? What can we learn of what might be called the topography of revivals, or the pattern of their incidence, and the configurations of secular and religious influences that checked or stimulated them? This chapter focuses on these questions as a means of broadening our understanding of revivalism at a crucial stage of its development.

Finney, Conservative Calvinists, and Methodist Enthusiasts

The most dramatic stimulus to the more egalitarian, more deliberately engineered revivalism experienced in all areas in the later years of the Second Great Awakening was the revivalism found at the turn of the century in western and southern frontier areas, particularly in the Cumberland region of Kentucky. These newer settlements, often deficient in regular ministry and permanent churches, threw up revised forms of theology, organization, and revival capable of meeting the needs of a harsher, cruder, and less socially stratified society than that found in the east. Frontier isolation, the evangelical or God-fearing background of migrants, and an expectation of revival helped give rise in the late 1790s and 1800s to a Great Revival notable for its huge outdoor meetings held over several days and nights. Here poorly educated but physically robust itinerant preachers encouraged intense excitement and emotional public conversions; they preached a democratic gospel that in practice seemed to reject the Calvinist idea of an elect and sought to bring home to all men their duty to seek their salvation through positive action.[7]

The frontier style of revivalism, however, even when pruned of its more egregious novelties, could at first make little headway against the restraint and propriety that marked the revivals of the Calvinist churches of New England and the east. The Presbyterians had been the first denomination in the west to use the camp meeting, but amongst the better-educated Calvinists of the east, traditions of conservatism in theology and means produced revivals that were less emotional and less obviously engineered. The central weapons were Sabbath-preaching by the pastor (sometimes assisted by neighboring ministers), supplemented by prayer meetings, house-to-house visiting, lectures, and days of fasting and prayer. Evangelists were rarely used, and intense and sustained public pressures on those seeking salvation were discountenanced.[8]

That in eastern Calvinist churches revivals generally conformed to a conservative model was in no small part due to the restraining influence of their most successful revivalist, Asahel Nettleton. One of the few itinerant evangelists at work there, Nettleton was no ranting frontier exhorter: "he was so reserved, and so entirely controlled by judgment rather than emotion, that some would have pronounced him austere."[9] In 1811, two years after graduating from Timothy Dwight's Yale, he had begun a decade of highly successful but emotionally restrained revival work in the Congregational churches of the villages and small towns of Connecticut, Massachusetts, and New York. Unprepossessing in appearance and lacking real eloquence he nonetheless had an extraordinary capacity to read his hearers' minds and tackle their psychological barriers to conversion. This ability was undoubtedly the consequence of his own troubled conversion—a ten-month oscillation between hope and despair—and the periodic doubts that afterward assailed him.[10]

Thus qualified, Nettleton had no need of noisy expedients; his services were generally well ordered. Nor did his Calvinism—of the strict Hopkinsian variety, emphasizing the utter dependence of the individual and the church on God's sovereign grace—allow any device that suggested he was attempting to "get up a revival." He set great store by "the ordinary means of grace"—preaching, prayer meetings, and private consultation with those seeking salvation, whether in their own houses or in "inquiry" (or "anxious") meetings. These meetings were to be used not to "work up" a revival but rather to sustain its progress. There should be no "promiscuous speaking at religious meetings," no hasty admission of converts, no facile multiplication of meetings. He was known to leave in the middle of a revival if he felt that too much might be expected from his presence alone. Aware, too, of the havoc wrought by the itinerant James Davenport in the eighteenth-century Awakening, Nettleton *always encouraged and strengthened the bonds of the regular pastors of the churches.*"[11]

By the early 1830s Nettletonian revivalism no longer exerted a near-monopolistic hold over eastern Calvinism, and Nettleton himself was a spent force. Amongst the complex causes of this erosion of older standards by a noisier, more calculated revivalism was the movement that began in western New York State in the mid-1820s, centered on the converted trainee-lawyer, Charles Grandison Finney. This area—the "Burned-over District," as it came to be known—had experienced a rhythm of revival boom and recession since its early settlement by New Englanders in the 1790s. And now in districts at a stage of development between pioneering crudity and full economic maturity, the cycle reached its climax under the auspices of a number of revival-minded pastors and evangelists. Of these, none was so successful as Finney. In 1824 he helped promote a series of revivals in the small villages of the Oneida region; the following year he blazed an even more remarkable revival trail amongst the "Presbygationalists" in the towns of the upper Mohawk Valley. He employed a theology that challenged "hyper-Calvinism"—the belief in human inability, limited atonement, and election—by urging on the sinner and the minister their active role in the process of conversion, and he used a variety of "new measures" consonant with these theological beliefs. He thereby provided a revivalism that stood midway between frontier extravagance and New England traditionalism for a population that found the former too crude and the latter too constricting.[12]

Reports of these revivals, and of Finney's part in them, began to filter eastward in the winter of 1825-26. Nettleton, Lyman Beecher, and other easterners attempted to check Finney's progress by calling a convention at New Lebanon in July 1827 to discuss the new measures, but Finney emerged unscathed and ultimately won his way into the pulpits of Philadelphia, New York City, Boston, and other towns and cities of the east.[13] Here he and his supporters—hyperevangelical laymen and pastors intoxicated by his success—proved strong enough to fend off the counterattacks of Princetonian, Old-School Presbyterians and conservative Congregationalists who likened Finneyite activity to the unsavory antics of Crazy Dow.[14] Even Nettleton had to turn tail. His fame spreading, Finney succumbed in 1832 to the promptings of Lewis Tappan and others to take up a New York City pastorate in the converted Chatham Street Theatre. When in 1835 Joshua Leavitt published Finney's *Lectures on Revivals of Religion*, a practical handbook on revivalism incorporating the lessons of over ten years' experience, its phenomenal sales testified to the immense influence of Finney and his techniques.[15]

Certain eastern Presbyterians and Congregationalists were sympathetic to Finney since they saw his revivalism as a practical expression of the more liberal theology gaining ground in New England and the older centers of Calvinism under Timothy Dwight, Nathaniel W. Taylor, and Lyman Beecher. Eager to establish revivals as a means of combating infidelity, republicanism, and Unitarianism, New Englanders had made adjustments to the prevailing stricter Calvinism. Taylor and Beecher in particular rejected the doctrines associated with the eighteenth-century "Consistent Calvinists," especially those of moral inability, total depravity, and a restricted use of means. Man's depravity, urged Taylor, was his own act and not a creation of God; he had the power to act as a moral agent and "to perform every duty which God requires." Consequently, the duty of the minister to preach the practicality of immediate repentance was parallelled by the sinner's duty to act in that knowledge. Dwight, Taylor, and Beecher all sought revivals on this basis.[16] Significantly, by 1831, when Finney's methods had lost much of their roughness, three Congregationalists from New Haven, the home of the New Divinity, could extend him an invitation. "Your views of doctrine and of measures," they told him, "are our views," and twelve months later Taylor himself urged Finney's immediate visit to Yale to be received "with universal and entire cordiality." Even Beecher, fired by his vision of evangelical unity, was ready to accept Finney's seven-month campaign in Boston during the winter of 1831-32.[17]

Charles G. Finney in his prime. Courtesy of Syracuse University Library.

Finney's entry into the east was no mean achievement. But suspicion of the new revivalism continued and served to aggravate the growing disharmony amongst both New England Congregationalists and Presbyterians of the middle states. The conflicts between Taylorites and Hopkinsians (including Nettleton) were coming to a head, and the heresy trials of the New-School men (including Albert Barnes and Lyman Beecher and his son Edward) indicated the tensions within Presbyterianism that would erupt in the schism of 1837. Each of these groups found an opportunity in the debates over new-measure revivalism to engage in long-smouldering disputes over doctrinal issues, especially that of the respective roles of man and the Holy Spirit in regeneration.[18]

Certainly, many of the means were radically different from those used in Nettletonian revivals. In new-measure revivalism, preaching was often more direct, specific, and theatrical and was often conducted by preachers who itinerated with the avowed intention of stirring churches and winning converts. Prayers were sustained over long periods, sometimes with specific requests for named individuals. At "social" or "promiscuous" prayer meetings, women might prove as vocal as men. In addition to the more reputable inquiry meetings, the "anxious seat" was employed. This was a pew set aside at the front of the congregation where those in a state of concern over their souls could go to be exhorted and prayed for by the minister and where a public commitment might be expected. Here, and in his work generally, the minister was sometimes helped by a "Holy Band," a close-knit group that included laymen dedicated to bringing waverers to salvation. In these high-pressure conditions, the aroused emotions found in any revival could explode uncontrollably. Meetings were often "loud and boisterous," groaning was not unusual, and even "muscular agony" was evident at times. Protracted meetings held over three or four days—or even much longer—served only to increase the likelihood of emotionalism. In general there was no rigid procedure, and the methods employed could vary from revival to revival. What was constant was the boldness, frenetic activity, emphasis on public pressures, and general readiness to experiment that marked the exponents of the new-measure revivalism.[19]

To conservative Calvinists the new measures smacked of ecclesiastical impropriety and theological heterodoxy. The Holy Spirit took second place to the efforts of minister and sinner. "If you will take hold, we can have three or four hundred converted," claimed the evangelist Jedediah Burchard. "It is as easy as to turn over your hand." This reeked of Arminianism: the sinner was being told in effect to convert himself. Conservatives deprecated the assumption that the mere employment of means would in itself prove effective. Further, the conversions that followed the threatenings, cajolings, emotionalism, trickery, and other public pressures characteristic of the new measures were rarely evidence of a real change of heart. When some real change did occur it generally went uncultivated, since admissions to the church were much too hurried: "the numerous converts of the new measures have been, in most cases, like the morning cloud and the early dew. In some places, not a half, a fifth, or even a tenth part of them remain." Equally detrimental, continued the critics, was the arrogance and egotism of presumptuous laymen and evangelists, the exclusion of broader Christian instruction in the face of terror tactics that produced an "animal religion," and the divisive effect that this new revivalism could have on the whole church society.[20]

It is tempting to measure the radicalism of the new revivalism by the expressions of horror that it drew from conservative Calvinists. Too sharp a contrast should not, however, be drawn between "worked up" and "prayed down" revivals. Old-school revivalists of the early nineteenth century stood in the traditions of orthodox Puritan theology, which saw conversion in terms of the operation of means on the unregenerate, without in any sense denying the supernatural character of the process of grace.[21] Nettleton would have been horrified had he been told to shun human instrumentality. He was extremely conscious of technique. He well understood when and how best to approach the anxious inquirer, how best to conduct meetings, what psychological weapons to employ. The conflict between revivalists like Nettleton and the new-measure men came not over the use of means, but over the type of means to be employed legitimately. Thus at New Lebanon both parties were fully agreed that "though revivals of religion are the work of God's Spirit, they are produced by means of divine truth and human instrumentality. . . . The idea that God ordinarily works independently of human instrumentality, or without any reference to the adaption of means to ends, is unscriptural."[22] Not only did earlier revivals have considerably less spontaneity than observers cared to admit, but the later "mechanical" revivals should not be regarded as inevitably created at will: attempts to promote revivals sometimes failed, while a flurry of conversions could sometimes take a church community by surprise.

It is, however, true that eastern Calvinist churches had come to adopt a more avowedly calculated and promotional revivalism reminiscent of early nineteenth-century frontier methods. Finney's role in this adoption had indeed been catalytic. Aided by the crumbling of an older Calvinism and a desire for revivals by those worried by the demise of the established churches, he more than any other individual was able to secure this change in practice. Even in Calvinistic Baptist ranks he made his influence felt. Their first professional itinerant evangelists, Jacob Knapp and Jabez Swan, both acknowledged Congregational, Presbyterian, and specifically Finneyite leadership in breaking down what Swan termed "double-extra Calvinism." Until about 1830 Baptist revivals tended to result from restrained methods similar to those employed by Francis Wayland as a pastor in Boston and later as president of Brown University. After Finney, however, itinerant revivalists, protracted meetings, and anxious seats emerged in Baptist circles, despite strong prejudice against them.[23]

It is easy, however, to exaggerate the uniqueness and novelty of this Fin-neyite movement. The two most scholarly treatments of American revivalism give such prominence to Finney's role in the creation of a new style of evangelism that they overlook parallel contemporary developments.[24] Yet we know that Finney's measures and the New Divinity were "not new in themselves, [being] only new among the churches professing Calvinism in the north and east."[25] That there were others besides Finney himself pressing the claims of a more urgent and promotional revivalism will be clear from investigating the most fervent evangelical denomination of that period, the Methodist Episcopal Church (MEC); and, since Finney's carrying of the new revivalism into the cities of the east has been regarded as a major turning point in the creation of modern urban evangelism, it will be helpful to give particular attention to the standing and character of Methodism in urban areas.

Methodism was wholeheartedly a revival movement: it had been born of a revival; its churches grew through revivals; its ministers preached revival; its success was talked of in terms of revival. Sometimes, when most of those who were converted were the children of Methodist parents, the revival served to consolidate, but just as frequently it sought to break new territory and reach new pockets of population to achieve overall growth. And grow Methodism did. From a membership of less than ten thousand in 1780 the MEC grew to embrace over two hundred and fifty thousand members in 1820; within another decade it had nearly doubled in size.[26] Although at first it drew its strength from frontier and western areas and the Atlantic states south of Pennsylvania, by 1830 its penetration of the northeast and even of Calvinist New England was well underway.

This phenomenal advance made the Methodist Church in little over a generation the largest of America's denominations. It owed much to the appeal of an Arminian theology whose individualistic, democratic, and optimistic emphases found a positive response in an expanding society where traditional patterns of authority and deference were succumbing to egalitarian challenge. In the late eighteenth and early nineteenth centuries, with the advance of a secular ideology that sanctioned the broadening of social and political opportunity, some of the stricter and exclusive Calvinist formulations seemed increasingly illogical and irrelevant; George Peck's wife was one of many New Englanders who "had often felt the repulsive force of the Calvinist doctrines of election and reprobation." Significantly, such disaffection often predated acquaintance with Methodism. When Deborah Millet confessed, "I was a Methodist in sentiment before I knew their doctrines," she suggested very clearly how Methodism met a felt need that the theology of the pulpit should present—in Tobias Spicer's words—"a system that seemed to harmonise with itself, with the Scriptures, with common sense, and with experience."[27]

The powerful rapport between preacher and people provided a further source of strength. Methodist ministers in the early years were largely men of the common people without an education that might distance them from their social origins; even the church's bishops were ordinary, unpretentious, homespun figures. The boisterousness of Methodist services and the constant interruption and criticisms of preachers by members of their audience suggested the strong sympathy between the two parties. The authority of the minister derived less from his formal status than from admiration for his driving sense of purpose and aggressive pursuit of souls, manifested in his acceptance of a debilitating regimen of constant travel in all conditions; it could derive too from his understanding and use of local superstitions in the name of religion and from a preacher's and the people's shared perception of a God that could and did intervene in human affairs through visions and dreams.[28]

Methodism benefited, thirdly, from the flexibility of its connectional organization. Though criticized by some for its "anti-republican" hierarchy and centralization, the vast majority of Methodists recognized that the system of circuits and stations, districts, annual conferences, and quadrennial general conferences provided the discipline and the potential for reaching all parts of the country and for maintaining coherence in a rapidly growing church. Moreover that church was flexible enough to sanction the use of instruments—most obviously the camp meeting—devised to meet a particular social or religious need. By encouraging experimentation in the quest for souls and by ensuring that it was the Methodist minister who first penetrated unchurched areas, the organization secured a respect from its members that protected it from the attacks of a dissenting minority of "republican" Methodists.

Of course, the very success of the church was self-reinforcing. The huge numerical advance, particularly in the 1820s, provided the best available proof to unconverted sympathizers that its prophecies would be fulfilled, that the millennium really was at hand, and that Methodism did provide the best avenue to spiritual well-being. Equally, as Methodist encouragement of thrift and industry began to reflect itself in the increasing social and political status of its members, and as "the first families" in some areas helped make the church more than a haven for the poor and laboring classes, so it suffered less social stigma and indeed came to be extolled as an agency of social improvement.[29]

One product of Methodist flexibility was its success in a variety of geographical locations. Surprisingly, perhaps, in view of its later blossoming on the frontier, Methodism's earliest footholds in America were urban ones. New York City, Philadelphia, and Baltimore provided its early focuses until, under Francis Asbury's guidance, the center of gravity shifted to rural areas and small towns in the middle states and the south. If the circuit system and itinerancy gave Methodists an advantage in underpopulated and newly

settled areas, the church also secured urban strength through its cultivation
of city "stations" and—in New England, at least—through its acceptance of
a pew-rent system. By 1810 in the three cities where Methodism was strongest—New York, Philadelphia and Baltimore—its combined membership,
white and black, was seven thousand. By 1820 the figure was ten thousand;
by 1830, fifteen thousand. For a more accurate assessment of Methodist
strength one should at least double these totals to include the unconverted
adherents of the various churches. This reflected a significant urban standing.[30]

Revivals were a central part of the life of these urban Methodist churches
in the late eighteenth and early nineteenth centuries. Baltimore's participation
in the "considerable revival" on the Eastern Shore of Maryland in 1774 was
only the first in a series of increasingly impressive revivals that affected her
churches at five- or ten-year intervals and that culminated in the movement
of 1818, when nearly a thousand joined the denomination. There were also
early revivals in New York City. Of the "remarkable" religious outburst of
1807-08, the seasoned campaigner Jesse Lee could announce that he "never
knew so great a revival of religion in the city before." Thereafter revivals
grew in frequency and extent until the widespread movement beginning
there in 1827-28. Ezekiel Cooper's ministry in the black and white churches
of Philadelphia in 1800 and 1801 contributed to a revival that he described
as "the greatest . . . I ever knew"; in the following decade alone there were
two more major revivals there. Nor were churches in smaller cities and
towns immune. In Providence, Rhode Island, the revivals of 1815 and 1820-
22 brought "very large accessions to the society"; in Albany, Boston, New
Haven, Newark, and Washington, D.C., for example, revivals became a
feature of church life, and even such an "unpromising" town as Charleston,
South Carolina, was affected at times.[31]

From the first, the Methodist churches demonstrated an "enthusiasm"
and lack of restraint in religion that brought persecution and ridicule from
other denominations. The early, rampant emotionalism of Methodist services
in urban churches was gradually curbed and guided. When Nathan Bangs
took over as preacher in charge of the city churches of New York in 1810, he
was offended by the "spirit of pride, presumption, and bigotry, impatience
of scriptural restraint and moderation, clapping of the hands, screaming,
and even jumping, which marred and disgraced the work of God." Revivals
had "degenerated into extravagant excitements." However, despite the opposition of many of the more recent converts, Bangs succeeded in establishing order and method.[32] Such correctives usually satisfied Methodists, who
regarded their style of worship as moderate, scriptural, and proper, but
their meetings continued to be more fervent than those of their evangelical
competitors. Revivals they agreed could sometimes be noisy, but it was
sheer presumption to question the way in which the Holy Spirit operated.

This more wholehearted, "enthusiastic" revivalism of the Methodist Church,
which existed side by side in the cities with the generally cautious methods

of the Calvinist and more socially respectable denominations, has received scarcely any mention in the analyses of the development of mid-nineteenth-century urban revivalism, perhaps because there were no spectacular divisions within the Methodist Church to parallel those found in Presbyterianism and because the Methodists are thought of as a rural and western denomination at this time. Yet the techniques and influence of Methodist revivals played an important role in the emergence of the urban revival movement of the late 1820s and early 1830s. The new measures that caused such controversy and tribulation in Presbyterian and Congregational ranks were in no sense new to Methodism.

Probably the most controversial new measure was the anxious seat or mourners' bench. The sensitivity of Old-School Calvinists over this measure seemed utterly misplaced to Methodists, who had long used a similar device—the "call to the altar"—in their services, both east and west, country and city. This call to the altar was not quite the same as the anxious seat, since there was no pew set aside for mourners. The latter merely came forward to kneel at the altar rail and the open area at the front of the congregation. However, the idea behind both devices was identical: to separate the penitents—those actively seeking salvation—from the rest of the congregation so that they could be made more easily and more intensely subject to the psychological and social pressures of the minister and of the community of the converted. According to one version, the practice was introduced in an urban, eastern setting in 1806. Aaron Hunt, the Methodist minister in the Forsyte Street Church, New York, had received news from a former colleague of a scheme recently adopted in camp meetings in the south and west. This was the enclosing of "a space in front of the stand, called an altar, where mourners and those who were considered capable of instructing and praying with them were invited to meet, apart from the great congregation." The device seemed well suited to eliminate the confusion caused by several little prayer meetings taking place simultaneously in different parts of the house.[33] In fact, Hunt was only one of several who were adopting the practice at about this time. As early as 1801 Richard Sneath, in Saint George's, Philadelphia, "invited all the mourners to come to the communion table." Far more important, however, than the precise pattern of adoption is that by the second decade of the century the call to the altar had become a standard feature of Methodist revivals. Indeed it sometimes happened that mourners would anticipate the minister's call and move to the altar before the invitation was given, so institutionalized had the procedure become.[34]

Methodists as a body were committed to the itinerant system and had long been criticized by other denominations for neglecting the pastoral relationship. There was thus no equivalent in Methodist ranks to the Presbyterian debate over the propriety of Finney's movements as an itinerant. Similarly, the various other measures opposed by strict Calvinists failed to bring controversy to the Methodist Church. Women praying in mixed, or promiscuous, assemblies; direct, pointed, and often colloquial preaching; and sustained sessions of private and public prayer were scarcely innovations in their denomination, and Methodists were amused that such issues should perplex the Presbyterians. Even the protracted meeting can be found in practice, if not in name, in eastern Methodism well before it caused dissension in Calvinist ranks. In the revival of 1820 in Bristol, Rhode Island, it was reported that "for about two weeks our chapel has been opened every day, in the morning, at two o'clock P.M. and in the evening till near midnight."[35] Although Methodists did not adopt the so-called "three" or "four days meetings" extensively until the late 1820s and early 1830s, this was not because they disapproved of protracting meetings but because in practice they already possessed a weapon that performed a similar task: the camp meeting.[36] This institution had been transferred to eastern areas as an adjunct and a spur to city revivalism shortly after its development on the frontier. In September 1803 the first camp meeting east of the Alleghenies was held just fifteen miles from Baltimore. Soon similar meetings were to be found in various northeastern locations. These outdoor meetings were less flexible, more expensive, more dependent on good weather, and less single-mindedly religious than protracted meetings, but they filled a similar place in the revival tool kit.[37]

Eastern Calvinists, then, had come to blows over the propriety of revival measures that Methodists had long used happily. Unlike other denominations, Methodists had been able, without appreciable stress, to introduce frontier revivalism into the eastern cities in modified form very soon after its development in the west. In this they had been aided by their theology and the mobility of ideas allowed by their organizational structure. Their theology encouraged every sinner to make some effort on his own behalf to effect his salvation. Methodists complained comparatively little over sinners supposedly putting too much faith in human instruments. The Calvinists' concern that the new measures put insufficient reliance on the Holy Spirit was generally absent in Arminian churches. As for Methodist organization, the very mobility of its preachers meant that revivalistic ideas and instruments could spread relatively quickly, while it probably made it more difficult for a minister with doubts about certain revival techniques to bind a church community perpetually to his own approach.

When eastern Calvinists eventually succumbed to a semi-Methodistic revivalism, this occurred as a result not only of the Finneyite onslaught from the west but also because of considerable pressure from within the cities themselves. It is clear that there were Presbyterians in the east anxious for a newer and more successful revivalism to combat the problems of their church in an urban environment and to meet the challenge posed by growing Methodist success. For the evangelical denominations were in competition: denominational self-sufficiency and aggression were corollaries of the era's prevailing optimism. Although much of the early opprobrium cast on

Methodism was now losing its vigor, there were still acrimonious battles between the Congregationalists and Presbyterians on the one hand and the Methodists on the other. There were numerous instances of local interdenominational cooperation, but the climate of relative interdenominational harmony that came to exist in the 1850s was still a long way off. In 1829 a convert from the Episcopalians explained why other denominations continued to abuse the Methodists: "the foundation of the present opposition to the Methodist Episcopal Church is *its continued prosperity*."[38] In that year the Methodist Church was the largest denomination in the United States, numbering almost five hundred thousand members, and in the five years from 1826 to 1830 the Methodists added twice as many converts as the Presbyterians.[39] There was interdenominational rivalry over securing converts. Methodists constantly complained of other churches "stealing" their converts. A Methodist in New York City noted sarcastically that while it was the Methodists who went out to draw the city's one hundred thousand reprobates into the church, yet "I find the Calvinistic ministers and people are welcoming them to their communion, crying, 'we are all *one*—we are all one!'"[40]

Some of the Calvinist churches were also adopting Methodist practices. Tobias Spicer's experience in New York State and New England prompted the reflection that "such had been the success of Methodism that [Calvinist] ministers . . . were obliged to bestir themselves or lose their hold upon their people. . . . They must . . . occasionally borrow our doctrines, and imitate our manner of preaching; they must borrow our tools, and invent some new ones of their own."[41] From Georgia there were reports in 1827 that "camp meetings, penitents at the altar, sudden conversions, and sudden admissions into the church, formerly the anomalies of Methodism, are no longer uncommon incidents with our brethren, especially the Presbyterians."[42] Even more strikingly, during the 1822 revival in Washington it was noted that "they are introducing all the habits and hymns, of the methodists into our presbyterian churches, after the regular service is closed by the clergyman, the congregation rise, and strike up a methodist hymn, sung amidst the groans and sobs of the newly converted . . . then [the minister] calls on the *mourners* to come forward, and he and others pray over them, as they loudly vent their sorrows."[43]

An important factor, then, in Calvinist adoption of Methodist practices was a hankering after that denomination's success in revivals. Such was the case in New York City in the late 1820s. In the winter of 1827-28, at a time when New York Presbyterianism was "generally in a cold stupid state," many of the Methodist churches were experiencing prosperous revivals of a kind they had known for several consecutive years.[44] Some Presbyterian laymen were eager to experience this kind of "vital religion" themselves. A female correspondent wrote to Finney's wife in 1827 of what seem to have been twice-weekly Methodist meetings "where the women pray before men."

With unconcealed envy she added, "They are delightful little meetings but a great prejudice exists against them."[45] For such Presbyterian laymen, lacking the theological scruples of their seminary-trained ministers, an obvious way of obtaining this type of religion was to recruit the arch-exponent of a more Methodistic, yet nominally Presbyterian, revivalism—Charles Finney himself. Despite clerical opposition, the laity, or at least a powerful part of it, secured Finney's entry into New York in late 1829.

Finney himself was undoubtedly influenced by Methodist revival practices and was to some extent attempting to emulate the successes of that denomination. The earliest sermons that he heard as a child in upstate New York were, he recalled in his *Memoirs*, delivered by "some travelling minister, or some miserable holding forth of an ignorant preacher who would sometimes be found in that country." Finney was later ready to recognize Methodist effectiveness, urging that all good sermons should have a Methodist directness and simplicity—qualities that characterized his own preaching style. He admired the purposeful approach of Methodists. In 1824-25 he investigated a recent revival at De Kalb in western New York, where there had been considerable excitement and "falling under the power of God." The local Presbyterians had criticized the Methodists, holding that such physical manifestations invalidated the revival. Finney, however, instead of siding with his own denomination, concluded that "the Presbyterians had been decidedly in error," and in the ensuing revival produced similar cases of "falling." Although he later rid his revivals of this extreme type of emotionalism, his debt to pragmatic Methodism remained. It is even possible that his decision in Rochester in 1830 to adopt the anxious seat as a main feature of his revivals was Methodist-inspired. In the Methodist revival there in 1827-28 the call to the altar had proved "singularly beneficial" and had involved "some of our wealthy and respectable citizens." When Finney arrived in 1830 he was looking for "some measure that would bring sinners to a stand." He "had found, that with the higher classes especially, the greatest obstacle to be overcome was their fear of being known as anxious inquirers." He decided to use the anxious seat, and the response among "the highest classes of society" was good.[46]

Certain of the claims made for Finney are clearly much too exclusive. He did not invent the new measures;[47] he did not even introduce the style of revivalism associated with them into the cities of the east. What he did succeed in doing was to give those measures a wider popular base and to make them palatable to a somewhat more respectable class of people than most of those reached by the Methodists. Finney gave a focus to the forces that favored new developments in revivalism and that envied the vigor and prosperity of the rapidly growing Methodist churches but that rejected the Arminianism, perfectionism, and alleged fanaticism or "enthusiasm" of a denomination that attracted eccentrics like Crazy Dow and appealed to the lowest classes in society—the poor white and the black. Finney perhaps gave Presbyterians and Congregationalists a chance to taste the urgent evangelism of Methodism without their having to suffer the indignity of joining a socially inferior church; many of his converts in Buffalo, Rochester, and Auburn in 1830-31 were from "among the more influential classes," and in eastern cities he was able to reach well-to-do groups like merchants, lawyers, and physicians.[48] Finney's undeniable successes in revivals could not be ignored, and having modified the tone of his revivalism when he reached the east his good standing among many in the Calvinist denominations was ensured. Hyper-Calvinism could have been successfully challenged only from within by a Finney and not from outside by the Methodists. But only in the context of the challenging influence of Methodism and the far-reaching attack on Calvinist standards that its success represented can Finney's progress be given any coherent, satisfactory explanation.

During the 1840s and 1850s many of the practices and emphases of the new measures took firmer hold in the major evangelical denominations. Early in 1853 a Methodist observed, "Revivals are no longer exhibitions of Methodist fanaticism in the estimation of our brethren of other churches. On the contrary, they too glory in them, and labor for them with great zeal and diligence, having become quite reconciled to the reproach of fanaticism and enthusiasm which they must endure from 'the wisdom of the world.' " The Episcopalian Benjamin Cutler participated during the 1857-58 revival movement in evening meetings for prayer and short addresses that, he said, "twenty years ago . . . would have been denounced as Methodistical." By that time similar changes of emphasis in all denominations meant, according to the *Oberlin Evangelist*, that "the long agitated questions about *revival measures* appear to be tolerably settled."[49]

The settlement, however, had not been achieved completely on the terms of the new-measure revivalists of the 1820s and 1830s. The new-measure "extravagances" of that period had been very largely brought under control. Already by 1840 some Unitarians believed that revivals were "conducted with more propriety than in some former instances"; Robert Baird's conclusion later in the decade was essentially the same. The professional revival preacher failed to achieve his anticipated preeminence. Even the anxious seat and similar techniques for securing public commitment found their popularity on the wane. The anxious seat continued to be used, of course, but not without criticism, and, significantly, it never became part of the armory of respectable post-Civil War revivalists such as Dwight L. Moody. The development of a greater decorum in worship was having its effect. "I sometimes go into a Wesleyan church to warm up a little," wrote James W. Alexander to Francis Wayland. "Why!—they are as genteel and formal as so many Presbyterians." Thus to talk of the broadening hold of new-measure revivalism implies not the multiplication of excitement and revival techniques, as in the 1820s and 1830s, but rather a wider acceptance of a psychology that saw revivals as capable of promotion and control and less than ever an occasion for evangelical bewilderment.[50]

Urban Adjustments

The later phase of the Second Great Awakening, from the late 1820s onward, illustrated the growing importance of urban revivalism.[51] Revivals could, of course, boast a lengthy urban existence: during the eighteenth-century Great Awakening, George Whitefield's work had embraced Philadelphia, "where commerce was suspended," New York, and the principal cities and towns of New England; in the early nineteenth century, Nettletonian revivals were experienced in many of the major cities.[52] But it was the amalgamation of the urban manifestations of Finneyism—the work of Finney himself and of men like James Patterson, Thomas Harvey Skinner, and Albert Barnes in Philadelphia, and Joel Parker in New York—and the older revival traditions of city Methodism that helped promote the first broadly based urban revival movement, one that reached its climax in the early 1830s. In April 1831, after four or five years in which the revival strain had grown more pronounced in cities both east and west, a delighted Methodist found it "no small consolation to see our large Atlantic and commercial cities, which exert so great an influence over the surrounding country, taking the lead in [the] present great revivals of pure religion. In Baltimore, New York, New Haven, and Boston, and other cities, God is doing wonders."[53] The pattern repeated itself a decade later, as cities played a prominent role in the revival movement of the early 1840s.

To many evangelicals worried about the "vice" and "demoralizing causes" of east-coast cities pickled in alcohol and swollen by European "Infidel" or Roman Catholic immigrants, these revivals were long overdue. Ministers were convinced that only revivals could cleanse the rapidly growing cities; that urban evangelistic efforts deserved priority, since "cities have an amazing influence on the community at large"; and that such efforts would hasten the advent of the millennium.[54] Even when millennial visions blurred in the following decades, the sense of revivalism's centrality in the spiritual well-being of the city (and hence the nation) lived on, to be well captured in Henry Clay Fish's rhetorical question: "*What can save our large cities* but a powerful revival of religion?"[55]

In facing up to the problems of city environments revivalism became the subject of adjustment, of changes in emphases that gave it a somewhat different character from the revivalism of frontier and small-town America. The revivalism of the early nineteenth-century frontier had, of course, considerably influenced the tone and forms of later revivalism. The egalitarianism of theology, the emphasis on action and premeditation, the strengthening of itinerancy, the introduction of camp and protracted meetings, and the use of the altar or anxious seat were all frontier characteristics that found urban expression. But city ministers were aware that the unique conditions of the "urban frontier" demanded changes in approach.

The sheer density of an urban population, with its internal mobility, its constantly changing character produced by migration from country areas and from northern Europe, and its cultural and social heterogeneity meant that the city minister, unlike the small-town pastor, had to search out a congregation and to work more aggressively than in an area where church attendance was the norm; unlike the frontier preacher, he was likely to encounter large sections of the population ignorant of evangelical Protestantism and unresponsive to its appeal. Since he could not rely on the support of a state church, he and his energetic laity (especially church women) needed a more organized revivalism that would reach unchurched groups considerably larger and more inaccessible than in other sections of the country.

The machinery they fashioned, impressive and vigorous, was aimed, through the conversion of the individual, at producing revivals—an approach that is well illustrated in their work with children and Sunday schools. The religious education and upbringing of the children of church members had always been a central feature of the church's work, both urban and rural. But Sunday schools were more than an arena for education: "Sunday School instruction must be regarded as only a means to an end, *and that end the conversion of the soul.*" The abundant reports of revivals originating in Sunday school conversions gave added meaning to the urgent promptings of one Methodist that "the proper training of the rising generation is the grand means to introduce the millennium." Often very young children were involved. Phoebe Palmer's children, for example, were "all intelligently converted to God before attaining the age of seven years." Although such conversions produced alarm and repugnance in some quarters—Horace Bushnell urged that a child could grow up a Christian and never have to undergo a traumatic and dramatic conversion experience—this did not prevent the conversion of children remaining an integral part of revivals.[56]

An awareness of the churches' dependence on the younger generation helped create in the 1820s the American Sunday School Union, which aimed to organize and direct local Sunday schools and give children the religious education they were denied in the public schools. Sunday schools were set up in both urban and rural areas, but city activity was broader and much more systematic. The lack of church interest in Sunday school activity complained of by a Methodist itinerant in certain newly settled districts was scarcely conceivable in a city like New York.[57] When a Methodist mission was established in religiously derelict areas of a city, Sunday schools might well be introduced simultaneously. When Chelsea Methodist Church was established in the upper part of New York in 1838, the Sunday school was one of its primary weapons; school officers who made concerted efforts to reach the "heathen children" in poorer parts of the same city through organized visiting did so because "the best shield against immorality is the Sabbath School institution."[58]

Similarly systematic in their approach were the Bible and tract societies, effectively organized in Baltimore, Boston, New York, Philadelphia, and other cities. Their work went beyond the mere distribution of Bibles or tracts. In essence the movement aimed to bring the "unchurched masses," "the multitudes who have, from infancy almost, never crossed a church threshold," into the church and then on to conversion. Only by the active, systematic work of church members could they be reached. As one of the Beechers told the American Tract Society in 1838, "Every man must be a revival man, and every women."[59]

This emphasis marked much of the other organizational work of the urban churches. Work amongst seamen on board ship and in special mariners' chapels characterized most of the large towns along the Atlantic coast. Concern here was primarily for the spiritual welfare and redemption of the sailor, not for his material conditions of life. Similarly, organized work among the poor by the various benevolent societies subordinated material relief to securing a "change of heart" amongst the "profligate and vicious" of the slum areas.[60] Even among the various immigrant groups, the emphasis lay on the revival as a central aspect of mission activity. The Methodists by the 1840s had many missions to the German population of the cities, and they had similar, though fewer, missions to Scandinavian, French, and Welsh communities.

City conditions prompted further adjustments in revivalism. The different work and leisure patterns of the large centers of commerce and industry generally precluded the sustained concentration on religion found in the early camp meetings and small-town protracted meetings, where for several days, perhaps a week, religious services were held from dawn to late evening. There were exceptions to this. Samuel Halliday recollected how in the winter of 1828-29, one of the most severe ever known in New York City, mercantile business came to a halt as rivers froze and canals closed. Temporarily unemployed laborers and mechanics were attracted to the four-day meeting, and in the ensuing revival, merchants and clerks closed their stores in order to attend during the daytime.[61] But in general, evangelical businessmen could not be expected to give up their normal activities in the face of competition from non-Christians. Instead the emphasis was placed on evening religious meetings conducted over a protracted period. The coming of age of the railroad, the growth of industry, and the intensification of commerce meant that in the cities secular and religious business had to learn to coexist even during a revival. Only in times of enforced business inactivity after the panics of 1837 and 1857 could the demands of the revival outbid those of secular activities, and even then there was no suspension of all business routine. The use of the noontime prayer meeting during the 1857-58 revival in all the affected cities was a clear acknowledgment that whole days devoted to religious services were no longer feasible. Each noon meeting was restricted in length and terminated by the ringing of a bell.[62]

Not only the daily time table of the workingman but also the much greater variety of available leisure activities prevented unrelieved attention to religion in the city. For the frontier settler or the resident of the New England township, the church provided a real and often the primary social focus. In the city the Sunday sermon had to compete with the counterattractions of theatres, lectures, taverns, politics and other extraecclesiastical activities that seduced urbanites in their out-of-work hours. "[The] impressions made by preaching are so soon obliterated from the mind by business and the influence of the world," complained a Philadelphian.[63] Evangelicals responded not only by denouncing the theatre, taverns, and the other evils that they saw but also by trying to promote the claims of religion through less conventional means. This was the reasoning behind the use of protracted meetings and other novel measures. A key factor in Finney's decision to take up a pastorate in New York in 1832 was the novel nature of the location—a theatre converted into a church—which would, he believed, cause a "*sensation.*"[64] To combat secular attractions there had to be more novelty, more of the untraditional in church life.

The most dramatic instrument that urban churches adopted from the 1820s onward was the professional itinerant evangelist. His work was, of course, by no means the primary feature of revivalism in the mid-nineteenth century: the norm was the pastoral revival conducted under the resident minister, possibly with the aid of local ministers. Methodism could boast only a handful of full-time itinerating revivalists—in particular John Newland Maffitt, James Caughey, and John Inskip—all of whom experienced considerable urban success. Methodism depended mainly on the regular ministry for revivals, and though the regular Methodist ministers generally stayed for only two years in one charge, that was considerably longer than the visits of Maffitt or Caughey. In the Presbyterian Church, the revival-minded pastor was a much more typical figure than the traveling evangelist. A Finney or a Daniel Baker might make the denominational headlines, but the pastoral revivalist in the mold of Albert Barnes was the figure on whom the churches depended most for revivals. Amongst Congregationalists, the Henry Ward Beechers outnumbered the Edward Norris Kirks (and Kirk himself itinerated for only a few years).[65] Nor were Elder Jacob Knapp and Jabez Swan the most typical of Baptist ministers.

Although it found precedents in frontier itinerancy, urban evangelism had characteristic features of its own. Frontier itinerancy had been fashioned as a practical means of coping with a shortage of ministerial manpower and a scattered population; indeed, the frontier circuit rider was both pastor and itinerating evangelist rolled into one. But the professional urban evangelist was not concerned with long-term developments in the spiritual life of the church. His interest lay simply in promoting a revival in one expectant church after another. Jacob Knapp openly admitted his deficiencies as a pastoral worker; when he took up a one-year pastorate in Albany, New York, "God

did not seem to smile on the undertaking." Urban evangelists, their advent
and activities well advertised by show bills, were employed as crowd pullers
to promote and popularize revivals, whose long-term consequences were
usually left to the local pastor. The itinerant's success lay in the production
of immediate effect through well-directed prayers and sermons characterized
"rather by brilliancy than depth of thought, by apt and striking illustration
rather than by strength of reasoning."[66] These methods might result eventually in a postrevival "reaction," but in the short term the glamour, mys-
tique, or personal appeal of a dramatic evangelist could produce electrifying
results.

One of the earliest of such evangelists was John Newland Maffitt, a Dublin-
born Methodist, who began his evangelistic work soon after his arrival in
America in 1819. From the 1820s to the 1840s he visited all the large cities
from Boston to New Orleans; his part in bringing President-elect Harrison
to conversion in the winter of 1840-41 ensured an even wider fame. His
compelling oratory, well-developed sense of drama, and distinctive physique
gave him enormous power over his usually overflowing audiences. He knew
exactly how to manipulate his hearers by his preaching and his fine singing
voice. He was known to leave his pulpit, stand in front of the congregation,
then announce that he would sing alone, and encourage all penitents to
come forward to the altar. Sometimes his egotism and vanity got the better
of him, as on one occasion in New York when he ran a ladder up against the
rear wall of the church and crawled in through an opening above the pulpit
to the enthusiastic response of his audience. About Maffitt there was a fero-
cious "diversity of views," particularly in the 1840s, when divorce and re-
marriage challenged his moral credibility and when he was faced with alle-
gations of "lasciviousness," "using intoxicating liquors," and "imprudent
conduct" ("little else," according to Maffitt, "than a black girl's coming
suddenly into his room and finding him attending to a call of nature"). In
view of this and his seemingly importunate demands for payment it is hardly
surprising that many Methodists had doubts as to the validity of his religious
experience, nor, in view of his extrovert nature and handsome features, that
so many of his "converts" were young women succumbing to "man-worship."
Maffitt was an undeniable showman, an entertainer, dependent on his ora-
torical techniques—"a bladder full of wind," as he was once called—who
highlights, albeit in an exaggerated way, the attempt of the churches to use
more glamorous and spectacular means to reach the unchurched.[67]

Few revivalists of the period cultivated Maffitt's brand of showmanship,
but other itinerants did attract a similar degree of attention. Some, like
Jabez Swan, operated in a small-town orbit; others—Charles Finney, Jacob
Knapp, and Edward Norris Kirk, for example—proved to be considerable
attractions in the larger urban centers. The character of their appeal could
vary considerably. Finney's strength lay in his commanding, logical preaching and in the glamour and self-perpetuating nature of his success. Knapp

was an unrestrained controversialist with a colloquial, "sledge-hammer" style of preaching who found no trouble in attracting (often unfavorable) attention, whether from unfriendly mobs or amused newspaper reporters looking for good copy.[68] Kirk's appeal was quite the contrary: his polished, fluent pulpit manner helped fill Congregational churches that would have rejected Knapp-style professional evangelism but which nonetheless wanted to enjoy the stimulus of an outside revivalist.[69]

That Kirk's success derived in part from his restrained style of evangelism suggests a further major modification of revivalism in an urban setting: the emotional, cruder excrescences of revivals were being pruned by ministers anxious not to alienate the more respectable, sophisticated members of their congregations. Even amongst Methodists and Baptists (churches of the poorer classes), the generation before the Civil War witnessed a growing prosperity. Methodism, which according to one itinerant preacher "in nearly all our large cities . . . was cradled in a hovel . . . quite unobserved by the more wealthy and honorable," was by the 1840s and 1850s building elegant churches with organs and rented pews; her ministers allegedly preached "to a much less proportion of the poor than formerly."[70] In 1842, Jacob Knapp, who was at his ease when preaching amongst the poor, criticized "the growing desire of [Baptist] ministers and churches to gather their converts from the ranks of the wealthy and the intelligent."[71] Partly through the rise in social status and prosperity of church members—perhaps as a result of that very membership—and partly because these denominations were attracting the more well-to-do, the poor were no longer the central object of their concern.

These more fashionable city churchgoers and their increasingly better-educated ministers wanted a more decorous and polished revivalism. Enthusiastic revivals were "unworthy [of] the attention of the more refined and intelligent ranks of society," and fit only for "the weaker portions of the community"; some Lutherans were terrified that rich and influential families, the "very bones and sinew" of the church, would be driven away by the new measures.[72] Emotional revivals affronted intelligence and social gentility; some even considered them socially disruptive. They could interrupt business, divide the churches. They bred a "presumption and boldness . . . through the lowest classes of society" by emphasizing the individual's own role in his conversion and his equality with all other men before God.[73]

Albert Barnes's appeal to his "highly respectable" Philadelphia congregation in 1841 well exemplifies the fears of conservative laity:

I am no advocate for suspending the proper business of life, or of breaking in upon regular employment. . . . I have no views of revivals which would not make men more sober, and honest, and industrious. . . . I have not one word to say in disregard of the urbanities and civilities of social life; of the respect due to rank and office. . . . I hold no views of religion which would not make men more courteous, refined, and truly polite and respectful in revivals and at all times.[74]

His statement signified that new-measure Presbyterians and Congregationalists were making adjustments in the face of urban gentility. Finney, for example, was able to quiet doubts about the boisterousness of his earlier revivals. In his first large-scale city revival, at Rochester in 1830, the most significant feature was its "phenomenal dignity." As he reached the eastern cities so his methods became ever more refined. "The only thing insisted upon under the gospel dispensation, in regard to measures," he announced, "is that there should be *decency and order.*"[75]

Methodists, too, were polishing the rougher edges of revivalism. As the design and furnishings of Methodist churches reflected the members' increasing wealth, there occurred a parallel movement toward propriety and decorum in the conduct of religious meetings. In Portland, Maine, a controversy over the introduction of pew-rents, an indication of growing prosperity, was closely connected with dissension over the issue of shouting and other departures from seemly behavior in prayer meetings.[76] Similar tensions existed in New York City in the 1810s and 1820s. As members of Methodist churches grew wealthier and as the numbers of Methodist ministers with formal ministerial training increased, so the cruder emotionalism of urban Methodist revivals was eliminated.

Despite these modifications in city revivalism, a great sea of humanity still lay beyond its net. At both extremes of the more highly stratified urban society existed sizable groups generally unresponsive or antipathetic to the evangelical appeal. On the one side stood "that part of society which is deemed respectable," the fashionable "votaries of pleasure"; rarely could these sophisticated upper classes be reached. When in the revival of 1857-58 a scheme of systematic house-to-house visiting in New York City was extended to the fashionable areas, including Fifth Avenue, the "number of rich people who were found never to attend any church was enormous." For this polite class revivals were the equivalent of "wildfire, fanaticism and disorder"; if attached to any church it was to the Episcopalian, with its social respectability and emotional restraint.[77]

At the other end of the spectrum were the urban poor—a "dense and dark mass, the population of alleys, and cellars, and garrets—the ignorant, the degraded, the grossly sensual, the idle, the worthless—the refuse of society." Neither the evangelizing activities of the Benevolent Empire and the city missions nor the Free Church movements in Presbyterian and Episcopal churches, which complemented the almost universally free seating provided by Quakers and Methodists, succeeded in attracting the growing numbers of urban slum dwellers. This was due partly to the problems of social environment, partly to the unbending Catholicism of the German and particularly the Irish immigrant population. Louis Pease's Five Points House of Industry, for example, failed almost wholly to win converts in that destitute and predominantly Irish Catholic community of New York.[78]

The urban evangelical's concern is all the more understandable when his experience is compared with that of the small-town minister. For instance, in 1842, the year that Finney, Kirk, Knapp, and Maffitt were attempting to win Bostonians from Catholicism, Unitarianism, and Infidelity, Jabez Swan contributed to a revival in the small town of Mystic, Connecticut, in which over four hundred were baptized, "and so thinned were the ranks of un-believers . . . that it was easy to believe that the whole community had become or was in a way to become experimentally acquainted with pure and undefiled religion." Mystic's experience was not normal, but neither was it unprecedented. In Bristol, Rhode Island, in 1812, according to William Rogers, "The whole town was apparently paralyzed . . . and business in general suspended for several days. . . . All political conversation for a time ceased."[79] One of Nettleton's revivals, in Salisbury, Connecticut, in 1815-16, provoked such interest that "husbandmen would leave their fields, mechanics their shops, and females their domestic concerns, to inquire the way of eternal life. Religion was the great and all absorbing theme in almost all companies, and on almost all occasions." At New York Mills in 1830 cotton production was halted as penitent factory workers held prayer meet-ings; Christians were "encouraged to pray for, and even to *expect*, the con-version of every unconverted person in the place."[80] Even when the com-munity was divided and there was opposition to revival, dissenters fre-quently found themselves reduced to silence if not to actual acceptance of the movement.

Of crucial importance in producing revivals of this kind was the cultural and ethnic homogeneity of a relatively tightly knit community such as a New England township, with its common religious traditions, its experience and expectation of periodic revivals, and a population small enough for all the families to be acquainted. In this environment, once a revival had broken out in the churches themselves (usually during the leisure afforded by winter) and had soon become common knowledge, it was often possible to bring the rest of the community into the revival's embrace after house-to-house visiting by pastor, evangelist, and church members. With the whole town aroused, with secular entertainments discouraged, and sometimes with regular daily business suspended, the backslider, the unconverted inquirer, or the nonconformist—Universalist, Deist or atheist—might come under intense psychological and social pressures to attend and submit. It was not by mere accident that the pastor or evangelist sought to influence "the great-est weight of character in the community."[81] If the leading families were sympathetic and involved in the revival, then they might exert considerable influence on the rest. The conversion of the principal lawyers, doctors, mer-chants, and other professional men in Pittsfield, Massachusetts, in 1821, and the presence at the services of the high sheriff of the county, provided what for Heman Humphrey was the key to the success of the revival and to the quietening of the drum-banging, canon-firing body of dissidents who tried to disrupt the services.[82]

The comprehensive sweep of small-town revivals and their success in bringing those communities into closer conformity with the social morality of evangelical religion—sobriety, observance of the Sabbath, shunning of "profanities"—encouraged many city evangelicals to see revivals as the key to urban problems. Revivals would reach the inaccessible pockets of population; they could provide the only viable antidote to the "interlocking sins" of drinking, gambling, Sabbath-breaking, and corrupting doctrines which were thought to cause the crime, vagrancy, poverty, and other social ills afflicting American cities.[83] Nor were revivals wholly unsuccessful in their aims. Many accounts noted that "all classes of the people" had been affected, rich as well as poor. Converts might include "persons whose previous character was not only doubtful, but openly vicious," as at Harlem Mission in 1843, when "a leader in mischievous rioting" and a prominent tavern keeper were involved.[84] Sometimes, when revivals broadened their hold, theatres, circuses, billiard halls, bar rooms, and other places of entertainment were closed for lack of customers.

City revivals, however, did little more than tinker with the problems facing urban evangelicals, because city populations were much too large and internally mobile. Gardiner Spring found himself hampered by the "wide dispersion [of Christians], the continual change in their place of residence."[85] How much more difficult, then, was the problem of reaching non-Christians. Further obstacles lay in the greater heterogeneity and stratification of city populations and, particularly in seaboard cities, their exposure to cosmopolitan influences. Evangelicals were faced by city masses with "vast varieties of habits, manners, customs, and opinions"; by non-English-speaking and foreign-born populations, as in New Orleans, with its large "French semi-infidel Catholic element"; and by visitors who came "to . . . corrupt the young with the lax notions of . . . the licentious capitals of Europe."[86] All this militated against the cultural uniformity essential to successful revivalism.

Rarely did evangelicals effectively break into these unevangelical or anti-evangelical cultures: revival converts were drawn mainly from the churches themselves (from the unconverted adherents and the Sunday schools), from lapsed churchgoers and backsliders, and from migrants from the country and immigrants from Europe who boasted an evangelical heritage. Even here the churches faced problems: for while "the man of profaneness in the country village is usually almost alone . . . and the burning *lens* of public indignation usually meets him wherever he goes," the urban sinner could often find anonymity and avoid evangelical pressures to conform.[87] Indeed (and again in contrast to the small-town experience), it was made easier for him by the general dissociation of the more sophisticated city elite from revivalism and its "enthusiastic" connotations.

When urban revivals did appear to match in extent those of smaller communities, they seem to have been the product of essentially small-town circumstances. In 1830-31 Finney's impressive revival in Rochester, a city of nearly ten thousand inhabitants, closed saloons, taverns, and theatres, and "converted the great mass of the most influential people." This was a brilliant evangelical achievement in an urban environment. Yet Rochester's outlook was in fact culturally much closer to the small town than to that of a larger east-coast city, since its amazing growth (from a mere 1,049 inhabitants in 1818) had been based largely on migration from the evangelical richness of rural New England. Finney simply appealed to Yankee consciences dulled during the canal boom of the 1820s.[88]

Similar features of homogeneity and small-town roots existed in Lowell, Massachusetts, a textile manufacturing town with a population in 1840 of twenty thousand. The many cotton and woolen factories were "filled with Protestant workers brought in from all the country round," especially young women over fifteen years old. The company refused employment to "any one who is habitually absent from public worship on the Sabbath, or known to be guilty of immorality."[89] These concentrations of like-minded operatives from similar cultural and religious backgrounds provided a fruitful field for revival work; the contagious effect of a factory conversion gave Lowell even greater resemblance to a small town, with its social network conducive to a speedy chain reaction.

Even the urban revival of 1857-58 can be interpreted partly in small-town terms. The unprecedented coverage of the revival by the secular press and national telegraph system promoted the rapid dissemination of news and increased the community interest essential to the spread of religious excitement. The clever psychological technique of dealing with people in their occupational groups—special meetings were held for businessmen, firemen, policemen, and even waiters—reproduced the sort of pressures and bonds of social sympathy more usually connected with small-town religion. Moreover, central to the revival in many areas was the work of the Young Men's Christian Association, established in the principal cities in the 1850s to protect the morals and piety of young men recently arrived from the country. They offered sociability and friendship in hostile surroundings. "Young men and youth are 'at home' here and must not hesitate to take part," announced a typical YMCA church-meeting poster in 1858; the conversion of young men through YMCA agency testified in some cases to a homesickness or disenchantment with city life.[90] For such people revivals could provide a simple, uncomplicated view of a culturally complex and threatening world. Involvement in a revival might also reflect a young man's sense of guilt for the betrayal of an evangelical background: ministers and laity spent much time ensuring the return of such apostates.

These urban manifestations of small-town revivalism were not parallelled by a reproduction of its numerical success. First, despite impressive growth, city church membership failed to expand at a rate commensurate with that of the whole urban population. Table 1 indicates Methodist strength in three fairly typical cities—Baltimore, Cincinnati, and New York—between 1820 and 1860. In all three cases there was in these forty years an overall

TABLE 1   Percentage of Methodists in the Total Population of Baltimore,
           Cincinnati, and New York City, 1820-60

	Baltimore	*Cincinnati*	*New York City*
1820	7.80	6.31	2.60
1830	7.78	4.60	1.95
1840	10.55	5.41	2.05
1850	7.22	2.90	1.73
1860	7.07	2.51	1.41

SOURCES: *Minute of the Annual Conferences of the Methodist Episcopal Church* (1820, 1830, 1840, 1850 and 1860); U.S. Bureau of the Census, *Fourth Census* (1820), *Fifth Census* (1830), *Sixth Census* (1840), *Seventh Census* (1850), *Eighth Census* (1860).

decline in the percentage of Methodists in the population at large. This decline was not steady; indeed the denominational growth of the early 1840s in all three cities almost returned to the high levels of the second decade of the century. It was only "the vast influx of foreigners" in the 1840s and 1850s that undermined the relative standing of evangelical Protestants, particularly in New York and Cincinnati. Secondly, even more significant than this evangelical decline relative to the whole urban population was the more rapid church growth in nonurban areas. Figure 1 compares Methodist strength in New York City with the rest of New York State—predominantly rural and small town in makeup. From this it is clear that until 1820 the Methodists were relatively stronger in the city than out of it, but thereafter, despite their participation in the major revival movements, the city Methodists lost ground as nonurban areas were cultivated. A tellingly similar pattern is clear from figure 2 which compares the experience of Boston with that of the remainder of New England. Methodist standing in both was comparable during the 1810s: here again the crucial decade was the 1820s, when the enormous Methodist gains were based largely on rapid expansion in non-urban areas. Thereafter the disparity between urban and rural strength grew wider not narrower. Revivalism had not proved the panacea that urban evangelicals hoped for.

British Contributions

The new revivalism, then, had been fashioned by various forces. The frontier had provided a forum for its most dramatic expression; Methodists had broadened its currency; Charles Finney had helped secure its acceptance by reluctant Calvinists; city evangelicals had refined it and given it system and organization. There remains an additional factor in its shaping: the influence of British evangelicalism. For while British Protestantism, with its Established Church and "fox-hunting clergymen," was often taken by orthodox American evangelicals as a measure of all that a virtuous and voluntarist American Protestantism was not, most of them recognized the common blood, the common faith, and the common purpose that they shared with their British counterparts. On the Anglo-Saxon race, blessed with free political institutions, lay the responsibility of defending evangelical truth against the attempted encroachments of Popery and Infidelity. The sense of American dependence within this partnership, noted by the Philadelphian Ashbel Green in 1799—he perceived in American evangelical circles a "kind of sacred emulation" of British missionary and humanitarian initiatives—gradually gave way to a growing self-confidence and feelings of full partnership with Britain in the grand enterprise of carrying the Gospel to the whole world. A buoyant optimism with a frequent millennial strain marks much of the transatlantic correspondence of the early and mid-nineteenth century. "England and America must love each other," declared the aged Methodist Freeborn Garrettson, for they "are the nations by whom God will work. . . . The leven is cast in, and it must defuse its salutary nature, till the whole is levened."[91]

This sense of oneness and joint mission was perhaps most powerfully felt by British and American Methodists. It is worth recalling that American Methodism sprang largely from Britain and was not an indigenous growth. The Irish immigrants, Philip Embury and Robert Strawbridge, supported by the British preachers Richard Boardman, Joseph Pilmoor, Robert Williams, and Asbury, first rooted Methodism in American soil. Moreover, British-born preachers and laymen played a disproportionately influential role in cultivating the tender plant: at the first annual conference of American Methodists in Philadelphia in 1773 there was only one American-born itinerant preacher. Even the persecution of the tory Methodists during the Revolution and the return to Britain of most English Wesleyan preachers did not remove British influence. Zealous Methodists like Richard Whatcoat and Thomas Vasey were sent to encourage the work. More importantly, Asbury remained. Throughout forty years, while traveling a quarter of a million miles and saving thousands of souls, he fired with the same urgency the indigenous preachers of the young church and came to be justly regarded as the father of the American Methodist connection. Second in stature only to Asbury was the able and irrepressible Welshman, Thomas Coke, nominated by Wesley to be Asbury's colleague as superintendent of American Methodism. Between 1784 and 1803 Coke made nine supervisory and preaching visits to America.

American relations with British Methodists in the period of the early republic were not entirely unruffled. A popular suspicion that British Methodists were arrogant anti-republicans persisted, reinforced by the tensions and animosities of the War of 1812. The problem was well illustrated by the

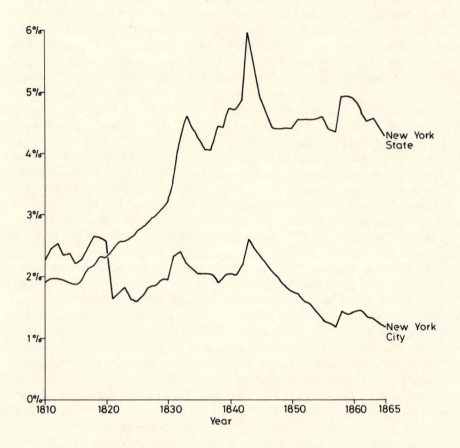

Figure 1. MEC Membership in New York City and in the Rest of New York
State As a Percentage of Their Respective Populations, 1810-65.

SOURCES: *Minutes of the Annual Conferences of the Methodist Episcopal Church* (1810-65); U.S. Bureau of the Census, *Third Census* (1810), *Fourth Census* (1820), *Fifth Census* (1830), *Sixth Census* (1840), *Seventh Census* (1850), *Eighth Census* (1860), *Ninth Census* (1870).

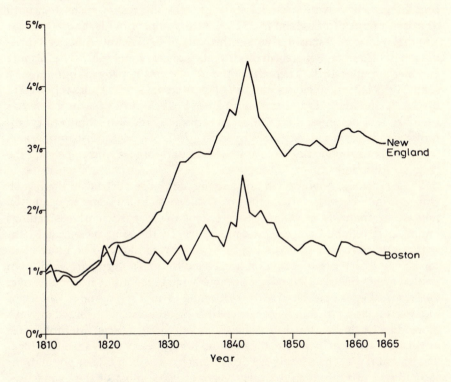

Figure 2. MEC Membership in Boston and in the Rest of New England As a Percentage of Their Respective Populations, 1810-65.

SOURCES: *Minutes of the Annual Conferences of the Methodist Episcopal Church* (1810-65); U.S. Bureau of the Census, *Third Census* (1810), *Fourth Census* (1820), *Fifth Census* (1830), *Sixth Census* (1840), *Seventh Census* (1850), *Eighth Census* (1860), *Ninth Census* (1870).

case of the luckless Joshua Marsden, a British Wesleyan missionary to the West Indies who arrived in New York in the spring of 1812 en route to England. Here, as a consequence of the embargo and war, he found himself in effective detention for over two years. He was not without Methodist friends and persuaded Bishop William McKendree to give him a ministerial position in New York City. But Marsden's tactlessly proclaimed loyalty to George III ignited Methodist passions. Some ministers tried to prevent his preaching. They were unsuccessful, but the ill feeling persisted until Marsden's return to England in 1814.[92] At a more formal level too the war strained relations, particularly over the issue of British and American jurisdiction in Canada, where Methodist allegiances were split. The dispute rumbled on until 1820. Thereafter official relations improved, but amongst some of the laity suspicion of the British persisted. George Coles reported in the 1820s an elderly lady's hostility to her English-born preacher: "He has been brought up under a tyrannical government; and if he thinks to tyrannize over us, it won't answer." Even in the 1850s Methodist immigrants from England found it necessary in some quarters to avoid appearing the "regular John Bull."[93]

These tensions, however, in no fundamental sense obstructed the British contribution. Through letters, the press, ministerial visits, and transatlantic migration, channels of influence were kept open, particularly as sailings improved in reliability, speed, and regularity. By the 1830s a Georgia Methodist could note that the crossing to England was likely to be more comfortable and faster than riding on horseback to the western part of his own conference.[94] British Methodism became a reference point in debates over questions of episcopal power, the stationing of ministers, and a variety of questions relating to church government.[95] Britain also contributed in ways more directly influential in the development of American Methodist revivalism. First, it helped meet the demand for aggressively evangelistic local and itinerant preachers badly needed to reach a swelling tide of population; secondly, it produced, in the early years at least, most of the evangelical literature necessary to support revival effort; thirdly, it contributed much of the refinement and polish that made Methodist revivalism palatable to more sophisticated American audiences; and, finally, the constant antislavery pressures emanating from Britain reinforced the element of social morality within American revivalism.

The neglected obituaries that litter the *Minutes of the Annual Conferences of the Methodist Episcopal Church*, although frustratingly uninformative in their recitation of the barest biographical data, offer a cumulative picture of the character and makeup of the itinerant preaching force. The minutes over ninety years yield nearly three thousand obituaries of itinerant Methodists who entered the ministry between 1771 (when Asbury arrived) and 1865. Although this total falls short of the total number of ministers operat-

TABLE 2   Country of Birth of Men Entering the MEC Itinerancy, 1771-1865

	North America	Britain	Other	Total in sample	Unknown
Number of ministers	2,335 (89%)	228 (9%)	51 (2%)	2,614	320

SOURCE: *Minutes of the Annual Conferences of the Methodist Episcopal Church* (1792-1881).

ing in these years, it is large enough to be considered a representative sample. Of those itinerants for whom there is a record of their place of birth, the British-born composed 9 percent (see table 2). A breakdown of this same sample into decennial groups based on the year that ministers entered the itinerancy indicates that there were proportionately more British-born in the period up to 1800 than in any later decade (see table 3). War was perhaps the major cause of the decline in the proportion during the 1810s, but from the 1820s there continued a steady and impressive increase until the 1850s, when over 10 percent of those joining the MEC ministry had a British background. War once more interrupted the pattern in the 1860s.

The proportion of 9 percent British-born was, if marked, hardly overwhelming. It is worth emphasizing, however, that this group excluded many American-born Methodists whose parents had learned their Methodism in Britain, that there were more British-born in such influential conferences as Troy and New York than elsewhere, and that the group was able to exert an influence greater than the bare numbers sugest, since it was working within a denomination largely sympathetic to British Wesleyanism. It is not possible to offer a precise total of British-born ministers. In the period from 1773 to 1900 the minutes record the deaths of 426 ministers of whose British birth there is no doubt and who entered the ministry in or before 1865. But this figure does not include those who were active in this period and lived on beyond 1900 (men like George Hughes, leading east-coast evangelist and perfectionist), or those whose connection with the itinerant ministry was broken before death, as in the cases of John Newland Maffitt and the scores who "located" after a few years' work.[96] And the list excludes local preachers and opinion-forming laity. But there are enough data to provide a picture of what sorts of Britons entered the ministry, why they came, and what they contributed to the revivalism and the growth of a denomination that provided the cutting edge of American evangelicalism.

Not surprisingly, a substantial majority—59 percent—of these 426 ministers were born in England; 31 percent were Irish-born (table 4). But these overall figures hide the shifting pattern within the whole period. In no decade before 1830 did the English-born entering the ministry outnumber the Irish; before then 61 percent were Irish and 36 percent English. Thereafter the proportions shifted so far that 65 percent English-born entered the MEC

between 1830 and 1865; the Irish figure for the same period was 24 percent. This change in emphasis may simply reflect shifts in the wider pattern of emigration from Britain, but this cannot be established from the statistics of emigrants, since they do not differentiate between English, Irish, Scots, and Welsh. Certainly the change does not reflect any absolute decline in the Irish contribution to the American ministry, for the number of entering Irish-born shows a steady decennial growth. Rather it suggests some caution on the part of the English, particularly those of a more conservative temperament, in the generation or so after the Revolution. For such men, British North America may have appeared a more appropriate milieu than the United States. One thing is sure: from the 1820s onward English Methodists who pondered emigration, as indeed did British emigrants generally, found the United States an increasingly attractive destination.[97]

Many of the influences that drew these men from Britain were similar to those operating on emigrants generally. Amongst the so-called push factors that drove thousands annually from the United Kingdom were poverty, food shortages, and general economic depression. The high representation of Irish in the American ministry directly mirrors the extensive economic deprivation and intermittent famine in Ireland during this period. If the picture in England was less bleak, it too experienced cycles of depression; it was during one of the worst of these, after the Napoleonic wars, that George Coles left London for the New World. More personal reasons could also operate: both Joseph Holdich in 1818 and Zachariah Davenport in 1832 left Britain as enfeebled young men hoping that a long voyage and a change of climate would restore their health.[98]

For her part, America pulled men to her shores because it represented one of the best hopes for economic advance. Abraham Owen and Alexander McMullen felt in some general way that the United States presented opportunities for "improving their worldly condition." A handful were fortune hunters in the strictest sense: after twelve years at sea George Sim in 1853 went prospecting for gold in California. But most looked more conventionally to farming, commerce, and industry to achieve their prosperity. John Cooper left Yorkshire "to engage in a special branch of woollen manufacture" in New England; when Joseph Marsh left England in 1821 he had already come to an agreement with a New England glass company to serve them for at least three years. Of course, economic attractions could be supplemented by other influences. A number, including John Buckley and George Stevenson, were drawn to join uncles, brothers, or other members of their families who had already emigrated. Some looked for educational advantage: the Scot, William Armstrong, believed he would find "better opportunities to satisfy his insatiable thirst for knowledge" in America. For S. Ravenscroft of Stoke, a "great admirer of republican institutions," the United States' attraction had to do with her social and political makeup; similarly Thomas Walters was drawn by the "freedom" of America. But it

TABLE 3   British-born Methodists Entering the MEC Itinerancy, 1771-1865

	1770s	1780s	1790s	1800s	1810s	1820s	1830s	1840s	1850s	1860-65
Total ministers in sample	12	50	99	191	277	426	719	521	446	91
Number of British-born ministers	4	7	11	18	12	30	55	40	46	5
Percentage of British-born ministers	33.3%	14%	11.1%	9.4%	4.3%	7%.	7.6%	7.7%	10.3%	5.5%

SOURCE: *Minutes of the Annual Conferences of the Methodist Episcopal Church* (1792-1881).

TABLE 4   Birthplace of British-born ministers of the MEC, 1771-1865

Date of entering ministry	England	Ireland	Wales	Scotland	Other (Isle of Man, Channel Isles)	Unknown	Total in sample
1771-89	5	5	—	—	—	1	
1790-99	4	6	—	—	—	1	
1800-09	2	15	1	—	—	—	
1810-19	4	10	—	—	—	1	
1820-29	16	16	1	—	—	—	
1830-39	56	22	7	2	1	—	
1840-49	56	26	3	4	2	—	
1850-59	94	29	6	7	2	—	
1860-65	13	4	1	3	—	—	
Totals	250	133	19	16	5	3	426
	(59%)	(31%)	(4%)	(4%)	(1%)	(1%)	

SOURCE: *Minutes of the Annual Conferences of the Methodist Episcopal Church* (1792-1900).

is not always possible to determine exactly why emigrants chose America: as George Coles admitted, "my mind was drawn towards the United States with an attraction which I could neither explain nor resist."[99]

There were identifiable religious forces at work, too—some of them from within British Methodism. John Wesley was only the earliest to encourage Methodist work in the New World. James Mather, for example, member of a thoroughly Wesleyan family, emigrated from Manchester in 1843 on the advice of Robert Newton, friend of America and British delegate to the MEC General Conference of 1840. Others found themselves driven from Britain by an apparent lack of opportunities. Benjamin Redford was in competition with so many candidates for the Wesleyan ministry that in 1843 he decided to enter the American itinerancy. Similarly, William Livesey, a Yorkshire local preacher, was recommended as a foreign missionary by the Wesleyan Conference of 1829; there seemed little hope of a speedy appointment, and in 1830 Livesey became a minister of the MEC.[100]

More importantly, a substantial number felt a particular religious call to a new continent waiting to be won for Christ. George Cookman visited America on business in 1821; on his homeward voyage he felt a "call of the Spirit" and returned to America in 1825 to preach. Another Yorkshireman, Isaac Milner, studied under an ex-missionary to the West Indies and developed a powerful desire to work in America, despite the "sacrifice [of] home, friends, relations and associations." Sometimes a persuasive American sowed the idea. John Emory, American delegate to the British Wesleyan Methodist Conference in 1820, was instrumental in encouraging John Summerfield to cross the Atlantic. There were those who needed little encouragement and for whom the attractions of America were obvious. In America, unlike Britain, married men could enter the traveling ministry; for Thomas Bottomley, as for others, it seems that this was a powerful attraction. Most important of all, America possessed a voluntarist church structure and a tradition of religious toleration. Isaac Milner felt "straitened" in England under an established church and looked for freedom in America; James Rusk sought to escape the claustrophobia and intolerance of the Irish Roman Catholic community that denounced him as a Methodist "heretic."[101]

This list of emigrants represented a powerful injection of evangelicalism into American religious life. The vast majority had known an evangelical Protestant upbringing, Methodist in the main. The denominational affiliation of the ministers' parents is known in 100 instances: 94 were Protestant, 61 specifically Methodist, and a large proportion of the 16 attached to the Church of England were sympathetic to Methodism. Even those who had not experienced conversion before they left Britain—a minority of those for whom the data have been examined (table 5)—generally brought with them a knowledge of evangelicalism that helped shape their later religious development. Most who crossed the Atlantic in childhood came with actively evangelical parents. William Wheeler's settled in Indiana in 1822 when their son was only ten. He was converted in the following year, but the ground had largely been prepared in his English home, where Wesleyan ministers had been frequent visitors. There is a similar pattern among immigrants who arrived unconverted in their late teens and early twenties and whose conversion within a year or so was little more than the climax of a process begun in Britain. Sometimes, though, that process was interrupted by the jolt of emigration. It took the guilt and nostalgia aroused by American Methodist preaching to "reawaken" these "apostates" and secure their conversions. In 1817 John Tackaberry left Ireland for Canada, where "evil company" kept him away from church for two years. Only the visit of an American itinerant preacher and transatlantic pressure from his Methodist brother in Ireland successfully led him from "wickedness" to salvation and eventually into the ministry.[102]

Most British-born ministers, however, seem to have brought a conversion experience with them. Some, like George Hollis of Rye and Joseph Odgers of Cornwall, had been converted in full-scale revivals. Others could boast the contribution of famed revivalists to their spiritual advance: Gideon Ouseley, the Irish outdoor itinerant, exerted a powerful influence over Thomas Burch and Moses Blackstock, as did the high churchman Robert Aitken over Henry Fox. More importantly, all this group, through their experience of a dramatic change from a state of sin to one of grace, reinforced the evangelical direction of American Protestantism and the centrality within it of justification by faith alone.[103]

From the available evidence it seems that nearly half of British-born preachers developed their skills before they set foot in North America (table 5). A few progressed no further than the ranks of exhorter in Britain. But the vast majority had acquired experience as local preachers, in some cases over many years. None could rival Charles French's record of thirty years "on the plan" in England or David McCurdy's twenty-three in Ireland. Nor had many begun preaching at twelve, as had the "boy preacher," James Davidson. But John Harris, city missionary and street preacher, John Hewitt, and Thomas Watson were just a handful of those who had served over ten years as local preachers. Smaller in number were those who in Britain had been

TABLE 5 Place of Conversion and First Preaching of British-born Ministers of the MEC, 1771-1865

	Britain	*United States*	*Canada*	*Total*
Place of conversion (where known)	221 (62%)	127 (35%)	10 (3%)	358
Place of first preaching (where known)	150 (48%)	161 (51%)	2 (1%)	313

SOURCE: *Minutes of the Annual Conferences of the Methodist Episcopal Church* (1792-1900).

full members of the Wesleyan itinerant ministry or ministers of other evangelical churches. William Gothard, for seven years a Primitive Methodist minister, and Charles Stokes, seventeen years a Baptist preacher, were representative of those who found in the MEC a congenial arena for their American work.[104]

These men carried with them considerable experience in revivals and conversion-minded preaching acquired within the most revival-focused wing of British evangelicalism. By no means all joined the itinerant ministry immediately upon arrival. Local preachers commonly combined their religious duties for a few years with a secular means of support. Abraham Owen spent seven years as a tailor and an exhorter before entering the itinerancy; Thomas Sparkes joined the New York Conference in 1832 after thirteen years in the wool business. But whether in the local or the itinerant ministry most of these newcomers revelled in the greater freedom for revivalism and soul-saving in their new home. William Gothard and Abraham Bowers found themselves carried away at times by their "enthusiastic" preaching; Henry Stead developed a name as a major revival preacher over half a century in the New York and Troy conferences; Robert Beatty became a noted revivalist in Wisconsin; and scores of others developed reputations for general and particular skills in revival work. Walter Prescott and William Armstrong were effective with children and Sunday schools. Charles Elliott and Thomas Thompson supported the Methodist mission to the Wyandot Indians. Welsh-speaking preachers gravitated toward the various Welsh missions. Some threw themselves into pioneer work on the frontier. George Ekin joined the Western Conference (of Tennessee, Kentucky, and Ohio) in 1811 fresh from preaching in Ireland, and in forty years gathered over ten thousand into Methodism; a generation later James Raynor and Richard Williamson tackled the new frontier of California and Oregon. Others took on the urban frontier: John Davies was one of the first to conduct religious services in the Five Points of New York; at about the same time John Perry was at work for the Philadelphia City Mission. Finally, there were those who specialized as advocates of entire sanctification. Both William Routledge and David Nash received the "second blessing" while in England and devoted themselves to advocating this Wesleyan doctrine in the United States.[105]

The most revivalist of American denominations, then, received from Britain throughout the period before the Civil War constant injections of evangelical ministers and, of course, an even greater injection of immigrants who contributed actively as Sunday school teachers, tract distributors, or other lay agents of an urgent revivalism. Britain also supplied much of the published material that supported the American Methodist advance. Particularly during the early years, when the MEC was too busy saving souls to spare the resources to support its own literature, Americans were dependent on books, tracts, and magazines sent from England; even after establishing their own Book Concern, they continued to rely on British authors, most notably Wesley, Coke, John Fletcher, Joseph Benson, and Adam Clarke. Not until the 1820s, particularly with the appearance of the instantly successful *Christian Advocate*, did a sense of self-sufficiency develop. Even then British books continued to arrive, not only recondite volumes of theology, but also practical evangelical manuals and biographies of popular revival preachers. Elbert Osborn was only one American specialist in protracted meetings fired by the writings of the single-minded English revivalist, William Bramwell; the *Memoir of David Stoner*, a like-minded contemporary of Bramwell, was equally popular. Moreover, few seekers of entire sanctification in the 1830s and 1840s went without reading the *Life of William Carvosso*, the Cornish Methodist. Through various channels, especially George Coles, assistant editor of the *Christian Advocate*, and the network of British-born preachers, Americans continued to receive regular consignments of books right up to the Civil War.[106]

Britain's greatest influence perhaps lay in the gradual refinement of American Methodism. The new revivalism, so strongly identified with that denomination, could make only limited headway for as long as sophisticated Americans perceived it as the crude fervor of the poor and the uneducated. This, as we have seen, was what Methodists feared in the cities; this is why many of them tried to raise the social standing of their denomination and to refine its practice. Some believed they would achieve this in part through a greater commitment to education, an approach opposed by "old-fashioned Methodists" for whom ministerial learning was an obstacle to "heart religion." Britain contributed considerably to this increasingly one-sided debate, mostly on the side of better education. Thomas Coke was the most persistent advocate of the first Methodist college in America; and after Cokesbury, as it was called, had twice been destroyed by fire, the cause of learning was left dependent on a Book Concern dominated in its early years by the English-educated John Dickens and John Wilson. Thereafter British Methodists promoted the cause by contributing financially to American colleges, by bringing with them to America a sound university or theological-college training, and by actively contributing to the establishing and running of seminaries and universities from the 1830s onward. Charles Elliott, educated "thoroughly" in Ireland, professor at Madison College, Pennsylvania, editor of the *Western Christian Advocate*, and later president of Iowa Wesleyan University, was only the most illustrious of those Britons who gave American Methodism social status by strengthening its literary and educational character.[107]

More direct agents in winning a wider approval for Methodism were those preachers who, without jettisoning their evangelical appeal, developed a polished pulpit style. Amongst those who secured for Methodism a hear-

John Summerfield. Courtesy of Drew University Library.

ing from the opinion-forming and well-to-do were several whose allegiance was to the respectable wing of British Wesleyanism. One of these, John Summerfield, was widely regarded after his premature death as the single most influential agent in broadening the social base of his denomination. Now scarcely remembered, he won in his brief career an extraordinary popularity, founded almost entirely on a unique pulpit presence, which drew audiences from all denominations and social classes. The precocious child of an engineer and Wesleyan local preacher from Preston, Lancashire, Summerfield had spent much of his childhood in the company of adults. As a child of twelve he taught persons twice his age. Later his father took him to Dublin, where his fascination with public speaking and a seven-month spell in a debtors' prison stirred him to become a self-taught lawyer for insolvents. In 1818 his conversion in a cellar prayer meeting drew him into the ministry. Early signs of tuberculosis began to blight his promising itinerant career, and in 1820 he sailed for the United States.

His impact in America was sensational and unexpected. So great was his popularity that within eighteen months the secular press in Philadelphia was carrying regular bulletins on his health. His written sermons offer no key to his success: much of his appeal lay in his youth, frailty, and "angelic benignity." Admirers considered him "chaste" or simple in style and language; he employed direct entreaty and a pathos made all the more effective by his own condition. There was nothing of the ranter or frontier exhorter about John Summerfield. In Ireland his audiences had often included persons unconnected formally with Methodism—members of the nobility and gentry—as well as influential members of the connection. This pattern persisted in the United States. In Philadelphia, Baltimore, and other eastern cities, his eloquence, "good sense and good taste" attracted many of the better-off into Methodist churches. Episcopalians in Albany welcomed him; in Washington his Foundry Chapel congregation included John Quincy Adams, John C. Calhoun, and some fifty other senators and congressmen. Above all, Summerfield won for Methodism a new status in New York City, where he was stationed in 1821 and 1822, by winning "the wonderful admiration of all classes," including "aristocratic" and "fashionable" groups who followed him from church to church. Summerfield was only twenty-seven when he died, but his work was done: Methodists had begun to secure recognition from the respectable.[108]

The relationship of religious revival and evangelical attitudes to black slavery is complex and incompletely resolved, but it seems clear that British Methodism's concern for the slave helped reinforce the antislavery tendencies in American Methodist revivalism. The doctrines of millennialism and disinterested benevolence preached in revivals gave a powerful impetus to much reforming activity and helped to shape the immediatist abolition movement of the 1830s; the evangelical experiences of Theodore Weld,

James Birney, William Lloyd Garrison, and other abolitionist leaders are relevant in explaining their brand of antislavery; the rhetoric and persuasive techniques of abolitionism in the 1830s closely resemble those of revival meetings. Yet revivalism and abolitionism were clearly not one and the same. In the south revivals remained central to the life of evangelical churches throughout the antebellum period, yet organized antislavery sentiment waned and Christians used the Bible belligerently in the defense of the "peculiar institution." Nor were revivals and abolitionism coextensive in the north; even Finney, who wanted an end to slavery, regarded radical abolitionism as an obstacle to soul-saving and viewed with apprehension an agitation that he felt could lead to civil war.[109]

Methodism well illustrates this uncertain relationship between revivalism and attitudes to slavery. The vast majority of northern Methodists, though they subscribed to the original Wesleyan view of slavery as sin, sought primarily to maintain church unity. A handful of radicals led by Orange Scott argued that no church harboring slaveholders could be spiritually pure; in various schisms in the early 1840s their supporters consolidated themselves into the Wesleyan Methodist Church and used revival meetings to win converts to abolitionism. Yet simultaneously many southern Methodists found tolerable any tensions they may have felt between slaveholding and an evangelical profession of faith. As far as the escaped slave Frederick Douglass was concerned, "Revivals of religion and revivals in the slave trade [went] hand in hand together"; in his experience, conversions and camp meetings, far from undermining slavery, actually lent a sanction to the institution.[110]

British Methodists almost unanimously used their influence to place religious revivalism "on the side of liberty, of emancipation." They did not have to agree with Frederick Douglass (indeed, they proved largely unsympathetic to his radical views) to perceive slavery as a "foul blot," a "damning sin," and "a dark leprous spot" on American society and its churches. Abolitionist Americans welcomed the pressure that Britain put on their churchmen, whether formally, as at the London sessions of the 1846 Evangelical Alliance, or more frequently and informally through private correspondence.[111] Even more effective was the influx of immigrants of an overwhelmingly antislavery disposition. There were few, perhaps, who went so far as to follow John Broadhead into the Scottite party. But Daniel Wise, who brought impressive editorial and preaching skills into the service of antislavery and who toyed briefly with the idea of leaving the MEC for the abolitionist Methodists, showed that it was possible to use the mother church as a forum for radical views. Indeed, a substantial group of mature immigrants from Britain, carrying with them well-formed attitudes to slavery, used the ministry of the MEC to advance antislavery and the broader reform of society. George Gold, for example, manumitted the slaves that he inherited from his uncle; George Cookman encouraged emancipation in

Maryland and won the genuine confidence of the slaves he met; James McClelland could draw on an experience of teaching emancipated slaves in the West Indies; Thomas Bainbridge and William Livesey supplemented their antislavery preaching with temperance work; and a large group of British-born found that their principles took them into service as chaplains in the Union army.[112] Probably most indicative of British attitudes to slavery and the south are the settlement patterns of these immigrants. Large numbers were determined to avoid settling in areas where the only Methodist church "perpetuate[d the slave's] bondage, and justifie[d] his degradation and oppression."[113] A comparison of the minutes of the MEC and the MECS for the period 1845-65 suggests that over three times as many British-born Methodists settled in free states as in the slave south.[114] To some extent this reflects the economic realities that shaped the pattern of settlement of immigrants in general. But it also indicates the antipathy toward slavery that many European Methodists carried with them. That antipathy only intensified the antislavery tendencies of the northern church and, ironically, turned even more defensive the church in the south. When British-born antislavery ministers did penetrate her borders their lot was persecution and eventual retreat, as in the case of Daniel De Vinne's disrupted mission to the slaves in Mississippi.[115]

The impact of British Methodists should, of course, be kept in perspective. First, they represented the most conspicuous but not the sole transatlantic connection. Scotch-Irish Presbyterians, and English and Welsh Calvinist Dissenters injected their own brand of evangelicalism, though in Britain this, as we shall see, was much less firmly focused on revivals. Secondly, the relationship between the immigrant and his new environment was a two-way affair; as well as influencing American revivalism, British Methodists themselves underwent some sort of metamorphosis in a different culture. It was not simply a matter of a change of loyalties—George Coles, for instance, became "quite a Yankey"—but rather of shifts in their outlook and practices.[116] The vast circuits of early nineteenth-century American Methodism and the extensive use of camp meetings, for example, provided a context within which newcomers with only a half-developed instinct for revivals could find much greater opportunities for soul-saving; similarly, the earlier and more wholehearted flowering of teetotalism in America presented an opportunity for temperance revivalism that Britain did not at that stage offer. Finally, British influence tended in the main to reinforce and not to challenge the established direction of American revivalism, which had itself been shaped very largely by the particular social and cultural environment of America itself. Even Britain's marked contribution in refining American revivalism was significant primarily because it coincided with similar indigenous movements toward education and social improvement. Yet for all these qualifications it is clear that revivalism in the United States had a substantial transatlantic dimension during this period, one which Turnerians with their frontier-focused lenses would do well to consider.

The Topography of Revivals, 1790-1865

It now remains to examine the incidence of religious revivals in the period of the Second Great Awakening and its postscript from 1790 to 1865. These were years when the new revivalism came to dominate the Protestant denominations and when those churches generally experienced formidable growth. From 7 percent in 1800, the proportion of Protestant church members in the population increased to 15 percent by 1855, suggesting that through revivals had come both an extension of evangelical influence and an intensification of the pressures on the unconverted to move from the category of congregational "hearer" to committed member. The pattern of these revivals is best traced through the annual returns of membership in the Methodist churches, not simply because the Methodists were more firmly associated with revivalism than other denominations, but also on account of the relative completeness and reliability of their statistics. In fact, the returns of the other evangelical churches, though less complete, serve to support the general picture presented by Methodist evidence and suggest that in terms of the incidence of revivals the Methodist experience was typical of evangelicalism as a whole.[117]

It is of course possible to find evidence of revivals in almost every year of this period if those of limited geographical and numerical extent are included. Five New York City churches, for example, claimed significant revivals in 1836, a year of general religious recession; ten years later Joseph Wakeley reported a limited revival at Trenton, New Jersey, during a period of similar "coldness."[118] Of greater interest, however (and this is what will be considered here), is the broader pulse of revival: the oscillation between periods of rapid overall growth, when membership increased at a rate faster than the population at large, periods marked by the multiplication of revival services, and—on the other hand—times of religious depression, when membership went into absolute decline or grew so slowly that it failed to keep pace with the overall growth in population. Between these periods of euphoric advance and frustrating depression there sometimes, but not inevitably, intervened years of gradual growth, when regular but unspectacular revivals kept the proportion of church members to general population largely fixed.

The precise course of these oscillations will be clear from table 6 and figure 3. Table 6 indicates the annual growth rates of the Methodists from 1791 to 1865 (including, after 1844, the MECS). These have been calculated by expressing the annual increase in membership as a percentage of the previous year's total membership. Figure 3 expresses Methodist annual membership as a proportion of the total population of the United States.

TABLE 6 Annual Growth Rates of American and British Methodists, 1791-1865

Year	American growth rate	British growth rate	Year	American growth rate	British growth rate	Year	American growth rate	British growth rate
1791	10.10	1.54	1816	1.45	5.28	1841	8.03	1.58
1792	3.98	3.32	1817	4.96	1.20	1842	6.35	-0.48
1793	2.52	1.04	1818	2.12	0.76	1843	16.92	2.05
1794	-1.53	14.19	1819	4.92	0.96	1844	10.38	1.68
1795	-9.48	8.47	1820	7.87	1.33	1845	-2.69	0.09
1796	-6.02	5.88	1821	8.18	9.16	1846	-3.52	-0.14
1797	3.53	8.02	1822	5.65	8.85	1847	-0.19	-0.78
1798	2.57	6.51	1823	5.22	4.97	1848	3.07	0.85
1799	1.96	6.67	1824	5.11	4.44	1849	3.23	3.64
1800	5.77	-1.00	1825	3.84	0.67	1850	3.21	4.54
1801	12.30	-2.14	1826	5.76	2.89	1851	3.90	-0.34
1802	19.02	3.88	1827	5.88	2.26	1852	1.50	-4.96
1803	19.99	3.43	1828	9.54	3.22	1853	4.40	-2.70
1804	8.71	0.77	1829	7.17	1.52	1854	4.07	-1.87

Year		
1805	6.02	4.81
1806	8.86	8.98
1807	10.74	6.97
1808	5.12	7.18
1809	7.27	4.47
1810	7.07	4.31
1811	5.73	5.31
1812	5.85	6.43
1813	9.70	3.86
1814	-1.48	7.08
1815	0.02	4.31

Year		
1830	8.69	0.47
1831	7.76	0.81
1832	6.91	3.80
1833	9.32	10.54
1834	6.51	4.79
1835	2.15	1.83
1836	-0.37	3.32
1837	0.60	6.21
1838	6.50	2.70
1839	7.14	3.35
1840	9.54	4.51

Year		
1855	2.95	-1.82
1856	1.16	2.12
1857	2.25	-3.72
1858	12.13	3.82
1859	2.40	6.55
1860	3.32	6.03
1861	-0.57	2.78
1862	-4.59	3.25
1863	-2.06	2.21
1864	0.53	0.34
1865	0.13	0.54

NOTES: The growth rate represents the annual net gain or loss expressed as a percentage of total membership in the previous year.

The American growth rate is based on MEC membership 1791-1844, 1861-65, and on combined MEC and MECS membership 1845-60.

The British growth rate is based on the total combined membership of the major Methodist denominations in England and Wales.

SOURCES: *Minutes of the Annual Conferences of the Methodist Episcopal Church* (1791-1865); P. A. Peterson, *Handbook of Southern Methodism* . . . (Richmond, Va., 1883); Alan D. Gilbert, "The Growth and Decline of Nonconformity in England and Wales . . . ," D. Phil. thesis, Oxford University, 1973.

Figure 3. American and British Methodist Membership As a Percentage of the
Population, 1801-70.

SOURCES: *Minutes of the Annual Conferences of the Methodist Episcopal Church* (1791-1865); Peterson, *Handbook of Southern Methodism*; Gilbert, "Growth and Decline"; U.S. Bureau of the Census, *Historical Statistics of the United States, Colonial Times to 1970, Bicentennial Edition, Part 1* (Washington, D.C.), p. 8; B. R. Mitchell and Phyllis Deane, *Abstract of British Historical Statistics* (Cambridge, 1962), pp. 8-9.

Together table 6 and figure 3 suggest four periods of rapid growth: 1799-1813, 1819-34 (including a slight lull in 1825), 1838-44, and 1857-58. They also indicate five periods of marked decline: 1793-96, 1813-16, 1834-37, 1844-47, and 1860-65. The pulsations of revival may be drawn as follows:[119]

DECLINE   STABILITY   RAPID GROWTH

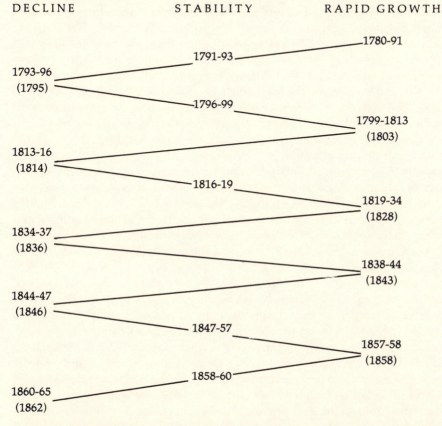

1780-91

1791-93

1793-96
(1795)

1796-99

1799-1813
(1803)

1813-16
(1814)

1816-19

1819-34
(1828)

1834-37
(1836)

1838-44
(1843)

1844-47
(1846)

1847-57

1857-58
(1858)

1858-60

1860-65
(1862)

This repeated pattern of growth and decline can be seen as a statistical expression of what might be termed the psychology of revivals. Local church revivals and broader revival movements grew essentially out of a climate of high expectancy cultivated by persistent preachers and an optimistic congregation. The more eager for conversion were the churches and the more they were able to attend single-mindedly to soul-saving, the more likely it was that an appropriate agent—a charismatic evangelist or a sudden death, for example—would precipitate a revival. As conversions multiplied, emotional intensity gathered to a pitch that could not be maintained indefinitely, and eventually the high state of religious interest collapsed: new converts were hard to find; recent converts often failed to make the grade. Such "sifting" of weak converts marked the period of the mid-1790s after the rapid evangelical advance of the previous decade; similar disenchantment with wavering "probationers" occurred in the mid-1830s and mid-1840s. Slowly, however, the "reaction" or emotional exhaustion that followed the peak of revival excitement came in turn to be replaced with renewed optimism and expectancy, and the cycle began again.

This psychological pattern remained constant, but the particular blend of secular and denominational influences that helped occasion or terminate the different revival movements varied from period to period. The religious depression of the mid-1790s reflected not just the sense of exhaustion that followed a decade of extensive revival. It also sprang from the bitter schisms over church organization that William Hammett and, more seriously, James O'Kelly and his Republican Methodists provoked in Virginia and the Carolinas. The O'Kelly division may have developed out of heightened political partisanship in Virginia; certainly the political excitements of the mid-1790s undermined church life in Georgia, where the Yazoo land frauds dominated public and private attention.[120] The renewed and rapid growth after 1799 appears to have been stimulated in part by the alleged challenge of the writings of Thomas Paine and other "infidels" whose popularity was seen to grow during the 1790s. Fearful that the Deists would "deluge the country with ungodliness," Methodists reacted with a day of general fasting and a more determined pursuit of souls. The unchurched newer settlements of Upper Canada, western New York, and the southern and western frontier provided an equal stimulus to action. Dramatic revivals consequently peppered both old and new sections of the whole country in the early years of the new century. They persisted for a decade, in part because the Republican policies of embargo and nonimportation produced unemployment and economic hardship that a number of churches were able to use to their advantage. Shortly afterward, the severe earthquakes that shook Mississippi, Louisiana, and the southwest drove thousands of alarmed and literally trembling sinners into the churches "to call on God for mercy and salvation."[121]

This period of revival drew to a close as in 1812 "the war-whoop took the place of thanksgiving and prayer."[122] The impact of hostilities on church membership was not uniform. Indeed there was substantial denominational growth in 1813. But on the frontier, where Indians were encouraged to arms by the British, in New England, where the British warships and privateers were often in sight, and in seaboard areas generally, the outbreak of war had an immediate and demoralizing influence on the churches. Methodist membership actually declined in 1814 and made only a slight advance in the following year. It took the "general rejoicing" on the return of peace to provide a context for gradual growth. In some New England towns revivals broke out almost immediately, but it was not until the winter of 1816-17 that a more general improvement occurred. Even then it was centered disproportionately on the northeast, on those areas where growth had been most stunted during the war.

What might be called the second phase of the Second Great Awakening got underway in 1819, and for the next fifteen or sixteen years a powerful surge of revivals proceeded with scarcely a check. All sections of the country were affected at some time or another, though there was much regional variation. Ohio and parts of Pennsylvania lost members in 1821, while Mississippi doubled in membership; Georgia Methodists made no significant gains until the mid-1820s. A peak was reached in all areas, however, during the late 1820s and early 1830s. Conceivably the return to this rapid growth had been prompted by the dislocation and suffering occasioned by the Panic of 1819 and the economic depression that ensued; far more certainly it was the burgeoning optimism and intense interdenominational competition for souls described earlier that ensured the continuation of this spectacular growth; equally clearly it was the "ravages of . . . the Asiatic cholera" that in 1832, instead of checking the progress of revivals, brought "hundreds, if not thousands . . . to deep concern for the salvation of their souls."[123]

The high tide of revival had ebbed by the middle of the decade. In 1836 Methodists experienced a decline in membership, only their second of the century; Presbyterians, too, lost ground and registered a membership total in 1837 that was actually lower than their figures for 1833-34. Some saw this as a consequence of the mounting antislavery excitement within evangelical churches; certainly Methodists found the slavery issue pressed on their attention after 1832 more forcefully than ever before. But that this agitation persisted well into and beyond the next period of revival suggests that other influences were at work. Some southern Methodists were convinced that "flush times," a "wild" pursuit of wealth, and speculation in cotton and slaves drew men away from religion. Almost all were agreed that one basic cause of decline lay in the drift toward promiscuous church admissions during the heady days of revival: many were admitted "who were but poorly instructed in the doctrines and duties of religion, and but poorly prepared to stand the trial of faith."[124] Backsliding in this group was virtually inevitable as the immediate excitement of revival waned.

This period of religious depression was short-lived. A resurgent revivalism extended its influence after 1837 to all parts of the country, urban and rural, and evangelical growth reached unprecedented levels. Probably the most crucial stimulus was the financial panic of 1837 and the ensuing six or seven years of economic depression marked by a decline in wages and acute unemployment. All classes were affected, but especially the poor and laboring men. Some workers—their infant trade-union movement shattered—turned for a remedy toward political activity. Others pursued more utopian, otherworldly ends, sometimes joining cooperative associations distinguished by religiosity and mysticism, and frequently providing a fruitful constituency for the evangelist. There was no straightforward correlation between unemployment and revivalism. Factory hands thrown out of work were more likely to channel their energies into seeking new jobs than the Lord: George Brown's Methodist Protestant church lost sixty members (unemployed factory hands in Pittsburgh and Allegheny) when they were driven to find work elsewhere. But most contemporary ministers accepted without question the primary significance of economic distress in drawing men of all classes into the churches. An Australian visitor considered that the economic crisis had "proved highly favourable to solemn reflection, and [had] led multitudes of gay and thoughtless persons to 'consider their ways,'" now that they had been stripped of their worldly goods.[125]

Spurred by widespread economic and social distress, the revival movement found its reinforcement in the Methodists' intensified efforts during their centenary year and located its continued and increasing momentum in the impact of the Millerite Adventist movement that reached a climax in 1843.[126] William Miller, a New York Deist-turned-Baptist, had predicted that Christ's Second Coming would occur in 1843. For a decade after 1833 he and his followers had conducted revivals in the north, east, and west, borrowing techniques and personnel from the more orthodox evangelical denominations. By 1842-43, with their prophesies of doom matched by an appropriate bleakness in the economy, the Millerites were counting their converts by the thousands. The orthodox were distressed by this "fanaticism" and by a considerable loss of members to the Adventists, but they more than balanced their accounts through the general religious excitement aroused.

Consequently the winters of 1842-43 and 1843-44 brought enormous gains to all denominations, especially the Methodists. In these two years the MEC added over a quarter of a million members, a staggering growth of nearly 30 percent. This represented in absolute terms the most dramatic increase during the first half of the century and the fastest rate of growth since the extraordinary years of the early 1800s. William G. McLoughlin has placed the end of the Second Great Awakening in 1835, after the Finneyite climax of the early 1830s.[127] But in strictly statistical terms the peak of the Awakening came in this adventist phase of 1843-44. McLoughlin, of course, is properly concerned with more than bare statistics; his terminal date is based on the year by which the Calvinists had largely come to reorientate their theology and redefine their revival practice and concept of the ministry. Yet his preoccupation with Calvinist developments has perhaps led him to underestimate the residual strength of revivalism in the later 1830s. Certainly the Presbyterian returns at that time indicate a weakening of the revival pulse, but this reflects more the problems of a newly divided denomination than the general condition of a revivalism that in 1844 was to make Methodism proportionately larger than in any other year of the period under review (figure 3).

This runaway growth could not last, and the ensuing, inevitable reaction produced a pattern of recession and sputtering growth in most evangelical churches for four or five years after 1843-44.[128] Scapegoats were sought and found. Had itinerant revivalists been too precipitate in receiving untested converts? And was not the frothy excitement of Millerism even more to blame for the straw conversions of these years? "Without a doubt," wrote a bitter Methodist, *"the Second Advent delusion has proved inconceivably the greatest calamity that has befallen us since our organisation as a conference."*[129]

The discrediting of Millerism made the religious recession more severe, but the revival momentum would have been lost anyway. Economic recovery during the later 1840s meant a return to a preoccupation with more secular affairs. Soon the "universal passion for gain" had conceived a "worldliness" and complacency in the churches that troubled single-minded evangelicals.[130] Others, like Heman Bangs, blamed the political diversions presented by the election of 1844 and later the Mexican War.[131] Meanwhile those energies left for internal church affairs were increasingly directed toward the resolution of the explosive issue of slavery. Arguments over the churches' responsibility to the slaves and to their slaveholding communicants brought bitterness to all denominations and schisms to the two largest, the Baptists and the Methodists. The years of division—1844 and 1845—saw few revivals, with acrimony and litigation consuming much of the churches' energies. Nor did formal division remove the tension. Particularly in free and slave border states—where "what had been a united, prosperous [Methodist] church, now presented the appearance of two hostile armies"—bitter rhetoric could spill over into violence. In 1846 on the Eastern Shore of Virginia, for example, mobs of southern sympathizers twice interrupted services of the MEC, on the first occasion ejecting the preacher physically from the church. The acrimonious battles between the two sides over possession of church buildings did not eliminate revivals entirely, but it was not until the end of the 1840s that a sense of prosperity returned.[132]

In the decade after 1847, a period when revival reports are strewn through the columns of the evangelical periodicals, Methodism grew at a steady if undramatic rate, maintaining its proportionate status in the population as a whole. A high percentage of its converts came not from the "irreligious" outside the churches, as in the Millerite phase, but from within her own "nurseries," the Sunday schools. The shift from gradual growth to spectacular revival came in 1857-58, a year of religious explosion explained in considerable part by the financial panic and the economic depression of that winter. Church-shaking as this revival was, its later reverberations were seemingly slight: immediately afterward the Methodist rate of growth reverted to the more modest dimensions of the early 1850s. The onset of political crisis in the winter of 1860-61, when "the excitements about secession [were] so intense that it [was] scarcely possible to concentrate public attention and interest upon any other subject," ensured a scarcity of revivals and a decline in total membership that continued during much of the Civil War. Not that war brought an end to evangelical activity: there were conspicuous revivals within the ranks of the soldiery; and arguably ministers like Pelatiah Ward, whose "thrilling appeals" brought a large number of men to the Union standard, were simply redirecting their revival skills to military ends. But in general, revivals did not flourish. Only toward the end of the conflict did (northern) Methodist numbers slowly begin to rise.[133]

What then can be concluded about the precipitants of religious growth and depression? Were there certain denominational or secular factors that operated constantly and predictably to produce and restrain revivals? The preceding analysis appears to support Whitney Cross's verdict that "the revival cycle had long been inclined to an inverse conformity with the business cycle, rising with hard times and falling with good." During the period under scrutiny there were three major economic depressions—those of 1819-21, 1837-43, and 1857-58—and other times of recession included the years of embargo, 1808-09, and periods of the middle and later 1820s. Furthermore, the long period of previously unparalleled prosperity from the early 1790s to 1807 was twice interrupted briefly, in 1797-98 and in 1801-03. All of these were periods of moderate or considerable revival. Conversely, in the period up to 1860, those years of absolute decline in church membership (1794-96, 1814, 1836, and 1845-47) were occasions of either prosperity or improving economic conditions. All of the foregoing suggests the accuracy of Cross's statement. But equally there was no mechanical or wholly predictable relationship between economic and religious phenomena. Some years of impressive church growth—1800-01, 1804-07, 1813, and 1830-32— were periods not of recession but of general economic buoyancy, while the minor depression of 1854-55 brought no obvious stimulus to revival. Even Cross, in his persuasive analysis of the reinforcement that economic conditions gave to religious fervor in the "Burned-over District," has to grapple with the problem of explaining substantial religious advance over a wide range of economic climates in the 1830s.[134]

The psychological motivation behind church attendance and conversion in times of epidemic disease is clear: when cholera threatened in 1832 and yellow fever raged in parts of the south in 1839 it was the very real fear of death that concentrated the mind wonderfully on the evangelical message of repentance and escape from sin. Far less clear is how the psychology of economic disaster might have turned the popular mind toward evangelical religion. Methodist and Baptist revivalism in particular, with its promise of salvation and its cultivation of social intercourse through regular and frequent meetings, may have offered to the unemployed and poor hope and comfort in their struggle for a better material existence. Some clearly found in the millennial strain of the orthodox denominations and in the more eccentric adventism of the Millerites an opportunity or promise of escape from a harsh world. Still others were led by their ministers to see "pecuniary embarrassments" as a providential punishment inflicted by a just God who teaches a people led astray by prosperity "that the silver and gold are his, and he gives it to whomsoever he pleases." And undoubtedly in many minds a combination of these reactions—guilt, escapism, and an overwhelming sense of dependence on God—operated to produce a positive response to evangelicalism.[135] It seems fair to suggest, then, that if the relationship between economic cycles and church growth was less than wholly predictable, the pattern of revivals was certainly influenced by periods of economic prosperity and depression. Secular setbacks did often induce an otherworldliness, perhaps seen most clearly in 1857-58; the unhampered pursuit of wealth in flush times did help divert attention from evangelical devotion. Sometimes, too, the depression pinched so hard that the movement of unemployed church members to find new jobs halted the drive to revival; this was the experience of George Peck in Ithaca after 1828, when the great gains of 1827 were lost.[136] But the economic climate was never the primary determining influence over revivalism; rather it served to modify or intensify a revival cycle that had a momentum and life of its own.

A second but more occasional factor in determining the pattern of revival was the impact of denominational schism. There is little doubt that the O'Kelly Republican Methodist secession of the mid-1790s hurt the mother church and that the Methodist and Baptist crises of 1844-45 helped terminate the final phase of the Awakening; nor were Presbyterians benefited by their division into Old and New School branches in the later 1830s, for thereafter their rate of growth was much lower than in rival denominations. At a more local level Methodists sustained losses through the divisions occasioned by Pliny Brett and his Reformed Methodists in New England in 1813, by the defection in 1816 of over a thousand Philadelphia blacks led by Richard Allen, and by the secession of revival-minded Stillwellites in New York City in the 1820s. But these occasioned no essential change in the direction of the revival pendulum. Nor, rather more surprisingly, did the more substantial secession of the Methodist Protestants in the late 1820s: conceivably their relatively circumscribed geographical base, focused on the Baltimore Conference, minimized its impact.[137]

Much more uncertain was the effect of heightened political activity. Contemporary evangelicals believed that party politics diverted attention from the serious issues of life and blamed the controversies surrounding the War of 1812 and the Mexican War for restraining the revival impulse, as they did the various presidential elections, particularly those of 1844 and 1860, and the sectional crisis of secession in 1860-61.[138] But political excitement was not necessarily a distraction; not only the tense election of 1800 but the boisterous campaigns of 1828 and 1840 all occurred during periods of flourishing revivals and above-average growth in membership. Such ambiguity in the effect of political excitement, when complemented by the complexity of the impact of economic recession, only serves to reinforce the conclusion that the revivals in the era of the Second Great Awakening are not to be satisfactorily explained as a product of a particular set of political or socio-economic conditions.

The only stable factor amongst the whole complex of influences that operated at times of revival was the existence of a desire for and expectancy of revivals in the churches involved. Essential to all revivals was a climate of opinion that regarded revivals as desirable, for a wide range of reasons that included the theological and congregational (an almighty and benevolent God demands that souls be saved; a new generation of children has to be brought into the church) to the social and economic (only through salvation of the individual will a wholesome and a prosperous society be created). Only within such a climate did economic and social dislocations work to intensify revivalism and political enthusiasm to weaken it. Without economic depression and despite the excitement of politics, revivals were able to flourish; without an appropriate theological and congregational climate there could have been none.

American evangelical religion, then, had made huge advances in the half century after 1790, both absolutely and in relation to the increase in the total population. Across the Atlantic, too, the most revivalistic of British evangelical churches experienced marked expansion during the same period. Figure 3 makes clear both the rapid progress of the best organized and most aggressively evangelical of American denominations during these years, and also the impressive, if less dramatic, growth of her coreligionists in Britain. Of course, in each country the nature of evangelicalism and its advance was affected by particular national and local characteristics. America's voluntarist church structure and expanding frontier society produced religious patterns quite different from those found in an industrializing Britain, with her established churches. Moreover, within the broad pattern of transatlantic advance there were national variations in annual growth: as British churches leapt ahead in the mid-1790s American evangelicals experienced lethargy; Americans prospered in the early 1800s, while Britain saw limited growth and even decline (table 6). But evangelicals in both countries regarded themselves, with justice, as part of a single community optimistically pledged to counter corrupting doctrines in an age of revolution. Increasingly, too, confident American Protestants provided an inspiration to a British evangelical community much less socially and ecclesiastically dominant than they. British evangelicals could not ignore developments in the New World; least of all could they shut their eyes to the attractions—and dangers—of her revivals and their practitioners. It is this close transatlantic relationship, as manifested in revivalism, that forms the subject of the remainder of this study.

part two

VOICES FROM AMERICA

two

English Calvinists and the New Revivalism

Late in 1826 Robert Everett of Utica, New York, wrote to his former ministerial colleagues in North Wales, reporting "a wonderful outpouring of the Spirit of the Lord on the congregations of this country" and offering one of the earliest descriptions of the startling revival movement in western New York.[1] Not that British Dissenters needed to be reminded of the vitality of American religion. Since the 1790s they had published intermittent accounts of transatlantic camp meetings and revivals, and American ministers had sent proud letters celebrating their country's religious progress.[2] The dramatic crescendo of revivals in America in the late 1820s and 1830s, however, and the expanding facilities of the religious presses transformed a periodic stream of revival news into a steady flow of private and published descriptions that "produced an unusual impression on the minds of our ministers and churches in town and country."[3]

The personal visits of a number of American ministers encouraged the developing British interest. William Patton, the pastor of a New York Presbyterian church noted for its "powerful revivals," was in England in 1825 and 1828. His friendship with John Angell James, minister at Carr's Lane Congregational Chapel, Birmingham, and one of Nonconformity's luminaries in the mid-nineteenth century, helped secure for American evangelicalism a powerful English spokesman. So too did James's association with another American minister, William Buell Sprague. Pastor in West Springfield, Massachusetts, Sprague toured Britain and parts of the Continent in the winter and spring of 1828; American revivals, he noted, were frequently discussed in distinguished metropolitan and provincial nonconformist circles. Through the printed word and personal conversation British curiosity was so aroused that evangelicals were "almost disposed to believe that there may be some truth in the idea of Jonathan Edwards, that the Millennium shall commence in America."[4]

What was it in the theology, activity, and mood of British churches that led them to focus attention on an evangelical fireworks display some three thousand miles away? How wholeheartedly did they espouse the cause of the new American revivalism? What practical consequences resulted from the application of American ideas and techniques? The variegated character of British evangelicalism prevents a straightforward answer to these questions. Denominational differences in emphasis and approach demand that Calvinist Dissenters be treated separately from Arminian Methodists, while the traditions and coloring of evangelical churches on the Celtic fringe forbid their being examined in harness with English evangelicalism. It was amongst evangelical Calvinists that the American revivalism of the 1820s and 1830s caused the greatest stir, for it challenged traditional evangelical methods and their theological supports. This chapter examines that challenge in the two most important denominations of English Calvinists, the Baptists and Congregationalists; the following chapter explores the impact of that newer revivalism on Wales (the area with the richest revival seam) and Scotland.

English Needs and American Example

Vast sections of Calvinist Nonconformity underwent a considerable revolution during the half century before 1820, when enormous strains (especially in the revolutionary decade of the 1790s) were placed on the structure of secular and church authority. Much of Old Dissent was jolted out of its exclusive, introverted, passive and generally unaggressive, outlook into a fervor and militancy that owed considerable debts to the Methodism of the Evangelical Revival. Baptists and Congregationalists worked to attract recruits from those groups alienated by or geographically remote from the Established Church; for the demographic, social, and cultural changes wrought by the Industrial Revolution had created an audience that wished to assert its "independence" from the traditional sources of authority—squire and parson—and that was unprecedently receptive to an evangelical appeal.[5]

The confrontation between Old Dissent and a newer, zealous evangelicalism fashioned a new theology and a more aggressive mode of action. By the third decade of the nineteenth century most Congregational churches professed a moderate, evangelical Calvinism that had been given its expression and, to an extent, had been molded by Edward Williams of Rotherham. Williams's theological system—"Modern Calvinism," as he called it—denied the more negative aspects of High Calvinism without surrendering wholly to Arminianism. High Calvinism insisted on the absolute and unconditional nature of predestination, arising out of the sovereign will of God, on an atonement made strictly for the elect, and on the total depravity of man, who can in his bondage do nothing until his will is renewed by the energy of necessitating grace. Such a theological system seemed to deny the sinner's responsibility for his own salvation. Williams, in contrast, urged that Christ's death was a price paid sufficient for the salvation of all, that man's depravity extends to his nature, but not to his will, which is entirely free, and that man can voluntarily make use of the means of grace. Similar theological developments marked the Particular Baptists, amongst whom Andrew Fuller in the late eighteenth century undermined the prevailing "hyper-Calvinism" of men like John Gill and John Brine, whose theology had to be countered before Baptists became *"a perfect dunghill in society."* Despite the challenge of Arminians like Dan Taylor and the counterattacks of High Calvinist Gadsbyites, by the 1820s Fullerism had become the prevalent strain in Particular Baptist churches.[6]

Moderate Calvinism provided an ideology that stimulated and justified the militant evangelistic efforts of Baptists and Congregationalists in the late eighteenth and early nineteenth centuries. Their evangelical drive—reinforced by the threat of an "Infidelity" and Deism given immediacy by the horrors of the revolution in France—took various forms. Most striking was the energetic involvement of settled pastors in "village preaching." Often in the face of local apathy or the firm opposition of clergy and magistrates, ministers like George Burder and William Roby carried the Gospel to the rural and small-town poor in "dark and destitute" places, distributing tracts, setting up prayer meetings, and founding Sunday schools. Full-time itinerating evangelists, supported by denominational, county, and local organizations, came to supplement the work of settled pastors. By such methods Congregationalists established five hundred new chapels between 1800 and 1830; Baptists reported a similar increase, or twofold growth, in the same period.[7] It was little wonder that a jubilant Nonconformist asserted in the late 1820s "that more has been effected for the religious instruction of the poor and ignorant of our . . . land, within the last thirty years, than during any preceding century of its history since Christianity was introduced into Britain."[8]

Theological and practical developments within English Dissent had brought it into much closer harmony with the mood of American evangelicalism. The urgent soul-saving, growing church membership, and buoyant optimism of much of American Protestantism found an echo (admittedly more subdued) amongst English Baptists and Congregationalists. But discrepancies remained. Most significant was the general absence in these English denominations of periods of extraordinary "ingathering" or revival. The religious excitement, the large numbers of dramatic conversions, and the setting up of special services were not typical of English Calvinists; nor were the contagious effects on the wider community and neighboring churches that marked New York's "Burned-over District" and even the more subdued New England revivals. Baptist and Congregationalist growth was relatively gradual and much less likely to be marked by short, powerful bursts of religious fervor that completely absorbed the attentions of church and congregation.

Their numerical increase was produced in two main ways, both of them gradual and unspectacular. On the one hand, churches might acquire new members through the efforts of an energetic pastor. This was the case at Portsea in Hampshire under the ministry of the Congregationalist John Griffin. Infused with a burning desire to save souls, Griffin gathered a large and prosperous church through traditional pastoral methods. But, significantly, it was noted that "no extraordinary revivals were experienced during his ministrations, the 'shower of blessings' seldom fell, but the 'dew of heaven' constantly descended on the 'garden of the Lord': continual and regular progress marked his course." Although the pastorate of Lewis Winchester, Independent minister at Andover, Hampshire, was said to have witnessed "a considerable revival of religion," only twenty-three members were added to the church between 1807 and 1813.[9] Denominational increase could also be achieved by establishing new churches through mission activity, especially village preaching. Here too growth was generally gradual. Opposition to or ignorance of evangelical preaching worked against single-minded efforts to save souls swiftly and in large numbers. The introduction of gospel-preaching, more than likely in the open air, followed by the setting up in private rooms and houses of regular meetings for prayer, preaching, and reading, conducted by lay brethren and ministers, and culminating in the building of a small chapel—this was the standard pattern of advance, which could take several years to reach its climax.[10]

There were occasional exceptions to this general rule of undramatic increase. James Sherman, for example, experienced numerically significant revivals within short periods while at Norwich, Bath, Bristol, and Reading from 1817 to 1836, in his own church, and in the neighboring villages where he had established preaching places; considerable emotionalism was not unknown in his services. But John Angell James's general assessment stood: "Of Revivals, strictly so-called, we know nothing in this country. It is true that religion is, I think, steadily advancing, but it is more in the way of silent and unmarked progress, than in that of conspicuous and noticeable movements."[11]

As denominations which saw their raison d'être in soul-saving but which had not experienced powerful bursts of revival, Baptists and Congregationalists sought to use American religious prosperity as a spur to revival at home. In 1828 and 1829 a number of leading ministers in both denominations published calls to action, demanding the positive use of "efficient and suitable means" to promote conversions;[12] England's dearth of revivals during an American glut was an indictment of her passive waiting on God's good time. The strictures of the visiting South Carolinian, Thomas Charlton Henry—"that [British evangelicals] had the means of producing revivals . . .

and that if they [did] not occur the fault" was their own—were taken to heart. At the same time local conferences of ministers and laymen discussed how best to achieve revivals. Tentatively they urged special services for prayer, humiliation, and fasting; independently and jointly churches held special meetings "for the outpouring of the Holy Spirit."[13]

The ostensible aim of such gatherings was the promotion of revival; yet they were scarcely revival meetings in the American sense of the term. First, they did not aim directly at reaching the unconverted during the service itself. Their primary aim was to increase the piety of existing church members and to sharpen the appetite for general revival. The "powerful, yet subdued feelings" manifested at these meetings did not amount to conversions. The services, though exhortatory, were solemn, quiet and undramatic: "We have . . . no scene of agitation and outcry to record; these were not made the necessary signs of revival." Second, the services were "once and for all" occasions, intended to supplement the regular Sunday and weekday services; they were not multiplied over a short period of time. Even the more regular weekly or monthly prayer meetings, aimed at "praying down" a revival of religion, were meetings preliminary to revival and not services during which conversions were sought. They had much more in common with the prayer meetings for revival in the late eighteenth century than with the American new-measure revival services and protracted meetings of the late 1820s.[14]

That English Calvinists had not wholeheartedly adopted an American mode of revival reflected their instinctive caution. Few of them would have denied the need for revival in the traditional sense of an increase in piety amongst church members and the gradual conversion of sinners in the congregation and from the world. But the English advocates of American revivals began to equivocate as doubts developed over their theology, practices, and excitement.

Theologically speaking, it was widely held that the too-vigorous prosecution of revival might demand too much of the individual sinner. This fear was apparent in the arguments over John Howard Hinton's *Work of the Holy Spirit*, a book that attempted to provide a theology of revivalism and put the argument against human inability in its strongest and most controversial form. Hinton argued that man possessed the means to turn to God. Since these means exist in man before the Holy Spirit ever begins to operate and since "*the possession of the means of repentance constitutes the power of repentance; therefore, a sinner has power to repent without the Spirit.*" Though Hinton went on to recognize the influence of the Holy Spirit, he had produced a provocative formula, one that harmonized with the immediacy of revival evangelism and that paralleled the promptings of Taylorite New-Divinity men in New England. In fact, Hinton was well versed in those developments in American Calvinist theology that allowed the preacher to make immediate demands on his unregenerate hearers; he concluded that the prevalence of American revivals resulted from American ministers being much less tainted with the "pernicious notion" of inability. By eliminating this "poison of the most direful kind," English Calvinists too would experience evangelical advance.[15] Not all were ready to forgive Hinton his bluntness and apparent heterodoxy. One reviewer of his work claimed that he had "involved himself in notions very little, if at all, different from that of the self-determining power of the will." This had not been Hinton's intention, but the criticism continued, especially from Baptist elder statesmen alarmed by the Socinian and Pelagian tendencies of this "new doctrine." They pointed out that in practice he reduced the Holy Spirit's influence to ineffectualness. If adulteration of their theology were the price, they wanted nothing to do with American-inspired revivals.[16]

Similar caution was clear in the debate over instrumentality. Though moderate Calvinists agreed that man had a duty to use means to promote God's work, there was, as in America, no unanimity on the type to be used. Calvinists were wary about deviating from those well-established methods that emphasized man's subordination to the Holy Spirit. Hence the nonconformist "revival services" of the late 1820s used only the most traditional and regular of means: prayer, exhortation, and fasting. Prayer was the most warmly advocated of the classical Protestant weapons; important too was the direct and forceful preaching of the Gospel, to arouse the sinner's slumbering conscience and make him susceptible to the Holy Spirit's influence. In addition evangelical ministers demanded behavior of their church members that was more accurately the consequence, not the means, of revival. The improvement of domestic religion, the rejection of worldly values and materialism, regular attendance at religious services, self-denying exertion for others—by such means the church would be revived, and conversions would follow.[17] Some Calvinists wanted to supplement these customary methods. In particular they turned to a frequent feature of American revivals reported in Britain, the inquiry meeting—the special meeting held after the main service, where the anxious conversed in private with the minister and his lay helpers. John Angell James established his own weekly anxious-inquiry meeting in 1829, reprimanding those who supposed that everything could be effected through the pulpit and urging the adoption of an "INDIVIDUALISING SYSTEM . . . in reference to *all* the members of our congregation who are yet unconverted." But the novelty, apparent lack of scriptural justification, and possible affront to the Holy Spirit prevented the widespread use of the inquiry meeting: for many its use savored too much of "technique."[18]

To Calvinists' caution over theology and means can be added their fear of revivals in which excitement, indiscretion, and fanaticism replaced a true invigoration of religion. "Mere excitements of natural sensibility" in religion were anathema, for animal feeling could subside as quickly as it arose, leaving in its wake religious and social disorder.[19] That revivals in the extremities of Britain, in America, and within Methodism had exhibited such unhappy features helped create a prejudice against revivals generally. So too did nonconformist experience of glossolalia and millennialist excrescences in the late 1820s and early 1830s. It was within the English and Scottish established churches that fascination with biblical prophecy was most evident, but Dissenters were not wholly immune from the virus. Most notably, Independents were among those affected by Edward Irving, popular minister of the Scots Presbyterian chapel in Regent Square, London. In 1825 Irving had adopted premillennialist views; in 1831 his chapel witnessed outbursts of "speaking with tongues." Millennialism in its postmillennialist form (Christ's Second Coming would follow a millennium ushered in through ordinary Christian effort) was generally an acceptable doctrine within orthodox evangelicalism. It was the cataclysmic, apocalyptic, premillennialist vision that worried Nonconformists. Irvingism was only part of general "agitation" in the evangelical world: revivals in the west of Scotland in 1830 were marked by premillennialism and "miraculous" manifestations. Although orthodox Dissent was relatively safe, it was often difficult for Nonconformists to be sanguine in the face of such curious excitements.[20]

Advocates of revival recognized that emotion had a place in conversion, that the heart had as crucial a role to play as the mind. "The unrestrained expression of real compunctions is not extravagant; it is only the imitation of them, by those who do not actually feel them that is outrageous," explained Thomas Jenkyn, expressing the frequently made distinction between "true" and "false" emotion, and "good" and "bad" excitement. Such evangelicals adduced two arguments to reassure those fearful of rampant emotionalism. First, English nonconformist churches were scarcely on the brink of uncontrollable religious fervor. At a time when pastors complained of congregational hearers sitting for up to thirty years without professing religion, the very last threat was one of overenthusiasm. The religious flame should be fanned, not smothered. Secondly, they argued that the character of revivals was largely determined by the nature of the society in which they occurred. Joseph Fletcher was probably referring to Wales and the American frontier when he explained that societies marked by "comparative simplicity, . . . limited intercourse with the world, and . . . inartificial manners of the people may [produce] the most undisguised exhibition of all the feelings of such as have been brought under religious impressions." In England, however, "we are accustomed greatly to repress . . . the indications of powerful feeling, and especially of religious emotions"; here a revival of religion would proceed with "greater tranquillity and less sympathetic excitement."[21]

Such cajoling did not remove the suspicion of revivals as a source of disruptive enthusiasm, theological heterodoxy, and practical negation of divine agency. In this climate the revival meetings and publications of 1828 and 1829 promoted no more than "mere public stir and excitement." "Alas! for England, on the subject of revivals!" bemoaned a disappointed John Angell James in 1831: "the little stir that was made about two years ago has nearly all died away; . . . it has not been followed by any visible general result."[22]

The good character of American revivalism was further challenged by the relationship of the American churches to the institution of Negro slavery. After the abolition of colonial slavery in 1833, British evangelicals were free to criticize American slavery without embarrassment. At a purely official level the remonstrations of British churches remained mild and friendly, urging American Christians to use their influence to bring the "peculiar institution" to an end. But many British Nonconformists were in their private capacity severely critical of the slave system and the "deeply-rooted prejudices against the free people of colour." If Americans could thus betray their espousal of liberty and freedom, might not their religious profession prove just as hollow and insubstantial? The American churches—Baptist, Presbyterian, and Methodist, in particular—had thousands of slaveholding communicants over whom they might wield enormous moral influence. "If the pulpit be once engaged against slavery it will fall." Calvin Colton, a colonizationist, noted British religious opinion inferred from the perpetuation of slavery "that our religion is hypocrisy, and American revivals an unholy excitement. With such views of our morality, it is not easy for them to entertain respect for our religion."[23]

The indictment of America's religion was never total. During the 1830s first- and secondhand reports of her revivals continued to uphold their essential integrity. At the same time English Nonconformists faced certain ecclesiastical and social challenges that made increasingly attractive the introduction of an aggressive American-style revivalism.

While British periodicals continued to describe the most powerful and least objectionable of American revivals,[24] a larger-than-ever flow of American evangelicals crossed the Atlantic. Few came primarily to conduct preaching tours or to seek conversions. Calvin Colton, for instance, arrived to solicit funds and books for the fight against Romanism and infidelity in the Mississippi Valley. Some, like John Codman, Heman Humphrey, and Gardiner Spring in 1835 and Robert Breckinridge in 1836, were sent as official delegates to the Congregational Union. Others came as reformers and antislavery men. The Presbyterian Samuel H. Cox of New York visited England in 1833 and returned two years later to help effect a union between abolitionists on both sides of the Atlantic. And there were many more who came, as did the Episcopalian Charles Pettit McIlvaine, essentially for pleasure or for the benefit of their health.[25] Inevitably these visitors were pressed to discuss revivals. English interest was well illustrated in Anson Phelps's report from

Liverpool in August 1833 that "Revd. Mr. Fraser [of New York] is Evrywhere beset to Preach Revival Sermons and Tell Something about the american Revivals. Even in country towns if its given out that he is to give some account of the American Revivals the places of worship will not contain the People."[26]

The most distinguished revivalist visitor was Asahel Nettleton, though by the time he sailed from New York in May 1831 his challenge to the growing influence of new-measure men had failed, and his triumphs lay behind him. His entourage, which included the New England ministers Joel Hawes, Nathaniel Hewitt, and Samuel Green, was steeped in temperance and revivals; though convinced that England was in dire need of a religious awakening they made no attempt to translate what was for most of them a visit for convalescence into a systematic revival campaign. However, Nettleton was subject to pressing invitations to preach, and he was occasionally lured into the pulpit, preaching for John Angell James, William Wardlaw of Glasgow, Thomas Raffles of Liverpool, William Wilson of Nottingham, and Robert Bolton, the American pastor at Henley-on-Thames. He was not a success. James later told Lewis Tappan that Nettleton "produced no effect by his preaching"; less charitably, James Sherman described him as "so cold and dead . . . that he seemed to have a special faculty for sending people to sleep." Yet Nettleton's fifteen-month trip was not wholly profitless, for his advocacy of temperance and his defense of the more restrained American revivals helped remove some prejudices.[27]

Of all the visiting publicists of American revivalism in the early 1830s the most successful was Calvin Colton. As a child and then as an ordained evangelist and Presbyterian pastor in western New York, Colton had had firsthand experience with revivals, and shortly after his arrival in Britain in 1831 he drew on this experience to advocate American revivalism before congregations of interested evangelicals. The promptings of his British friends led to his publishing the *History and Character of American Revivals* early in 1832. Here Colton argued that "*extra* efforts and *extra* measures" were "in some form indispensable to a revival," and he defended the vast majority of American revivals, in particular those of New England, from charges of extravagance, impermanence, and spuriousness.[28] The work was especially useful as an antidote to the influence of the novelist Frances Trollope, whose impish *Domestic Manners of the Americans* in the same year graphically and unsympathetically described American camp meeting and revival scenes, brimful of noise and emotionalism.[29]

Colton's book was better suited to commend American revivals to Britons than another work that appeared later in 1832, William Buell Sprague's *Lectures on Revivals of Religion*. Though well received—it carried the impeccable credentials of enthusiastic introductions by John Angell James and George Redford—it could have been seen as a useful anti-revival weapon.

For Sprague had written his book as a corrective to Finneyite revivalism and some of its measures, theology, and excitement. As such, the book contrasted strongly with Colton's ardent advocacy of American revivals. But the differences were more apparent than real. Despite his cautions, Sprague emphasized the need to seek and work for a revival, and Colton himself claimed to have read Sprague's book "with great satisfaction . . . the views generally expressed accord . . . with my own sentiments."[30] The differences between the two approaches can be explained in terms of religious context: Sprague in America was faced with a Christian world that needed regulating; Colton was addressing a Christian community that had to be roused. Their emphases were bound to differ.

As time passed English Nonconformists became increasingly eager to see for themselves the operations of revivals and the voluntary system in religion. Congregationalists persuaded Andrew Reed and James Matheson to travel as their representatives to the American churches in 1834; Baptists, through Francis Cox and James Hoby, followed suit a year later. All four traveled extensively and returned impressed by the "moral magnificence" and solid foundations of American religious life. On revivals, they declared most of their doubts removed.[31]

Reed offered the fullest treatment. Having participated in various kinds of services and conversed with leading evangelicals, he was ready to approve the vast majority of American revivals—those marked by genuine conversions and promoted by "regular" means. In contrast, the new measures had produced some extravagances. Protracted meetings often exhausted and dissipated religious feeling; the anxious seat offended against the Scriptures and the rights of the congregation and could produce precipitate and short-lived "conversions"; "rash" and "raw" itinerant evangelists could undermine pastoral authority and congregational stability. But Reed denied that new measures were synonymous with "extravagance and disorder." The anxious seat could be used effectively and with propriety. Most important, in light of later English (and Reed's own) adoption of the measure, he argued for the discreet use of the protracted meeting in urgent cases; it was giving it an undue importance compared with ordinary means that troubled him. He happily endorsed its use in the 1834 revival at Northampton, Massachusetts: the extra services were appointed only after it was clear that religious feeling had already been awakened by more regular means; and the meetings, spread over a few weeks, did not weary the community through overconcentration. Essentially what mattered was not the measures themselves, but the spirit in which they were used. New measures sparingly and wisely employed could have beneficial results; regular means adopted in the wrong spirit might well have no effect.[32]

Reed allayed many British fears over American revivals and the new measures. In one sense, Nonconformists had little option but to accept his judgment. The Dissenters' campaign against church rates, against the virtual monopoly held by the Established Church of baptismal registers, marriages, and funeral rites, and against other disabilities, reached a new and bitter stage in 1833 and 1834. Nonconformists saw these as part of a whole range of wider ecclesiastical abuses that grew out of the union of church and state. Only disestablishment would remove these and allow an unfettered evangelical attack on irreligion and immorality. Dissenters were happy to translate evidence of American prosperity into an argument for the supremacy of the voluntary system. As James had noted in 1833, he and his colleagues looked to American revivals as proof of the greater vitality that resulted from disestablishment.[33]

Conversely, high churchmen who saw the attack on the union of church and state as "blasphemous and anarchical" swooped eagerly on any evidence that suggested that large parts of the United States were "rapidly sinking into heathenism" and that the American voluntary system was unable to cater to the religious needs of her rapidly growing population. Mrs. Trollope provided fodder for the establishmentarians. So too did John Bristed's complaint that in a society with no national church the "unbaptised infidels" were "the most atrocious and remorseless banditti that infest and desolate human society." William Hull argued that under the American system the people's control of the minister's purse strings produced a ministry which, to make itself popular, contrived a system of excitements by which it could hypnotize an ignorant congregation. From this there grew a "reign of fanatical imposture and intolerance" in which "Roman priests, and American revival-men" were ascendant.[34]

Dissenters rushed to arms in defense of Americans and, by extension, themselves. America, they maintained, demonstrated a higher level of individual piety and greater supply of churches and pastors relative to population than Britain. Voluntarism had produced enough inventiveness, energy, and benevolence to deal with the spiritual needs of the people. The religious advances during the first three decades of the century had shown that only through the efforts of voluntary bodies like the American Home Missionary Society and the American Sunday School Union would the vast Mississippi Valley be evangelized. Dissenters eagerly concurred with President Andrew Jackson's remark to a delighted Cox and Hoby that "human legislation in matters of religion may make hypocrites, but it cannot make Christians."[35]

Nonconformists' interest in American aggressive revivalism was further stimulated by the problems they faced in reaching Britain's unchurched. Precise data were lacking, but one estimate put the proportion of regular churchgoers to total population at less than one-sixth; another calculated that some four million of churchgoing age remained "spiritually destitute." Widespread lack of religious instruction promoted crime, created a climate favoring the advance of "Popery" and "infidel doctrines," and ensured that "profane swearing, Sabbath-breaking, and drunkenness [emerged as] the prevailing sins of [the] nation." The problem was most apparent in the cities, where concentration of population dramatized evangelical shortcomings. The failure of London evangelical churches to reach the urban masses was greater in degree, but little different in kind, from the lack of success in provincial cities and industrial centers. Many considered rural "ignorance" and "superstition" an equally acute problem, exacerbated as it was by the anti-evangelical character of the clergy, high rate of illiteracy, and general rural conservatism. The attachment of rural gentry and landlords to the Established Church frequently led them to outlaw evangelical preaching, sometimes driving out tenants if they encouraged Dissent.[36]

Nonconformists saw insidious movements ready to gobble up those areas unseasoned with evangelicalism. Algernon Wells identified in 1839 three major forms of "Error": Popery, Infidelity, and Puseyism. The former had always been a useful evangelical rallying cry, and the sprouting of Roman Catholic churches in the decade after the Catholic emancipation act gave substance to the threat. In fact it was not until the great migrations from Ireland during the 1840s that Roman Catholicism represented a substantial challenge to Protestant evangelicalism. The exaggeration of the popish threat is more easily understood in the context of growing concern over Puseyism, "the extensive and alarming diffusion, by divines professing to be reformed but not Protestant, of semi-papal doctrines concerning the christian ministry, sacraments and way of salvation." The Tractarian threat (identified in the late 1830s) represented, because of its growth from *within* the church, a force even more insidious than Jesuitism. The pervasiveness of Infidelity was equally exaggerated. The anti-clericalism of much of the workingman's literature was not "heathenism." It was true that Robert Owen's socialist and communitarian ideas held an appeal for radicals and Chartists in the late 1830s and early 1840s. But orthodox Dissenters tended to overestimate his anti-religious influence. Chartists loyal to Christian teachings but hostile to the organized churches, with their indifference or antagonism towards Chartism, "undoubtedly far outnumbered either the infidels or the active church members." Atheism or even skepticism was much less prevalent among workingmen than more limited anti-church or chapel feeling.[37]

Such misjudgments were understandable. Evangelicals could see how feeble was their hold on masses of the poor and the working class at a time when economic depression, social dislocation, and political unrest were intensifying. The good harvest and trade boom of the mid-1830s came to an end in 1836; there followed six years of unrelieved economic depression. Unprecedented unemployment in manufacturing districts was accompanied by high food prices and inadequate relief. Faced by hunger and destitution, thousands of workingmen responded sympathetically to the appeals of

Chartism and radical movements. The disruptions of 1839-40 and the riots of 1842 ensued.[38]

In the face of threatened social collapse Nonconformists reacted in various ways. While the middle-class emphasis of nonconformist leadership prevented general sympathy for radical Chartist methods, a few liberals, Edward Miall in particular, proved sympathetic to the democratic demands of the Charter. But Dissenters were unanimous that only the spread of evangelical religion could defuse the social and political crisis. Purely secular remedies would prove impermanent if men's hearts were not changed. At a time when a revival of the "feudal distinction" between rich and poor was provoking bitter social tensions, some ministers, sandwiched nervously between both poles, saw it as their duty as representatives of "the mediate classes" to take evangelical religion to the extremes of society. It would, however, have to be a religion divested of its elitist and partisan trappings: the poor had been alienated from formal religion as a result of the "disastrous conjunction of religion with bigotry, religion with oppression, religion with ignorance, religion with indifference to the present social welfare of the masses." Such a purified religion would provide the key to social harmony and national prosperity. The active promotion of a universal evangelicalism, already established as the duty of the Dissenter-as-evangelical, now became the responsibility of the Dissenter-as-patriot.[39]

The New Measures Adopted

This combination of English needs and American example stirred evangelical Calvinists to adopt a more aggressive evangelism in the 1830s. Alan Gilbert points to an internal reordering of priorities within Nonconformity in this period: as the social catchment area that had provided the basis for their growth continued to shrink, Nonconformists began to put organizational consolidation before the conversion of outsiders.[40] But the aggressive strain was far from dead: evangelical Calvinists were confident of achieving a revival of religion through better direction of effort, increased manpower, and a little novelty. In this reenergizing of Dissent, American influence was particularly apparent in three areas: those of lay participation, itinerant preaching, and protracted meetings.

To provide the manpower necessary for this evangelical drive, a bevy of Baptist and Congregational ministers sought to encourage greater lay involvement in the work of missions and revival. American experience provided a constant spur to these activists, encouraging them to promote prayer meetings conducted by laymen, to improve lay-directed tract distribution, and to establish maternal associations. The latter—groups of praying mothers who met to secure the conversion and spiritual welfare of their families— had originated in New England in the second decade of the century. When

Samuel Green of Boston visited Europe in 1831 he found no such associations and claimed to have acquainted London and Liverpool with their purpose and organization. London and Reading had certainly acquired maternal associations by 1835, thanks to the efforts of Andrew Reed's wife, James Sherman, and John Hinton. They were never wholly popular and occasionally ran into outright opposition.[41] A more attractive import was the Bible class, where lay teachers sought to prepare young people for conversion and missionary work through the study of the Scriptures. In the late 1820s and 1830s Bible classes sprang up in British evangelical churches as a means of prolonging the attachment of senior Sunday scholars to the church.[42] Similarly encouraging was the success of American Sunday schools, dependent on lay teachers, in securing the conversion of young children. This, rather than secular learning, argued Andrew Reed, was the proper business of English Sunday schools, "the nurseries of the church." Challenging those skeptical of early conversions, Francis Cox noted that his American experience "would lead to this conclusion, that *those who had professed the earliest, had persevered the longest.*"[43]

Itinerating agents working in "home missions" were irked by the discrepancy between their position and the superior status of American itinerants. The home missionary was the poor relation of the denomination—badly paid, uneducated, and generally ill-equipped. Dissenting ministers valued the pastoral function and the settled order of their churches too highly to allow any real emphasis on itinerant work: bringing sinners to conversion, instructing them, and sustaining the piety of the church membership were tasks best performed by the settled minister. The itinerant might successfully gather converts, but his irregular ministrations would result inevitably in church decline. Moreover, itinerant evangelism savored too much of vulgarity for the more genteel middle-class elements in Dissent. Outdoor itinerancy in particular had frequently been accompanied by mobbings and other social disorder.

"Lady-like preachers" could not, however, prevent more vigorous open-air preaching and tent services in the 1830s and 1840s or the extension of the existing system of itinerancy. More attention was paid to training and financing home evangelists and to supporting pastors who itinerated close to their charges.[44] Most important, evangelical Calvinists adopted a relatively novel evangelism much nearer to the American model: the itinerancy of full-time evangelists who visited both untenanted preaching stations and, more significantly, the churches of settled pastors. On his return from the United States Francis Cox demanded "journeys exclusively for the revival and diffusion of religion." Charles Hill Roe, secretary of the Baptist Home Missionary Society (BHMS), was an enthusiastic advocate of appointing evangelists to visit society stations and, when invited, to hold public revival meetings in neighboring churches. "When will our denomination learn wisdom from the Bible's examples—from our Welch brethren's efforts and success—from the American churches' zeal—and from the plans and prosperity of the Methodists, which are daily before our eyes?"[45] Consequently, in the later 1830s full-time evangelists began to conduct revivals, albeit on a relatively limited front. By 1841 the BHMS was supporting the visits of evangelists to "decaying, sleeping, sinking, poor, neglected little churches" for perhaps several weeks at a time. Generally these agents were ministers who had given up thriving pastorates. Thomas Pulsford was the most strikingly successful of the group. As pastor in Torrington, Devon, in the early and mid-1830s he had made a reputation in village preaching. Now, in 1839, he put settled work behind him and, in part inspired by Finney's *Lectures on Revivals*, began a career as an "evangelist." He traveled over the whole country, the industrial north in particular, to conduct revivals that brought fame to himself and significant additions to the churches.[46]

Protracted meetings were the most novel means of promoting a revival of religion in the 1830s. John Angell James of Birmingham attributed their introduction amongst Congregationalists to George Redford, who held meetings in Worcester in 1837. But as early as April 1834 a young Baptist minister of Boston, Lincolnshire, arranged a week's revival meetings in imitation of the American practice, "being the first of the kind ever held in this country."[47] Within a year, five similar "four days meetings" had been held in the same area, and by 1836 their use had spread into Baptist and Congregational circles farther afield. Multiplication of services was not in itself novel. The "cholera revivals" of 1832-33 had seen Baptist meetinghouses open daily for scripture-reading, sermons, and prayer. But these services had been established in panic during a period of manifest congregational need. In contrast, the protracted meetings were established to create the very church climate that predated and prompted the extra services of the cholera year.[48]

In the later 1830s and early 1840s evangelical Calvinists gave protracted meetings considerable currency. American influence was directly instrumental. First, Finney's magisterial *Lectures on Revivals* appeared in Britain in 1837, sold quickly, and reappeared in 1839 in a new edition designed specifically for a British audience.[49] According to John Keep, they were "scattered like leaves of autumn all over the kingdom." Their direct, practical advice on all aspects of revival procedure made a considerable impact, favorable and unfavorable. "Seize[d] . . . with greediness" by laymen in particular, the book unquestionably helped launch revival activity in general and protracted meetings in particular.[50] Second, there were present in Britain at this time a number of American ministers prepared to make available their expertise in revivals. The most notable were Nathaniel Sidney Smith Beman, Edward Norris Kirk, and William Patton. Beman and Patton had been prominent New-School men in the Presbyterian schism of 1837-38.

Arriving in Britain in 1839 as delegates from the New School General Assembly they succeeded in winning Congregationalist sympathy for the new
denomination. Both were associated with the new revivalism. Beman had
found himself in the center of the new-measure controversy in 1827 in the
Troy revival with Finney. Loud groaning and "liberal" theology proved too
much for some of his congregation, and the strong-willed Beman was brought
before the presbytery for trial. Patton's career was less stormy, and he
acquired a name for successful revivals in his New York ministry. Both men
were active in the various May meetings in 1839 and found their services in
demand, though of the two, Patton's impact in Britain was apparently the
more marked. In particular, he achieved "a great deal of good" at a series of
protracted meetings in Birmingham. The congregations were clearly impressed by the genuine article.[51]

Kirk's visit is of even greater significance. Though he is probably best
known as the Boston Congregationalist under whose ministry Dwight L.
Moody was later converted, when Kirk left America in April 1837 for a
two-year visit to Europe he was already established as a prominent new-
measure revivalist. In 1828, after four years at Princeton, he became pastor
of the Second Presbyterian Church in Albany, New York. His congregation,
composed of a number of the elite of Albany society, "eminent lawyers,
merchants, and statesmen," soon discovered in Kirk a most un-Princetonian
appointment. His uncompromising preaching and new measures offended
many who wanted only "the simple intellectual presentation of the truth."
They urged Kirk "to 'tone down' his doctrines, [and] to 'beware of offending
the tastes' of his congregation." He refused and was dismissed. Setting up a
new church in a poorer area of the city, he continued to employ the new
measures, in particular the "continuous meeting" and the calling on sinners
to rise or come forward for prayer. Eight years later he could claim to have
added over one thousand to his church and to have assisted other churches
in about thirty protracted meetings.[52]

Kirk's career to this point helps explain his warm reception in England. In
his ministry he had struck a balance between the educated and refined
"formalist" and the emotional itinerant revivalist. In rejecting the self-satisfied
traditionalism of Second Presbyterian Church he had not adopted "Methodistic" or "enthusiastic" extremes; he could not jettison his Princetonian ac-
cretions completely. He was fully aware of the secular and purely physical
sources of "religious" emotionalism. As a proven pastor, he knew the problems of maintaining a permanent ministry, but he also appreciated the value
of novelty in the routine of church life. This struck a sympathetic chord
amongst British Congregationalists, a denomination much of whose tone
was middle-class (especially in the metropolitan churches, where Kirk's
most effective work took place) and which valued order, education, and
pastoral authority, but which saw too the need for some fire and urgency in

Edward N. Kirk. Courtesy of Drew University Library.

religion. Kirk provided this. James Sherman, writing in 1860, considered him the most effective American preacher that he had ever heard addressing an English congregation. But "Bishop Kirk"—as John Keep disparagingly characterized him—was able to wrap his radicalism in a cloak of urbanity and thereby make revivalism palatable to an audience that had previously associated it with vulgarity, emotionalism, and disruption.[53]

Kirk had come to Europe to broaden his experience, not to promote revivals, but soon he was participating in protracted meetings, most memorably in Carr's Lane, Birmingham, and in Surrey Chapel, London. The latter was one of the largest and most strategically placed of London churches, with James Sherman, one of the great popular preachers of his time, as its minister. When Sherman took the pastorate in 1836 he had already spent nearly twenty years in energetic evangelistic work in the Countess of Huntingdon's Connexion in Bath, Bristol, and Reading; he was temperamentally suited to the task of rebuilding the church to the strength it had known in the heyday of its former pastor, Rowland Hill. In this "he was ready to sanction, or to adopt any lawful means that seemed likely to secure [conversions]. He was not afraid of novelties." Consequently, Sherman collaborated with Kirk in November 1838 in a week of special services designed to maintain the revival that had broken out in the previous year.[54]

Kirk took the lead, preaching on a variety of subjects that centered on revivals and their "progress and principle" in America. Kirk was aided by a number of ministers—including Caleb Morris, Charles Roe, John Stevenson, and Sherman himself—for whom this was but one episode in a general association with revivalism and American evangelicalism. The novelty of such services in London and the distribution of special handbills caught the evangelical imagination. Some 800 "spectators" attended Kirk's first sermon, and a special reporter was dispatched to document the proceedings. "Whole weeks, morning and evening, were devoted to services." What Kirk called the "Philosophy of Revivals"—"the principle of constantly holding the minds of the people fixed on the truth" through daily meetings—seemed vindicated, as interest grew daily more intense in the crowded chapel. "On one occasion we had the vestry and three rooms in the parsonage filled with souls crying for mercy." Private conversation with the individual and the visits of church elders supplemented these "anxious meetings." By the second week of December (with Kirk now gone) 140 persons, from "the most respectable" and "the meanest" sections of the community, were "under concern." The older church members had doubts over the unusual methods and the speed of admission to membership, but 251 new additions were made during the church year of Kirk's visit.[55]

Events at Surrey Chapel proved contagious. Early in 1839 Baptists and Congregationalists arranged meetings lasting from three to six days at Shadwell, Clapham, Chelsea, Tottenham, Walworth, and other districts of

London. In east London, Andrew Reed set about reawakening Wycliffe Chapel, a church already revived once since his return from America, and established a week's special services over the New York period in 1838-39. Within less than a year he had received over two hundred persons into his church. Over the next few years similar meetings sprouted all over the country, some of them the work of an experimenting pastor, as at Rochford, Essex, and others promoted by itinerating Baptist evangelists. William Barnes, Charles Roe, and other Baptist home missionaries were in considerable demand, as were "on-call" pastors like John Craps. Most popular of all was Thomas Pulsford. On occasions "the Baptist evangelist," as he was called, remained for no more than a few days' sustained evangelism. At other times he could be found conducting two services a day, every day, for several weeks, as at Bridlington in the latter part of 1840. It was men of Pulsford's kind, the English equivalent of American new-measure men, who gave the protracted meeting its most passionate endorsement within English Calvinist Dissent.[56]

At the time when the United States was experiencing the second phase of the new-measure movement—the revival period of 1837-44—parallel developments were occurring in England. Many Baptists and Congregationalists were for the first time dabbling in untraditional means that emphasized human instrumentality in the scheme of awakening and regeneration. Inevitably these "instrumentalists" manifested some diversity of approach. Protracted meetings—taken as a generic term embracing any extra meetings that aimed at awakening religious concern—conformed to no single type. Methods and emphases differed according to the temper of the minister, his assessment of church needs, and the particular social and theological blend of his congregation. In the Wycliffe Chapel revival in 1840, for example, Andrew Reed refused to use the inquiry or anxious meeting, despite its successful use elsewhere. He insisted on seeing all inquirers individually and in private: the inquiry meeting might sometimes prove advantageous, but on this occasion, in the emotion-charged atmosphere of the inquiry room, "human sympathy" might prevail over spiritual considerations in bringing the inquirer to a decision.[57]

The social makeup of the individual church may have determined the character of revival meetings. Perhaps it was significant that Reed was a London Congregationalist: since novel revival methods were often distasteful to fastidious middle-class congregations, it was from the elite of London Independency that objections to the "enthusiasm" of revivalism were to be expected. Moreover, the new measures did take hold in poorer Baptist churches, especially in the north, more strikingly than in middle-class Congregationalism. But the difference was at most one of emphasis. If working-class men and women—the artisan class in particular—formed the bulk of

Baptist and Independent congregations, there was often a leavening of
"middle-class respectability" in revivals. This was the case in Francis Cox's
protracted tent services in Hertfordshire in the summer of 1841; "persons
of all ages, classes, and characters" participated in Pulsford's Stockport
revival of 1843.[58] Social class was no more important a determinant than
theology: the "Antinomianism" of a number of Baptist congregations, including the poorest, provided a barrier to the use of revival techniques,
whereas Independency's moderate Calvinism and urgent desire to save souls
could overwhelm its impulse toward middle-class respectability, as witnessed by Kirk's efforts at Surrey Chapel.[59]

Variations in the character of revival services should not obscure certain
common features. In most cases ministers made considerable efforts to prepare the congregation psychologically for revival meetings. They used their
routine services to discuss them, aroused expectations through special prayer
meetings, and visited "lukewarm" members and unconverted adherents.
Once the required pitch of excitement had been achieved, the starting of
protracted meetings, and especially the arrival of a respected "evangelist,"
acted as a detonator. To be sure that his arrival would set off a revival,
Pulsford came to rely—as had Nettleton, Finney, and other successful itinerants—on handbills, placards, and word of mouth sending his reputation
ahead of him.[60]

The services themselves varied in frequency and venue. At their most
intensive, meetings might be held four times daily for four or five days, as at
Shakespeare's Walk Baptist Chapel, Shadwell, in 1837. But protracted
meetings that ignored the inflexibility of English working hours might prove
more than ever dependent on the women of the congregation. Consequently,
some ministers, especially in industrial areas, postponed their weekday
protracted meetings until holiday periods. The Baptist minister at the mill
town of Haworth, Yorkshire, held four meetings a day during the first two
days of the Shrovetide holiday week in 1836. His hardy congregation en-
dured some twelve hours of services between five in the morning and ten at
night. But this solution was not wholly satisfactory: holidays were too in-
frequent and allowed no real flexibility over the timing of extra services.
Increasingly ministers came to sandwich the working day between early-
morning and evening meetings and to extend the period of special services
from a few days to one, two, or even several weeks. Sometimes services
were held out of doors; other experimentalists may have followed James
Gallaway's example of tent preaching. But most meetings were held securely
within the chapel walls.[61]

They were also, in the main, denominational and single-church occasions,
though sometimes—as at Sheffield in 1840, when the two Baptist churches
held services jointly for two weeks of the revival—there was a pooling of
effort, and there were occasions when union took place across denomina-

tional lines. The minister and his lay assistants might well supplement the day's prayer meetings and addresses with tract distribution, lecturing in the streets around the chapel, and visiting from house to house. This work directed attention to the day's climax, the evening service. Here the minister might aim his address at a particular group in the evangelical community; Andrew Reed on separate occasions singled out "professors," the unconverted, fathers, mothers, and the young. Specificity was matched by immediacy, as the sinner was reminded of "the great importance of immediate decision for God." Consequently many evening services ended with large numbers emotionally unsettled and ready to remain for a special inquirers' meeting. The more conservative ministers apart, the revival-minded regarded these meetings as legitimate and effective. Pulsford used them more or less nightly. However, few ministers—not even Pulsford—intensified the psychological pressures by conducting the anxious meeting while the public service was in progress. Nor was the anxious seat, so common in Methodist and American circles, a favorite device. Occasionally English revival services encouraged dramatic and public "confessions" of past sins, despite the general dissenting emphasis on private testimony of spiritual experience. Testimonies of wife-beating, swearing, drunkenness, and Sabbath-breaking no doubt stimulated temporary interest in the revival, but they were not typical. Equally, there were numerous protestations of good order and denials of "false enthusiasm" in revival meetings. Ministers perhaps protested too much. The tense, expectant atmosphere of revival services, heightened when the chapel was "crammed almost to suffocation" and moved by an adult baptism or electrified by the announcement of a death, could easily induce hysteria. Even the most circumspect ministers found their congregations affected by occasional bouts of extreme emotionalism, though the more prudent were quick to treat these as signs of "human infirmity," not true religion.[62]

In winning converts these services achieved considerable success, despite the problems posed by bad weather, or counterattractions like political elections. Gallaway's West Bromwich revival produced some two hundred "deeply anxious," of whom he expected over one hundred to join the church. In the two Baptist churches in Sheffield the figures were similar; Reed had three hundred "under concern." These were the most dramatic figures, but elsewhere results could be almost equally remarkable. Occasionally revivals went beyond securing conversions, to the "moral elevation" of the neighborhood. Though the part played by temperance in this English wave of revivals appears more limited than in the corresponding Welsh and Scottish movements, some of the more committed teetotalers achieved their ends. Moses Saunders reported that as the result of the Haworth revival of 1836 "the streets and roads were quiet, the public-houses had little to do, and the beer shops . . . were for a time forsaken." But the effects of revival on the broader community were rarely so marked.[63]

Sometimes the converts were old enough to be particularly susceptible to the revivalist's promptings to consider the afterlife, but usually they were young, often adolescent. A large proportion were drawn from Bible classes and Sunday schools; rarely did the revival represent "an extensive ingathering of souls from the profligate and abandoned world." Alan Gilbert has argued that at this period, with previous external sources of converts drying up, Nonconformity was increasingly having to recruit new members from within. Sunday schools ceased to play a supporting role to aggressive itinerancy and became an important area of recruitment in their own right; as the nineteenth century proceeded the chapels drew their new members more and more from the pool of unconverted adherents.[64] The evidence from this period of revival supports Gilbert's argument. Pressures on unconverted hearers were intensified. Delinquent family members were coaxed by the regenerate in the household; masters brought servants, and parents their children. For the revival tolerated all kinds of persuasion, uses of authority, and perhaps the manipulating of guilt to bring the unconverted churchgoers to the brink. Further, insofar as conversion was predicated upon experience of at least some elementary evangelical instruction—concepts such as "sin," "grace," "salvation," and "regeneration" would otherwise have been unintelligible—it would have been surprising had not most converts been established members of the congregation or Sunday school. It was often discovered at inquiry meetings that those inquirers who did not actually belong to the congregation were lapsed churchgoers anxious to return to the fold. Sometimes, too, they had learned their evangelicalism elsewhere, for inadvertent proselytism brought gains to both Baptists and Congregationalists at each other's and the Methodists' expense.[65]

The adoption of new-measure revivalism coincided with an upsurge in Calvinist nonconformist recruitment in the later 1830s and early 1840s. Figures for Congregationalists are not available in this period, but it seems likely that their pattern of growth resembled that of the Baptists, for whom figures do exist. Limited local evidence suggests that Baptists experienced peak years in 1828 and in 1833 (as indeed did most Methodists). More extensive returns suggest stable nonconformist growth between 1834 and 1838, the Baptists' annual increase oscillating only slightly from a high mark of an average 4.7 additions per church to a low of 3.7 (figure 4). The figure jumped to 7.9 in 1839, 8.8 in 1840, and a huge 13.1 in 1841. These figures were more impressive than Methodist growth rates, in part because Methodists suffered from internal quarrels over teetotalism, in part because Baptists were probably the greatest beneficiaries of the Barkerite schism within the Methodist New Connexion, occasioned by disputes over paedo-baptism, formal creeds, and centralized ecclesiastical organization.[66]

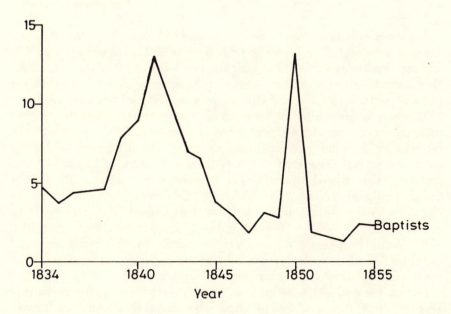

Figure 4. Baptist Growth Rates, 1834-55 (England) and Combined Methodist Growth Rates, 1830-55 (England and Wales). The Baptist growth rates represent the net increase in membership per church per annum; the Methodist growth rates represent the annual net gain or loss in membership expressed as a percentage of total membership in the previous year.

SOURCE: Gilbert, "Growth and Decline," pp. 38-39, 106.

These periodic upswings were attributable to a complex of internal and external pressures. The dramatic revival of 1832-33, for example, at first appears identifiably related to a single stimulus—the threat of cholera, which approached from Asia across Europe in the summer of 1831, reached the ports of northeastern England later in the year and hit London in February 1832. Panic and fear filled churches across the country; united interdenominational prayer meetings were held; and "cholera converts" continued to be received by the churches until well into 1834. But there were additional stimuli to revival. The impact of American revivalism, as in 1827-28, undoubtedly encouraged conversions and revival services: the publication of Colton's influential *History and Character of American Revivals*, for example, coincided with the advent of cholera in London and gave focus to evangelical effort. Moreover, both peaks—1827-28 and 1832-33—coincided with a period of high social tension; more specifically, Eric Hobsbawm and George Rudé offer evidence that in some areas religious revival followed upon the frustrations and failure of agricultural revolt in 1830.[67]

During the mid-1830s the pace of growth slackened a little, perhaps in keeping with a natural rhythm of religious boom and slump, perhaps because an improved economic climate brought a reduction in social tension, perhaps because evangelical attentions were too consumed by political concerns. The last interpretation was offered at the time. Referring to the bitterness in 1834 between Church and Dissent over the disestablishment issue, John Angell James concluded that "all hopes of a revival of religion are at present checked; the heads, hearts, and mouths of our people are full of the secularities of religion." It has been suggested that during the Victorian era revival consistently coincided with political agitation relating to specifically religious objectives,[68] but this was not true of the 1830s.

This chapter has argued that the upswing in recruitment from 1839 had an American dimension (as indeed did certain other signs of religious upheaval: the beginnings of significant Mormon emigration to America and the establishment of Millerite Adventist groups in Britain).[69] The adoption of special techniques undoubtedly helped stimulate revival, in the Calvinist denominations at least. Furthermore, the upswing coincided with a further period of social tension linked to economic depression. But the precise nature of the relationship is not easily determined. In Lancashire and the West Riding (J. F. C. Harrison's English "Burned-over District"),[70] for example, the revivalism of the poorer Baptist and Congregational churches perhaps offered working people a hope and security in a bleak world. Others may have found an escape in the otherworldiness of the evangelical message; in its offer of emigration Mormonism represented escapism taken to its extreme. But for those whose experience of social dislocation was more that of the concerned observer—perhaps the more middle-class elements of Dissent—religious revivalism possibly offered a means of spreading an evangelical doctrine that would, they thought, ease tension and harmonize social relationships.

During the mid- and late 1840s the era of revivals gave way to a period of much-reduced increase, and the exuberant confidence and high expectations associated with the "revival system," as some called it, began to evaporate. Baptists and Congregationalists complained of an annually declining rate of growth. If economic and social distress had contributed to the revival boom in the late 1830s, then a continuing decade of less severe but still trouble-some commercial depression seemed equally effective in dulling spiritual appetites and cutting off the funds essential to the effective operations of home missionaries. Political events, too, were blamed for diverting church energies into "the things of the passing world," as activist ministers joined in the agitation over the Factory Education Bill, the Dissenters' Chapels Act, and the Corn Laws.[71]

It was the "revival system" itself that took most of the blame for the decline. Critics argued that the calculated use of new measures ("bellows-blowing, and systems of mechanical apparatus") by an irresponsible revivalist simply overwound the psychological mainspring of a gullible congregation. They did not lack damaging evidence. During the 1840s Townhead Chapel in Sheffield lost a number of those added during the revival who had "made a profession without a renewed heart." The annual accessions at Surrey Chapel in the two years after 1838 were the lowest of the next ten years and tempered James Sherman's initial enthusiasm. By the mid- and later 1840s, with revivals at a premium, the revival system had lost many supporters. Thomas Pulsford now found himself treated with "derision" in certain sec-tions of the denomination. By 1847 his funds had dried up, few churches outside his previous orbit applied for his services, and the BHMS had to conclude that "the system with which his name was so closely identified, had been brought . . . to a close." This evidence, and the reports of relapse in American churches, emphasized to traditionalists that the older pattern of gradual, steady growth was more stable and less harmful than the explosive American strategy.[72]

The new revivalism was further questioned by the apparent sprouting of heretical views on the sinner's role in conversion—a development seemingly attributable to the fertilizing effect of American revival theology. Orthodox Nonconformists did not reject the New Divinity as a whole. Writers like Moses Stuart and Albert Barnes had a wide and sympathetic audience. In-deed, the work that ultimately gave greatest offense—Finney's *Lectures on Revivals*—at first received the qualified endorsement of some of the intellec-tual leadership of Nonconformity: George Payne, one of the foremost Con-gregational theologians, John Harris, tutor at Cheshunt College, and John Angell James. It was possible to see Finney as simply driving home in strong language the arguments of British authors like Thomas Jenkyn and John Howard Hinton. Finney's works, despite their "vulgarity," "rash and hazardous phraseology," and "theologically discordant diction," were welcomed because they pressed on the sinner his duty and ability to repent immediately, at a time when the prevailing tendency of nonconformist preaching and theology was "too scholastic, stiff and cold."[73]

Views changed quickly once the revivals exposed the tendencies of this theology. John Angell James, who in late 1840 thought that "responsibility can[not] be too much dwelt upon and pressed home," had in under two years concluded "that our danger. . . lies in going over to the opposite extreme, to the neglect of Divine sovereignty." The uncritical reading of Finney's works and his imitation by others had given unprecedented circulation to the view that men could convert themselves. The early sympathizers with American revival theology withdrew from their exposed position. Doctrinal purity, particularly on the crucial question of salvation, was essential if evangelicals were to counter successfully Puseyite notions of sacramental efficacy and the priestly character of the ministry. Nor would it do to encourage those young pastors and ministerial students attracted by novelty and especially the directness of the American approach to salvation: nine students were expelled from Glasgow Theological Academy for heresy in 1844.[74] American-style revivalism had been introduced to provide English Calvinists with a sharp evangelical edge: but could they, when using it, avoid self-inflicted wounds?

three

The New Revivalism in
Wales and Scotland

Charles Finney's *Lectures on Revivals* arguably achieved their most enthusiastic reception not in England but across the border in Wales. The rapid sale of the Welsh translation enhanced the reputation of the Welsh as a people who read nothing but theology. More dramatically the study of the *Lectures* was considered the major stimulus behind the "powerful awakenings" in North Wales in 1839 and 1840 and in South Wales in the following three years. This revival was said to have drawn some twenty thousand new members into the churches and was especially marked amongst the Independents. The Congregational minister Thomas Rees possessed firsthand knowledge of the movement and was in no doubt about Finney's influence: the revival had been "chiefly promoted" by his *Lectures*, which had "been instrumental in the conversion of hundreds if not thousands of our countrymen."[1] Indeed, the revival was popularly known as Finney's Revival. In attributing a wave of revivals to the circulation of a single publication, however, Rees's analysis bordered on the simplistic. The *Lectures* may have provided a major—perhaps the most influential—immediate factor in the outbreak of revival, but the book's success is only fully intelligible in the context of particular theological and practical emphases in Welsh Dissenting churches, without which it would have remained untranslated and unsung. Only in an evangelical community peculiarly attuned to revivalism could the publication of such a work produce an immediate and electrifying effect. Welsh Nonconformity provided that community.

Finney's Revival

When Calvin Colton visited Wales in 1834 he concluded: "The Welch are a very religious people. There is perhaps no other christian people in the world, who manifest so much religious susceptibility, or who can be brought so much under its power." Colton was writing a century after the first stirrings of the Methodist Revival had projected Welsh religion onto the course that brought Wales this reputation for highly charged evangelicalism. The spiritual warmth of that revival had thawed the perimeters of cold Dissent, with its rationalist and unitarian tendencies, infusing at least some Dissenters with a concern for the salvation of souls. This change in mood produced a drive toward expansion: in the second half of the eighteenth century Dissenting congregations doubled in number. But the greatest growth was to come in the nineteenth century, triggered by the anti-climactic separation of the Calvinistic Methodists from the Established Church in 1811 and abetted by the accelerating process of industrialization, to which Dissent proved eminently more adaptable than the Establishment.[2]

In the north in particular Methodism spread rapidly, while older Dissent tightened its grip on the south, especially in the industrial concentrations of Monmouthshire and Glamorgan. Nonconformity was blessed with considerable advantages. Its use of itinerant preachers stood in utilitarian contrast to the inflexible parochial system of the Establishment. The identification of the Established Church with the Welsh landowning and gentry classes, the wielders of local power, aided its estrangement from the vast mass of the population who turned with increasing confidence to Nonconformity. Welsh-speaking farmers, laborers, miners, and ironworkers found their spokesman in the nonconformist preacher, a man of similar social background, a "tribune of the people." This gave to Nonconformity a power that strengthened, and was also itself nourished by, a germinating sense of nationalism. Consequently, if in the first years of the century the Church could still outbid Dissent (in numbers if not in potential), by 1851 Dissent apparently outnumbered the Establishment in attendance by about three or four to one.[3]

The growth of Dissent and the broad revival of evangelical religion were marked by a myriad of local revivals (of diverse character) that observed a fairly regular rhythm of boom and decline. Thomas Rees noted five such clusters of revivals in the first half of the nineteenth century. The earliest, between 1807 and 1809, drew several thousand into the churches, chiefly in the south; North Wales was similarly affected from 1815 to 1820; and both sections were equally involved in the movement of 1828 to 1830, when an estimated thirty thousand members were added to the four major non-established denominations. Finney's Revival a decade later was itself followed by the great "cholera revival" of 1849, which took firmest hold in the industrial areas of the south.[4]

What were the major instruments of these revivals? Apparent to all commentators was the central place of preaching. Since the mid-eighteenth century, preaching had become generally more extempore, animated, colloquial, and colorful. Its passion, appeal to the imagination and feelings, and great variety of intonation were best exemplified in the "hwyl"—the musical, semi-chanted, emotional climax to the sermon—which at its most effective could reduce a whole congregation to tears. In the hands of an experienced minister (especially the itinerant who could polish his small stock of sermons), preaching developed into something of a sophisticated art form. Moreover, the preacher himself came to take on the character of a folk hero, and the prospect of a visit from a celebrated preacher invariably promoted intense excitement and expectancy. This was especially true of Calvinistic Methodism, where itinerancy was the norm, but Baptists and Congregationalists also used itinerancy as a supplementary agency. Nor was it the preachers alone who traveled. Thousands would journey for many miles to hear their favorites at the annual association ("sasiwn")— one, two, or three days of services held by a number of churches of a particular denomination and carried on wherever possible out-of-doors.[5]

Preaching was not the whole story. Congregational singing, prayer meetings (sometimes spread over a number of days), and inquiry meetings for those under concern were a fairly regular feature of Welsh revivals. So too were "society" meetings, which aimed to cultivate a fuller Christian life among church members through mutual encouragement and rebuke and the relating of "experience." In time of religious excitement they proved of enormous value, especially when they took inquiring nonmembers into their embrace. Yet in general it was the preaching service that provided the dramatic focus. Even allowing for predictable exaggeration, there was significance in the claim that through a single sermon at the Pwllheli Association in 1831, the Calvinistic Methodist John Elias kindled a conflagration of 2,500 conversions in Caernarvonshire: it was the sermon and not the prayer meeting through which, in the first instance, impressions were sought.[6]

Clearly the practice and character of Welsh evangelical religion shared a number of common features with the evangelicalism of the American frontier. The isolation—through language and geography—of much of the population of rural Wales and the expanding, unsettled, and "disoriented" character of the working population in the industrial belt offered grounds for comparison with the isolated, moving, and restless population of the American West. Since in both regions the Established Church system was either weak or nonexistent, the work of evangelizing a "deprived" population was left to the voluntarist, revivalistic churches. In these new social conditions, churches in both countries found themselves adopting novel roles: just as American frontier Presbyterianism stood ready on occasion to become the church of the ordinary man, jettisoning its eastern traditions of respectability, so early nineteenth-century Welsh Dissenters in the industrial belt surrendered their middle-class character and set about providing for the religious needs of the workingmen.[7]

Those mission instruments most typical of the American frontier—itinerant and lay preaching and camp meetings—were employed with corresponding vigor, and often with similar effect, in Wales. They were developed to meet similar needs: itinerancy and supplementary activity of laymen made the most of thin resources to evangelize "dark" areas; camp meetings and associations recognized the problems of social isolation. Great outdoor gatherings for religious purposes offered to the American frontiersman and the poor Welsh farmer or ironworker one of the few opportunities for large-scale social intercourse and entertainment.

In both countries, too, the character of preacher and people, and their mutual relations, were conducive to revivals. First, preachers addressed audiences of common people possessing limited education, a narrow range of intellectual experience and little social refinement. In both places there was a critical absence of a large, educated, middle-class body that might have tempered this lack of intellectual and social sophistication. In addition, geographic isolation slowed the entry of new ideas and delayed the erosion of old superstitions. An English Wesleyan Methodist in Merthyr in 1830 discovered that "the people on the mountains [were] serious believers in fairies, ghosts and spirits." Some elements in both "frontier" areas accepted the existence of a God and a Devil who interfered directly in the affairs of man, and the sense of nearness to God or the Devil, Heaven or Hell, was of course heightened by the often precarious nature of life. The preaching of death and salvation was assured of positive effects where life expectancy was markedly shortened by the reality, in Wales, of industrial disasters or cholera epidemics and, in America, by factors like disease or violence. Secondly, the preachers themselves drew on much the same social and intellectual background as their hearers and could rely on powerful bonds of sympathy. American Baptist and Methodist frontier ministers were men of the people, sometimes farmers themselves, with little education and refinement; they spoke the same language as their audiences. The same was true of Welsh Dissenting ministers, men of low social origin, whose sermons were saturated with biblical metaphor, and who were in full rapport with an audience which spoke the same biblical language.[8]

A limited education and intellectual outlook, a fair grounding in evangelical doctrine, and a firm bond between preacher and congregation provided a recipe for a revivalism of some potency: by the 1830s and 1840s in Wales "jumping" was "getting pretty much into disrepute," but "physical manifestations" reminiscent of American frontier revivals were still not unknown. In the 1829 revival at Merthyr some individuals suffered fits, and six years later at the Bala Association "strong men [fell] down dead like logs of wood, their limbs stiffened, their eyes glaring." If these more extreme manifestations were unusual, enthusiastic singing, audible congregational responses during sermons, and weeping during emotional preaching marked most of the services of Dissenters.[9]

But the comparison must not be strained. Not all aspects of Welsh religion fitted snugly into a frontier model. There were, for example, forces making for broader education and for less emotion in religious exercises. More importantly, Welsh revivals possessed something other than the expansive, missionizing character of frontier revivalism: in many areas there was a degree of religious continuity, stability, and community that ensured that the Sunday school, for example, emphasizing spiritual feeling and gathering in the younger generation, became a more valuable institution than the itinerant ministry, which represented dynamic, quick growth rather than settled, orderly progress. In the first half of the nineteenth century, when "ingatherings" through the Sunday schools were ever more common, itinerancy was seen increasingly to have passed its golden age and to be open to abuse. Thus there was a side to Welsh revivalism much closer to the practices of New England than to the religious style of the frontier. New England revivals were less an instrument for reaching a rapidly growing or mobile population than a means of drawing into the church the younger generation of a community where profession of evangelical religion had long been the social norm and which was relatively stable in its population.[10]

In rural and small-town Wales and New England a homogeneous population, bonds of tradition and custom, and a history of evangelicalism produced a social cohesion that was of enormous importance in the spread of religious sympathy. If the young American frontier communities and the Welsh industrial population were less socially stable, they each had a certain mental homogeneity shaped by their common evangelical traditions and sense of struggle against the arduous conditions of life. Thus within all these communities an event such as the conversion of an "infidel," the death of a church deacon, or any other dramatic occurrence might easily detonate a whole host of conversions. Moreover, this social and religious sympathy was checked in neither Wales nor America by the operations of a powerful Established Church seeking to throw its social weight against the workings of revivalism. In Wales the Church did not possess sufficient numbers or prestige for the task; and in those New England areas where there was an establishment, it was itself a church of revivals.

With revivals so integral a part of Welsh religious life the widespread reading of Finney's *Lectures* is unsurprising, especially as the book appeared at a time when the revival pendulum was on the upswing. There had been no major revival movement since that of 1828-30 and its recrudescence during the cholera threat in 1832. After a period of lull, and with a new generation of young adherents to gather into the churches, the expectations of church members provided a powerful impetus to the renewal of the revival cycle. A handbook on the promotion of revivals would be read avidly. Nor was it surprising that the catalytic agent of the 1839 revival was transatlantic in origin. Welsh-American bonds created one of the closest of transatlantic communities. Constant emigration from Wales to a country of allegedly abundant material wealth and enviable political and religious freedom promoted a remarkable awareness of American conditions. In these circumstances American religious prosperity was contagious.[11]

Some of the most colorful of all the episodes in this story of cross-fertilization centered on the Welsh immigrant, Benjamin Chidlaw of Ohio. Chidlaw had been a child in 1821 when his parents had set out from North Wales on a route that eventually took them to the Welsh settlements of Lower Sandusky. Here his nonconformist upbringing brought him into close sympathy with the prevailing evangelical temper, and in 1829 he made a public profession of religion. Six years later, becoming a licensed Presbyterian minister and eager to equip himself properly for the task of preaching to Welsh-speaking congregations, Chidlaw decided to return to Wales. For two months the raw young preacher learned much from his native countrymen, especially William Williams of Wern, John Elias, and John Jones (Llanllyfni). In return, Chidlaw set evangelical imaginations alight with his addresses on temperance.[12]

Attitudes toward temperance in the 1830s in Wales—as in the rest of Britain—were in a state of flux. The efforts of the expatriate Robert Everett in forming a temperance society in Utica, New York, had served as a direct stimulus to the birth of the Welsh Temperance Society in 1831. But the moderate approach of such societies soon came under attack from total abstainers onto whose side Chidlaw threw himself with gusto. He was happy to relate that a "preacher from America was an attraction, and temperance was a new subject. The chapel [at Mivod] was crowded. Much interest was excited on the subject of total abstinence, and a temperance society was organised, the first in that part of Wales." If in fact Chidlaw and the teetotalers did not immediately succeed in provoking a close alliance of total abstinence with all Nonconformity, within a few years the value of teetotalism to the churches seemed to be powerfully exemplified, for during the revival of 1839-43, taking the pledge and admission to church membership were regarded as complementary and often functioned as mutual stimuli. A number of ministers testified that "the readiness with which the Total Abstinence principle was received and acted upon" was the means, together with the reading of Finney's Lectures, by which great numbers were added to the churches.[13]

Chidlaw returned in 1839, by now more experienced in handling revivals. Occasionally on his preaching tour of North Wales' Congregational churches he held four-day meetings. More usually, he remained in one station for one or two services—in country chapels at noon and in villages or towns in the evening. Frequently he would follow his services with inquiry meetings ("the new measure I . . . introduced"), where from five to twenty inquirers might present themselves for conversation, prayer, and encouragement. The holding of inquiry meetings immediately after the sermon, and not on a separate occasion, may well have been unusual in the parts of Wales Chid-law visited, but this practice was not so new as he believed and was known in other areas at an earlier date.[14]

It was at Llanuwchllyn in December 1839 that Chidlaw made the most dramatic use of the inquiry meeting. After prayer and a sermon on repentance, some 150 people responded to his request that those who were seeking or had found salvation should stand up. The enthusiastic scenes at Llanuwchllyn made Chidlaw's a name synonymous with revivalism, though, as he himself realized, he was merely capitalizing on a religious awakening that was already under way in the village. It was noteworthy, however, that one of the focal points of the 1839-43 revival was the very county (Merionethshire) in which Chidlaw operated so successfully, and that one of the foremost figures of the revival in South Wales—William Williams of Llandeilo—was allegedly stimulated by Chidlaw's work.[15]

Despite the steady transatlantic stream of men and ideas, the *Lectures* could never have been so influential had not Finney's theological assumptions knitted in well with contemporary developments in Welsh Calvinism. As in America, much of the Calvinist theology that underpinned the majority of revivals of the early nineteenth century frequently spilled over into the "hyper" or "high" variety. The doctrines of election and reprobation, the total depravity of man, and his complete inability to do anything toward his salvation were widely held in the three major Calvinist denominations, and in particular amongst Calvinistic Methodists; many were reluctant to employ any but the most traditional of means.[16] However, the second, third, and fourth decades of the century witnessed a controversy in all three denominations between moderate and hyper-Calvinists that was ultimately to achieve a considerable liberalizing of beliefs.

To an extent this easing of hyper-Calvinism had been prompted by the Wesleyan Methodists, whose preaching of a full, free, and present salvation, the moral agency of man, and the possibility of falling from grace was directly or indirectly effective in winning Calvinists from antinomian views.[17] A less easily documented stimulus was to be found in changes in the contemporary social and political climate. Broad social developments that promote a refashioning of a person's view of the world may lead ultimately to a reconsideration of his relationship to his God. Was it accidental that the egalitarian emphases in American society in the Jacksonian era and the increased sense of individual participation in politics were paralleled by theological developments that asserted the "democratic" and "egalitarian" nature of Christ's atonement and the participation of the individual in determining his spiritual fate?

In Wales the early nineteenth century was a time when egalitarian and liberal ideas were broadening their hold. It is true that during the French Revolution Dissenters remained generally loyalist and that great preachers of the early nineteenth century like John Elias and Christmas Evans were strong Tories in politics. But there was another side. The democratic spirit of Nonconformity was well embodied in Joseph Harris, Baptist minister and reforming editor of *Seren Gomer*, and in Samuel Roberts ("S. R."), minister and radical publicist, who advocated franchise extension, Catholic emancipation, the abolition of religious tests and church rates, and the improvement of tenant conditions. Moreover, despite the coolness and opposition of much of articulate Nonconformity to disruptive egalitarianism or leveling causes like Chartism or Rebecca, the links between Nonconformity and these movements were undeniable. Clearly there was a sufficiently extensive drift toward social and political action and "democracy" in the first few decades of the century for it to be likely that the theological thinking of many Dissenters was affected. The exclusive, quietist implications of predestinarian Calvinism were replaced by an assertion of the inclusive, egalitarian aspects of the Gospel and the capacity of the individual to act for himself. It was surely significant that some of the most eager liberalizers of theology were also strong political liberals, that the stricter Calvinists came under fire for authoritarianism and exclusiveness, and that the denomination most moderate in its Calvinism—the Independents—was the most radical politically.[18]

The pace at which modifications were made in High Calvinism varied considerably from denomination to denomination. The enormous influence of the strict Calvinist John Elias within Calvinistic Methodism meant that it was only during his failing years of the 1830s that the issues began to be thrashed out thoroughly. Amongst Baptists the wheels of theological change turned more quickly; by the end of the 1820s Baptist theology was generally moving to more liberal ground.[19] The most rapid and wholehearted adoption of moderate Calvinism, however, took place within Congregationalism, where there was no formal Confession of Faith to protect orthodoxy. John Roberts of Llanbrynmair, student of Edward Williams, was the most forceful exponent of what came to be known as the New System. In 1820 he published his celebrated *Galwad ddifrifol ar Ymofynwr am y Gwirionedd* ("A Serious Call to Inquirers for the Truth"), better known as "The Blue Book," at a time when (as he reported to his brother in America) moderate Calvinist views were "greatly gaining in popularity in Wales." He encountered bitter opposition from the older generation of ministers, but by 1840 the New System had been adopted generally.[20]

It was during this confused period of theological transition that Finney's *Lectures* appeared. Not surprisingly, given their exhortation to use calculated means and their fundamental acceptance of "modern" views of atonement, election, and ability, the *Lectures* were most readily accepted amongst the Independents, the denomination that had traveled farthest in their theological direction. Two letters sent to Finney in 1840 made clear to him the extent of Congregationalist acceptance. The first, acknowledging that his works had in "great measure" promoted the conversion of "several thousand souls," was significant in that amongst the ten Congregational ministers of North Wales who signed the letter were several prominent defenders of the New System in the recent theological battles. Notable were Michael Jones of Llanuwchllyn, one of the seven contributors to John Roberts's "Blue Book" and Chidlaw's ally in the revival of 1839, and Lewis Everett, whose older brother Robert had contributed to the "Blue Book" and had emigrated to America in 1823 to become pastor of a Welsh church in Utica, New York.[21] The second letter, from James Griffiths of Saint David's, conveyed a similar resolution of thanks to Finney, passed by some fifty Independent ministers of southwest Wales.[22]

For these ministers and men of similar minds, Finney was a powerful and articulate ally. His work helped push them further along the road of moderate Calvinism and "led them to seek the revival of pure religion in a more suitable manner than they had done before." In the revival of 1839-43 they used promotional techniques that were for many churches more focused and carefully calculated than ever. The Congregational minister at Henllan described the new approach: in addition to "plain," "pungent," and "earnest" preaching, "prayer-meetings . . . were organised, on the principles recommended by the great Revivalist, with a view to producing strong, striking, and instantaneous impressions"; hearers were divided into classes ("the children of believing parents," "unbelieving husbands of believing wives") that allowed for greater specificity in the appeals for immediate repentance; hymns were chosen with an eye to their psychological propriety; "all legitimate means, psychological and moral, that could be thought of were employed to arrest the attention and awaken the conscience."[23]

Some Welsh ministers were none too happy with the effects of Finney's influence. White-hot denunciations issued from the elderly Morgan Howell, a lifelong battler against every variety of heretic—whether Finney, Pusey, or the pope himself—and one who, in a more trenchant moment, was heard to remark "that it would have been a blessing if the ship that brought over Finney's work had been buried in the Bay of Biscay rather than for it to have been brought to [Wales] to poison minds." Others were more restrained but no less critical, believing that through the influence of men like Finney and John Jones of Talsarn, the 1839-43 revival lacked spontaneity: it had been "reasoned up" through unevangelical argument; the absence of excitement and noise and the emphasis on calculation threw doubt on the revival's integrity.[24] Amongst the criticisms of Finney's early revivalism in western New York State had been the charge of overemotionalism and overdependence on noise; now, in a country where religious excitement had a long pedigree, Finney-inspired revivals were regarded as too "quiet" to be the work of God. But there was no irony in this: the excitement and emotionalism of Finney's early revivals had been misleading. Finney's essential aim in revivals was to persuade the mind of his hearers. He did not aim simply at arousing the emotions, nor did he deny the value of such appeals, but primarily he aimed to persuade through cool reasoning. And in contrast to the traditional fiery diet of the Welsh this was tepid fare.

There was, however, no general disillusionment, and Finney received urgent pleas to visit Wales during both his trips to Britain: he had, after all, helped promote a revival that had brought positive and substantial gains to the churches. But while the glory was Finney's, the explanation of the revival necessarily has to extend beyond the work of a single man. The flourishing Welsh-American connection and the contribution of Benjamin Chidlaw, the developing tandem relationship of temperance and revivalism, the developing upswing in the established religious pendulum, the solace provided by religious meetings in a time of severe economic recession—all these factors served to reinforce the drive to revival. More fundamentally, the *Lectures* were well received because they gave positive expression to a growing emphasis on individual responsibility and participation found in both theology and social thinking and because they offered a comprehensible method of perpetuating a revival system regarded as essential to the churches' livelihood. The success of the *Lectures* was ultimately attributable to the fact that they expressed forcefully and cogently what many were thinking and others were groping toward but which few had been able to articulate so clearly. The *Lectures* were novel, but not so novel as to conflict with the experience of their readership nor to encounter blank incomprehension. Their success was substantial testimony to the assertion that there is nothing more powerful than the impact of an idea whose time has come.

Scottish Revivals and Schisms

In Scotland, too, in the 1830s the cause of evangelicalism lay almost wholly in the hands of Calvinists: in the Church of Scotland, other Presbyterian bodies, and the smaller Congregational and Baptist churches. These denominations could invoke a history of revivals that included such dramatic landmarks as those at Kirk o'Shotts in 1630 and Cambuslang and Kilsyth in 1742-43 or more recent but lesser explosions as at Moulin in 1798-1800 and Lawers in 1815. But a fairly strict Calvinism kept evangelism and efforts for revival within bounds. In the 1820s even revivals of the most traditional variety had no prominent place in the life of Scottish churches. Yet there were stirrings in the early and mid-1830s that presaged a new wave of revivals, a new kind of revivalism, and a much-modified Calvinism within the Scottish Protestant churches and made it clear that the Welsh and English pattern was repeating itself north of the border. A functioning machinery stood ready: evangelical Calvinists regularly used Bible classes, Sunday schools, tract distribution, city missions, and open-air preaching. In the Glasgow area, for example, there were encouraging signs of revival. In Kilsyth, the Presbyterian William Burns attracted large numbers to his weekly prayer meetings and held a series of revival lectures; John Hercus successfully brought his Greenock Congregational church to a revival in 1830 after establishing a regular weekly prayer meeting in the previous year.[25]

Significantly Hercus's moderate success was prompted by a visiting American minister, "Mr. Fraser of New York," who had arrived "quite unexpectedly" and stayed to preach for seven or eight weeks. Other Scottish evangelicals too were in touch with American developments. In Glasgow a revival society set about publishing narratives of American revivals, correspondents exchanged evangelical news and religious periodicals, including Leavitt's *New York Evangelist*, and visiting Americans were closely questioned. Glasgow evangelicals interrogated Asahel Nettleton on the nature of his country's revivals when he made his visit in 1832. His fight with Finney over the new measures tempered his verdict, but he could not avoid defending "legitimate" revivals at a time when Scottish evangelicals were giving increased attention to the subject.[26]

Of even greater significance in keeping aggressive American revivalism in Scottish minds in the early 1830s was the work of David Nasmith, an energetic representative of the harder edge of Scottish evangelicalism and a man best remembered for his organization of city missions to the poor. By 1830 he had added to his first enterprise in Glasgow another twenty missions in Scotland and Ireland. A restless young man, Nasmith sailed in July 1830 for New York, anxious to visit a country whose lack of city missions he regarded as a personal challenge. Within three weeks of his arrival he had met William Patton and the philanthropist Arthur Tappan, called a meeting of fifty ministers and laymen, set up a New York City mission, and secured funds for the support of two missionaries. Thereafter he traveled widely in New England, the east, and the south. Before his return to Scotland in December 1831 he had established additional missions and young men's societies in New Orleans, Augusta, Charleston, Baltimore, Richmond, Alexandria, Washington, D.C., Philadelphia, Boston, and elsewhere.

If Nasmith had overextended his energies (none of these American societies continued to operate successfully for long), his travels had at least brought him into contact with many revival converts and prominent Calvinist ministers sympathetic to revivalism. He carried back an urgent longing for similar revivals in Scotland and immediately set about holding meetings to explain American revivals and to encourage "prayer for the outpouring of the Holy Spirit." During the following winter of 1832-33 he continued to organize revival meetings, temperance societies, and maternal associations.[27]

The revival Nasmith sought did not come until the later 1830s. By that time the earlier, smoldering interest had been fanned first by a temperance reformation and drive to teetotalism that owed much to American example. Of course, the progress of teetotalism was largely a symptom of a revival whose leading ministers regarded teetotalism as a concomitant of conversion. Yet the desire for total abstinence may also have helped promote revivalism. The identification of so many ministers and laymen with "liquor-selling and liquor-drinking Christianity" cast a doubt on the quality of their religion, and to some at least it seemed that evangelicals would have to introduce a new kind of religious effort before there could be a complete revolution in drinking habits.[28]

Secondly, there seems good reason to believe that the economic depression of the late 1830s and early 1840s created conditions in which revivals could flourish. It is true that at this time in the rural areas of the Lowlands, Highlands, and Islands—where there is evidence of a number of revivals—prosperity was returning after the period of low agricultural prices from 1832 to 1836. But the real focus of the revival movement was the industrial belt from Renfrewshire and mid-Ayrshire to mid-Fife and the northeastern outposts of Dundee and Aberdeen. Here an industrial and commercial revolution was being fed by an industrial proletariat of highland and lowland peasantry and Irish immigrants. Population was growing at a bewildering pace. In the coalfields, textile mills, and ironworks the economic boom of the mid-1830s had given way by 1837 to a general depression that helped feed Chartism and related forms of social and political protest. Some felt that the depressed conditions of working people and the twelve- to fifteen-hour days they worked allowed no time for religious concern. Nevertheless, many of the affected laboring groups did turn to evangelical religion. Colliers in Lanarkshire villages, mill workers in the jute manufacturing city of Dundee, Perth men and girls from the "manufactories and large workshops," Shotts ironworkers, and servants, quarrymen, factory workers, and colliers in the carpet-manufacturing town of Kilmarnock were drawn into the revival.[29] Significantly, it was the group hit hardest by the depression, the handloom weavers, whose economic status had been mortally affected by the recent introduction of the powerloom, which made perhaps the major contribution to an evangelical explosion that helped set the tone of the whole revival movement. In the Kilsyth revival of 1839 William Burns found weavers (elsewhere regarded as "Radical or opinionative" and their shops "hotbeds of anarchy") to be "well-read, sober," and "among the best friends and upholders of the hands of the minister." For handloom weavers and others living marginal existences, the revival perhaps offered spiritual succor and support.[30]

Thirdly, by the 1830s the harsher Calvinist formulations were already being softened in some churches, especially amongst the Independents, but the strict emphases of Calvinism would have to be modified further before revivals could occur in large numbers. As in Wales, American influence proved a major agent of change, particularly in Congregational and United Secession churches. John Kirk, reflecting on the Calvinist upheavals of the 1830s, recalled how "there were two books which had very great influence in suggesting those ideas which ripened into a true revival of religion": Reed and Matheson's *Visit to the American Churches*, whose descriptions of American special services were to draw activists like Kirk into enthusiastic imitation, and, of even greater value, Finney's *Lectures on Revivals*, inexpensive and widely circulated.[31] Finney was not of course the only New-School Presbyterian theologian to influence Scottish Calvinist thinking. Such writers as Moses Stuart and Albert Barnes were influential liberalizers who exploited the theological shifts encouraged earlier by the extensive reading of Timothy Dwight's works. But at the popular, less intellectually sophisticated level, Finney had no rival.[32]

There were stirrings of revival in Scotland throughout the 1830s in the shape of city missions, the revival of outdoor preaching, and the multiplication of prayer meetings. But not until 1838 did revival meetings really arrest public attention. Late in that year and early in 1839 protracted meetings were held in parts of southern Scotland following reports of Edward Norris Kirk's meetings in Surrey Chapel, while John Kirk conducted successful services northwest of Glasgow.[33] Then, in the summer of 1839, Kilsyth experienced a revival explosion whose tremors were felt across Scotland. The sexagenarian pastor, William Burns, tried to control a revival that affected hundreds from all denominations. Meetings were held at all hours in church, church yard, loom shops, factories, and market square. "The state of society is completely changed," Burns observed. "Politics are quite over with us. Religion is the only topic of interest." Out of curiosity and disbelief crowds flocked from the whole Glasgow area, and in September between ten and twelve thousand crowded into the communion tent. Letters from eyewitnesses were sent to relatives all over Scotland and read out to interested congregations. The "kind of laudable jealousy" that had helped multiply conversions in Kilsyth itself now began to operate elsewhere.[34] During 1840 the revival movement became general, though the focus continued to be the industrial belt, and the Glasgow region in particular. Soon the elements of surprise and relative spontaneity disappeared, but it was not until the mid-1840s that the drive to revival finally lost its impetus.

This wave of revivals saw the introduction of a number of American revival techniques, particularly protracted and inquiry meetings, which found little favor amongst the more traditionalist and cautious Calvinists. But it was in the area of theology, not methods, that the most acrimonious and divisive quarrels developed. The contemporary American schisms were reenacted on the Scottish stage—not least because the two leading exponents of a more liberal theology were both much affected by their reading of Finney. In the remote Presbytery of Elgin the newly licensed minister,

James Morison, beyond the supervision of denominational authorities, increasingly questioned one of the central orthodoxies of the United Secession Church—that Christ had not been sent to die for all men—and was soon unequivocally to uphold the universality of the Atonement. If his mind had been in part turned in this direction by John Brown at Edinburgh Theological Hall, it was Finney who gave coherence and definition to his thinking. "I do strenuously advise you," he wrote to his father, "to get Finney's Lectures on Revivals, and preach like him; I have reaped more benefit from the book than from all other human compositions put together." In Morison's first and enormously popular tract, *The Way of Salvation*, published in 1840, he sought clearly to urge on unbelievers their ability and obligation to repent at once. In its tone and message Finney's influence was unmistakable. Morison's views continued to drift further from orthodoxy, until by 1843 he had concluded that the influence of the Holy Spirit was resistible and election conditional: man simply had to believe in order to be elected and justified.[35] Similar developments were taking place within Congregationalism. John Kirk, after an orthodox ministerial education, had become pastor of a humble church in Hamilton, where during 1840—by which time he had become "to some extent a pupil of Finney"—he began to shift his position. Most Congregationalists, especially in the Lowlands, already held moderate Calvinist views. But when in 1842 Kirk outlined his "new views" it was clear that he had gone several steps further, in Morison's direction. Several capable Congregationalists in the Glasgow area responded positively to Kirk's preaching. One of these was Fergus Ferguson, Jr., "the boy preacher," student at the Glasgow Theological Academy and a member of Kirk's congregation. As the son of a church deacon who had spent much time "reading the works of Finney, Dwight and Independent writers" Ferguson's response was predictable.[36]

Temperamentally John Kirk was a radical. In 1831 he had thrown himself into the Reform Bill agitation; during the 1830s and 1840s he attacked church establishments, denounced the Corn Laws and American slavery, and suffered for his undeviating teetotalism. Fergus Ferguson, Sr., and Henry Wight were of a similar liberal mold. Such minds would welcome theological formulations based on egalitarianism, freedom of the will, and the responsibility of the individual. Theologically conservative evangelicals might well prove politically Tory: Thomas Chalmers regarded Radicalism as nothing less than an "aspect of infidelity and irreligion"—and others considered that serious soul-saving excluded vigorous political activity. But there can be little doubt that changing social and political attitudes helped erode the old Westminster Confession of Faith.[37]

It will be recalled that though English Calvinists reacted warily to the "new theology," they experienced no significant denominational disputes or schisms. When James Morison visited Manchester in 1845 and preached universal atonement and God's love, his hearers, attuned to Methodist and Congregationalist preaching, found nothing startlingly new in his message. In Scotland the popular hold of a much stricter variety of Calvinism ensured more pronounced and extreme reactions to the new views. In March 1841, Morison, at the center of a popular storm in Kilmarnock, was suspended from the ministry of the United Secession Church. Within a year his father, Robert Morison of Bathgate, had been similarly ejected for his views of the Atonement; in May 1843 two other ministers, Alexander Rutherford of Falkirk and John Guthrie of Kendal, were suspended. Through their writings and energetic evangelism these four men shook the United Secession Church.[38]

Though Congregationalists also experienced schism, their more moderate Calvinism and the looseness of their denominational structure allowed for greater toleration of new views. Many churches sympathetic to the revival movement remained within the Scottish Congregational Union. But there were important exceptions. In 1844, blaming American influence, the committee of the Glasgow Theological Academy expelled nine students tinged with "self-conversionism." One of those expelled was the young Fergus Ferguson, a member of John Kirk's church at Hamilton. Within a year, eighty sympathizers in Glasgow's North Allen Street Church had split away from their church and invited Ferguson to be their pastor. Divisions grew up between as well as within churches. Four Glasgow Congregational churches withdrew from fellowship with five others in the Glasgow area known to espouse the new doctrines, including Kirk's church at Hamilton and the senior Fergus Ferguson's at Belshill.[39]

The most fundamental and turbulent of church schisms in the 1840s, the "Ten Years' Conflict" in the established Church of Scotland, had its roots not in theological dispute, but in differences in approach to the relationship of church and state. Yet the great disruption cannot be divorced from the swelling evangelical wave of the 1830s. Those Church of Scotland ministers who played the most dramatic part in the revival—Burns of Kilsyth, W. C. Burns, the Bonars, James C. Lorimer, and Alexander Cumming—were later to join the Free Church, and most evangelicals withdrew from the Established Church at the time of the disruption. Indeed, "evangelical" and "non-intrusionist" were often synonymous. Undoubtedly the experience of flourishing churches reinforced evangelicals' self-confidence and their commitment to spiritual independence. Once completed, the disruption ceased to be a symptom of revival and became a cause of it, as minister after minister found himself in need of church and congregation. In an intensive evangelistic drive, Free Church ministers preached out-of-doors and in barns, sheds, and wooden churches to attract and maintain congregations.[40]

Schism was not the whole story. The more committed evangelical wings of the different denominations often worked together in revival services. Even more striking was the cooperation forced upon those single-minded evangelicals who had been expelled from their churches. In May 1843, on the heels of the suspensions of Guthrie and Rutherford, James Morison called a meeting of excluded ministers and disaffected members of the United Secession Church, intending to create an association that would "be on a revival ground, and take cognizance only of revival matters." The resulting Evangelical Union soon won the cooperation of the ostracized "new views" group within Congregationalism, which for several years had conducted protracted meetings with the Morisonians, though not all joined formally what was intended at first to be a loose association of like-thinking evangelicals and not a fully fledged denomination. The Evangelical Union was also able to attract disaffected evangelicals from the Relief and Free Churches. However, the Evangelical Union could not long remain simply a cooperative association. Most important, the request for preachers from newly formed Morisonian churches demanded a theological academy that would train students in the distinctive theology of the Union—the universality of the Atonement, the universal love of the Father, and the universal and resistible influence of the Holy Spirit. Here, in evangelism and theological similarity of outlook, lay the Union's cement, for the various member churches differed widely in their internal organization and church government. It was revivals and their promotion that mattered most.[41]

The Scottish revival of the 1830s and 1840s had thrown up a new denomination entirely committed to soul-saving and revivalism. If it was a small denomination—in the early 1850s it had about forty ministers and a somewhat larger number of churches—it spread its influence widely through its newspapers and itinerancy; if the energies of its major figure, James Morison, were largely consumed in the running of the academy at Kilmarnock, he was still able to find time for some revival work. John Kirk was even more influential. In addition to his evangelical pastorate in Edinburgh and his editorial duties on the *Day Star* and *Christian News*, the first Scottish newspapers to direct popular attention to evangelism and total abstinence, Kirk spent significant periods annually in the 1840s and 1850s itinerating in Scotland and England. It was as a direct consequence of such influences that Cumberland and Northumberland and other areas of the north of England became exposed to the "new views" and revival services of the Evangelical Union.[42]

The advent in Scotland of America's revival methods and moderate Calvinism had helped promote a remarkable revival and a number of church schisms that had produced a new revivalistic denomination. Of course, American influence was only one amongst several and had only limited effect on the actual course of the revival. But America and her revivals remained firmly in mind. William Buell Sprague and Jonathan Edwards, as well as Finney, were read at revival meetings; American example was invoked in popular tracts; and it was during the course of the revival that

Charles Livingstone (brother of David) left Scotland to take up his studies at Finney's Oberlin. A little later William Cunningham, after a visit to America on behalf of the Free Church, reported on the favorable state of American theology and religion.[43] Moreover, when some Evangelical Unionists welcomed Finney into their (somewhat suffocating) embrace during the American's second visit to Britain in 1859-60, their hospitality represented an acknowledgment of Finney's role not only in advancing the cause of applied evangelism but more particularly in acting as midwife to their denomination.

four

James Caughey and
Methodist Revivalism

Languishing in the historical shadow of the two most influential nineteenth-century American evangelists, Charles G. Finney and Dwight L. Moody, can be found a group of lesser-known but once highly effective itinerants. One of these was an Irish-American, James Caughey, who in the early railway age became one of the first full-time revivalists of the "urban frontier" and who—if remembered at all—is recalled largely for his influence on William Booth, the founder of the Salvation Army.[1] Yet in his own time Caughey was an enormously popular and powerful figure, especially in Britain. His reputation as another Wesley or Whitefield derived initially from six years of revival campaigns held during the 1840s in the industrial areas of the midlands and the north of England in which tens of thousands were allegedly converted or "entirely sanctified." This represented success that no visiting *denominational* revivalist had previously achieved or was going to achieve again in the nineteenth century. The better-remembered Lorenzo Dow, an agent in the emergence of Primitive Methodism, was an historically more colorful character but a much less-disciplined revivalist; Finney probably had a wider influence than Caughey, but this was achieved primarily through his publications rather than his visits, which were much less successful in purely revivalistic terms; Moody's campaigns were broadly interdenominational and derived their strength from that very strategy.

Caughey's itinerancy of 1841-47 can be set in a context of a well-established Methodist to-ing and fro-ing across the Atlantic, though few came to Britain quite so single-mindedly to save souls. In 1820 John Emory, the MEC delegate to the British Wesleyan Methodist Conference, returned home after settling the long-standing dispute over jurisdiction in Canada (and taking with him a less than symbolic gift of two Chinese pigs)[2]; thereafter a steady flow of delegates and unofficial "fraternal messengers," including William Capers, Wilbur Fisk, John Price Durbin, Joshua Soule, and George Peck, attended several annual British Conferences. Less formally, others came to visit relatives or convalesce after illness.[3] All served to reinforce the widely held view amongst British Methodists that in the "fine and improving" United States the Methodist Church was "likely to become the most extensive and pure in the Universe."[4]

British and American Methodists liked to see this traffic as an expression of their fundamental unity. But inevitably, given the contrasting social and ecclesiastical complections of the two countries, there were considerable differences. To some extent these were manifested in the tension over Negro slavery (though the tone of British Wesleyan criticism was generally more moderate than that of other British evangelical denominations).[5] They were apparent too in church structure and organization: most obviously, the American Church was episcopal, had replaced the district chairman with a presiding elder, and did not use band meetings. But the most telling differences came in the field of revivals.

British Methodism and American Revivalism

British Wesleyans, much more than Baptists and Congregationalists, were a revival denomination. They possessed an Arminian theology that sanctioned an unrestricted appeal to all men. At times the whole connection might be ablaze with revivals, as in the mid- and late 1790s and the early 1820s; on these occasions some churches claimed hundreds "set at liberty" in a matter of days in intense and emotional meetings. The American new-measure revivals of the 1820s consequently made much less impact in Wesleyan than Calvinist circles: British Methodism was sufficiently revivalistic not to need an overseas spur to action. In the later 1820s, as American revival news arrived, Wesleyans in Scotland, Cornwall, and the industrial areas of northern England were themselves scoring revival successes that offset the slow advance of the middle of the decade.[6] American stimulus was only one amongst many and did no more than help set in motion an existing revival machinery. In contrast, the response of the Calvinist evangelicals, possessors of no such machinery, had been to attempt the building of a revival structure where none existed before.

Nonetheless, the religion of American Methodists in the first half of the nineteenth century was clearly more emotional, revival-centered, and tolerant of innovation than that of British Wesleyans. The Oxford origins and Anglican connections of Methodism were more conspicuous in Britain (English Methodism's first institution for ministerial training was established decades in advance of a similar American college) and, according to John Durbin, the "wealth and respectability" of many Wesleyans compared favorably with the status of most American Methodists. In consequence, revivalism was less extensive and its manifestations less crude. Wilbur Fisk, thoroughly shocked when a "Wesleyan preacher in England seriously asked me whether

I thought *revivals* were, on the whole advantageous to the church," concluded that "what we in America term revivals are comparatively rare" in Britain.[7]

Wesleyan uncertainties over revivals could be explained in large part by the far-reaching effects of an earlier flirtation with American revivalism stimulated by the visits of Lorenzo Dow. Son of a Connecticut farmer, Crazy Dow had deservedly acquired his nickname. Asthmatic and epileptic, he cut an extraordinary figure with his long hair, thin face, flashing eyes, stooped shoulders, harsh voice, crude gestures, and unkempt dress.[8] Driven by an aggressive belief in his special calling and claiming visionary powers, Dow ran into trouble with his Methodist superiors in America for unsupervised outdoor itinerancy. Late in 1799, aged twenty-two, he left for Ireland convinced he was to be God's instrument in the cataclysmic overthrow of Popery. For sixteen months, often hungry and footsore, he traveled the length of the country, from Antrim to County Cork. He would preach two or three times a day wherever he could find an audience—in Methodist chapels, private houses, and out of doors, offering the gospel of salvation to his generally poor and unsophisticated hearers and denouncing Popery, Calvinism, and various brands of Infidelity; then he would move swiftly on. It was not an easy progress. A victim on one occasion of smallpox, on others of Roman Catholic mobs, he met his most persistent opposition from local magistrates and from Methodists themselves. A majority of Wesleyan preachers, unhappy about the "irregularity" of Dow's movements and echoing the view of a Cork preacher that "he follows his own feelings too much— he is Quakerized," voted in Conference to "hedge up [his] way." Not least they feared that the hostile mobs that Dow attracted might transfer their attentions to the Wesleyans' official "Irish Missionaries," the outdoor itinerants Gideon Ouseley and Charles Graham; the "government will immediately conclude we are at the head of these disturbances, or the occasion of them; by which means they will deem us enemies, and take away some of our privileges." This was no unreasonable fear. Local magistrates, their nerves strained by the tensions of the recent rebellion and its aftermath, were thoroughly suspicious of itinerating speakers, particularly from abroad. Dow's eccentric appearance, fervent republicanism, explicit hostility to George III, lack of "proper *Credentials*," and itinerancy throughout those areas involved in the uprisings of 1798 ensured that he was on a number of occasions apprehended by magistrates afraid he was one of those "who go about to stir up the minds of the lower class . . . to politics, riot and rebellion." Thomas Coke, well aware of Dow's indiscipline in America and in sympathy with the concerns of Dublin Castle, threatened to report the American to Castlereagh, Chief Secretary for Ireland, should he continue to itinerate without proper authority. Undeterred, however, the ungovernable revivalist remained until January 1801.[9]

Similar concerns marked Dow's second visit, when he itinerated in the

Lorenzo Dow. Courtesy of Drew University Library.

northwest of England and in Ireland between December 1805 and April 1807. Once again the civil authorities were quick to threaten with imprisonment and fines a foreigner who refused to take the oath to the king and whom they suspected of participating in the triangular revolutionary traffic between Ireland, England, and France. The denominational authorities similarly found it difficult to look with equanimity on a figure who exposed and reinforced the tensions within Methodism.[10] During the 1790s and 1800s many in the rapidly changing industrial society of northern England were finding Wesleyanism too restricting for their spiritual needs. "Modernists" confronted "primitives." Revivalistic groups within and outside the parent denomination—including the Magic Methodists of the Delamere Forest, the Quaker Methodists of Warrington and Macclesfield, the Band-Room Methodists of Manchester, the Revivalists of Leeds—sought a return to "primitive" simplicity and a break from formalism.[11]

In this setting Dow's influence operated in two major ways. First, he helped give increasing cohesion and momentum to a number of these disparate revivalist groups, particularly in Cheshire and Lancashire. Often obstructed by Wesleyan ministers and trustees and of the opinion that "a hardiness" hung over "Old Methodist" chapels ("so I don't have such good times in them as in Ireland and America"), Dow was increasingly attracted by the spiritual warmth and spontaneity of the "Third Division" of Methodists.[12] Amongst the Christian Revivalists, Free Gospellers, and Quaker Methodists of Warrington, Macclesfield, and other towns of the northwest (as indeed among the freewheeling followers of the female preacher Alice Cambridge in Dublin), Dow found a welcome rejection of the customary European "stress . . . upon forms, names and tradition"; frequently, in their emphasis on inner prompting over outward form, these groups stood close to Quakerism, for which Dow himself had considerable sympathy. The American denounced "party spirit" and drew attention to those of his revivals which—as in the Wesleyan chapel at Congleton—worked against schism; but in general his work strengthened the separatists and increased their numbers, while his itinerancy amongst revivalist societies having "no particular intercourse or communion together" reinforced the drive for that cohesion already being encouraged by "insiders" like the Quaker Methodist Peter Philips.[13]

Secondly, Dow encouraged the use of the camp meeting. For several years the *Wesleyan Methodist Magazine* had reproduced reports of these dramatic outdoor meetings in America; they had excited intense interest amongst Wesleyan experimenters, but no action was taken before Dow arrived. Drawing on his own experience in the southern and western states, the American persuaded a group of revivalists at Harriseahead, on the edge of the Potteries, to hold the first English camp meeting at Mow Cop in Staffordshire in May 1807. Their leader, Hugh Bourne, an enthusiastic Wesleyan local preacher, had heard Dow speak on camp meetings in the previous month and had acquired some of his tracts on the origins and methods of conducting them. Field preaching was an established part of the eighteenth-century Methodist practice, but the idea of large crowds spending the whole day in religious exercises, as at Mow Cop, with preaching, prayer, exhortation, and singing taking place simultaneously in separate groups, was quite new. The American practice of multiplying meetings over several days (they were, after all, *camp* meetings) did not, however, take root in British soil, despite Bourne's efforts to set up tents on the campground. Conference sought to stifle these camp-meeting men, whom it rightly regarded as in sympathy with the revivalist schismatics of the Potteries and the northwest, but the weapon used—a restrictive resolution against these meetings "even supposing [them] to be allowable in America"—fanned rather than choked the revival flame. Ten months after Bourne had ignored the resolution, he was expelled from Wesleyan Methodism and within three years headed a recognizable group of Camp-Meeting Methodists. Their union with William Clowes and other "primitives" in 1811 resulted in the establishment of the Primitive Methodist Church.[14]

Dow's contribution to the emergence of the most revival-minded denomination in England in the first half of the nineteenth century was reflected in his movements during his third and final visit to Britain in 1818-19. Effectively excluded from English and Irish Wesleyan chapels by the resolutions of the 1807 Conferences, he held most of his indoor meetings in Primitive Methodist chapels in the church's heartland of Derbyshire, Nottinghamshire, and Leicestershire. The denomination did not forget its debts to America. Not only did camp meetings continue to nourish the earthy, noisy revivalism of laboring men and women, but from the late 1820s the reports of the Primitives' own missionaries to America—William Summersides, Thomas Morris, Ruth Watkins, and others—ensured an acquaintance with the new measures. Particularly in 1838 and 1839, after Summersides's return and the serialization in the denominational magazine of Finney's *Lectures on Revivals*, evening protracted meetings were adopted and during the 1840s spread throughout the denomination as a means of promoting revivals.[15]

Dow and camp meetings had not inoculated Wesleyan Methodists against revivalism as such, but they had injected them with a fear of the schismatic tendencies of revival and a sense that American evangelicalism was less well disciplined than it ought to be. These feelings were rekindled when the new-measure revivals made their debut. When the most likely champion of these measures, James Caughey, arrived to give them effect, he would find a residue of distrust for things American that no amount of practical success could ever remove.

Caughey's Itinerancy, 1841-47

James Caughey was born in the north of Ireland on 9 April, 1810. During

James Caughey. Courtesy of Drew University Library.

his youth his family, "of Scotch ancestry," responding to those forces that were driving thousands of Irishmen annually to emigrate, set sail for the United States. Little is known of this stage of Caughey's life. At some time he repudiated his family's Calvinism, probably before 1827, when a J. Caughey held a post in the Methodist Sunday School Association at Newburgh, New York. By 1830 he was employed in a flour mill in Troy, and along with thousands of others in the "Burned-over District," he found himself swept along by the tide of revival. Two years after his conversion he was admitted as a preacher on probation into the Troy Conference. He received deacon's orders in 1834 and after a further two years was ordained elder.[16]

Such scanty information conceals many of the formative influences on Caughey's mind. It tells nothing of the close associations made in adolescence and young manhood. From his unknown teachers he learned enough to study the Scriptures in Hebrew and Greek and to allow discerning English Methodists to label him "well read," "a philosopher" and "a clever man." From his immersion in the revival he derived his single-minded belief in the unfolding conversion of the world and his conviction that any evangelical minister worth his salt must be a revivalist. In these early years, too, he acquired that sense of the direct intervention of God and the Devil in his daily activities which remained with him throughout his life and which made him peculiarly susceptible to what he called "impressions." In every detail of life—what text he should choose, what itinerary he should follow— he felt himself guided by a special Providence or checked by satanic agency. His denominational critics in both England and America feared that he came dangerously close to claiming supernatural revelations, all the more disquieting once Millerism, a movement dependent on "fanatical impressions and revelations," had upset the equilibrium of the MEC.[17]

Caughey's description of the circumstances surrounding his decision to visit Britain reinforced such fears. In 1839 he began to feel doubts about his plans to marry. Plagued by anxiety he spent three days in prayer. In the twilight of a July evening

a light, as I conceived from heaven, reached me. My soul was singularly calmed. . . . The following, in substance, was spoken to my heart . . .: "These matters which trouble thee must be let entirely alone. The will of God is, that thou shouldst visit Europe. He shall be with thee there, and give thee many seals to thy ministry. He has provided thee with funds. Make thy arrangements accordingly; and, next Conference, ask liberty from the proper authorities, and it shall be granted thee. Visit Canada first; when this is done, sail for England."

This splendidly specific "message" illustrates very well the tendencies of Caughey's mind. He was essentially a pragmatist, not a mystic. Later he was to explain that he had "heard no audible voice," had seen no "visible manifestation" at the time of this "visitation." The "call" to leave is best explained as a practical resolution of his "mental troubles." Where better to turn than neighboring Canada, where a few years earlier he had participated in revivals, and Ireland, where he could search out surviving relatives and family friends?[18]

Caughey's work in the 1830s had given him a thorough grounding in the technique of revivals, camp meetings, and religious excitement. As a circuit preacher in the small but developing agricultural and manufacturing communities of Essex and Clinton counties of northeastern New York he tapped the evangelicalism of a population whose roots lay predominantly in New England, secured a local reputation as an effective revivalist, and won invitations from churches farther afield. In 1835 he contributed to a major protracted meeting in Montreal; in 1837 in the manufacturing town of Pittsfield, Massachusetts, he was present to help when over three hundred were converted in a period of only six weeks. Even so, when Caughey prepared to leave Whitehall in September 1840 with private funds for two years' travel and a certificate of "good standing" from Bishop Robert R. Roberts, there was little to indicate that he had the ability to flourish in the unfamiliar environment of industrial Britain.[19]

Caughey arrived in England in July 1841 after several months' work in Montreal, Quebec, and Saint John's. Traveling immediately to Manchester, where ministers were gathering for the annual Wesleyan Methodist Conference, he found that his despondency bred of uncertainty evaporated in the company of John Hannah, secretary to the Conference, William Lord, and Thomas Waugh, all established friends of American Methodism. Waugh, the most influential and respected of Irish Methodists, secured Caughey a Dublin pulpit for his first British sermon, after which "The American" was invited to conduct a series of special services in the city's Wesleyan chapels. Within five months he could claim seven hundred converts in a revival "unequalled in the entire history of Methodism in Dublin." Such an impetus virtually guaranteed him similar successes when he moved on to Limerick and Cork.[20]

However, at Bandon, in County Cork, during the late summer of 1842 Caughey encountered some of those constraints on growth that had plagued Irish Methodism throughout the century. Constant emigration, "the frowns of papists"—the vast majority of the population—and "the contempt of the Establishment" had long rendered difficult a regular Methodist increase. "The congregations are tolerable," Caughey wrote after two months' work, "but our doings excite but very little interest beyond the families of Methodism." Caughey's techniques were well designed to reinvigorate well-established churches nestling within a friendly evangelicalism; they were less well suited to expansion into a hostile environment. Caughey was no Gideon Ouseley, the Irish itinerant preacher of the late eighteenth and early nineteenth centuries, whose audiences had been generally poor, often hostile, and reachable only through outdoor preaching. Nor was he a Lorenzo Dow. Caughey's audiences, sympathetic and evangelically minded, indoor, and "highly respectable," reflected the changing character of Irish Methodism.[21]

According to his original schedule, with his Irish mission over, Caughey —moderately successful, but his reputation as a revivalist still unmade in Britain—should now have returned to America. But in May 1842 he had written to the Troy Conference asking for a "located station" that would free him indefinitely for itinerant work outside the conference, yet keep his status as a fully accredited minister of the MEC. His request granted, Caughey pondered his itinerancy. Inevitably he sought and received an "impression": "Liverpool is constantly before me," he wrote, "although I have no official invitation"; the great port would be "the pass" into England. He was correct: in the next six months Liverpool was to provide the setting for the biggest revival he had experienced so far in Britain. In the North Circuit, where special services had been held some two or three years previously, the revival-minded superintendent, Abraham Farrar, and his colleagues John H. James and Joseph Beaumont, warmly welcomed the uninvited evangelist. His protracted meetings flourished. In the South Circuit the going was not so easy. Caughey's invitation had come from the circuit leaders against the better judgment of William Atherton, the superintendent, who was "not at all enthusiastic" about the proposed visit and had reservations about revivals in general. Caughey did not perceive it, but later battlelines were already forming, for Atherton was to preside over the Conference of 1846, which effectively excluded the American from Wesleyan pulpits, while Farrar and Beaumont were to be the American's chief defenders.[22]

It was difficult for Caughey to treat non-cooperation seriously, for he was becoming a much-sought-after figure. Liverpool was indeed the pass into England. His successes there prompted invitations from other large northern cities, and in the next four years Caughey's efforts in the industrial and urban areas of the midlands and the north demonstrated his increasing mastery of urban revivalism. His movements determined generally by ad hoc considerations, his invitations, and his "impressions," Caughey adhered to no precise overall strategy and itinerary. After Liverpool his major campaigns, apart from that in Birmingham in 1845-46, were conducted in Yorkshire: in Leeds, Hull, Sheffield, Huddersfield, and York. In each of these seven centers his meetings interrupted a period of decline or only limited growth and contributed to marked increases in membership (see table 7 and figure 5). These campaigns were supplemented by a series of shorter efforts in other northern centers, notably Nottingham, Lincoln, Sunderland, and Chesterfield. Eventually, after nearly six years of revivals, interrupted by relatively short periods of convalescence, including two trips to the Continent, Caughey could claim to have been instrumental in over twenty thousand conversions and to have brought nine thousand to experience "entire sanctification."

TABLE 7 Wesleyan Methodist Membership and Growth Rates in Seven Towns and Cities Visited by James Caughey, 1842-46

	Liverpool (Oct. 1842-Apr. 1843)			Leeds (Apr.-Sept. 1843)			Hull (Oct. 1843-May 1844)			Sheffield (May-Sept. 1844)		
YEAR	MEMBERSHIP	GROWTH RATE	YEAR	MEMBERSHIP	GROWTH RATE	YEAR	MEMBERSHIP	GROWTH RATE	YEAR	MEMBERSHIP	GROWTH RATE
1838	3,141	14.47	1838	7,286	4.74	1839	3,050	9.63	1839	4,416	-3.64
1839	3,186	1.43	1839	7,967	9.35	1840	3,275	7.38	1840	4,591	3.96
1840	3,231	1.41	1840	8,079	1.41	1841	3,424	4.55	1841	4,604	0.28
1841	3,154	-2.38	1841	7,727	-4.36	1842	3,286	-4.03	1842	4,462	-3.08
1842	3,096	-1.84	1842	7,695	-0.41	1843	3,107	-5.45	1843	4,334	-2.87
1843	3,166	2.26	1843	7,574	-1.57	1844	3,358	8.08	1844	4,307	-0.62
1844	3,500	10.55	1844	8,103	6.98	1845	4,042	20.37	1845	5,171	20.06
1845	3,581	2.31	1845	7,909	-2.39	1846	3,935	-2.65	1846	5,226	1.06
1846	3,643	1.73	1846	7,776	-1.68	1847	3,790	-3.68	1847	5,143	-1.59
1847	3,606	-1.02	1847	7,390	-4.96	1848	3,654	-3.59	1848	5,021	-2.37
1848	3,651	1.23	1848	7,317	-0.99	1849	3,749	2.60	1849	5,310	5.76

	Huddersfield (Dec. 1844-Apr. 1845)			York (June-Sept. 1845)			Birmingham (Dec. 1845-May 1846)	
YEAR	MEMBERSHIP	GROWTH RATE	YEAR	MEMBERSHIP	GROWTH RATE	YEAR	MEMBERSHIP	GROWTH RATE
1840	2,545	−0.47	1840	2,200	6.28	1841	2,976	5.57
1841	2,456	−3.50	1841	2,562	16.45	1842	2,932	−1.48
1842	2,339	−4.76	1842	2,800	9.28	1843	2,954	0.61
1843	2,212	−5.43	1843	2,850	1.79	1844	3,169	7.28
1844	2,274	2.80	1844	2,855	0.18	1845	3,140	−0.92
1845	2,481	9.10	1845	2,850	−0.18	1846	3,286	4.65
1846	2,820	13.66	1846	3,060	7.39	1847	3,663	11.47
1847	2,894	2.62	1847	3,023	−1.21	1848	3,628	−0.96
1848	2,956	2.14	1848	3,000	−0.76	1849	3,601	−0.74
1849	2,827	−4.36	1849	3,058	1.93	1850	3,366	−6.53
1850	2,785	−1.49	1850	2,900	−5.16	1851	2,633	−21.78

SOURCE: *Minutes of Several Conversations between the Methodist Preachers . . . at their . . . Annual Conference,* 1838-51.

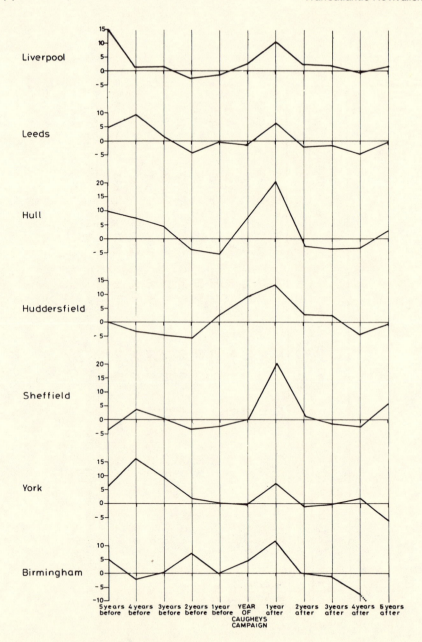

Figure 5. Wesleyan Methodist Growth Rates in Seven Towns and Cities Visited by James Caughey, 1842-46.

SOURCE: *Minutes of Several Conversations between the Methodist Preachers . . . at their . . . Annual Conference, 1838-51.*

These figures were no doubt overgenerous, but even at a more modest estimate Caughey's successes reflected his extraordinary energy, the receptivity
of his audiences, and the appropriateness of his modus operandi. These
factors are perhaps most easily identifiable in Sheffield, the city of his greatest
triumphs, where during the summer of 1844, "the revival . . . surpassed
anything I had ever before witnessed."[23]

Sheffield in 1844 was a fast-growing city of some one hundred thousand
inhabitants, the majority of whom were in some way connected with the
city's iron and steel industries. The growth of industrial Sheffield had offered
great opportunities to its evangelical churches; by mid-century evangelicalism held a virtually unchallenged influence over the major Protestant denominations. This had been aided by the general cooperation of a predominantly evangelical Established Church that was too weak and inflexible to
have successfully checked the growth of evangelicalism, had it been that
way inclined, and by the absence of a resident aristocracy of any real social
significance. In other words, two forces that elsewhere acted as powerful
brakes on revivalism were here too weak to do so. By midcentury the Methodists stood clearly in the fore among the various Sheffield denominations.
Within the old parish the various branches of Methodism claimed twenty-
four places of worship, the Church of England thirteen.[24]

Methodist strength·was based on a strong tradition of revivals, particularly
within the predominant Wesleyan branch. In some areas of Wesleyanism,
revivalist sections of the church had broken away. This was not the case in
Sheffield. Despite suffering losses during the Kilhamite disruption of 1797
and the Warrenite agitation of the 1830s and despite undoubted upward
social movement, Sheffield Wesleyanism remained undeviatingly revival-
minded. Wilbur Fisk, troubled by the coolness of so many English Methodists
to revivals, was relieved that at least in Sheffield "no Methodist . . . asked
me whether I thought religious revivals advantageous to the cause of Christianity."[25]

The question would have been superfluous. In every decade since the
1790s the Wesleyans had experienced a marked revival. From 1794 to 1796,
during a decade of acute social and political tension, which spilled over into
connectional politics, the Sheffield circuit experienced a revival whose earthy,
noisy meetings contributed to an explosion throughout the West Riding.
One of the converts, William Miller, much influenced by William Bramwell
(minister at Sheffield during the later stages of the revival) entered the Methodist itinerancy in 1799. His growing reputation as a revivalist was enhanced by the Sheffield revival of 1803-04, his first year in the circuit. Bramwell
himself, probably the most effective revivalist of his generation, returned to
Sheffield between 1810 and 1812: more members were added to the Wesleyan
society than during any other two years of the decade. The revival of the

1820s, which began in 1821 under John Nelson, "son of thunder" and intimate friend of Bramwell, was less clear-cut, for growth continued for every year until 1828, the peak year coming in 1824-25. But as if to remedy the absence of the really dramatic, Sheffield Wesleyanism experienced between 1831 and 1834 its most spectacular revival for a generation, when over fifteen hundred were added to the two city circuits. In its early stages the revival was stimulated by the savage cholera epidemic of 1832 and the efforts of ministers like Richard Treffry, Sr. Later the dominant personality was a Manx clergyman, Robert Aitken, whose preaching irregularities had resulted in his withdrawal from the Church of England and his employment during part of the 1830s in Wesleyan pulpits, even though he was never formally received into Methodism.[26]

Consequently, when Caughey arrived in the city he entered a veritable crucible of revivalism. Few cities could claim to have experienced the ministries of four of the best-known and respected English revivalists of the first half of the nineteenth century. As in the other northern cities where Caughey worked, he entered churches whose members had learned that revivals could be expected and worked for at regular intervals to restore their churches to full prosperity and to draw a new generation into the church. In other words, the anticipation of revivals, encouraged by a pattern of revival boom and slump, was in some ways self-fulfilling: there was a powerful *internal* force driving the churches toward revival. By 1844 the membership of the two Sheffield circuits had dropped from the record figure of 4,950 reached in 1834, to 4,307. Once again it was time for reinvigoration.[27]

There were also considerations of a more secular kind, for the Methodist responded not simply as a chapel-goer, but as a member of the broader society. In 1844 Sheffield and the northern industrial areas were slowly emerging from a period of economic depression and social tension. Trade prosperity was returning, Chartist strength declining. To much of the Wesleyan membership and to a Wesleyan leadership recognizably in sympathy with authority and disturbed by social and political disruption, a revival represented a force for social harmony. During the Chartist agitation of 1839-40 a Methodist local preacher argued that only through revival would "good order and society, virtue and sobriety characterise our crowded cities [and] our rural districts; and all classes of society be distinguished by mildness, courtesy, benevolence and good-will." Sheffield Wesleyans could regard Caughey as an appropriate instrument in the creation of that harmony. Unlike Lorenzo Dow, whose unrepentant republicanism had alarmed secular authorities, Caughey was untainted by social or political radicalism. His antagonism toward the *"Chartist conspiracy,"* as he called it, his regret over the *"villanous and successful attempts . . . to blow up premises"* and his confessed lack of understanding of the *"secret combinations* among the workmen" exposed a mind that examined all issues through evangelical lenses, that considered unimportant all that could not be explained in evangelical terms, and that saw secular prosperity as dependent on a community's religious well-being.[28]

Caughey's campaigns in Sheffield and the north took place during the lull between the peaks of Chartist activity in 1842 and 1848; this might suggest that Edward Thompson's thesis of a process of oscillation by a "floating population" between political radicalism and religious excitement is applicable to this later period. There was, after all, a degree of Methodist influence in both personnel and institutions within Chartism: in the Sheffield area Chartist camp meetings and love feasts on a Methodist model were employed particularly during 1839-40; and during 1842, a critical year for Chartist disturbances, the Wesleyans suffered marked losses. But the hypothesis does not work. *At the same time as* the earlier period of disorder, in 1839-40, the Wesleyans, becoming increasingly "respectable" in character and tone under conformed Tories like James Dixon, experienced their greatest increase in membership during the entire decade from 1834 to 1844. Moreover, the great majority of Caughey's converts were in regular church membership or attendance and outside the group most susceptible to Chartist persuasions.[29]

The receptiveness of Sheffield audiences to Caughey was a product not only of their entrenched psychology of revivalism and of favorable secular circumstances but also of the persuasive techniques and dramatic appeal of the revivalist himself. A truly powerful personality was capable of producing results that ran counter to broad connectional trends. William Miller and his colleagues in 1803-04 had produced in Sheffield significant growth at a time of connectional decrease. Caughey himself, after Sheffield, was to continue his spectacular work for three more years while Wesleyan Methodism was recording its lowest triennial increase in nearly thirty years, and the revival flame was sputtering in the other denominations (figure 4).[30] An examination of the particulars of Caughey's campaign does much to explain his success.

Caughey's arrival at Sheffield in May 1844 reflected the role of anticipation and contagion in revivalism. (Caughey himself well understood the importance of expectancy: "set all *your people a-praying*," he would exhort his intending hosts.) The connectional system had helped spread his reputation, and he was eagerly awaited. The city was littered with handbills and placards announcing his impending campaign. On Sunday, 12 May, Caughey held his first services, at Ebenezer Chapel on the outskirts of the town. The relative remoteness of the chapel worried him. But after his very first sermon, 29 professed conversion; Caughey found it unnecessary to threaten imminent departure—a tactic he was known to use when things were not going well; and by the end of the first week the number of converts stood at 132. From the beginning, Caughey's primary methods—preaching, prayer and appeals to the penitent—were clearly taking effect.[31]

Regular, frequent preaching was central to Caughey's work. "Hammer on a rock long enough, and it must break in pieces . . . God's word is as a hammer to break the rocky hearts in pieces before the Lord." This was Caughey's justification for a working life that was nothing less than a continuous protracted meeting. For most of his stay at Sheffield, and in Britain generally, he preached six evenings a week; on occasions during his career eight to ten sermons weekly were not unusual. Such efforts would have killed a weaker man, but despite occasional "violent attacks" Caughey's strong constitution kept him itinerating for thirty-five years, a span rivalled by few of his contemporaries. Only in the later 1860s did he retire from active work, "on account of broken health."[32]

In the pulpit, Caughey cut an impressive figure. His commanding height, keen eyes, and strong, dark, not unattractive features gave him an assurance and presence reinforced by his "easy" and "natural" pulpit manner, by an unshakable conviction of his utter rightness, and by a complete absence of self-doubt. "His voice," it was said by one of his Sheffield hearers, "was music of the gamut range. When tremulous with emotion, it had a bell-like ring never to be forgotten." But Caughey was no Ranter. Even a Wesleyan critic admired "the general delicacy and beauty of his accent, pronunciation, tone, and emphasis." But he did possess the revivalist's necessary plainness of style. His nonstop flow of language was to the point, often ungrammatical, and "crowded with provincial idioms" and arresting Irish-American pronunciations. His strength lay in the telling anecdote and in blunt denunciation and frank exposure. Essentially Caughey's "strange fascination" lay in his capacity for stating evangelical commonplaces in novel and arresting, yet simple, ways. He was not an original thinker; he more or less ignored speculative divinity and doctrinal preaching. Instead he relied on a vast store of anecdotes and real-life illustrations to bring to life the fundamental evangelical doctrines. Even the smallest incident could be turned to good use, as when, gesticulating violently, he knocked a nearby brass candlestick out of its holder. Unperturbed, Caughey continued his appeals to the penitent, using the incident successfully to unsettle "the *lightless backslider*" who would, like the candlestick, "be removed out of his place suddenly, unless sudden repentance prevented the *terrible catastrophe*."[33]

Some recalled the "Irish wit and humour" of Caughey's sermons, but it was for inspiring terror that they were best remembered. Directing his attentions primarily at "undecided" hearers ("How long halt ye between two opinions?" was his favorite text), Caughey spent most of his time trying to frighten his audience into the Kingdom of God. He spared none of their delicate feelings in his descriptions of the horrors of Hell, the terrors of the Devil, and the severity of the law of God. On an audience that accepted the terrifying reality of Hell, the effect could be electric. With his audience "broken down," Caughey would switch suddenly to a theme of mercy—of Christ's atonement and God's willingness to save sinners: "Decide now I tell you, you are reaching the point on which your destiny turns; the fearful crisis approaches that decides your fate."[34] A generation later, in Dwight L. Moody's campaigns, the emphasis on God's love would predominate; with Caughey it still held second place to "hell and damnation." Nevertheless, it was an indispensable element in a preaching scheme erected on such anti-theses.

To intensify the pressure on his hearers, Caughey often addressed his sermons to individual members of the congregation, never mentioned by name, but described in unusually precise detail. Such descriptions were usually broad enough to embrace more than a single person, but specific enough to make individuals feel they were being selected for special attention:

Now, there are several characters here before me tonight, my discourse will particularly concern. The first is a man who has heard me often before, both here and elsewhere. The next is one, who has heard me before, but not here: he has heard me in_____. Another, is a woman, who has heard me once before only, and that in this chapel: she was here on Sunday night. The last is an old, grey-headed man, who has never seen my face before, either here or anywhere else.[35]

Caughey would proceed to "expose" their characters, implying that his particularizing was of divine inspiration and maintaining that he had received on the individual's behalf "a message from God," often a prophecy of impending death. "This year thou shalt die" was an alarming text that Caughey used repeatedly with conspicuous success on audiences for whom death was always close at hand, whether from day-to-day industrial diseases like "grinders' asthma," or from a dramatic epidemic, as with cholera in 1832.

Caughey reinforced his demands for immediate decision by encouraging the restitution of goods fraudulently obtained. This was a product both of the concern of many Wesleyans for social harmony and an ordered community and also of a revivalist tradition in which the restoration of ill-gotten gains was regarded as a necessary concomitant of genuine conversion. Less directly Caughey encouraged teetotalism in penitents and church members. In 1841 Conference had ordered that Wesleyan chapels be closed to teetotal meetings; most Wesleyan ministers saw teetotalism as unscriptural, tainted with radicalism, and associated with overbearing lay influence. Caughey respected this official ruling and kept the friendship of temperate but not wholly abstemious Wesleyans; he demonstrated much less moral self-righteousness than some other visiting American Methodists. But if not abrasive, Caughey's teetotalism was firm and, through his lectures in Sheffield's only Primitive Methodist chapel, well publicized. Not all Wesleyans would have been pleased with his association with total abstinence, but in

Sheffield he was in relatively sympathetic territory; teetotalism had taken root there in the mid-1830s and had the support of "many intelligent and good people."[36]

In the meeting for prayer (or "knee work," as he called it) Caughey sought to capitalize on the effects of his sermons. Experience had taught him that prayer meetings held immediately after preaching—a practice regarded with caution by many English Methodists—were an essential antidote to procrastination; during these meetings he regularly used the well-established American device of the call to the altar. Leaving his pulpit, he would wander from pew to pew encouraging the anxious to go forward to the communion rail or penitent bench. His presermon prayer meeting in the vestry would already have strengthened the resolve of many to move. Now they were guided forward by special helpers. Others were shamed into obedience with the shout: "Come out, man! and save your soul now." At the rail Caughey, aided by local preachers, would instruct penitents how to "get liberty" from their sins, while the rest of the congregation sang hymns, joined in the prayer or shouted hallelujahs. At Ebenezer "the noise was sometimes tremendous." Occasionally, however, the excitement went beyond the acceptable limits of weeping and "piercing cries of mercy": in Sheffield's Norfolk Street Chapel, the proceedings stimulated "fits of the wildest fanaticism, carried on with . . . fervour," and on one occasion in Ireland there were cases of jumping and physical jerks.[37]

Caughey's use of the call to the communion rail was not restricted to Sheffield. Some saw it as the "most remarkable" feature of his work, for although an integral part of American services, it was not universally employed in British Methodism. Wesley had never used anything like this, nor had Bramwell and other revivalists in the early nineteenth century: penitents were dealt with in scattered groups about the chapel or in a special penitents' meeting. Only in the later 1820s and 1830s did the call forward to the penitents' bench or penitents' form make its appearance, and even then it was not a regular feature of Methodist revivals.[38] Its attraction lay in the public pressure it imposed on the undecided and in its removal of the confusion that accompanied scattered prayer groups. Both good order and souls were protected. Inevitably one looks for an American stimulus to the use of this "new measure" (which was indeed described as "the American custom"). The visit of men like Richard Reece to America in the 1820s provides one explanation, for they gained firsthand knowledge of the practice. The transatlantic supply of books and journals also kept British audiences well informed of American practices, while Caughey himself was a traveling salesman for the measure who probably won as many customers as he repelled.[39]

Caughey's results at Ebenezer reinforced enthusiasm for his "special services." He could claim some 486 conversions in a little over three weeks—a dramatic achievement even by American standards. At the same time 262 were "entirely sanctified," for the preaching of entire sanctification (or "purification," "perfect love," or "holiness of heart," as Caughey variously called the doctrine) formed an integral part of his work. He saw the "blessing of purification" as much more than an inessential appendage of the Christian experience. "So long as you are only justified and not purified you are only half a believer; and do you think Christ can be satisfied with your being half a believer?" In his preaching of this (and the other major Wesleyan doctrines), Caughey was essentially orthodox. Together with other British and American Methodists he held that there was a spiritual state beyond simple regeneration, which though not representing an *absolute* "sinless perfection" or release from the temptations of sin, gave the Christian a sense of purification, greater mental equilibrium, and a triumphant acceptance of death. Advance to this state could take place only *after* justification (though sometimes it could be realized simultaneously), but in contrast to Calvinist belief, it could occur before death. Moreover, entire sanctification, though the result of gradual preparation, was achieved "in an instant." As with justification, there was an identifiable moment at which the individual realized his new spiritual status; hence it was not only the unconverted who were subjected to the high-pressure conditions of revival. And in Sheffield, where the doctrine had been absorbed into the Wesleyan bloodstream, thanks to a long line of ministers fully committed to its transfusion, Caughey's exhortations were eminently successful.[40]

After three weeks at Ebenezer Caughey took over the pulpit of Carver Street Chapel, the finest Wesleyan chapel in Sheffield and one of the most impressive in the whole connection. It possessed large galleries, an organ, and elegant fittings appropriate to the advancing social status of much of its membership. But social pretension did not stand in the way of revival: within four weeks there were 1,160 cases of conversion and entire sanctification, which gave meaning to the chapel's nickname of "the converting furnace" and which, wrote Caughey, went "beyond anything I [had] ever seen before, in the same space of time." By the time he transferred to Brunswick Chapel in the East Circuit his success had developed an unstoppable momentum. Here the campaign reached its climax. His name drew thousands, many traveling from Hathersage, Eyam, Grindleford, and other villages up to twenty miles away. At times the police were called to control the crowds, hundreds of whom never gained entry. Those who did find seats, spiritual squatters who brought food for the day to keep possession of their places, were often "crammed to suffocation" in a chapel that could hold nearly two thousand people. Remarkably, since it was July, Caughey worked with "much ease, and . . . success"; nor was this the only summer period when he broke the rule, well-established on both sides of the Atlantic, that revivals were essentially a winter phenomenon. When he left Sheffield early in Sep-

Caughey in Brunswick Chapel, Sheffield, in 1844. From a print donated to Sheffield City Libraries by C. H. Lea. Courtesy Sheffield City Libraries.

TABLE 8   James Caughey's Sheffield Campaign, 12 May to 8 September 1844

	Ebenezer	Carver Street	Bruns- wick	Norfolk Street	Bridge- houses	Total
Number of days' services	20	29	26	24	2	101
Justified—"From the world"						
Appointed to east and west circuits	285	591	734	534	61	2,205
Not appointed	13	60	25	26	—	124
Appointed to other circuits and churches	25	72	116	83	8	304
Total	323	723	875	643	69	2,633
Justified—"In the church"						
Members of east and west circuits	145	150	104	82	11	492
Members of other circuits and churches	17	31	65	26	2	141
Total	162	181	169	108	13	633
Entirely sanctified						
Members of east and west circuits	225	292	332	306	24	1,179
Members of other circuits and churches	34	76	87	58	1	256
Total sanctified	259	368	419	364	25	1,435
Total justified	485	904	1,044	751	82	3,266
Total justified and sanctified	744	1,272	1,463	1,115	107	4,701

SOURCE: *Agency and Progress of Wesleyan-Methodism* . . . (London, 1845).

tember the grand total of cases of conversion and entire sanctification approached five thousand (see table 8). Some may have doubted the value of the professed experiences, but this remarkable figure is almost certainly reliable, since Caughey was determined to avoid the charge of exaggeration, and since the records were compiled by scrupulous circuit secretaries from lists of names and addresses collected during the services—a practice well-established in Sheffield and elsewhere.[41]

Caughey's converts came from no single social group. According to the superintendent of the East Circuit, "The work was not confined to the lower orders." After his work in Ebenezer, where the members were "generally poor," and in the more assertive, influential Wesleyanism of Carver Street, Caughey remarked on the social variegation of his hearers, who included "the rich and the poor; the educated and uncultivated; the refined and intellectual, on the one part,—the vulgar, and those of the *baser sort*, on the other." If Wesleyanism did not embrace the leaders of the community (it was to be another short generation before Carver Street could boast a mayor and master cutler), it was nevertheless more likely to attract men of greater social standing and education than were the Primitives and the various Reformed Methodist bodies. Shopkeeper Wesleyanism had arrived. Abraham Sharman, for example, a leader of Carver Street, was a grocer. Albert Bradwell, son of a tradesman, reported an education that had included Aristotle, Hobbes, Hume, Locke, Voltaire, Leibnitz, and Kant. And there was a similar story in other areas where Caughey worked of a middle-class leavening of working-class Methodism.[42]

If there *was* a lowest common denominator amongst Caughey's converts, it was religious and not social. Almost all boasted or concealed an evangelical background. Though nearly 80 percent of the converts in the Sheffield revival were described as being "from the world" (table 8), most attended Methodist services regularly. Occasionally Caughey attracted "scoffers" and "infidels" seeking cheap and eccentric entertainment, but even this audience might betray an acquaintance with evangelicalism. Albert Bradwell, a professed atheist before becoming one of the revival's more interesting converts, had in fact "found salvation" in a Methodist chapel as a youth. Only later had he fashioned his own system of "infidelity." His mocking attendance at Caughey's services backfired, as evangelical embers were rekindled and guilt over his apostasy was aroused. Yet Bradwell, as Caughey realized, was a special case: few converts had ever come so close to repudiating their evangelicalism.[43]

Caughey's converts sometimes included "some of the wildest and most dissipated characters." But this was unusual. Most of his hearers outwardly led a sober, Christian life. "I do not charge you with swearing, with sabbath-breaking, with whoremongering, with adultery," Caughey told them. Their sin lay in *"mental rebellion"*; he criticized them for "refus[ing] to yield to God's claims," for having remained regular hearers for years without wholeheartedly seeking salvation. This unregenerate group, central to the work of all Methodist revivalists, provided the major source of Caughey's converts; most of them were young people, between sixteen and thirty years of age, brought up in Methodist families that had themselves pɔobably experienced the earlier revivals of Aitken, Miller, and Bramwell. Nor was Caughey slow to approach young people *under* sixteen who were still members of Sunday schools and catechumen classes: he was pleased to find that the primary concern of Sheffield Sunday school teachers was to bring pupils "to an *early and . . . experimental acquaintance with God.*"[44]

The evangelical background of the "justified" reflected the profound changes in Wesleyan Methodism over one or two generations. As revivalism had come indoors the Methodist mentality had altered. The sectarian aggression of Wesley's day, or even Lorenzo Dow's, reflected in the commitment to reach through outdoor preaching well beyond the walls of Methodist chapels, had now given way to denominational consolidation, the pastoral tending of flocks, the building of finer and more substantial chapels, the education of ministers. Insurgency into the "darkness of Paganism" was absorbing relatively less time than in the past. Open-air preaching was in decline; most converts were recruited from within the familial orbit of Methodism, for the children of Methodists offered a much more fruitful field for labor than did that class of the community "saturated . . . with Infidel, Socialist, Chartist and blasphemous notions."[45]

The remaining 20 percent of Caughey's converts in Sheffield constituted an embarrassing group for diligent Methodists, for they were drawn not from the explicitly unconverted church adherents, but from within the church membership itself. The figure may seem high. In fact it was considerably lower than the returns for Liverpool and Leeds, where 50 percent or more of those converted were already society members. Some of these were backsliders from a previous state of grace. But large numbers had been admitted into society in a state of "awakened concern" without ever having experienced a "new birth." Caughey was scandalized. He pointed to American Methodism, where frequent revivals and a searching style of preaching exposed anything less than full-blooded commitment. He proved his point as his direct sermons released a stream of self-questioning amongst confused church members. Had they ever been truly converted? Could they remember the exact time and place of their change of heart?—as they surely should, given that "the work of conversion is so momentous, that no man can pass through it, and not know it." In Sheffield congregations superintended quite recently by James Dixon, a minister who had never insisted "upon instantaneous and sensible conversion in all cases" since "the work of the Holy Spirit is often gradual and gentle," Caughey sowed doubt and confusion; many who had thought themselves converted took out a double indemnity at Caughey's communion rail.[46]

The reconverted element in Caughey's revivals contributes just one explanation of the great discrepancy between the total number of conversions (3,266) claimed by the revivalist, and the much lower figure of 800 or 900 that represented the actual increase in the two Sheffield circuits for the revival year. In addition there were hundreds on trial. There was also the customary revival wastage: about 5 percent of the converts "from the world," the magic of their conversion rapidly evaporated, never presented themselves for church membership. Furthermore, many of the converts—some 15 percent of the total—joined churches of other denominations and Wesleyan churches outside the Sheffield circuits. Caughey, like other Wesleyans, did not want to be accused of proselytizing members of other denominations, but few of his audiences were exclusively Methodist. At Leeds, indeed, a huge proportion of his converts—600 out of the total 1,600—were members of other denominations or from circuits outside the city, and many of those converted would have remained with their own churches.[47]

Tensions and Explosion

Caughey's passage at Sheffield had been smooth. He had received the cooperation of leading laymen and ministers; there had been no concerted efforts to disrupt his meetings; the press had proved generally favorable. His experience was not always so placid. In Hull in 1844 "all hell" had been let loose against him; the next year Huddersfield socialists turned him into a useful whipping boy in public debate; in Lincolnshire in 1846 the revivalist received an unprecedented "flailing from the public papers." Particularly harmful were the criticisms of respectable Christian laity. The Whig *Morning Chronicle*, for example, saw Caughey's Birmingham revival of 1846 as stark evidence of popular ignorance and the pressing need for improved education. The revival fostered "family disunion," "spiritual pride," and a fanaticism that would bring genuine religious fervor into disrepute. "Nothing that has grown of the transatlantic fusion of puritanism and democracy ever produced a more appalling frenzy than the ministrations of Mr. Caughey have engendered among the sturdy hammerers of the iron town."[48]

External criticism was an occupational hazard; attack from within the revivalist found more damaging and less forgivable. Wesleyan Methodists gave Caughey a mixed reception. By the time of Caughey's itinerancy the advancing prosperity and respectability of early-Victorian Wesleyanism was eroding support for "Pentecostal excitement." Caughey's meetings were at a reasonable remove from the boisterous tumult of an earlier generation, but they were still sufficiently noisy and confused for charges of "enthusiasm" and "disorder" to stick. Caughey, as a good revivalist, defended the noise on the familiar grounds that as great a change as conversion could scarcely occur without considerable distress. Similarly he rejected the charge that "many persons [were] merely frightened into religious life," that when the revivalist left, his "mushroom converts" disappeared with him. Relevant here are the Wesleyan membership returns for each of the seven major centers that Caughey visited. Table 7 allows a comparison of the members in society during the year before Caughey's arrival with the returns for the fifth year after his departure. In only two cities—Birmingham and Leeds—was there an overall decline between the two dates, but in none of the centers was the total for the revival year itself maintained. Though there was slippage after Caughey's revival, many of his converts stuck.[49]

As a further part of his defense, Caughey took refuge in the primitivist argument that he was simply returning to an aggressive, revivalistic Methodism strong in the past but now found only in certain parts of the country. Ministers like Thomas Harris, Francis West, and James Everett agreed with him, convinced as they were that organs, theological institutions, and growing "formalism" would suffocate genuine Wesleyanism unless they were balanced by men like Caughey, struggling to see "old Methodism revived with new energy." Yet there was more to Caughey than is suggested by this atavistic interpretation. His critics, after all, believed that "he had struck out a new line of things," and regarded him as "a perfectly new phenomenon in Methodism."[50] Why did they believe that he had introduced an unhealthy trend in revivals?

Methodists were at this time engaged in a debate over means and human instrumentality that corresponded closely to the instrumentalist debate in contemporary Calvinism. Although their views on human ability were in theory more generous than the Calvinists', Methodist theology did not give man carte blanche over means. During the 1830s protracted meetings and penitent benches caught the imaginations of experimenters, and the incidence of "special services" spiralled upward in the early and mid-1840s. Caughey arrived in Britain when less adventurous Methodists were afraid that these new techniques savored of "getting up" a revival and undervalued the regular means. His holding of daily services for months on end condemned him on both counts. Though the revival prayer meetings of the late eighteenth and early nineteenth centuries had often gone on until the early hours of the morning for several days in succession, they had been extended and repeated on an ad hoc basis, often at the request of congregations that felt spiritually starved: sometimes in Bramwell's meetings "the enthusiasm excited was so great that . . . 'the people *would not go home'*"; Dow's arrangements were notoriously impromptu. Caughey's meetings, in contrast, were premeditated, part of a preconceived campaign to stir a religious awakening, more or less without regard to the initial receptiveness of the audience. Other elements of calculation and contrivance in Caughey's meetings—penitent benches, particularizing in sermons, "death warrants," the repeated use of the same text—came under similar attack, though the additional charges that he planted "decoy penitents" at the altar to encourage the shy penitents to come forward and that he deliberately regulated the interior lighting for dramatic effect were probably unfounded. Under attack, Caughey was unflinching. But despite his emphasis on prayer, it was difficult for him to escape the charge of revivalistic engineering; when, infrequently, he tried to adopt a noninstrumentalist explanation of revival as simply God-given (as when he claimed that "a revival is a miracle"), the argument rang hollow.[51]

In Caughey, then, there was a blend of the old and the new, though not in equal proportions. His equability in the face of noise and excitement, his appeal to "Old Methodists" and certain similarities between his style and message and that of, say, William Bramwell, had been less significant than his innovations. To achieve success at a time when "native springs of spontaneous revival were drying up" he had refrained from using some of the traditional procedures—outdoor preaching, for instance, still a part of rural and semi-rural evangelism, played an almost nonexistent role in his work.[52] As his use of the term "revival campaign" suggested, he had set about giving revivalism a more premeditated, professsional character than the "spontaneous" revivals of an earlier generation.[53] His movements, determined not by Conference fiat but by his own estimate of his likely success, had been advertized in advance and had been supported by the sale of his books and portraits and by often liberal contributions from churches that had themselves profited financially from his visits.[54] His every act, his every idea had been determined by its implications for the conversion of souls. With James Caughey the day of the revival technician who was paid for his services had arrived.

For several years Caughey remained generally unhampered by his Methodist critics. Wesleyan Methodists were as worried as any other evangelical denomination in the 1840s about the challenge of Tractarianism, Roman Catholicism, and the seemingly impenetrable conditions of crowded cities, and even the most myopic had to concede the merits of Caughey's urban performance. Equally, it was difficult to challenge Caughey's personal integrity. Charges of vanity and hypocrisy carried little weight against a man so patently sincere and single-minded. Though the annual Wesleyan Conferences from 1843 to 1845 discussed Caughey's case vigorously, no formal decisions were taken.[55]

When, however, in the summer of 1846 Caughey entered his sixth year of itinerant work in Britain, Conference lost patience. Significantly his opponents turned for direction to Jabez Bunting, unchallenged leader of the "High Church" party in Methodism. On Bunting's suggestion the president of Conference, William Atherton, brought forward a resolution which proposed that the American bishops be "affectionately requested" to recall Caughey to the United States, on the grounds that he

has now been for several years in this country, and has visited many of our principal circuits, subject to no ecclesiastical supervision, responsibility or control, such as those to which all other Methodist ministers . . . are required to submit;—[and] that such an irregularity is dangerous to the good order, peace and unity of our Body. . . .

The point at issue was essentially one of connectional discipline and the authority of the pastoral office. The value and necessity of revivals (of the nonmechanical variety) was not really in question. "I am afraid lest any impression should get abroad that we are against revivals of religion," announced Bunting. What worried him and those ministers like Atherton, Robert Newton, George Osborn, and John Scott, who joined him in seeking to control Caughey's movements, was the damage that irregular movements could inflict on good order and pastoral care. Lorenzo Dow had shown that these were not illusory worries; Bunting himself had bitter memories of the critical, insurrectionary spirit bred by the Bramwell and Sigston revivalists in Leeds. Was Caughey reawakening the irregularities of the past?[56]

The American, it appeared, had worked with responsibility to no one but himself. He had arrived without invitation; for five years he had worked without official recognition from the British Conference; his movements had excluded regular ministers from their pulpits and interfered with regular services; his enormous popularity had pressured superintendents into arrangements for which they had little appetite; his great successes had stimulated invidious comparisons and jealousies. Perhaps worst of all, he had provoked others into demanding similar freedom from superintendence. Men such as David Greenbury, a Sheffield local preacher and converted coal porter and pugilist, had broken with regular practice and had taken up appointments for months at a time in various circuits; they "frightened [Conference] into the belief that *irregular* preachers were springing up like mushrooms, and [that] if Mr. Caughey were not sent back, the Connexion would soon be overrun with them."[57]

Caughey certainly had by British standards been at fault in his treatment of Conference. His attitudes to Methodist authority and to pastoral care had been formed in America, where revival discipline was less rigorous, where there was more room for individual initiative, and where circuit itinerancy had long been central to Methodism. Moreover, in Britain he was not susceptible to many of the sanctions operating against Wesleyan ministers. Financially independent, he could not be threatened with the withdrawal of support from connectional funds; he was not responsible to district meetings; he had no hope of advancement in British Methodism. Yet his defenders in Conference could point to two constraints on his behavior. First, Caughey's "location" had not severed his connection with the American Methodists, and to rejoin the MEC itinerancy he would need to produce "proper testimonials of . . . good conduct." Secondly, he could only make headway with the support of the ministers in whose circuits he worked. Most of the time he operated at the invitation of a superintendent and eager ministers and laymen.[58]

This defense of Caughey did not impress Robert Newton, secretary of the 1846 Conference and, as chairman of the Manchester District, instrumental in bringing Caughey's case to Conference. Caughey had never worked in Manchester; an invitation had been issued and then rescinded. But through the encouragement of William Atherton, now stationed in Manchester and critical of Caughey after the Liverpool episode of 1842-43, and of some recalcitrant members of the Sheffield district whose attempts to censure Caughey at their own meeting had failed, a ringing indictment of the revivalist was inserted in the minutes of the Manchester District Meeting to be read at Conference. It was Caughey's misfortune that Atherton was Conference president and that on the day that Newton made his case against Caughey one of his most influential supporters, Joseph Beaumont, was absent. Beaumont had taken Caughey's part in Liverpool in 1842-43, and his friendship with Caughey was later strengthened when his daughter was converted under the American's ministry. Beaumont allegedly possessed "important documentary evidence" that might have deflected the attack on Caughey, but in Beaumont's absence, and "amidst much clamour, many objecting to the resolution" for the revivalist's recall, Caughey's opponents triumphed and the resolution passed, on Monday, 10 August.[59]

Up to this point (the carrying of the resolution) the decision of Conference was clear, but the next step aroused much confusion and bitterness. Two days later Conference turned to discuss the minutes of the Sheffield District, which referred critically to the activities of "unauthorised Preachers, preaching for hire" and moving from circuit to circuit. The objects of concern were David Greenbury and another local preacher, and not Caughey. Inevitably, however, the American's name cropped up in the debate, and it was moved from the floor that Caughey should no longer be employed in Wesleyan pulpits. Thereupon the president "declare[d] it to be the decision of Conference that no Superintendent is at liberty to employ the Rev. J. Caughey, Mr. Greenbury, or any other such person during the next year." The president regarded this to be "as binding as any law of the Connexion." But unlike the resolution of two days earlier, the decision was not entered into the minutes, and the way lay open for constitutional arguments, ambiguity, and rumor. Hard-liners spoke of a "second resolution," Caugheyites of the absence of any permissive or restrictive resolutions apropos of Caughey's movements beyond a request to his bishops that he be recalled.[60]

One of the difficulties in the way of applying the presidential decision was that not all the district chairmen, let alone ministers, were present at Conference. Caughey continued to receive applications for his services throughout September and October, while Atherton and Newton sought to inform and correct ignorant or recalcitrant superintendents. Caughey himself had to wait for over a month to be told officially of the decision, though his abrupt exclusion from the Wesleyan pulpit in Gateshead in early September would have made its terms clear enough to him. Angered by the decision, he refused at first to be bound by it and continued to accept invitations from various circuits, including Huddersfield and Nottingham. But as his temper cooled and as Conference pressure on superintendents took greater effect he found it easier to comply with the "earnest request" of his bishop to plan his return. Still he equivocated, as his publishing commitments, lack of appetite for a winter crossing, and, most important, pressure from the major branches of Reformed Methodism held him back for a ten-month spell of revivalism and temperance work in the midlands and the north in Primitive, New Connexion, and Wesleyan Methodist Association chapels.[61]

Caughey's exclusion sent partisans rushing for their pens and produced waves of protest around the connection. Various circuits and special meetings issued testimonials to the revivalist's capabilities and good character; in pamphlets and journals, Conference came under fire. Caughey did not lack ministerial support, but most of his public defenders were incensed local preachers, leaders and trustees, and other prominent laymen ready to take matters into their own hands if their pastors would not act for them. The tone of their attack ranged from the mild to the vitriolic, but the argument in essence was always the same: Conference's inflexible standing by connectional discipline in a decade when denominational growth was low, relative to overall population and the increases of past decades, demonstrated that Conference's position was "in effect, one of distinct opposition to revivals of religion and the salvation of souls." Church order was important, but was not an end in itself: "is there not reason to *fear* lest [Methodism] should become a mere compacted frame work of ecclesiastical guards and precautionary regulations . . . ?"[62] Thrown on the defensive, Conference sympathizers tried to cast doubt on Caughey's revival figures and stooped on occasion to impugning the American's integrity on the slavery issue.[63]

Despite the acrimony, there was no explosion. Most ministers bowed to the Conference decision, while leading Caugheyite laymen, such as John Unwin of Sheffield and J. B. Melson of Birmingham, urged loyalty to Wesleyanism. Melson assured Caughey at a farewell meeting in July 1847: "Your name shall never be made the symbol of disaffection, or the watchword of a party." Caughey was genuinely relieved: "*Peace*—no *splits*—no *divisions* in Wesleyan Methodism, is . . . my sincere motto." He left peacefully, urging his sympathizers to be "quiet, kind, and loving." That there was no division in Wesleyanism in 1846-47 was very largely a tribute to his refusal to stir things up.[64]

In the short term Conference had succeeded in avoiding a split. Yet Methodism was on the eve of the most bitter and devastating internal conflict of her history. The schism of 1849-50 and the consequent expulsions and secessions from Wesleyanism had a variety of causes, each the outgrowth of divergent views on the true locus of authority and control and reinforced by social and educational lines of division. Buntingite orthodoxy maintained an emphasis on church order and on the minister's authority and unique responsibility for his church; reformers in contrast had a vision of religious democracy and of greater lay and local participation in spiritual matters. The debate over Caughey and his revivalism was integral to this brewing

James Caughey. Courtesy of Drew University Library.

conflict. His support derived from the "low church" side of the denomination, from those who wanted to increase the power of lay and local opinion and eliminate what they regarded as a popish authoritarianism.[65]

Caughey's expulsion was not the best way of soothing that raw nerve of Wesleyan Methodism that his visit had helped to expose. It contributed to the rapid waning of confidence in the representativeness of Conference and in its evangelistic commitment, while Conference itself retained a suspicion of the reformers and a fear that some sought nothing less than the destruction of the connection. Certainly the sides taken by Methodists over the Caughey affair corresponded closely, though not identically, to those drawn up in the later schism. The anti-Caughey forces generally took the Conference position. Bunting's position needs no elaboration: he was the prime target for the reformers; Atherton, though not a Bunting man, was "scarcely a reformer"; George Osborn was the minister who pressed the loyalty oath in the *Fly Sheets* debate of 1849; and the expulsions of that year had the "entire concurrence" of Robert Newton, lifelong friend of Bunting. Caughey's ministerial supporters numbered men such as Joseph Beaumont, a leader of the "moderate conservatives" against Bunting's power. They were unhappy about the schism and expulsions but remained loyal to Wesleyan Methodism. Also included was James Everett, who had stirred up opposition in York to Conference's policy towards the revivalist and who was probably the author of the *Fly Sheets*. Everett was expelled from Wesleyan Methodism along with Samuel Dunn, another Caugheyite, with whom he was appropriately and immediately to establish an organ of revivalistic Methodism, *The Wesley Banner and Revival Record*. Significantly, the scene of Caughey's most successful revival, Sheffield, spawned one of the strongest bands of Reform Methodists in the whole country, led by Abraham and John Sharman, John Unwin, and other prominent lay supporters of Caughey.[66]

The conflict caused by Caughey and by his revivalism, then, was both prophetic of and contributory to the great upheaval in Wesleyanism. It challenged the belief of contemporaries like Richard Reece and James Dixon that revivals were the great healing medicine for churches racked by disunity and party division.[67] Revivals depended upon and fostered a critical individualism. They emphasized the capabilities of the individual and his need to act. Once fostered, individualism in spiritual affairs might run rampant and challenge connectional authority. Revivals needed careful guidance, even at the best of times. Yet how likely was this when the master of ceremonies was not a careful, painstaking pastor, but an apparently cavalier American revival tactician who had no long-term interest in preserving church order? Far from bringing peace and cohesion to the unsettled ranks of Wesleyan Methodism, James Caughey brought aggravation, divisiveness, and an unsettling passion for souls.

five

"A Great National Mercy": Charles Finney's Itinerancy in Britain, 1849-51

Most American ministers made some response to the call to "save the West" in the first half of the nineteenth century. Charles Finney was no exception. In 1835, after three years of intermittent revivalism in New York City, he left the metropolitan east for the Western Reserve of Ohio to become professor of theology in Oberlin Collegiate Institute. Oberlin had been founded in 1833 as a "manual labor school" by John Jay Shipherd, a new-measure minister known to Finney from his "Burned-over District" days. Shipherd's plans for evangelizing the midwest had quickly run into financial troubles, and only the disruption of Cincinnati's Lane Theological Seminary had ensured Oberlin's continued existence. At Lane, most of the revival-minded student body walked out after the trustees, supported by the president, Lyman Beecher, had prohibited all discussion of the slavery issue. Shipherd offered collegiate shelter to the homeless students, secured funds from the ubiquitous Tappan brothers, and attracted Asa Mahan, a sympathetic Lane trustee, to the presidency. Together these men approached Finney to become head of the seminary. Finney accepted, not because he professed a wholehearted abolitionism, but because at Oberlin he saw the opportunity to breed "a new race of ministers" crucial for the continued existence of driving revivalism. In accepting he bade farewell to his days as a full-time evangelist, but during the 1840s and 1850s he still found time to conduct winter revival services in Boston, Rochester, Hartford, Providence, and, nostalgically, in western New York. In autumn 1849 Finney, now fifty-seven, prepared to travel once more. This time his destination lay not in the eastern states, but across the Atlantic.[1]

On 6 November 1849, Finney and his newly acquired second wife, fifty-year-old Elizabeth Atkinson of Rochester, disembarked at Southampton. It was an important moment. If it was not the first time that an American evangelist had set foot in Britain primarily to conduct revival services (Dow and Caughey could both lay claim to that), it was the first occasion when a revivalist with an established reputation in both countries had arrived to do more than adorn conventions or repair damaged health. During the decade between Edward Norris Kirk's departure and Finney's arrival, a number of American ministers associated with revivalism graced British Calvinist circles. But none came primarily to preach. Kirk himself made a return visit in the summer of 1846 to attend the World's Temperance Convention and the Evangelical Alliance. He was accompanied by a distinguished cluster of fellow Americans, one that included Lyman Beecher, now an old man but still retaining "some of the old fire"; Emerson Andrews, the robust, un-sophisticated Baptist evangelist, much influenced in his youth by Asahel Nettleton and Lorenzo Dow, and a number of others, such as Robert Baird and Samuel H. Cox. Possibly the most distinguished of all visiting evangelicals was Francis Wayland, president of Brown University and a man of wider interests and greater intellectual power than most of his coreligionists. As a representative of the polished side of American evangelical Protestantism, he served his countrymen well. But he rarely stood in a British pulpit, and he certainly did not conduct revival meetings.[2]

In pondering his chances of success in Britain, Finney knew that in some quarters Finneyism was a synonym for revivalistic extravagance and that his perfectionist doctrines were viewed with suspicion. But he was also aware that his *Lectures on Revivals* had won him many sympathizers and that his association with Oberlin guaranteed him a reasonably broad base of opera-tion, for the college had established its reputation on both sides of the Atlantic as a crucible of reform activity, particularly of abolitionism. In this, Oberlin owed much to John Keep, a committed new-measure man, president of Oberlin's board of trustees, and the champion of the blacks in the early crisis at the college over Negro admission. In 1839 Keep embarked with one of his colleagues, William Dawes, on a mission to "Oberlinize England" and to raise funds. The college was in desperate need of money, for after the finan-cial panic of 1837 the Tappans's benefactions had dried up. The uncom-promising position of the two Oberlin men on slavery and their presence at the World's Anti-Slavery Convention in London in June 1840 won them a host of friends, especially amongst Quakers, and ensured that they would not return empty-handed.[3] Their work for the good reputation of Oberlin was later reinforced by Lewis Tappan, in England after a thirty-two-year absence to attend the 1843 Anti-Slavery Convention.[4]

These visitors and the growing circulation of the *Oberlin Evangelist* in Britain helped suggest that Finney was, by association, a man "of temperance, peace and abolition." In fact, though Finney did want abolition, his position on the Negro was equivocal. Tappan himself had earlier considered Finney "unsound on the slavery question," since he refused to regard black men as the social equals of whites and since he put the conversion of the individual before *all* reform movements. Some years later a cynical compatriot of

Finney remarked that "the antislavery cause has nothing to hope, but much to fear from his influence in England." But English Nonconformists did not see it this way, and Finney's identification with Oberlin ensured that he was free from the attacks of skeptical Dissenters who generally "associated with the word *revival* all that [was] . . . detestable in American slavery."[5]

Houghton, Birmingham, and Worcester

Early in 1849 Charles Hill Roe of Birmingham, at one time a traveling evangelist but now a settled Baptist pastor, and Potto Brown, a Huntingdon-shire layman, wrote to Finney asking him to visit Britain to hold special services and offering him financial support. His coming, Brown told him, would be "a great national mercy." Finney repaid the compliment by travel-ing first to Houghton, the small village where Brown had helped to mold a lively evangelicalism out of unpromising materials against the opposition of "Tory magnates and Establishment bigots." Brown was a strong-minded man of fifty, a flour miller of wealth and influence in St. Ives and Hunt-ingdon who was known for his building of schools and support for the Anti-State Church Association and temperance cause, for his practical streak in business and religion, and for his broad-based interdenominational evan-gelicalism. Brought up a Friend, he later became a Congregationalist (though he never lost the Quaker emphasis on the search after individual truth), encouraged the visits of evangelists like Thomas Pulsford, built a number of Union chapels in Huntingdonshire villages, and manned the first of these, in Houghton itself, with James Harcourt, a Baptist minister "in full sympathy with the spirit of religious revival." Indeed it was Harcourt who, after read-ing Finney's *Lectures on Revivals*, urged on Brown the need to bring the American to Britain.[6]

Brown had sensibly encouraged a winter campaign to allow the participa-tion of agricultural laborers who at other times of the year could have attended evening services only at the risk of dismissal from employment. Soon the calm rhythm of rural life gave way to considerable excitement: Union Chapel proved too small, and Brown was driven to set up a large tent that would hold at least a thousand. Some walked thirty miles to attend. Though Finney himself held daily services for only three weeks he stayed long enough to ensure that the revival continued well into the New Year and spread into neighboring villages. There was coolness from some neighboring "timid" nonconformist ministers in Huntingdon and St. Ives and obstruction from the Established Church, which until recently had held a monopoly on religious services in the village: a Houghton gardener, for instance, employed by an influential Anglican family, was reportedly in danger of losing his job should he not repudiate the conversion to which he had been brought by Finney's preaching. But there was sufficient evangelical cohesion in the small village to ensure the success of the revival. Fifty new members were added to Union Chapel in the five months after Finney's departure (some led shivering to be baptized in the Ouse) and by 1851 the numbers in church membership stood at 285, an eightfold growth since the church was first constituted seven years earlier. A later generation had some doubts as to the long-term value of Finney's work, but for Brown and Harcourt the benefits were self-evident.[7]

Next Finney turned toward the midlands to fulfill his promise to help Brown's ally, Charles Roe. In 1842 this restless, energetic man had taken up a settled pastorate in the Heneage Street Baptist Chapel, Birmingham, after seven arduous years as the itinerating secretary of the Baptist Home Missionary Society (BHMS). But he never lost his enthusiasm for itinerant evangelism: "Our settled ministers are much too stationary in the country," he complained to Finney. "We go out collecting for our societies and Sunday Schools and chapel Anniversaries but seldom to save souls. Seldom to purely evangelise." Finney he saw as the man to strengthen the hands of those "struggling for the Revival of the Churches and the establishment of the Revival System." Eventually, in 1851, Roe was to resign his pastorate and emigrate to the United States, carrying with him the hope that his ten children might forge more successful lives there and a heart made heavy by Britain's "anti-revival position."[8]

Roe claimed his congregation had been waiting for seven years for the American's arrival. But Finney could not be certain of consolidated, city-wide support until he had won over John Angell James, the brightest star in the Birmingham evangelical firmament. Of simple habits, and generous in disposition and girth, James was now in his forty-fifth year as pastor at Carr's Lane, where he had seen his own congregation grow to some two thousand persons. At the same time he had done much to establish evangelical colonies in the city and its environs and to promote ministerial education. He was a figure of great influence, not least because of the enormous popularity of his short work, *The Anxious Inquirer after Salvation Directed and Encouraged*, a sort of instruction manual for those "awakened from sin" but as yet a step short of salvation. As with so much of James's work, this book demonstrated a Finneyite practicality, growing as it did out of his own experiences in inquiry meetings and his knowledge of penitents' psychology.[9]

James's endorsement of Finney would be of critical importance to the success of the American's mission. Temperamentally, of course, he was too much of an evangelical to resist a quickening of the pulse when Finney arrived, and Roe was able to tell Finney that James was offering the American his pulpit. The promise was kept, though not without misgivings. James had earlier burned his fingers in the cause of new measures, and like so many of his colleagues he remained unconvinced that evangelists as a breed should be cultivated, especially after James Caughey's operations in Birmingham in 1846. These doubts were rekindled as the unorthodoxies of Finney's revival theology surfaced once more. Through the pages of the *Biblical Repertory and Princeton Review* and its critical notice of Finney's *Lectures on Systematic Theology* (James was a regular reader of the American evangelical press) and from London correspondents James received indictments of Finney's views that made him question the wisdom of his friendly overtures. At a meeting with Birmingham Independent ministers late in December and in frequent correspondence during January and February, Finney and James (whom the American regarded as "a good and a great man") respectfully and frankly exchanged views.[10]

Finney's *Systematic Theology*, based on his lectures to Oberlin students and first published in 1846-47, represented the maturation of his theological thinking after twenty years of evangelism and was founded on the premise that man is a free moral agent with a moral obligation to repent. The *Biblical Repertory*, an Old-School organ, had condemned the publication, not on the grounds of faulty logic—"If you grant his principles, you have already granted his conclusions"—but because its premise was unscriptural: it did not follow that because man has the obligation to repent, God must therefore have given him the ability to do so.[11] James did not swallow whole the Old-School criticism of Finney, but he did feel that the revivalist had not sufficiently proved his orthodoxy. Did not his views lead inexorably to the denial of God's role in conversion, of the depravity of man's soul, and of the doctrine of election? Fortunately for Finney, however, James conceded that many of the differences between them were more apparent than real, the result of the American's use of deliberately provocative language to strengthen commonplace orthodoxies, and he kept his pulpit open, not least because James's good friend George Redford argued in Finney's favor. "After all," James was to write to William Sprague, "there is so much deadness prevailing that one would welcome any instrumentality that is likely to infuse a little more life, providing it be not the life of a lunatic or a maniac"—and Finney was neither.[12]

After preaching at Carr's Lane on five or six occasions Finney worked in several of the Independent and Baptist churches in and around Birmingham. His major efforts were concentrated at Heneage Street and the large but pastorless Ebenezer Chapel in Steelhouse Lane. Until his departure in mid-March, with his health in danger of breaking down and with the revival "in its most interesting and powerful form," Finney played almost daily to packed houses. He and Roe between them secured the addition of seventy-five members to Heneage Street in the twelve months preceding June 1850, a figure well above the church's average annual increase; indeed, new members acknowledging their debt to Finney were still being received months after his departure. Amongst Birmingham evangelicals generally, however,

Finney's three-month stay was little more than an absorbing interlude, regarded with great interest but attracting little organized support. "The ministers," Finney later complained, "were not then prepared to commit themselves heartily to the use of the necessary means, to spread the revival universally over the city."[13]

A similar record of moderate but not spectacular success was achieved at Worcester, a cathedral city of thirty thousand inhabitants and "a quiet retreat for persons living upon their money," where Finney worked until early May. He had intended the visit as no more than an opportunity for recuperation and a friendly call on an American acquaintance converted by Finney years before. This was before he met one of American evangelicalism's greatest admirers and a leading Congregational theologian, George Redford. Redford had written an introduction to Sprague's *Lectures on Revivals of Religion* and had been an early advocate of protracted meetings. One of his works, *The Great Change*, was directed at unawakened but regular churchgoers, a group at an earlier stage of spiritual development than James's "anxious inquirers"; its essential message—"Try, sinner!"— clearly illustrated the immediatist, Finneyite quality of his evangelicalism. He read Finney's *Systematic Theology* with considerable admiration for the powerful logic of the ex-lawyer, got Finney to agree to bring out an English edition, and set about removing some of the "objectionable phraseology" himself. Redford's respect for Finney was fully reciprocated, and the relationship flourished until the latter returned to America.[14]

Helped by William Crowe, the pastor of Silver Street Baptist Chapel, a member of the BHMS and an emancipationist whose children had settled in America, Redford persuaded Finney to stay to conduct special services. The city's small chapels, hedged in by a dominating and a nonevangelical Church of England, were scarcely a promising arena. But they were soon filled with the curious from Worcester and the towns around. Even a few Anglicans, who "had never known what true religion was," allegedly participated. The numbers involved, impressive by Redford's standards, ensured additions to the churches for several months and warranted a further series of special services the following year.[15]

There was no careful orchestration behind Finney's movements. After six months in Britain it was still not clear how long he would remain. During the summer of 1850 Oberliners and British sympathizers vied for his services. Eventually he chose to stay to supervise the publication of his *Systematic Theology* and to accept some of the flood of invitations to conduct special services that issued from all parts of Britain. Most of the requests of course came from Congregationalists and Baptists; some originated among Methodists (in at least one instance he was regarded as a useful replacement for Caughey); and a few were from Quaker and Union chapels. Many of Finney's greatest admirers were laymen; they were also likely to be associated with social and moral reform. Benjamin Parsons, for example, a minister in the Countess of Huntingdon's Connexion who tried unsuccessfully to attract Finney to his chapel in Ebley, Gloucestershire, was closely identified with teetotalism, education, antislavery, Sabbatarianism, and opposition to the Corn Laws and church rates. However, Finney's eager correspondents, with some notable exceptions, were not amongst the most influential or prominent in the denomination. Thus when the revivalist eventually found himself pressed by one of those exceptions, John Campbell of the Moorfields Tabernacle, to occupy his London pulpit, Finney accepted, and embarked on the major phase of his work in Britain.[16]

London

Echoing the sentiments of his fellow evangelicals, Campbell complained to Finney in that year that "a general deadness prevails over the land."[17] In addition to the continuing problems of confronting Puseyism, Popery, and Infidelity and of reaching "the mass of people beneath us"—problems discussed earlier[18]—Nonconformists in the late 1840s and early 1850s began to recognize challenges from other quarters. First, there were the problems associated with returning economic prosperity. In some instances the prosperous middle classes were leaving city centers for the growing suburbs, weakening once-thriving congregations. It was claimed that in London the Dissenting chapels were "fast being reduced to the poorer classes of tradesmen and to the operative multitude" and that without remedial action "the whole mass of . . . influential families [would] be lost to Nonconformity, and, to a great extent, to true religion." Access to wealth and the opportunity for entry into municipal life afforded by the reform of municipal corporations in the 1830s seemed to encourage a pursuit of material goods and secular status. Aided by "mixed marriages," lower standards of church membership, irregular church attendance, and a "fondness for light reading," concerts, and other "worldly pursuits," this political and commercial spirit helped blur the dividing line between "the church" and "the world" so crucial to successful revivalism.[19]

Secondly, there was the challenge to faith itself, which derived not from geology or biological evolution—the full implication of these for scriptural integrity was not fully realized until later in the century—but from German higher criticism. Previously, rationalist attacks on evangelical Christianity, as from Deism in the eighteenth century, had come from without, and the blow had been parried. Now the questioning came from within, encouraged primarily by rationalist German divines, most notoriously David Friedrich Strauss of Tübingen, who did not jettison all biblical teaching but who sought by applying secular scholarship to revelation to give natural, rational explanations to the miraculous and to expose many happenings described in Scripture not as history but rather as myth. Jumpy conservative theologians were thrown on the defensive. An infallible Bible, read by every man for himself and central to his religious experience, was crucial to evangelicalism in general and revivalism in particular. But as Strauss's works appeared in translation during the 1840s, as English writers like Thomas Carlyle and Americans like Theodore Parker and Ralph Waldo Emerson openly abandoned the Bible as the sole lexicon of truth, no one could prevent the doubts from spreading, especially amongst younger ministers receptive to novel and exciting ideas.[20]

At the head of the dissenters' counterattack stood John Campbell. A large, energetic Scotsman, he had left Kilmarnock in 1839 to become pastor of Tottenham Court Chapel and Moorfields Tabernacle, a century earlier the scene of George Whitefield's labors. He carried with him a university education, moderate Calvinist beliefs, a record of soul-saving in Scottish Congregational churches, and an enthusiasm for aggressively evangelical schemes. Gradually his commitments as Congregationalism's most effective journalist and editor and his growing huskiness of voice led him to fill his pulpit with some of the leading ministers of the denomination for a few weeks at a time.[21] His invitation to Finney came as no surprise to those who recalled his earlier enthusiasm for Finney's *Lectures on Revivals*, the undisguised interest in American revivals in the pages of his *Christian Witness*, and the implicit approval he had given to James Caughey's fervent evangelism.[22]

Campbell believed that metropolitan success would spread news of Finney's arrival denomination-wide and open churches to him across the country. One of Campbell's Glasgow correspondents later told of "an astonishing change of feeling respecting [Finney] in the North" after Finney's acceptance in London. Campbell's support of Finney in the *British Banner* and the influential *Christian Witness* gave the American further status. Moreover, at the Congregational Union's annual meeting, Finney was welcomed by the chairman, John Morison, who devoted his opening speech to the subject of revivals, and by James, Redford, and James Sherman. Their introduction and Finney's own address to some five hundred ministers (who received him with "loud acclamation") helped offset the suspicion of heterodoxy surrounding him and did much to thwart those Americans who attempted through their letters and publications to discredit Finney in England.[23]

Any disadvantages of Finney's liaison with Campbell were to be found in the realms of personality. Both were men of strong wills, and while there was no apparent discord there was little of the warmth that marked Finney's relationship with Potto Brown. More important, Campbell's strength of purpose could easily spill over into belligerence. His critics found him "dogmatic," "master of no one subject, yet working vehemently in all," "narrow and sectarian and one-sided," "superficial," "vituperative," and "terribly thin-skinned." During Finney's stay he was in occasionally bitter dispute with ministerial colleagues critical of the way he used his journalistic power to link the Congregational Union with causes rejected by many of its membership. The blessings of Finney's association with such a prickly individual were at best mixed.[24]

At Moorfields and in London more generally Finney could expect a warm reception. A major supporter was Henry Allon, pastor at Union Chapel, Islington, son-in-law of Potto Brown's business partner, a useful link between Houghton and the London evangelical world, and probably one of the men responsible for getting the revivalist to London for a brief visit in the previous November; on that occasion Finney had preached at the Baptist chapel in Borough Road, where his Oberlin colleague, President Asa Mahan, had been conducting protracted meetings for several months.[25] Other sympathizers included influential laymen of George Williams's and George Hitchcock's stature.[26] Enthusiastic young men and women from the Tabernacle congregation, copying the practice of contemporary evangelists, had distributed several thousand handbills announcing Finney's arrival and reporting his earlier successes. But not all the auguries were good. Campbell wondered whether the summer was the best time for constant services, especially after endless May meetings had left the evangelical vanguard "jaded." Finney himself, aware that his major successes had been achieved in small towns, must have felt twinges of concern as he looked out on metropolitan, unchurched London, with its huge population, challenging extremes of wealth and poverty, and peripheral revivalism. Even his resting place at the Tabernacle, handicapped by its irregular and constantly changing ministry, could not boast particular prosperity.[27]

Finney met the challenge in the way that he knew best, preaching on five weekday evenings and twice on the Sabbath over an uninterrupted period of eighteen weeks. After Edward Norris Kirk, Andrew Reed, and James Sherman, protracted meetings of this kind were no longer regarded in London as revolutionary, but they were still noteworthy, especially when a man not far from his sixtieth year was seen to cope so successfully with the extraordinary physical and mental demands of the work. As Campbell, two years his junior, enviously told Finney, "The Lord seems to have created you for public speaking. You could speak . . . for ever."[28]

In the pulpit, Finney—a tall, thin, dominating figure—retained much of his earlier magnetism. His greying, thinning hair and lined features betrayed his age, but his intense, pale blue eyes, and clear (his critics said "nasal") voice penetrated into the farthest corners of the Tabernacle. His hearers were compelled to listen as he carefully and logically built up his case. At times he was utterly severe, sparing none of his audiences' more delicate feelings. Campbell even claimed that the American could "thunder and lighten" as successfully as the fiercest of Ranters, but his preaching rarely matched this description. Rather was he charged, when criticized, with "dryness" and "dullness"; for unlike Caughey his fascination as a preacher lay primarily in his highly analytical, argumentative approach. (Unlike Caughey, too, he rarely preached for less than one and a half hours, and often for over two.) As in his *Systematic Theology*, he would take a proposition and, analytical in the extreme, explore its implications to the verge of heterodoxy—and sometimes beyond. Once his hearers granted his basic proposition they were compelled to follow where he so logically led. As R. W. Dale, shortly to become John Angell James's assistant at Carr's Lane, later explained, "The iron chain of the elaborate theological argument which sometimes contributed the substance of [Finney's] discourse . . . was fastened to an electric battery: every link of the chain as you touched it gave you a moral shock; but even in Mr. Finney's sermons the supreme impression usually came at the end; the effect was cumulative."[29]

Finney's sermons were directed primarily at the unconverted, and their major burden—the sinner's duty immediately to repent—needs no recapitulation.[30] Otherwise his task was the encouragement of believers themselves. First they had an obligation to work for the conversion of London and the world through vigorous practical effort; laymen and women represented a huge army, underutilized, badly deployed, and lacking in motivation.[31] Secondly they had a responsibility to themselves—the pursuit of a higher standard of Christian living and obedience to Christ's command: "Be ye therefore perfect, even as your Father which is in Heaven is perfect" (Matt. 5:48). Finney had developed his perfectionist views during the 1830s, turning to the Methodist doctrine of entire sanctification and to the perfectionism of John Humphrey Noyes as he searched for a means of keeping revival converts from relapse, and in 1843 he himself achieved this sanctified state. But Oberlin perfectionism differed from Noyes's antinomian variety in maintaining that man, though sanctified, might still be tempted to sin, might do wrong, and would thereby lose his holiness: Finney rejected the sexual communism and the "ultraist" practices of the Oneida Community.[32]

Waves of criticism, even from Finney's old allies, engulfed Oberlin after its leaders had embraced perfectionism, and in Britain, too, dissenting voices were heard. Even if informed nonconformist observers were aware that the Oberlin doctrine had no "tendency to licentious practice" and might even have a "holy tendency," they could not concede its theological validity. Man might have a duty to seek perfect sanctification, but in practice he would never attain it. Though regeneration and sanctification were to be differentiated—the first *in a moment* communicating life to the heart of the unbeliever, the latter *gradually* strengthening that life after its communication—they were never to be wholly separated. Sanctification was simply "the advancing process of personal purity," "a loving of the Lord with all the soul, and heart, and strength, and mind," crucial to Christian development. It was never to be achieved before death in its sinless entirety.[33]

Orthodox evangelicals were appalled to discover that Oberlin perfectionism had some currency within Nonconformity during the 1840s, particularly in areas where Nonconformists were already semi-contaminated through their close proximity to a dominant Methodism. "The Wesleyans are mightily strong in [the West Riding of Yorkshire]," wrote William Lamb, Congregational minister at Wakefield, to Finney in March 1845, enthusiastically telling the American of how he and two neighboring ministers, J. Millson of Pontefract and Edward Weeks of Dewsbury, had "fully embraced the doctrine of Entire Sanctification. . . ."[34] The discomfort of the orthodox was not removed by Asa Mahan's visit to Britain nor by the publication of his *Scripture Doctrine of Christian Perfection*, for of all the Oberlin luminaries Mahan was the most fervently committed to the doctrine. Mahan was not without sympathizers—as reputable a pastor as James Sherman expressed an interest in his views—but he found many pulpits barred to him.[35]

Finney was less unbending and more tactful than Mahan. The preaching of perfectionism, in contrast to Caughey's campaign, was not an integral part of his services. "The London papers give flowing accounts of Finney's sermons and audiences," James Alexander reported in September 1850. "There is no allusion to his later doctrines of perfectionism." Moreover, Finney's position was much less extreme than his fiercest detractors and his own unnecessarily provocative language suggested. George Redford correctly believed that Finney stopped short of preaching absolute perfection, and he told him, "After all I can make out of your views of Perfection you differ very little from ordinary theologians." Finney may have believed that there was a rational hope of achieving sanctification, but he maintained that he "would creep on his knees all the way to the Atlantic ocean" to see a man who was wholly without sin.[36]

Finney supplemented the call to repentance and the demand for heightened piety with revival methods that exploited the impressions created under his preaching. He had not totally abandoned the anxious seat and was not afraid to use this in England. On at least one occasion in London, clusters of penitents thronged the front seats of the chapel, weeping in as emotional a scene as Mrs. Finney had ever witnessed in America. Yet Finney was not being hypocritical when he protested, with reference to Caughey's activities: "I fear and dread an unintelligent bluster and excitement." He had too much experience to attempt hurriedly to kindle a religious fire that might quickly burn itself out or to organize a revival carnival within a denomination whose members might be offended by too public a demonstration of commitment. Finney consequently used the inquiry meeting much more than the anxious seat. Here he would pray and talk with those moved by his sermons. Sometimes, as at Carr's Lane, the meetings were not held until a day or so after the main services to avoid late meetings and overexcitement. More usual was the meeting that immediately followed the main service. Inevitably tens, and sometimes hundreds, crowded the vestry or lecture room. Unlike Caughey, Finney did not make the call forward an automatic part of his daily labor. He had been at the Tabernacle for three or more weeks before he first asked for inquirers. Campbell, afraid of confusion, was cautious: "Mr. Finney, remember you are in England, and in London; and that you are not acquainted with our people. . . . You will not get people to attend here." Finney confidently ignored the advice, and about a thousand attended the meeting.[37]

The Finneys continued in this way at the Tabernacle until mid-September. A continental holiday, a recuperative return to Houghton, and a visit to Worcester to put the finishing touches to the English edition of his *Systematic Theology* allowed a ten-week respite, after which Finney returned early in December to work at Campbell's chapels for an additional four and a half months.[38] His second spell in London followed much the same pattern as the first. If he had slightly fewer preaching assignments, he was still the devoted soul-saver. He rarely paid social calls. He eschewed sightseeing. True to his insistence on the primacy of individual regeneration in schemes of social reconstruction, he showed no apparent interest in humanitarian or social reform. He generally avoided public discussion of the slavery issue. Only in the sphere of temperance, so integral anyway to the spiritual cleansing of the sinner, did he step outside his regular preaching commitments. The intemperate state of Britain seemed justification enough, for, as Finney told the Leeds Temperance Society, he "had seen more drinking since he came to England than he had seen [in America] in the last fifteen years."[39] Even so, when Finney reluctantly took his leave of London, and Britain, in April 1851 to take over the presidency of Oberlin, it was for his single-minded evangelism that he was celebrated.

Finney's London campaign had caused a considerable stir. He had continued to cast his spell until the very end, though one may doubt his claim that on the Sunday of the religious census (30 March 1851) "many thousands" failed to gain access to the Tabernacle.[40] Campbell, well aware of the discrepancy between momentary drama and long-term reality, spoke of the "furious tempest which kept raging in London for ten long months," but was convinced that Finney had "done great good." Certainly the curiosity inspired by the American's reputation—carefully exploited by a phalanx of eager laymen who distributed addresses, posted bills, and shouldered large placards round the streets—drew in large numbers of "the unsophisticated, the men not Gospel proof, and sermon hardened." Some two-thirds of his congregation were strangers to the Tabernacle, a remarkable proportion even for evangelically minded London pastors. Of course, these were not total strangers to the churches; very few would have been ignorant of the rudiments of the Gospel. Most were evangelicals from Dissenting and Methodist churches; a few were Roman Catholics; some were Anglicans.[41]

The latter group included a number of clergy, at least one of whom, Hugh Allen, rector of Saint Jude's, Whitechapel, was subsequently to promote a revival in his own parish through "intensive preaching" and a large number of scattered prayer meetings. Certainly, many low-church Anglicans felt an evangelical kinship with Nonconformists: they preached to convert, took comfort in extempore prayer, encouraged evangelical lay workers, distributed tracts, and nourished millennialist expectations. Their difference from Dissenters lay in their loyalty to the Establishment, their firm attachment to the Prayer Book, and their generally higher social standing. In general, on the subject of revivals they stood close to the more cautious Nonconformists, hungry for souls and critical of "a mere intellectual religion," but prevented by their social milieu and generally (if mildly) Calvinist assumptions from sanctioning too unrestrained a revivalism. Using only "orderly arrangements" (days of fasting, "fervent and united" prayer, Bible reading, direct preaching, and the cultivation of domestic religion), these clergy ensured that "unsound revivals . . . occur[red] less frequently in the Church of England than in most other denominations of Christians."[42]

Finney's experience with Anglicanism indicates that in London, as indeed elsewhere, he reached not only the curious and unsophisticated amongst the city's lower classes and "poorer sort of small tradesmen" of whom the regular Tabernacle congregation was chiefly composed, but also a group of more sophisticated and intelligent hearers.[43] Finney's strength lay in the fact that unlike so many of his cruder predecessors and imitators, he did not abuse his audiences' intelligence. Popular American evangelicalism of the early and mid-nineteenth century may have nurtured an anti-intellectualism and distrust for polished learning,[44] but Finney himself had considerable respect for man's intellectual faculties. He demanded that, instead of paying unthinking allegiance to old dogmas, men use their minds positively to erect logical constructs on scriptural propositions. He could appeal with considerable success to lawyers and other community leaders in America, and to men of "wealth and intelligence" in Britain. The dramatic effect of his preaching and writings on such thinking men as James Cranbrook, lapsed-evangelical-turned-Unitarian minister, and John Moore, a Methodist preacher with a penchant for metaphysics and philosophy, illustrated the effect of his sharp and powerful mind on unbeliever and believer alike.[45]

The reasonably well-read middle classes generally marked the upper limits of Finney's social appeal; he was rarely able to poach from the classes above, broadly the preserve of the Established Church. Similarly, those at the bottom of the social scale were underrepresented in Finney's London congregations. The greatest concentrations of lower-class hearers were in fact to be found within the Tabernacle Sunday school, for in Britain to an extent not true of the United States, the Sunday schools were often seen as suitable havens for the instruction of the children of the poor, where they could be kept from mischief, but as insufficiently "respectable" for the better-to-do. The highest proportion of "poor working men" in his congregations was probably at Heneage Street, Birmingham, and at Houghton, where agricultural laborers, a customary audience of Baptists in rural areas, contributed a colorful band of converts that included "Old John Clark the drunkard," "Barnes the blasphemer—Ellis the pugalist [sic]—and Bass the harlot."[46]

In practice, of course, social categorizing was subordinated to the classification of hearers according to their spiritual state. The "thoughtless," the "inquiring," and the "pious" were singled out and respectively awakened, brought to decision, and spring-cleaned. Finney was reluctant to employ the Methodist practice of revival bookkeeping. He seems to have dealt with thousands of "inquirers." Between 150 and 200 entered church membership at the Tabernacle, and many more joined other churches. In addition considerable numbers confessed to all sorts of crimes, and apparently paid thousands of pounds in restitution. John Campbell captured the buoyancy that Finney had stimulated when he addressed the autumn meeting of the Congregational Union in 1850. "All things considered," he said, "the state of religion in the metropolis is highly encouraging as compared with what it was more than twenty-two years ago. . . . As to the churches generally . . . never since I knew them were they more tranquil, more active, or better conditioned than at the present time," and his audience apparently agreed.[47]

Constraints on English Revivalism

Finney returned to Oberlin in the summer of 1851. No doubt he had mixed feelings about his English campaign. On the credit side, he had won large numbers of converts and the endorsement of a number of leading Dissenters, which impressed those Americans who had suspected that a man so closely associated in their own country with schism and irregularity would fail to find a toehold on the stern face of English orthodoxy. Less favorably, Finney would have recalled his "solitude" in Birmingham and Worcester and the reluctance of some of London's principal ministers to open their pulpits to him. Moreover, some, like George Hitchcock and George Williams, were unhappy about a possible second visit, and Potto Brown himself, Finney's staunchest friend, had to write despondently that "we have not had the cooperation of many ministers in promoting your return."[48]

At one level, Finney's failure to achieve spectacular success can be explained in terms of timing and itinerary. Arguably, he arrived a decade too late. Had he appeared in Britain in the later 1830s or early 1840s he probably would have been able to cash in on the revival upswing. Certainly this had been the period of peak interest in special revival services, Americana, and

Finney's own *Lectures on Revivals.* Moreover, in 1850 Finney was almost
sixty, though his remarkable energy suggests that he was not seriously handicapped by his age. In terms of tactical advantage, Finney's initial movements
were unrewarding. Houghton, Birmingham, and Worcester may have benefited from a degree of revival, but by April 1850, six months after his arrival,
it was still not generally known that Finney was in Britain. In a noncon-
nectional system he needed an introduction to the Congregational Union, a
London base, and a denominational publisher to ensure a more general
recognition. Even then Finney paid little attention to Wales and Scotland,
areas where he was assured of a warm reception. But perhaps he was un-
wittingly wise: had he visited Scotland his most uncritical patrons would
have been Evangelical Unionists[49]—a church ostracized by the other evangelical denominations in Scotland; had he visited Wales he might well have
been handicapped by the complications of language and an emotional style
of religion from which he had long since sought to dissociate himself. And,
in fairness to Finney, once he had decided to confine his activities to England, he was certainly ready to employ that evangelical nonconformist
circuit developed by Baptist and Congregational home missionaries and
evangelists, by Evangelical Unionists in England, and by determined laymen.

Finney's essential problem was not so much tactical error as the fact that
the revival current running through this evangelical circuit was much less
powerfully charged than that Caughey found pulsating through Methodism.
Congregationalists and Baptists, as has been shown already, were not
wholeheartedly committed as denominations to revivalism, and the skepticism with which the new measures were regarded was not markedly altered
by Finney's presence. Finney's methods in England had been considerably
less provocative than in his younger days, but he could still prove unsettling.
Laymen were encouraged to disparage their ministers; Redford noted that
some of Finney's support came from those "who [were] disaffected towards
their pastors and ha[d] given us trouble in time past"; straw converts later
became backsliders: two of Hitchcock's relations "turned back into the
world," their conversions the result of "mere excitement for the moment,"
achieved, according to George Williams, "not [by] the power of God but
[by Finney's] powers of reasoning or the influence of a mighty mind over
others"; and the pastoral office was generally overshadowed. By all means
seek a revival through the traditional means, wrote Daniel Griffiths of
Cannock, but "itinerant evangelists, fast-days, protracted meetings, anxious
seats, &c., are not necessary." Nor was there universal rapture over Finney's
message. Some of the Tabernacle congregation stood aloof; Campbell himself made public his criticisms; and when eventually in 1851 Finney's *Systematic Theology* was published, the *Evangelical Magazine* branded it "a
dangerous book," "essentially destructive of all *true theology.*"[50]

Finney by reflex action labelled London a city "cursed with hyper-calvin-
istic preaching." The description was inaccurate, bred of Finney's exaggerated

sense of his own centrality in the breakup of American Calvinism and of his unwarranted reading of his American role into an English context, where High Calvinism had long been a minority evangelical taste. Yet, there was point to Finney's criticism. Implicit in it were three charges frequently levelled against nonconformist preaching by evangelical visitors, like John Keep, who believed that no "English Preacher . . . would stand head & shoulders above our American Preachers."[51] First, few Nonconformists could claim, as could Finney, that the majority of their sermons were addressed to the unconverted. Austin Dickinson reported that "ministers [in England] do not preach to sinners, and they scarcely know what conviction of sin means," and his view was later confirmed by Reverend Robert Young of Albany Chapel, London, who concluded: "It is an unusual thing to preach . . . wholly and expressly to the unconverted as a class."[52] Secondly, even when sinners were the subject of concern, their obligations and ability to repent immediately were rarely pressed with Finney-like vigor. There was a powerful corps within Nonconformity suspicious of the instantaneous conversions so achieved. "In Britain," reported Calvin Colton, "they estimate the evidence of a genuine conversion somewhat according to the time it has occupied." Evangelical stalwarts like Andrew Reed and John Angell James may have had their doubts, but in 1853 the president of the Congregational Union found it perfectly acceptable that sudden and striking conversions were being replaced by more gradual, gentle conversions, especially in the case of Sunday scholars and children of religious parents.[53] Thirdly, Finney's simple, near-extempore, colloquial pulpit style contrasted starkly with the sermons of fashionable midcentury Nonconformity. The reading of sermons which sought to satisfy good taste and the intellect through "excessive verbiage" and "a more smooth, soft, dulcet strain of address" but which failed to stir the conscience worried the more fervent of native and visiting evangelicals. Set together, these three characteristics shed much light on Andrew Reed's conclusion after his return from the United States that "they make the better evangelists; and we the better pastors."[54]

This approach to preaching and the attitudes that underlay it were major obstacles to the acceptance of a direct revivalism. Those attitudes were determined in part by the social composition of Nonconformity. The educated, middle-class leavening of Congregationalism in particular cushioned that denomination against revivalistic extravagance, protecting it from the one-dimensional theology of crude revivalism. Religious sociologists see certain social groups as particularly susceptible to a fiery, immediatist, ecstatic revivalism—groups such as the American frontier folk, and the workingmen and -women of industrial England in the eighteenth and early nineteenth centuries, which these sociologists would describe as socially uprooted, culturally unstable, and suffering from "anomie" and "relative deprivation." English Nonconformists in contrast could point to the support of middle-class respectability (together with solid artisans and poorer folk from stable rural communities) for whom religious excitement and novelty were less important than regular attendance and the gradual cultivation of Christian virtues. The better-educated, in particular, could not immediately jettison layers of received nonconformist wisdom to make way for a novel revival theology and method. To have accepted Finney would not have meant the scrapping of all carefully acquired traditions, but it would have involved an affront to middle-class propriety. When some of the more impulsive laymen of Campbell's congregation set about placarding London to announce Finney's visit, the "delicacy and propriety" of "not a few worthy people" was much affronted, even though Campbell had promised Finney that in London Congregationalism he "would be free from all constraint from proud rich men, terrified for the disturbances of the proprieties of great and easy people."[55]

But there were other factors, too. After all, Congregationalists and Presbyterians in America also included a sizable proportion of the educated and socially better-to-do. Yet they were much more ready than their English counterparts to embrace religious revivalism. One differentiating factor was tradition and historical circumstance. Initially the American colonies, New England in particular, had been settled by men committed to the concept of regeneration and a distinct demarcation between the church of "visible saints" and the world at large. The gathered churches that they formed, and which in Britain in the eighteenth century represented a minority way of religious life, were in New England at that time a powerful influence in the life of the small townships. Acceptance of nonmembers into the church was achieved in some instances through the Half-Way Covenant (which allowed children of church members to become members themselves with restricted rights before they actually gave evidence of being "savingly converted") and in others through local church revivals. Whereas English Nonconformists generally ignored such means, Calvinists in New England became closely identified with these "outpourings of the Spirit of God." Congregationalists, Presbyterians, and Calvinistic Baptists stood at the center of the eighteenth-century Great Awakening, but in England the Evangelical Revival of the same century had drawn much of its strength from Arminian Methodism and had secured only secondary support from the older Calvinist denominations. Though the excesses of that Awakening led to considerable heart-searching in American Calvinist ranks, the concept of periodic regeneratory revivals was much too deeply engrained in their thinking to be excised. At Northampton, Massachusetts, where under Jonathan Edwards some of the Great Awakening's greatest excitements were witnessed, revivals continued to punctuate the life of the township, massively Calvinist in disposition, at periods of between three and ten years, until at least the 1830s. Having no firsthand experience with this revival pendulum, mid-nineteenth-century English Nonconformists lacked the essential psychological equipment of their American counterparts.[56] "If I were asked why revivals are so frequent in America, and so rare in Europe," wrote Yale professor Chauncey A. Goodrich, "my first answer would be, that Christians on one side of the Atlantic expect them, and on the other side they do not expect them."[57]

As influential as the constraints on revivalism within the nonconformist churches were a number of external constraints determined by the general structure of religious and secular society. At least one historian, influenced by Frederick Jackson Turner, has used the interpretive key of the American frontier to explain the prevalence of revivalism in nineteenth-century America and its lesser significance across the Atlantic.[58] The religion of the late eighteenth- and early nineteenth-century frontier certainly had possessed a novel character. The raw, unsettled state of that society, the uneducated, uncultivated character of the people, and the necessity for ministers to use persuasive means of recruitment determined that revivals would be marked by excitement, a lack of theological subtlety, an emphasis on itinerancy and dramatic conversion above pastoral care, and on institutions like the camp meeting that catered for the social needs of a culturally starved population. Revivalism took on a new look. In Britain, however, where there was no frontier to give constant stimulation to revivalism, then—so the argument runs—revivals remained on the periphery of religious life.

That the edge of American revivalism was sharpened during the Second Great Awakening by the peculiar conditions of the frontier is not in dispute. Yet Britain also had her frontier areas—those areas harboring unsophisticated and unlearned populations unsettled by the dislocations of the Industrial Revolution—where an excited and emotional revivalism flourished into the nineteenth century. Moreover, in America in the later stages of the Second Great Awakening and during the middle years of the century, revivalism's center of gravity shifted eastward and toward the cities. This suggests that it is not helpful to attribute transatlantic differences to the frontier. Just as fruitful an area for investigation is the sphere of tradition and the role played by religious institutions. America was traditionally a country of revivals: the ministry's role was regarded as primarily evangelical; when America was confronted with the challenge of a newer kind of revivalism in the early nineteenth century, she did not have institutions of sufficient authority to put it down. Old-School Presbyterians protested; Congregationalists checked the entry of Methodism into New England; but the structure of ecclesiastical authority in America was too loose and its power too limited (especially after disestablishment) for the new men to be held back for long.[59] But in Britain, where revivals had little traditional importance in church life, limited mainly to Methodism, they faced entrenched ecclesiastical opposition and inherited prejudices. Francis Wayland wrote during his visit to

Britain in 1840, "I am struck with the great difference between an old and a new country. Here everything is fenced around by precedents; you cannot move without infringing on vested rights. If you attempt any reform, you are called upon to consider how it will affect the landed interest, or the aristocracy, or the church."[60] He was not referring specifically to revivalism, but his diagnosis was as applicable to that as to other areas of British life.

As Finney's experience made clear, the most powerful and conspicuous of these institutional checks on revivalism was the Established Church, regarded by most American and British evangelicals as "an incubus resting on the nation to a great extent, so far as revivals and piety are concerned." Calvin Colton was appalled at the way in which Anglican wealth, social status, a system of patronage, and the guarantee of state support dissipated the Church's drive to save souls. There was none of the evangelical aggression and hard sell typical of American voluntarism. Nor, it seemed, was the Church's doctrinal position conducive to the spread of revivals. The doctrine of conversion (involving the mature individual's conscious passing from a state of sin to a state of grace), essential for religious revivalism, had no universal currency in the Church of England. Infants were regarded as being regenerated by baptism; clergy were often held to possess the power to forgive sins; the burial service implied that all who died passed to heaven. Membership was open not to a select band who had earned it through their justification by faith, but—because of the territorial, national, and pastoral conception of the Church—was available to all men as of right: there was none of that sectarian exclusiveness and sense of separation from the con-taminating world so characteristic of the most urgently revivalist churches. All was summed up in her commitment to dry and repetitive liturgical forms that crushed the urge toward a more freewheeling and emotional style of worship. True, the Church did possess an evangelical wing wedded to the concept of conversion, but it was neither strong nor enthusiastic enough to shift the Established Church from its broadly anti-revival stance.[61]

Had the Anglican Church been operating on an equal footing alongside other denominations, then her position on revivals would have been no more significant than most. But she was the national church, the church of the governing classes, the nobility and gentry, who both contributed to and were infected by the Church's distaste for revival excitement. Evangelicals had long been numbered in their ranks, of course (the Clapham sect was scarcely socially obscure), and a concern for the spiritual condition of the poor—sometimes for secular ends that were demonstrably conservative—had marked much of their thinking. Sometimes, as with Sir Culling Eardley's sanctioning of tent services, and the Earl of Shaftesbury's later support for Dwight L. Moody's revivalism, men of considerable social rank espoused novel and aggressive evangelical means.[62] But in general amongst these classes revivalism into the 1840s and beyond had meant popular ignorance,

Methodistic extravagance, theological sterility, outdoor preaching, social disruption, and political radicalism.

The hold of the Established Church had never been vise-like. Extensive parishes, changing population patterns, new industrial settlements, non-residence—all these weakened Anglicanism's power.[63] (It was no accident that so many of the most striking English revivals were in newer industrial areas and noncathedral cities, like Sheffield, where the power of the Church had been weakened by its failure to come to terms fully with the social upheavals of the Industrial Revolution.) Nevertheless, the united front of anti-evangelical clergy and the socially influential was often capable of spiking the evangelicals' guns. The annual reports of the Protestant Society for the Protection of Religious Liberty during the 1820s illustrated the ways in which local magistrates—often clergymen or Anglican laymen—used the Vagrant Act to impede outdoor Methodist itinerants. In the 1830s and 1840s, as Baptists and Congregationalists began to intensify their own home missionary efforts, their agents were subject to discrimination by high-church and Puseyite clergy and the local gentry, especially in small towns and rural areas where patterns of social and religious deference were well established. In Somerset in 1843 the BHMS agent found that children who attended the Baptist Sunday school were theatened with expulsion from the day school run by the local high-church clergy. Equally, the itinerating agent might well find that the local gentry's threats of expulsion from tenancies or the withholding of poor relief had taken the edge off his hearers' appetites.[64]

Even without such blatantly obstructive means, the very climate of hostility to revivalism created by men of "property and rank and influence" could prove fatal to evangelicals' plans in a society marked by deference and the percolation of ideas of correct behavior downward through the social scale.[65] In America—or so it appeared to both British and American evangelical commentators—republicanism had promoted the "intermingling of classes" and had bred in all men, including the poor, "a firmer spirit of independence, which is less disposed to yield to the authority of custom or fashion."[66] But in Britain the pressures from above to conform to a code that honored refinement and decorum and rejected unambiguous revivalism led to a compromising of evangelical principles. There was some truth in this analysis, though one may dispute the implicit assertion that Americans were free from pressures to conform to the code of behavior embraced by the dominant social group. So often, however, in America that dominant group was itself revival-minded. This was particularly true in small-town and rural America, whether in older or newer areas of the country. Such communities could be almost wholly consumed by revival, as dissenting individuals found themselves under pressure from the majority and were sucked into the whirlpool of conversions. In the Nashville region in 1821 "many of [those affected by the current revival were] among the most respectable in the country, men of education, men of talents"; instead of blocking the progress of Methodism in their areas, community leaders in many growing communities—men like Gideon Taber of Schenectady, a farmer and representative in the state legislature—encouraged involvement in revivals. For such people evangelical religion represented not a threat or a challenge, but—as James Dixon put it—"an instrument of national order, virtue and peace," and the "conservative power [in] American society."[67] Of course, near-total involvement in revivals could occur occasionally in small communities in Britain where the Established Church was weak—in Wales, or the small mining communities of Cornwall or Shropshire, for example. But often the power of the Church of England in smaller communities tended to the social ostracism of the revival-minded.

Perhaps the best guide to the relative social status of aggressive evangelicalism in America and Britain was the standing of the Methodist churches, in both countries the major channel of revivals. From being one of the smallest denominations at the time of the Revolution, by 1844 the MEC had become the largest Protestant body in America. Size conferred status. "The relative social importance and respectability of Methodists as a body, is greater in America than in England," wrote John Durbin in 1844. "There are no offices, either in our State or General Governments, except the Presidency that have not been filled by members of the Methodist Church. Her ministers are occasionally professors in state universities, and often chaplains to Congress and State legislatures. I have heard of no case in England of high office having been held by a Methodist." A decade later Frederick Jobson concluded that American Methodism "may be spoken of as having the prestige among the churches which the Church of England has in our own country."[68] Revivalism and the American laissez-faire church system had placed Methodism in a position of numerical dominance and that dominance in the interdenominational scramble for souls gave her influence over other churches. Methodism had played a major role in the first half of the nineteenth century, introducing a more engineered revivalism and helping erode Calvinist defenses. In England, too, Methodism helped stir up the Calvinist Dissenters, but English Methodism lacked the same social status and remained uncommitted to the full-blooded revivalism that marked the American branch. Its influence in winning significant social acceptance of revivalism was never as potent.

Many years later, when writing his *Memoirs*, Charles Finney reflected on his first mission to England and recalled a proposal made to him at Worcester by a number of wealthy laymen that they finance the building of a transportable tabernacle for Finney's use throughout the country. The plan appealed to Finney; it would allow him to reach "the masses, irrespective of denomination," and would free him from the restrictions imposed by an Independency that was itself "so hedged in and circumscribed by the . . .

Establishment." But the Worcester ministers, wary of "a scheme which might disturb the existing churches," cautioned against the American's preaching "in an independent way" around the country, and Finney deferred to their advice.[69] Two decades later Finney had come to regret his decision. He had never been a rigid denominationalist, but the interdenominational aspects of his revivalism had for most of his life been held in moderate check by the strength of the prevailing denominationalism. He was not to know that within a decade of 1850 interdenominational revival meetings conducted outside the regular chapels would flower in both Britain and America. Had Finney seized his opportunities in 1850 he might have secured the personal benefits from anticipating broad evangelical trends (as he had done in the 1820s and 1830s). In actuality, when Finney returned to participate in the revival movement of the later 1850s he was to be simply one prestigious but scarcely radical member of a large band of revivalists devoted to its promotion.

part three

"TRANSATLANTIC MARVELS"

SIX

Transatlantic Revival

In August 1858 an American minister likened the current revival in that country to Pentecost, the sixteenth-century Reformation, and the eighteenth-century Awakening in colonial America; a little later the octogenarian Heman Humphrey wrote of his expectation "that the next revival may spread over the whole land; that not a single church may be passed by."[1] Such euphoria and optimism typified the mood of American evangelicals following a year of mass conversions. As the American revival lost momentum in 1859 a remarkable wave of revivals spread over Ulster, Wales, much of Scotland, and parts of England. Hundreds of thousands were said to be converted; religious emotion ran high; even the secular press was forced to take note. Evangelicals in both countries, dazzled by these "transatlantic marvels"[2] believed they stood at the brink of a new religious age. From a twentieth-century perspective, however, this movement appears much less than an "awakening." It marked no fundamental upheaval in the broad patterns of religious and secular life. Rather its importance lay first in demonstrating the ability of revival churches on both sides of the Atlantic to capture popular attention on a national scale and secondly in providing the most striking example yet of the interrelated character of transatlantic revivalism. The tendency of British evangelicals to turn to the United States for inspiration and example meant that once the American revival had burst into flame a British conflagration was assured.

Annus mirabilis

The American revival of 1857-58 more than fulfilled the hopes of single-minded evangelicals that 1857 should be "marked in the history of the church as the great revival year."[3] Northern and southern churches had experienced two minor peaks of revival since the mid-1840s but no major revival movement (figure 6). Now, through denominational protracted meetings and interdenominational or union prayer meetings, often directed by the laity, all the Protestant churches throughout the country shared in the excitement. Even many of the more cautious Episcopalians, Unitarians, and Universalists showed sympathy for a wave of revivals that seemed remarkably well ordered and free of the "enthusiasm" and "human machinery" of earlier "ingatherings."[4] By the end of *annus mirabilis* each of the evangelical denominations could report huge accessions: of the largest bodies, the Presbyterians (Old and New Schools) added almost thirty thousand members by examination, the major Baptist churches baptized almost one hundred thousand new members, while the two main branches of Methodism reported a staggering net increase of nearly one hundred and eighty thousand, a growth of 16 percent over the previous year.[5]

Many of these converts were drawn from a group that had become the most likely and dependable source of new members: young persons belonging to the denominational Sunday schools, often children of church members. Evangelical churches had come increasingly to view Sunday schools as the "nurseries" where "our revivals begin." It seemed crucial that during America's "national adolescence" (one minister noted that in 1850 over half the white population was under twenty years old) evangelicals should use the Sunday schools "to Christianize America in the bud." By 1857 there were over eleven thousand such schools in the United States; from their ranks had come in recent years four out of every five Methodist converts and in parts of New England five out of every six new members of Congregational churches.[6] This general pattern persisted into the revival year of 1857-58, when all denominations shared the experience of the Old-School Presbyterian Church, in which "the great body of [converts are] from the ranks of the young, from the Sabbath school and the Bible class."[7]

David O. Mears of Massachusetts was just one fourteen-year-old who felt a powerful sense of "duty to take a decided stand upon the subject of religion." His decision, and those of many others, owed much to the influence of churchgoing parents who had presented their infants for baptism and had brought them up "in conformity to the word of God," impressing on them their ultimate responsibility to "be saved from their sins." During adolescence, a time of growing guilt over inadequate Christian commitment and developing fear of "the wrath to come," pressures from within the family and Sunday schools intensified until "many a glad parent was seen embracing his converted children [and] brothers and sisters were rejoicing over each other." This search for salvation grew not only out of a sense of religious duty, however; occasionally it represented a recognition of secular responsibility. Young persons had been taught to see their conversion as a patriotic step toward becoming good evangelical citizens who would help "get the start of error, infidelity, Socialism, anti-marriage, anti-property, anti-legal fanaticism, anti-Sabbath and anti-Christ"; one of the Sunday school's foremost tasks

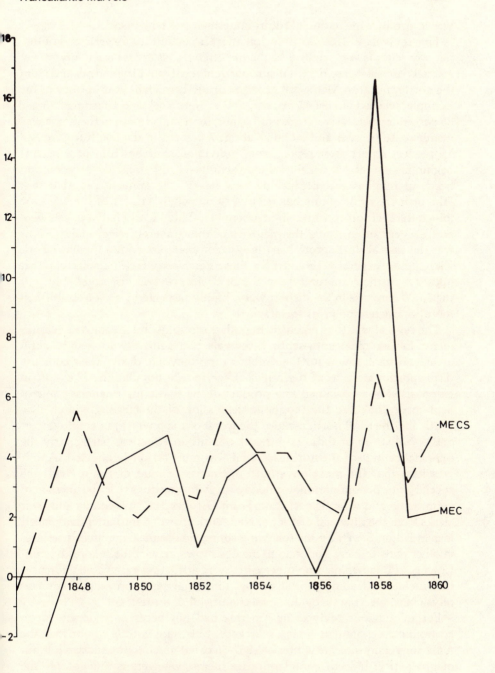

Figure 6. MEC and MECS Growth Rates, 1846-60.

SOURCES: *Minutes of the Annual Conferences of the Methodist Episcopal Church* (1846-60); Peterson, *Handbook of Southern Methodism.*

was to produce the nation's "future statesmen and patriots."[8]

The revival of 1857-58 drew on more than dutiful American youths. Sunday schools were central to the life of churches across the country, yet revival converts were drawn disproportionately from urban areas and from the northern states. Methodist growth during the revival year in Boston, for example, reached almost 22 percent, and in New York and Cincinnati 25 and 26 percent respectively. Yet overall denominational growth in the north was nearer to 16 percent and stood at about 7 percent in the south (figure 6).[9] Moreover, report after report from individual churches told of a revival beginning—as at Morrisville, Pennsylvania—"with married persons and heads of families"; at Bridgeton, New Jersey, the minister reported that "the proportion of adults has been very unusually large"; of the 177 who joined the Methodist church in Steubenville, Ohio, all but half a dozen were adults. Very often, too, "the majority of the converts [were] males." This was the case at Burlington, New Jersey, for example, and in the New York City region generally. Frequently these converts were "persons of great influence in the community": in the Bridgeton revival just noted many of the 2,500 converts in the district were "highly respected . . . for established moral character and great social worth."[10]

The revival was thus eccentric in both geography and much of its recruitment. Earlier nineteenth-century revivals had generally looked to rural areas and small towns for their momentum; they had drawn their converts disproportionately from the ranks of the female population. The shift in emphasis is best explained as a product of the shattering financial panic of September 1857 and the economic depression of the ensuing winter. The south and the rural north escaped the worst of the poverty, unemployment, and social strain of those months: it was urban America, particularly the financial centers of the northeast, that was most seriously affected. And it was here that the most novel and distinctive feature of the revival, the special interdenominational midday prayer meetings for businessmen, germinated and took firmest root. From October 1857 merchants and their clerks from the financial district of New York crowded into brief daily meetings in Fulton Street; by the following spring similar male-dominated services in other parts of New York and in the downtown areas of Baltimore, Boston, Chicago, Philadelphia, and other cities were attracting variegated audiences that included "leading capitalists, prominent lawyers and judges, eminent physicians, merchants, bankers, mechanics [and] tradesmen."[11]

Earlier religious revivals in America had not necessarily depended on economic recession for their occurrence, but there is little doubt that the mass conversions of the winter of 1857-58 owed much to the sudden jolt out of prosperity; indeed, contemporaries themselves were convinced of "the connection between the prostration of business and the revival of religion." But why, in the words of a Maine Calvinist minister, should "the depressed state of business [have] proved a most favourable circumstance"? For some, the answer was that business stagnation gave men more "time to reflect," or, as a more jaundiced observer put it, "religious demonstrations are only made when business is so flat that nobody can find anything to do."[12] But this hardly goes to the heart of the matter. More fundamentally, we need to ask: what was the psychological motivation that drew Americans in hard times into the evangelical churches? The answer is at least threefold.

First, evangelical churchmen were able to capitalize on a prevalent feeling of guilt within the business community for its "departure from God."[13] With increasing urgency during the previous decade ministers had pressed on American businessmen their duty to deal honestly with their customers and employees and, at a time of burgeoning national prosperity, to make socially responsible use of their wealth. A flood of publications in 1856 and 1857 encouraged Christian stewardship and methodical giving to charitable organizations (particularly through the newly established American Systematic Beneficence Society), denounced the ostentatious American pursuit of the "almighty dollar," and warned that "upstart prosperity, . . . walk[ing] on stilts, . . . in due time will stumble."[14] While accepting that there were discoverable economic causes for the financial collapse, most men recognized that in September 1857 God had intervened directly in human affairs: "In the very heart of a land abounding with elements of wealth, he lays his hand upon it, and locks it up for a season." The "paralysis" was God's punishment for moral disease, for "violated laws, and forgotten precepts of social and individual morality," for the adulteration of goods and the deceptions of advertising, for "artifice" and "tricks of the trade" in selling, and for Sabbath-breaking in the course of business. Racked with guilt over these sins and over their "wicked speculation" and *"monomaniacal haste to get rich,"* men who had lost all or part of their wealth rushed to find forgiveness. The hardware manufacturer who confessed at the Fulton Street meeting to overcharging his retailers exemplified those who accepted their responsibility for the economic collapse.[15]

Secondly, a number attended revival services as a means of finding what the Universalist Adoniram Patterson described as "strength and consolation." The noon prayer meetings offered considerable comfort to one New York businessman, representative of many others, who unequivocally claimed:

Prayer was never so great a blessing to me as it is in this time! I should certainly either break down or turn rascal, except for it! When one sees his property taken from him every day, by those who might pay him if they were willing to make sacrifices in order to do it, but who will not make the least effort, even for this end, and by some who seem designedly to take advantage of the times, in order to defraud him—and when he himself is liable to the keenest reproaches from others if he does not pay money, which he cannot collect and cannot create—the temptation is tremendous to forget Christian Charity, and be as hard and unmerciful as anybody. If I could not get some half hours every day to pray myself into a right state of mind, I should certainly either be overburdened or disheartened, or do such things as no Christian man ought.[16]

Thirdly, evangelical religion offered hope. An omnipotent God had intervened to punish American wickedness; surely, then, he would intervene to restore prosperity if Americans supplemented the standard recipes for economic recovery—contraction of the credit system, restraints on the expansion of banks, and so on—with a return to the paths of righteousness. George Peck, Methodist minister at the "small and greatly depressed station" of Scranton, Pennsylvania, where unemployment and poverty had crippled the community, injected a sense of purpose and hope through special services that directed attention "to the one infallible source of help in the time of need." Significantly, most of the forty who had "professed faith" by late January were "heads of families in the prime of life," men and women desperate to fulfill the needs of their hungry dependents. Similar hope was nourished in Henry Ward Beecher's regular services in Plymouth Church, Brooklyn: in emotional prayer meetings businessmen who had lost heavily in the crash "sobbed and laughed and told their dreams."[17]

Broadly speaking, then, the revival drew its recruits from two quite separate groups: children and adolescents who sought salvation to fulfill their secular and religious duty and adults, very often men, who turned in their anxiety and muted hope to religion at a time of financial crisis. Additionally, some evangelical Americans hoped to fulfill two further objectives: the inauguration of an era of harmony in the churches and in society at large, and the creation of a perfect Protestant republic freed from the taint of Catholicism, socialism, and infidelity.

Eighteen-fifty-six and 1857 had been years of occasionally bitter dispute within and between churches. The three great ecclesiastical separations of the 1830s and 1840s, when Presbyterians, Methodists, and Baptists suffered schisms that grew largely out of north-south sectionalism, had not ended the wrangling over the churches' relationship with slavery. In the summer of 1857, after the New-School Presbyterian general assembly had declared slavery a sin in the sight of God, the southern presbyteries withdrew. The two branches of the MEC, one advocating slavery's moral and permanent propriety and the desirability of its extension, the other firmly convinced of its immorality, came to sometimes physical blows in the border states, where their jurisdiction overlapped, particularly in the Virginia and Baltimore conferences and in Missouri, where Methodists were tarred and feathered by sympathizers of the southern church.[18] More damaging was the division within the northern branch between the "ultra abolition party," whose leading lights included Hiram Mattison and William Hosmer of upstate New York, together with the more temperate Daniel Wise of New England, and the larger party of moderates, led by the bishops, who put revivals and soul-saving before antislavery agitation. The major question of dispute was:

should slaveholders be allowed to continue as members in good standing within the church? At the general conference at Indianapolis in 1856 the ultras failed in their bid to exclude the several thousand slaveholding members in the border states, but only after a protracted and acrimonious debate that persisted into the following year. Similar battles between firm abolitionists and more conservative evangelicals marked other northern denominations and the major benevolent organizations, the American Home Missionary Society, the American Bible Society, and the American Tract Society. [19]

In this context nonabolitionist evangelicals in the north came to regard the preservation of church unity as one of their major tasks. Abel Stevens gave expression to their determination to avoid the slavery issue: "The Church needs peace in all her borders; . . . the prayer goes up for . . . an evangelical peace. . . . Let us then . . . turn universally to our great ostensible work—the evangelization of the land and of the world." For these men the revival of 1857-58 represented a substantial victory. In cultivating it they had inaugurated a brief period of church harmony. Old-School Presbyterians in the summer of 1858 reflected on "a year marked by unusual peace," the Dutch Reformed Church told of "divisions . . . healed," Congregationalists of "disturbing influences . . . greatly lessened," and not even the Rochester antislavery convention of northern Methodists in December 1857 could shake the "gratifying tone of conservative good sense and good temper" in that denomination. [20] Equally significant, much greater interdenominational cooperation prevailed than in any previous revival. Union meetings became the order of the day, some held in churches under denominational or YMCA auspices, others in theatres, music halls, or huge mobile "union tabernacles" associated with no single denomination. The extent of union varied from place to place—the revival in Boston, for example, developed primarily within the individual churches—but everywhere the general absence of sectarian argument occasioned remark. [21]

At the same time many saw the revival as a means of soothing tensions in society at large. During 1856 and 1857 sectional bitterness reached a new pitch over the violence in "Bleeding Kansas," the Sumner-Brooks affair in Congress, and the Dred Scott decision. Even northern evangelicals of a cautious temperament generally questioned the southern position on slavery, maintained the benefits of free labor, and advocated colonization or compensated emancipation as a means of ending the "peculiar institution." They upheld the duty of all citizens to fulfill their political duty and vote according to their conscience; indeed Ronald P. Formisano has argued that in Michigan during the 1850s the Whig and Republican parties, the political agencies of antislavery, relied heavily on evangelical Protestantism. [22] Nevertheless, most evangelicals were anxious to curb sectionalism, "to inculcate reverence for authority," and to preserve the Union from a threatened conflict stimulated by southern secessionists and the "idio-sin-crazi-ness" of northern "fanatics." Only through religion would harmony come. As one Baltimore Methodist argued, "The perpetuity of the country depend[s] upon a higher power than the mere politician looked to as a security against threatened evils. Righteousness alone exalts and saves a nation."[23]

At the time that he spoke, in October 1856, the immediate prospects for a revival were poor. The country was in an "almost continual uproar" from "the sirocco of political excitement" of the presidential election: a Philadelphian complained that " 'Buchanan,' 'Fremont,' 'Fillmore,' 'Kansas,' 'Buch and Breck,' 'Hurrah!,' 'Yankee Doodle,' etc., etc., are to be heard at nearly every corner." Furthermore, the intensity and moral fervor of the campaign made conventional religious practice less than relevant. Men carried their religion into politics. According to one view "the present political contest is a religious movement, a revival of religion, 'a great awakening' to be classed among the moral reformations of the world"; certainly the national convention of the Republican party that preceded the election "had assumed the character of a great revival meeting, filled with camp-meeting fervor and a crusading enthusiasm."[24]

Evangelicals, who were in consequence quite unsurprised by the absence of any general revival movement in the winter of 1856-57, found two sources of comfort. First, they could point to a number of local revivals in individual churches suggesting better times to come. The Methodist minister in Burlington, Connecticut, for example, explained that attending political meetings had "got the inhabitants in the habit of being 'out at nights' and was seized upon . . . as an argument for holding religious meetings" to which oxteams and sleds brought penitents through storm and snow.[25] More importantly, evangelicals were well used to regular political distractions and had come to appreciate the concept of oscillation between political and religious excitement. In both spheres periods of activity were followed by periods of lull. As the excitement of the election winter declined, ministers and laymen were confident that religious activity would increase.[26]

The revival of 1857-58 was thus related to the evangelical drive "to harmonise sectional differences" and to the relative cooling of the political temperature during that year. "The revival is the great event of the times," exulted one Presbyterian minister. "Kansas, Cuba, or even the Russian War . . . fade in comparative importance." The radical abolitionist and disunionist William Lloyd Garrison was well aware of the diversionary aspect of the revival, labelling it an "emotional contagion" that turned attention from reform and "practical righteousness" into "a pharisaical piety and sectarian narrowness." The slavery issue did not go away, of course; but even in Kansas, where the storm over the Lecompton constitution raged during the early part of 1858, some Methodist preachers reported "a great work."[27] Elsewhere, to maintain the harmony that prevailed generally, posters carried the injunction "no controverted points discussed"; others carefully avoided singling out politicians for special mention for fear of giving offense. Some politicians, in fact, recognizing the soothing effects of the revival, came to its support; President James Buchanan himself became a daily attender of the meetings at Bedford Springs, Pennsylvania, and took "a deep and solemn interest in knowing all that he could of the progress of the great revival."[28] Most significantly, it was the northern business community, particularly of New York, economically tied to the south and aware that it had much to lose from disunion and civil war, that rallied most enthusiastically to a movement that offered hope of sectional peace.

Southern evangelicals, too, sought to preserve the Union through the spread of "conservative christian influence"; for example, various members of the MECS proposed a less sectional name and urged an aggressive campaign that would check the "tide of Freeloveism, Fannywrightism and Abolitionism" and would recruit anti-abolitionist converts as far north as Boston. But there was a further stimulus to the south's pursuit of revival deriving from her growing sense of isolation and embattlement over the slavery issue. When northerners claimed that southern religion was "severed from morality" and British churches in "pious horror" refused to receive her preachers on a formal basis, she defiantly pursued a revival to vindicate an institution she considered compatible with "right and the Bible." During the winter, when the revival gathered pace in the north, there was little sign of a similar movement in the southern states; indeed such opponents of slavery as Charles Finney believed that "the people there were in such a state of . . . vexation, and of commital to their peculiar institution . . . that the Spirit of God seemed to be grieved away from them."[29] What such observers ignored was that in the south winter was not, as in their own section, the season of revivals: meetinghouses were not equipped to deal with the colder weather, while the Methodist convention of changing preachers' stations during these months worked against successful protracted services. But from March 1858 onward southern churches threw themselves urgently into the task of copying northern successes and cultivating their missions to the blacks, so that they could point to divine blessing on their social institutions and say, "God prospers us as a church." They were rewarded as the revival spread across the south during that summer and autumn at the very time when the southern economy was on the upturn after a season of low prices for staple crops. By the end of the year only the North Carolina and Louisiana conferences had failed to record impressive gains.[30]

Finally, many Americans turned to the revival as a means of achieving a better, perhaps even perfect, society. The optimistic millennialism of the 1820s and 1830s had not been entirely undermined by the second adventist disappointments of the 1840s. There was no shortage of evangelicals who saw in the gathering religious excitement a means of combating the corruption and crime of growing city populations and the infidelity of the "Socialism, Owenism, Fourierism, Abolitionism, and all the various *isms* and schemes for the reform of the great evils of society" that ignored the need for individual regeneration.[31] Most heartening of all, the revival would challenge Roman Catholicism, much strengthened in the 1840s and 1850s by waves of Irish and German immigrants and by the domestic missions of such groups as the Redemptorists. To Protestant eyes these missions—held not just in New York, Cincinnati, Baltimore, and Pittsburgh, but also in the deep south—were sinister and dangerously competitive imitations of evangelical protracted meetings. They spread a code of beliefs and practices that was held in New York, for example, to be "mostly responsible for the moral degradation and the criminal and pauper expense of our city." Popery unchecked would undermine the fundamental American values of individualism, republicanism, and enlightenment. Through its "music, and candles, and pictures, and romantic humbuggery," through its "priestcraft" and its enslavement of women in convents by "priestly ghouls," it encouraged unthinking emotion, "superstition," dependence, conspiracy, and "despotism."[32]

Protestants saw the revival that began in 1857 as an excellent opportunity to prove that "Popery, except in the stagnant populations of southern Europe, is a thing of the past [and] is out of place amid the new ideas and aims of the new world." It was no accident that the first major religious movement since the great influx of Irish Catholics should be marked by unprecedented Protestant cooperation, nor that during the revival a Methodist deputation from Ireland (*"the pope's nursery for English-speaking priests"*) should return home, after two years' work, with seventy thousand dollars to "unseat the hoary despotism of the Italian priest in the Celtic mind." Proportionately the number of converts from the Catholic community was small, but evangelicals achieved enough for many to believe that the death of Popery was not far distant.[33]

Elsewhere, too, there seemed to be abundant signs of the moral transformation of society. The penitent owners of gambling saloons made them available for daily prayer meetings; southern grocery keepers rolled out their barrels, poured their contents on the ground, and "abandoned the traffic in ardent spirits"; the chief of police in Atlanta, Georgia, maintained that the revival had so reduced the rate of crime that he could dispense with half his force; in the fourth ward of New York City many "haunts of sin and shame" were shut up and "hundreds" of prostitutes allegedly "rescued."[34] That such reports may have been exaggerated is less significant than that they were believed. They reinforced the conviction that evangelical Protestant morality, the morality of small-town and rural America, would inevitably triumph. At the same time the revival saw the broadening of the influence of perfectionism, the doctrine that regenerate men and women must aspire to a second and higher stage of Christian experience, a doctrine that had potent social implications: sanctified Christians had a duty to work for the perfection of society.[35] Taken together, the evidence of multiplying conversions, the influence of perfectionist teaching, and reports of fundamental improvement in social morality prompted the question: "Why should such a work cease till the Millennial dawn?"[36]

The work, of course, did cease. During 1859 ministers spoke increasingly of "lull" in religious activity (figure 6); most new members of churches were said to be the old fruits of the previous year. Some unhesitatingly blamed "the return of commercial prosperity" for attracting recent religious enthusiasts "into secular pursuits with a zeal and devotion." Others blamed renewed tensions over slavery.[37] John Brown's raid, the election of 1860, and the secession of the southern states scarcely offered a hopeful climate for church growth. Indeed, once sectional conflict had reasserted itself as the principal concern of the nation, religious revivalism no longer acted as a palliative but arguably intensified that conflict. The recent revival had visited both north and south and was taken by the people of both sections to have sanctioned their social arrangements and political positions; further it injected a rhetoric of cleansing and purification into party politics.[38] The moralistic tone of the 1860 campaign owed much to the revival of *annus mirabilis*. The revival had ceased, but its influence lived on, for in the longer term it was to aggravate not ameliorate sectional tensions.[39]

"The Work of Grace" in Britain

Well before the American movement broke out in 1857, British churches were directing renewed attention to revivals. The publication late in 1853 of the report on the religious census, which emphasized the weakness of the churches in "chief manufacturing districts" and their general failure to reach the working classes, seemed likely to stir at least some of them out of their "languor and death."[40] The 1854 Wesleyan Conference agreed to hold "Special Religious services daily throughout the kingdom" in the New Year; within Primitive and Reform Methodism revival services were on the upswing from 1855.[41] At the same time Congregationalists and Baptists sought noncontentious revivals dominated by prayer and introduced their own kind of special services: meetings in halls and theatres designed to attract urban workingmen through popular addresses by prominent ministers on subjects secular and religious. This was the period when the young Charles Haddon Spurgeon was beginning his London ministry and was pulling thousands into Exeter Hall and then the Surrey Gardens Music Hall.[42] Evangelical Anglicans, too, were active. While Robert Aitken conducted high-church revivals in Cornwall, the Black Country, and the north, and while some low-churchmen directed outdoor preaching at "the humbler classes in society," Lord Shaftesbury sponsored the Religious Worship Act that allowed Anglicans like Hugh Stowell, John C. Miller, Hugh McNeile, and John C. Ryle to officiate at special services in Exeter Hall, London, and in unconsecrated buildings in other cities.[43] Often these services were designed to bring hearers to a decision, though there was no attempt to secure public expressions of conversion.

The pace of revivals quickened in the winter of 1857-58. As on earlier occasions of upswing, economic distress appears to have helped. In October the chairman of the Congregational Union attributed the "increasing conformity to the world among professing Christians" to the current prosperity of trade and commerce.[44] By the end of the year the economic picture had changed dramatically to bring back bleak echoes of the 1840s. Trade was depressed, wages fell, unemployment spread, and in some areas there were significant increases in pauperism and in the numbers receiving poor relief. From Sheffield, where a recession in the steel industry helped lower wages during Christmas week to about a third of the total of the previous year, came reports of a major revival; in Bradford, though some of the distressed mill operatives held "meetings of bitter complaint," Frederick Jobson rejoiced that "religiously, our societies prospered."[45] The shock of recession may well explain the jolting into activity of Methodists generally during this winter. But it is also worth recalling that the peak of revival in Britain did not come until 1859 and 1860, by which time trade and price indexes were again on the upturn. Indeed, one of the most remarkable of William Booth's revivals, in St. Ives in 1861, occurred at the height of the fishing season, when it was thought that the local population "would be too much absorbed in catching pilchards to think about saving souls."[46] Economic recession may have given a stimulus to revival, but it cannot explain the sustained movement of these years. Once underway, the revival took on a momentum of its own.

In this context news of the American movement began to break early in 1858. By summer English and Scottish evangelicals had a good grasp of transatlantic events. American newspapers, including Horace Greeley's *New York Tribune*, were gutted for "revival intelligence," which was in turn condensed and republished in the various denominational magazines and newspapers or in tract form. Americans like William Patton who happened to be in Britain gave public addresses and were subjected to furious evangelical questioning. So too were Britons newly returned from "the work of grace."[47] During 1859, the coverage of American events reached saturation point. A flood of tracts and addresses from distinguished members of the major evangelical denominations applauded the revival; British editions of some of the most successful American publications, especially Samuel Prime's *Power of Prayer*, sold rapidly.[48] American eyewitnesses remained in great demand: they included Baron Stow, exhausted by his work in Boston, Emerson Andrews, and particularly Bishop Charles McIlvaine. The bishop's generous attitude to the revival found a sympathetic response from his "old friends" in the evangelical wing of the Established Church and from Archbishop Sumner himself.[49] Only as the American movement itself declined and British evangelicals found adequate demonstration of revival nearer home did the fascination with America dwindle.

This sympathetic reaction, so much more widely based than the response to American revivals a generation earlier, is explained first by the movement of British churches under American stimulus to a more instrumentalist, promotional conception of revival. Equally significant, the descriptions of the American revivals that reached Britain emphasized that earlier excrescences were now generally absent. There had been "less passion—less religious excitement" than in 1831-32. The revival "was not a forced movement, got up for the occasion": by generally avoiding anxious seats and "a ponderous and complicated machinery of means" and by giving prayer pride of place, the Americans had ensured that there would be "less of man and more of God." This was precisely the language British evangelicals, particularly Calvinists, wished to hear. Though prejudice against American revivalism persisted, not least because of the "foul blot of . . . slavery" and "widespread political corruption," reservations were remarkably limited.[50]

American-style revival services quickly sprang up all over England and Scotland, often encouraged by the highest denominational authorities. The prayer meeting in particular captured the experimenters' imagination. Daily, noon meetings were encouraged in churches, public halls, and business premises, some of them quite blatantly aping the Fulton Street model: they were union meetings, often under the aegis of the YMCA and sometimes specifically for businessmen, at which hymns, extempore prayer, and short addresses were blended into a mixture demanding little in time or sustained concentration. At these and similar evening meetings, laymen played a major contributory, and often directing, role; as in America, the 1850s had seen a new level of lay involvement in church work, in part a consequence of the sense of individual autonomy and responsibility constantly nourished by evangelical preaching. In fact, ministerial encouragement of lay participation was more limited than in the United States. Many evangelical Anglicans were "rather shocked" by the idea of lay leadership in public worship, and Nonconformists too were afraid that the proper procedures would be washed away by a wave of embarrassing improvization. More than one observer noted the greater fluency of Americans in lay prayer meetings and remarked how traditional reserve and social deference made for awkwardness in similar British attempts.[51]

Two particular examples of American-inspired services deserve attention. In Scarborough, Benjamin Evans, thirty-three years a Baptist minister, powerful supporter of home missions, and admirer of Finney, turned his admiration for American voluntarism into a didactic analysis of the American movement that was to stimulate a religious revival. For the first three months of 1859 the ordinary weekday services of the different denominations were cancelled as Anglicans, Baptists, Quakers, Plymouth Brethren, and Primitive, Free Church, and Wesleyan Methodists joined in twice-daily "united revival services" dominated by hymn-singing and prayer, and followed by inquiry meetings; except for the Sunday services there were no sermons.[52] A rather different series of meetings was held under Anglican auspices in Hertfordshire. William Pennefather, rector of Christ Church, Barnet, is best remembered as the cofounder of the annual Mildmay Conference on mission work and the man responsible for bringing Dwight L. Moody and Ira D. Sankey to Britain in 1873. But well before moving to Mildmay Park in 1864, Pennefather had won a wide reputation as a mission preacher apparently oblivious to the distinctions of denomination and social class. In the summer of 1858 he gathered together twenty clergymen and Dissenting ministers and some six hundred laymen (ranging from nobility, gentry, and bankers to "large numbers of the middle-class and peasantry") for four days "to glorify God and pray for an outpouring of the Holy Spirit on England such as had been witnessed in America." They adopted many of the features of the New York revival and jettisoned the Prayer Book in favor of extempore prayer. Similar services were held in the following year. Though the meetings were sustained for a much shorter period than at Scarborough, the dispersing ministers were able to continue revival meetings "after the American mode" in their own churches.[53]

The most explosive repercussions of the American revival took place in the Protestant enclave of Ulster, where one of the most extraordinary of nineteenth-century revivals reached its peak in the summer of 1859. A generation of intensifying evangelical activity had followed the Union of Presbyterian Synods in 1840; revivals, for so long mainly the preserve of the Methodists, became part of the religious life of the dominant Calvinist denominations. After stirrings of renewed revival in 1856 and 1857, accounts of the American movement produced more concerted efforts in the following year. Emigrants' letters, pulpit readings of accounts of the revival, and the return from the United States of impressed Irish ministers played their part. Robinson Scott extended his American fund-raising mission on behalf of Irish Wesleyans into the revival year; Presbyterians, equally curious, sent two of their ministers, William Gibson and William McClure, to report.[54] These men, and various North American visitors (Michael Bosner, John Cooke, Theodore Cuyler, John Graves, Edward Payson Hammond, and Walter and Phoebe Palmer) encouraged lay-directed prayer meetings and camp meetings "in . . . the American style."[55] Of course, once the revival had been set in motion in the agricultural villages and small towns of Ulster, as well as in the larger manufacturing centers, it increasingly assumed an independent character. Most significantly, the appearance in March 1859 of physical prostrations in Ahoghill, County Antrim, gave the revival a new and dramatic dimension that did much to shape its course. By summer the "sleeps," "trances," and "marks" that characterized so many of the crowded revival meetings had affected a sizable proportion of the more impressionable and less well-educated converts; factory girls in overheated rooms were the most likely victims. These manifestations were reminiscent of the even more convulsive physical phenomena of the Kentucky Revival at the turn of the century. But their degree and extent were unique in midcentury revivals, and it was the fear bred of this uniqueness that actually helped spread the revival amongst potential converts, for revival reports make plain the sense of an advancing and inescapable wave of physical prostrations felt by "sinners" terrified that they too would be afflicted.[56]

These characteristics attracted scores of evangelicals from other parts of Britain. If the majority concluded that the prostrations, which were anyway dying out by the end of the summer, were unnecessary to conversion, they also rejected the criticisms and ridicule of much of the secular press, and in particular the *Lancet's* characterization of the revival as hysterical disease. They returned home to tell of the salvation of thousands, a fall in crime rates, and a general improvement in the tone of religious and secular society. They noted that the fractured morality of "slave-ridden America" and the dead weight of Roman Catholicism in "Papal Ireland" had not prevented spiritual and social uplift in either country. Surely England and Scotland, lacking similar moral injuries, could emulate those countries' achievements.[57] In the west of Scotland in particular, geographically and religiously proximate to Ulster Presbyterianism, a wave of prayer-meeting revivals, conversions, and even some physical prostrations reached a crescendo in the second half of 1859, though the movement continued there and in eastern and Highland Scotland into the following year.[58] In England the exhortations to revival were never quite matched by the reality of achievement. But the winter of 1859-60 saw even more special prayer meetings and revival services than twelve months earlier.[59]

Meanwhile, Wales was in the grip of a revival that demonstrated clearly the powerful effect of social and religious contagion. Welsh churches, with their experience of periodic revivals, were reckoned to be in a state of relative decline in the mid-1850s. By 1857, according to David Charles, president of Trevecca College, "the rising generation were strangers to the manifestation of any very general influences of the Spirit of God upon the churches."[60] It was only a matter of time before the ingathering of another generation would occur. When a revival eventually broke out in Cardiganshire in the winter of 1858-59, the rest of Wales consciously set about emulating her achievement. By the spring of 1860, the village-to-village, county-to-county advance of revival had allowed the four major evangelical denominations, representing four-fifths of the worshiping Welsh, to estimate their total gains at approximately eighty thousand, a huge proportion of a population numbering not much over one million.[61]

Why did this revival, which in the context of Welsh religion was bound to occur sooner or later, begin in 1858? In the summer of that year a rather unstable young man, Humphrey Rowland Jones, returned to Cardiganshire, the county of his birth, after four years in the United States. In America Jones had sought to show the shortsightedness of those Welsh Wesleyans who in 1854 had rejected him as a ministerial candidate. In Oshkosh and other Wisconsin settlements he won a reputation as an effective exhorter. During the general revival of 1857-58 he worked with some success in the Welsh towns of Steuben and Remsen in Oneida County, New York, where the whole community of several hundred people was allegedly converted. Jones returned to Talybont, Cardiganshire, in September 1858 solely to "promot[e] a similar movement to what was going on in America"—no doubt to show the legitimacy of his earlier ministerial ambitions. He immediately attracted attention in a community already well informed about the American revival. With David Morgan of Ysbytty Ystwyth he began a protracted series of prayer meetings in the Wesleyan and Calvinistic Methodist chapels, and "in a few weeks the upper part of the county was in a blaze." Morgan was initially suspicious of Jones and his methods, but he had been converted in 1841 during the later stages of Finney's Revival, took a firmly instrumentalist view of means and was prepared to adopt the central feature of the American revival—the united prayer meeting—in his later perambulations. Indeed he was soon to be accused of Finneyism for his "personal and intimate manner" of addressing penitents in the "big *seat.*" The work of Jones, Morgan, and the son of Samuel Griffiths of Horeb, a recent arrival from America, justified the contemporary conclusion that the Cardiganshire revival was American in origin and style.[62] Eventually, given the country's multiple subsidiary links with the United States and the competitive instincts of local churches, the harnessing of the American and Cardigan thrust of revival created an unstoppable momentum throughout the whole of Wales.[63] Partly because of the language barrier, partly because the Welsh revival was well underway by the summer of 1859, the Ulster revival made only a minor impact in the principality; there were few physical manifestations.

New and Returning Heroes

For contemporaries one of the most singular features of the revival in the United States was the rather secondary role played by major revivalists. This was what Spurgeon had in mind when he remarked: "Providence had sent Caughey, and Finney, and such wide-famed revivalists, *packing*, that honour might be given to the Lord alone."[64] In fact, many full-time revivalists were at work during the American revival; some of those who were not were to be found in Britain. A few came too late and too briefly to make a major impact. William Taylor, his reputation made as a California street preacher in the 1850s, arrived in England in May 1862. He remained until early in the following year, holding special services for two or three weeks at a time in English and Irish Wesleyan chapels; then he sailed on to Australia.[65]

But a few established American revivalists came for long enough to make their presence more generally felt.

Foremost was the indefatigable Caughey. He returned ten years to the month after his reluctant departure in July 1847. In that decade he had continued to work at a pace matched by few ministers. Despite—perhaps because of—the complaints of British Wesleyans to the American Conference, the demand grew in America for Caughey's services, while the condensed American edition of his *Letters*, outlining his major English revivals, raced through numerous reprints; he was not the first or the last nineteenth-century revivalist to find his reputation enhanced by a successful itinerancy in Britain. In the towns and cities of Canada and the northeastern states of the Union his unstinting efforts (ten sermons a week for most of the year) won friends and a constant flow of conversions. His triumphs only reinforced his determination to return to what he regarded as unfinished business in England. After a series of successful revival services in New York, Newark, and Philadelphia in the winter of 1856-57, he prepared to cross the Atlantic.[66]

Caughey had remained in touch with James Everett, John Unwin, and other British friends, and his impending return had been rumored since the late 1840s. Wesleyans contemplated his arrival with trepidation and were relieved to find that when he disembarked at Liverpool the American Methodist deputation to the forthcoming British Conference (Bishop Matthew Simpson and Dr. John McClintock) was on hand to encourage his obedience to the denominational authorities. Simpson feared "that their advice would not be heeded." But Caughey provoked no connectional storm: not until January 1861, when invited to lead prayer in a union meeting, did he officiate in a Wesleyan building. There was no need. Non-Wesleyan Methodism, within whose revival circles he had become something of a folk hero, welcomed him with warmth and enthusiasm. From the moment he began his work in Sheffield, "the King of the Revivalist Preachers" could tap a reservoir of goodwill. The United Methodist Free Churches (UMFC) in particular—a denomination generally committed to giving space to revivalists and sustained by so many of Caughey's "spiritual children"—were to ensure that he would never go short of preaching invitations.[67]

Sheffield was a sensible place to launch his new campaign: it harbored many friends, Reform Methodism was strong, and men like Richard Poole and John Unwin had kept it a major center of revivalism during the 1850s. Thirteen years after his earlier triumph, Caughey's techniques remained as effective as ever. For over a year, working almost daily in non-Wesleyan chapels, he stood at the center of an extraordinary revival that numbered converts "by the cart load."[68] When he moved on to Hanley, Manchester, Hull, and Louth in 1858 and 1859, a time of gathering revival momentum generally, he was well placed to repeat his Sheffield success. By the summer of 1859, when he returned to America, the various church secretaries reported over eight thousand converted and three thousand or more "entirely sanctified."[69] Few of his contemporaries could match these totals. On Caughey's third visit from August 1860 to August 1862 he once again wisely directed his attentions to the urban centers of the midlands, Lincolnshire, and the industrial north, though he once strayed south, making a three-month visit to Bristol in 1862; again the UMFC chapels welcomed him; again he scored impressive statistical successes. Only in the last few months of his stay, in the summer of 1862, when his health began to give way, was there any sign of a decline in his effectiveness. Even then his results in Nottingham, Leicester, and Walsall won the approval of revivalist colleagues and contributed several hundred converts to the approximate total of seventy-five hundred recorded over his two-year stay. He was never to repeat this sustained performance. His fourth, and final, visit to England was interrupted by ill health and occurred in the fallow period of the mid-1860s, when most churches experienced only very limited growth. But for short periods Caughey was still able to recapture past glories, as in London in 1864 (the center of his orbit had now shifted south) and in Exeter and the southwest in the winter of 1865-66; he had not lost his capacity to conjure up revivals in times of general denominational stagnation.[70]

This particular problem did not face the elderly Finney, who returned to Britain at a time of incipient revival. Encouraged by Potto Brown, Neville Goodman, and other Huntingdonshire laymen, Finney had been contemplating a second visit since at least 1857. His plans hardened as, from his Boston and New York pulpits, he watched the spread of American revival and wondered whether he should "see if the same influence would not pervade" Britain. He vacillated as Oberlin colleagues tried to prevent his departure, but eventually his determined wife made up his mind for him. In December 1858 he and Mrs. Finney set sail for Liverpool.[71]

Superficially the omens were good. The Finneys were welcomed at Houghton; their arrival was announced in John Campbell's *British Standard*; immediately invitations and letters of welcome arrived from all over Britain, and there was evidence of conversions in their early work in Huntingdonshire. But in fact they had cause for concern. American events and Finney's arrival had reopened the debate over revivalism and demonstrated once again Nonconformity's ambivalence toward special efforts. George Hitchcock and George Williams, once sympathetic to Finney's methods, were now more interested in the special Sunday services in Saint Paul's, Exeter Hall, and elsewhere than in the American's more systematic revivalism; others shared their views.[72] Theologically, too, Finney was suspect and, ominously, had lost the support of his earlier defenders. John Campbell had in 1850 given Finney the benefit of the doctrinal doubt, but now, chastened by the *Rivulet* affair, he closed his pulpit to him and gave Samuel Tregelles and other nonconformist theologians space in his newspaper to erode any remaining confidence in Finney's orthodoxy.[73] Nor was Campbell's the only pulpit lost. Few of Finney's influential supporters of 1850 were now available: John Angell James was an old man (he was to die within the year) and his congregation less than sympathetic; Redford, who had recently left Worcester for an Edgbaston retirement, told Finney that his old church was divided over asking for the American's help; Charles Roe had emigrated to America.[74] Only Potto Brown and James Harcourt remained.

Finney's early movements reflected this new situation. Huntingdonshire, where Brown had strengthened his influence, remained his base for the first two months, while he conducted services in Houghton and Saint Ives. Only in late February did he move to Borough Road, London, where Harcourt was pastor. Thereafter, apart from a brief, semi-recuperative return to Huntingdon in May and June, Finney was determined to avoid the error of his earlier visit and avoid evangelical backwaters. Recognizing the importance of city revivalism, he scolded British evangelicals for the "impression extensively prevalent . . . that it was a thing quite Utopian to attempt to move [the] large cities [of Britain]."[75] At the same time his lack of standing among leading Congregationalists drove him into churches more firmly wedded to revivalism. First, he returned to London in the summer of 1859 to preach for two months in the four UMFC chapels of the East End. Next he made good his promises to John Kirk and other Morisonians (who, as Kirk reminded him, "for the last 22 years at least . . . have thought of you, read your every line almost and loved you . . . as one of themselves"). Beginning in late August, when the impact of the Ulster revival on Scotland was at its peak, Finney spent over three months in Evangelical Union pulpits working for Kirk in Brighton Street, Edinburgh, officiating at the reopening of the younger Ferguson's church in Glasgow, and contributing to the elder Ferguson's revival efforts in Aberdeen. He never met James Morison, who was absent, ill.[76]

Finney returned to the Congregational fold in the new year to hold revival services in the north of England. His immediate success at Bolton suggested his error in never before tackling those industrial areas where Caughey and other revivalists had been most impressive; it also threw into relief the limited success of his earlier efforts. In the quiet of Huntingdonshire, where a celebrity could easily attract public attention, Finney's return drew in excited crowds and prompted conversions; in the small commercial town of St. Ives the Finneys caused a considerable stir. But the visit had little wider significance and, in Huntingdon at least, the number of converts proved fewer than originally expected. The sharpest contrast between Finney's own estimate of "a glorious work of grace" and the reality of the achievement is found in his six weeks' work with London Methodists. The quarterly statement of the UMFC Third Circuit, issued after Finney's departure, noted an increase of thirty-four full members on the quarter and a *decline* of fifteen in the num-

Charles G. Finney in old age. Courtesy of Drew University Library.

bers on trial. Richard Poole in 1857 and Caughey in 1864 made a much more dramatic impression. Even in Edinburgh, where Kirk's church was packed regularly, where seventy had professed conversion by the month Finney left, and where the revival continued after his departure, one reporter noted that "he has done nothing towards the originating, and very likely will do but little towards extending, the Revival in Scotland."[77]

In Bolton, however, Finney was to participate in what the local newspaper regarded as "the most extraordinary spiritual movement ever known" in the cotton-manufacturing town. Arriving when the various evangelical churches were already trying to promote a revival, Finney began work with the Congregationalists in Duke Street Chapel. But growing crowds and flourishing relations between Independents and Methodists—Finney himself stayed with an influential and "very unsectarian" Methodist mill owner, James Barlow—quickly suggested the use of the Temperance Hall for union revival services. Here Finney recaptured some of his past vigor, delivering with considerable energy six or more sermons weekly to audiences of over a thousand. Though he looked older and now preached in spectacles, his simplicity, his vigorous logic, and his colloquial and anecdotal style could still rivet his audience. His efforts, and those of his wife in her ladies' prayer meetings, helped gather an alleged total of two thousand inquirers and twelve hundred converts over three months. Inflated these figures may have been, but the revival undoubtedly captured widespread popular attention.[78]

The Finneys' results in Manchester and Salford, their final stop before returning to Oberlin, proved anti-climactic after their Bolton achievement. Various factors were blamed. It was noted that "trade has been brisk. The working and middle classes have been employed until a late hour. Many of the higher classes are out of town"; and that "the Whitsuntide holidays . . . interfered with the regularity of the meetings." Finney himself blamed the lack of harmony between the Congregationalists, in whose chapels he worked, and the Methodists.[79] Perhaps, too, Caughey's efforts in the previous year had left the Methodist community too drained for new revival efforts. But there were other, less local, reasons. Finney's Manchester experience was in keeping with the broad pattern of only limited success that marked most of his work in 1859-60. First, his age worked against him. Though in Bolton he showed his old energy, he could not maintain this vigor indefinitely: on arrival in Manchester he was, by his own admission, "exhausted."[80] More important, Finney missed the benefits that others drew from working consistently within the same denomination or connection. Barriers may sometimes have been nonexistent in times of revival, but denominational partitions generally prevailed; other revivalists sheltered profitably within denominational itinerancy, and, as in Caughey's case, they were often able to exploit the revival momentum within a particular connection. Unfortunately for Finney, when he did commit himself to a single denomination (in Scotland), his choice, as will be seen, was a constricting one.

Phoebe Palmer. Courtesy of Drew University Library.

Walter C. Palmer. Courtesy of Drew University Library.

Two Americans who did take advantage of connectional organization were Walter and Phoebe Palmer, a unique couple in midcentury evangelism. Brought together by their common New York Methodist background, they married in 1827 and never lost the optimism and energy of that city's growing Methodist community in the early nineteenth century. Walter, a physician with a "large and lucrative practice," used his earnings to support the temperance, missionary, and Sunday school work that was always his primary interest. Phoebe, daughter of a Yorkshire Methodist, Henry Worrell, was the dominant personality of the pair. Central to her work was the legendary Tuesday meeting, a regular and interdenominational weekly prayer meeting established in 1835 and opened to men from 1839, where laymen and ministers met on equal terms to "inquire after the Way of Holiness." The Tuesday meeting was one of the primary contributions to and expressions of the upsurge of American interest in entire sanctification during the 1830s and 1840s.[81] It acted as a focus for a kind of connection within a connection, attracting some Methodist opposition but winning the warm approval of such influential ministers as Nathan Bangs and Leonidas Hamline.[82] Mrs. Palmer's utter commitment to propagating holiness, and perhaps too her tendency to look for the hand of God in the most everyday of occurrences, laid her open to charges of "mysticism" and "fanaticism." But, like Caughey, she generally removed these fears by her complete pragmatism and interest "in every form of practical Christianity." In addition to her work for the sick and the poor in her native city, from 1840 she and her husband conducted regular and effective evangelistic expeditions in churches and camp meetings throughout northeastern America and Canada.[83]

By 1857 the Palmers had become celebrities whose sense of their own centrality in a widening revival movement was heightened when in October in Hamilton, Canada West [Ontario], they presided over a revival regarded by some contemporaries as causally connected with the seminal New York movement of that year.[84] This feeling of being at the center of events helped persuade them, once they had seen the American revival through its most rewarding stages, to turn to Britain, where there were signs of developing revival and where Mrs. Palmer and her Tuesday meeting were well known. Her works on holiness had circulated in Britain for several years. Edward Weeks read some of them "with pleasure and profit" in 1853; by 1857 demand was sufficient to warrant English editions of several of her books, particularly *Faith and Its Effects* and the fast-selling *Way of Holiness*, which soon ran into further editions. Two earlier schemes to visit England (in 1845 and 1856) had fallen through, but now, in June 1859, after constant invitations, the Palmers disembarked at Liverpool.[85]

Several weeks spent in London and in Belfast Methodist chapels at the height of the Irish revival formed the prelude to a series of special revival services in the northeast of England and in Scotland in the autumn and winter of 1859-60 that gave the Palmers' itinerancy its early impetus. In Brunswick

Chapel, Newcastle-on-Tyne, where the couple arrived for thirty-five days' services in September, the minister was the elderly Robert Young, district chairman, ex-president of Conference, lifelong friend of revivals, sympathizer of Caughey, and correspondent and admirer of the Palmers for some time.[86] Young's aegis and the anticipation aroused by American, Irish, and Scottish events offered the Palmers promising conditions for evangelism. Thirteen hundred professed conversion by mid-October, when the couple moved on to other circuits in the same district (Sunderland and North Shields). Similarly impressive results followed here. Young and his colleagues unhesitatingly ascribed that year's district increase of nearly sixteen hundred members to "the proximate instrumentality" of the Americans. The Palmers returned to Tyneside in May and June after visiting sympathetic Methodists in the Glasgow and Carlisle areas.[87] Thereafter they may have been guilty of a tactical error: whereas Caughey had continued to work very largely in those urban and industrial areas where a minimum success could be more or less guaranteed, the Palmers consciously turned down the many pressing invitations from "promising" large towns to attend to smaller, out-of-the-way places where often, especially in southern England, the "religious thermometer . . . has been very low."[88] Partly for this reason, in addition to the slackening of the pace of revival generally, some of their early impetus was lost. They did not wholly ignore urban and industrial areas, however, and eventually returned to them for a sustained period in 1863.

In fact, whatever the venue, the curiosity aroused by this novel American couple guaranteed them substantial audiences at their twice- or thrice-daily services. If some of the ingredients in their services—the call to the communion rail, for example—were not new and others—the emphasis on conversion and holiness—were part of the customary proceedings in many Wesleyan chapels, the particular blend offered by this lay husband-and-wife duet was unique. The Palmers ordinarily worked closely with the minister to produce a well-orchestrated service that to the unsympathetic observer had all the elements of performance. The Newcastle arrangements were typical. There a circuit preacher opened the service with singing and prayer; Dr. Palmer then read and expounded on a chapter of Scripture. This was followed by "a brief and appropriate address" from the minister, after which Dr. Palmer announced the hymn and invited intending leavers to depart. Few did so, for the peculiar attraction of the service was yet to come. "Mrs. Palmer now modestly walks within the rails of the communion, not to preach according to the modern acceptance of that term, but simply to talk to the people. . . . She speaks deliberately. . . . Her voice is clear and musical." Her address (*not* a sermon) "on the duty of Christians to be holy, and to exert all their powers to bring sinners to Christ," was in style emphatically anecdotal and very heavily flavored with sentimentality. On completion of her address, her husband "in a very affectionate manner" invited penitents to walk forward to the communion rails while the rest of the congregation continued to sing hymns. Prayer and the recording of penitents' names brought the service to a close.[89]

In mood much of the Palmers' service stood between the close reasoning of Finney's sermons and the full-fledged sentimentalism of Moody and Sankey's work a decade later; in pattern and style their services were close enough to the instrumentalist revivalism of much of American Methodism and to Caughey's practice to offer cautious Wesleyans grounds for concern. Their offense in some eyes would have been compounded by their lay status— and worse still, Mrs. Palmer was a woman. Yet for three years they continued to be welcomed into Wesleyan churches. They were to some extent protected by their determination not to supersede the minister—both, for example, steered clear of the pulpit itself. But their vulnerability was made clear in the summer of 1862, when Conference resolved that superintendents should exclude from their chapels persons "not amenable to our regular discipline." That the minutes of 1847 (relating to Caughey) were specifically invoked and that those of 1807 (Dow's case) were mentioned in the broader debate indicates that the Palmers and the American aspect of the problem had contributed to Conference's decision.[90]

More significant, however, were the cases of native evangelists. Some of these were, in the eyes of the authorities, "no better than religious charlatans, who make considerable sums by working in a violent and irrational manner on the physical and emotional susceptibilities of uneducated crowds." Even more troublesome were Richard Weaver and William Booth. Weaver, collier-turned-evangelist with a racy style, "broad vulgarisms," and powerful presence, was especially effective amongst the "fustian jackets" and the "unwashed." Wesleyans were horrified to find him attacking "the black-coated and well-seeming," as "hard headed formalists, if not hypocrites," sometimes "addicted to sensual and secret sin."[91] Booth presented a somewhat different problem. In the mid-1850s as a young man he had achieved remarkable results as a Methodist New Connexion evangelist in Guernsey, the west country, the midlands, and the north, employing special services modelled on Caughey's methods. The New Connexion Conference at first approved of his itinerancies, but in 1857 those critical of his emotionalism, "penitent-form revivalism," and challenge to connexional order managed to persuade Conference that he should be given a regular circuit. Some of his lay supporters, temperamentally akin to Caughey's champions a decade earlier, boiled with resentment: "The only way for such men as you and Caughey to escape the mental rack and handcuffs," one of them wrote to Booth, "is to take out a licence to hawk salvation from the great Magistrate above, and absolutely refuse to have any other master." For four years he ignored this advice but when in 1861 the Conference rejected his application to return to evangelistic work he withdrew from the New Connexion and offered his services as a free-lance revivalist to sympathetic churches. Almost at once he was at the center of an emotional revival in the various branches of Methodism in Cornwall. Wesleyans were terrified lest such an untamed creature should prey on their vulnerable societies.[92]

The Palmers were saddened by the Wesleyan resolution of July 1862 but were neither temperamentally suited nor strategically placed to challenge it, for soon after the meeting of Conference, when she was in Ireland, Phoebe suffered a major breakdown in health that kept the couple out of revival services for several months. By the time she had recovered, the Primitive Methodist Conference, too, had directed "station authorities to avoid the employing of Revivalists, so called."[93] The only major branch of Methodism officially still in full sympathy with the Palmers' style of revivalism was the UMFC, and from late 1862 onwards much of the Palmers' work took place in that group's chapels and in those of the New Connexion, which, despite the Booth affair, had left the initiative in matters of revivalism to each individual circuit.[94] But the Americans never fully lost the support of Wesleyans, many of whom declined to regard Conference's decision (the act "of a few mistaken persons," and not "the voice of the body") as binding.[95]

For the final year of their visit, then, the Palmers were far from friendless as they itinerated in the midland and northern strongholds of Reform Methodism. Their performance in statistical terms continued to match that of the most effective periods of their tour. During the first eighteen months, for example, according to Mrs. Palmer's estimate, "at most places" they "witnessed an average of not less than one hundred saved weekly." In Wales in 1862 they claimed over one thousand converts in three or four months. Now, in Wolverhampton, Birmingham, and Walsall in early 1863, they calculated that in twelve weeks about fourteen hundred had received "forgiveness of sins" and two hundred "the blessing of purity"; soon afterward a total of thirteen hundred justified and sanctified were recorded in Manchester and Nottingham over a period of eight weeks.[96] These figures were comparable with those achieved by Caughey. When the Palmers finally sailed out of Liverpool in October 1863, they could reflect with pleasure on a record that was by contemporary standards enormously impressive.

The final member of this group of Americans itinerating in Britain was Edward Payson Hammond, an earnest young New Englander bred on small-town Congregationalism, converted at seventeen, college-trained, and intent on devoting his life to missionary work. Hammond's trip to Europe in 1859, when he was twenty-seven, was designed as a brief interruption of his studies, not as a major evangelistic enterprise. He visited Ireland for a fortnight to watch the revival and defend the American movement, toured the Continent, and visited John Angell James (whose *Anxious Inquirer* had been his "guide . . . to Christ and heaven"). Then, instead of returning to America, he attended the Free Church College in Edinburgh, a base from which he could lend a hand to neighboring Congregationalists in Musselburgh. Predictably, given Hammond's proven sympathy for revivals and the percolation of Ulster news throughout Scotland, emotional revival services became daily events in Musselburgh. Hammond was given most of the credit.[97]

Thereafter he never looked back. For twelve months he itinerated in various Scottish milieux—villages, towns and cities, mining areas and agricultural regions—holding crowded daily services for a week or two in each place and generally associating with Congregationalists or Free Churchmen. Hammond estimated that during 1860 some seventeen hundred had been "awakened" in his revivals, a figure nowhere near those of Caughey, the Palmers, and other Methodists but still a considerable achievement, given that many of the churches he visited had only a limited acquaintance with revival methods. He regularly supplemented his earnest, "unstilted" sermons, noted for their "marvellous knack of making mundane themes the medium for conveying precious spiritual truths," with a separate inquirers' meeting. These were methods much less challenging to conservative evangelicals than the more robust methods of the Methodists. Hammond may also have benefited from the levelling effects of his lay status: it seemed to a Glasgow editor that Hammond, lacking "the pride of office . . . of a thorough clerical training," was more approachable than most of the ministry. Of most long-term significance, however, were his services exclusively for children and his readiness to regard children no older than five as potential converts. Within the decade he was established on both sides of the Atlantic as "the children's evangelist."[98] Hammond's departure in 1861, unlike the departure of other Americans at this time, marked less an end than a beginning.

These Americans scarcely constituted a united phalanx amongst the activists of the British revival movement. Their movements were never coordinated and rarely overlapped. True, Finney, Hammond, and the Palmers found themselves in Scotland during the winter of 1859-60, and Caughey and the Palmers (friends of some standing within the holiness connection of the MEC) were in Rochdale simultaneously in 1861.[99] But such convergences were not planned. In fact, on at least one occasion, at Manchester, Finney was reluctant to begin work, principally because Caughey had been there in the previous year; probably recollecting their joint presence in Cincinnati in 1854, Finney asserted that "he always found he could do nothing after Mr. Caughey."[100] Yet there were certain features common to their itinerancies.

The enthusiasm and numbers that greeted the Americans suggested not only the drawing power of popular personalities, but also the increased prominence of evangelists. In the revival movement of the 1830s, when the American churches sustained a burgeoning itinerancy, British evangelicals had made only cautious efforts to promote evangelistic agency; enthusiasm had waned during the reaction of the mid-1840s. In the late 1850s the emphases were reversed, for as itinerant evangelists came to play an unaccustomed secondary role in the American revival, they participated increasingly in British church life. British itinerants could be divided broadly into two categories. The first, the ministerial group, was most firmly based in the various branches of non-Wesleyan Methodism, where historically there had prevailed a more mobile conception of the ministry than in other nonconformist denominations and where special services had been employed increasingly in the 1840s and 1850s. Foremost in this small group were William Booth and James Codd Milbourn, who had held revival services throughout the midlands and north during the late 1850s and early 1860s. Such men were often conscious imitators of Caughey.

Numerically much larger was the group of lay evangelists, whose growing importance was typified in the opportunities made available to Hammond and the Palmers. The emergence of full-time lay evangelists during the 1850s in part developed out of the encouragement of general lay involvement in the work of church recruitment. It also reflected increasing lay prosperity and experience of public meetings. This, however, was more immediately true of the better-off laymen—Reginald Radcliffe, Gordon Forlong, Henry Grattan Guinness, Hay McDowell Grant, and Brownlow North, for example—than those like Richard Weaver, William Carter, an ex-chimney-sweep, and "Mr. Bamford, the converted navvie," who emerged from the ranks of workingmen and were welcomed for their capacity to speak to the working class in its own language. The very success of these pathbreakers goes a long way to explain the increasing proliferation of lay evangelists during the later phases of the revival in the 1860s, when the earlier "spontaneity" had disappeared.

More challenging to traditionalists than lay evangelism was the emergence of a new strain of female preaching, forcefully represented by Phoebe Palmer. The female ranting associated with the Methodists earlier in the century was well on the wane by the 1850s, though some direct descendants of these women itinerants were still operating at that time in Primitive and Free Methodist circles. But at the same time a more decorous, middle-class female preaching was emerging, just part of the general broadening of women's activity in church life during the 1860s and developing in particular out of the laicism, search for novelty, sensationalism, and emphasis on holiness typical of the revival generally.[101] The supply of invitations reaching Phoebe Palmer suggested a widespread disregard for the resolution of the 1803 Wesleyan Conference, which had placed a broad restriction on the speaking of women in public, especially in sexually mixed assemblies. From the outset in the northeast Mrs. Palmer came under fire from scriptural literalists insisting that her practices were "diametrically opposed to an inspired apostle's precept," a reference to Saint Paul's injunction that "women keep silence in the churches" (1 Cor. 14:34-35). Robert Young and Catherine Booth (on Tyneside herself during the Palmers' northeastern successes) sprang to Mrs. Palmer's defense, the former emphasizing her "extraordinary call" and both adducing counterarguments from the Scriptures.[102] The affair was a major element in the controversy over female "prophesying" that continued through the

1860s and subsided when female preaching in its more sensational form declined in the next decade.

Yet on strictly secular feminist issues, Mrs. Palmer's views, like most contemporary women preachers', were not radical. "We do not intend to discuss the question of 'Women's Rights,'" she wrote in her *Promise of the Father*, a work designed to remove the prejudice against women speaking in the churches but specifically disclaiming any commitment to revolutionizing women's social or domestic relationships.[103] Here she stood on the same ground as Mrs. Finney, who, it was said, confined herself in Edinburgh "to the sphere of a true lady, according to the most stringent notions of 'women's place,'" and whose meetings in Bolton were regarded as remote from "eccentric exhibitions" of "women's rights." Mrs. Finney's public work on this visit was actually far more prominent and was better integrated with her husband's efforts than in 1850; at her daily prayer meetings, sometimes interdenominational affairs attended by two or three hundred people, this gentle but articulate sixty-year-old coaxed and prayed with many who were later converted at Finney's own services.[104] Unlike Mrs. Palmer, she abstained from work in sexually mixed meetings (in Calvinist Nonconformity, women's active participation in mixed public prayer was not widely encouraged) and received no prompting to do so from her husband; Finney himself, though accused in 1827 at New Lebanon of encouraging women's speaking aloud in "promiscuous assemblies," was not the radical in this area that his opponents had sometimes claimed. But Mrs. Finney's work did make considerable impact, particularly in Scotland. Her daily ladies' prayer meeting in Bristo Place, Edinburgh, continued for many months after her departure, and similar meetings sprang up in direct imitation elsewhere. The work of both Elizabeth Finney and, less palatably, Phoebe Palmer demanded that the evangelical community reassess women's status and increase their active role in church life.

The Americans' challenge to conservative evangelicals was positively welcomed by those with whom they worked. There was no ad hoc thrusting into standoffish churches. Instead they itinerated according to pressing invitations from admirers who promoted them as established soul-savers and champions of American freedom (for they were unanimously antislavery and, later, anti-Confederate). Often they arrived to continue special services already begun, but sometimes the revivalist—Caughey in Manchester and Finney in Huntingdon—came specifically to invigorate a "slumbering" church. Invariably they were treated as celebrities, and the expanding techniques of publicity, another aspect of growing sensationalism, trumpeted their "Revival Services." Placards, show bills, and printed circulars were more intensively used than ever before; reinvigorated religious periodicals were now supplemented by secular newspapers that, as in America, "no longer deem[ed revivals] beneath their notice."[105] The Americans' celebrity status did not, however, bring them huge material reward. The Palmers, sustained by the doctor's private means and the sale of Phoebe's books, gave their services free; Hammond generally worked "without fee or reward"; Finney, supported by wealthy laymen like Brown and Barlow, received occasional generous donations but worked for no personal profit. Caughey, whose crowd-pulling capacity was legendary (well over a thousand *paid* to attend four hours of speeches at his "Farewell Soiree" in Sheffield Music Hall in August 1858), was financially comfortable, but his personal lifestyle was beyond reproach, and he contributed generously to evangelical causes.[106]

The interdenominational emphases of this period of revival were generally well represented in the Americans' operations. All at some time or other supervised union prayer meetings and revival services. The Palmers' work in Newcastle, in which five denominations cooperated, was described as the Evangelical Alliance Revival; in Hammond's Annan revival Presbyterians joined Dissenters; Caughey attracted non-Methodists to his services in Manchester in 1859. The accelerating movement during the 1850s toward interdenominationalism and the use of unconsecrated buildings resulted in ministers taking over temperance halls and theatres for joint special services. This was Finney's experience in Bolton; in Huntingdon, he considered the Institution Hall suitably "neutral ground" for united prayer meetings; in Aberdeen he preached in the music hall.[107]

Yet the Americans were all essentially *denominational* revivalists. Caughey and the Palmers stayed within the Methodist fold, generally moving outside church walls only when the pressure of numbers dictated; Hammond worked under Scottish Calvinist auspices; Finney's operations were conducted through denominational channels. Cooperation between the churches meant interdenominationalism, not extradenominationalism. The work of the American revivalists was much more in keeping with the denominational special services that had developed during the previous thirty years than with the swelling undercurrent of work outside the churches apparent in this period. This extradenominationalism grew first out of a sense of the churches' failure to reach the working class and was perhaps best represented by the theatre-preaching of ministers and of lay revivalists like William Carter and Richard Weaver. In various London and provincial theatres Carter managed to make contact with workingmen on the fringes of society, beyond the orbit of the regular churches and conventional preaching. At about the same time the Booths, rejected by so many of the principal churches, were being driven to work independently. In 1863 they conducted meetings at Cardiff in a circus; at Walsall they worked in the open air. Such relatively spontaneous movements had, however, to be given permanent form and organization if they were not to evaporate. Consequently, Carter was to establish his own Church for Theatre Converts; the Booths set up a Christian Mission in East London in 1865 that in time metamorphosed into the Salvation Army.[108]

Whatever the erosion of denominational constraints, the Americans still regarded the British evangelical churches as hidebound by denominational prejudice. "Sectarianism, I am very sorry to say," Caughey told his American readers, "still runs very high in England." Finney, carrying rather less than pleasant memories of his work in Manchester and Edinburgh, echoed these sentiments: in England and Scotland, he was to write, "the members of the different churches keep more closely within the lines of their own denomination than in [America]."[109] His Scottish experience in particular soured his views. A number of conservative Scottish evangelicals associated his name with revivalistic extravagance; more damaging, his sponsorship by the Evangelical Unionists brought onto his head all the scorn and suspicion reserved for that denomination by orthodox evangelical churches. Reginald Radcliffe was to discover in Scotland in 1860 that after dissociating himself from the Morisonians, his "popularity considerably increased." Finney was unable to make a similar break, even though Morison himself was unfriendly to the idea of Finney's coming to work in his church. The American thus found himself generally ostracized by evangelical denominations (Congregationalists and Presbyterians) elsewhere ready to receive him.[110] Union meetings were much more common in the Scottish circles in which Hammond and the Palmers worked, though Mrs. Palmer noted that they attracted more suspicion than in England.[111]

All the Americans, of course, aimed at getting immediate commitment from their audiences. Yet in many of the particulars of approach—the precise form of service, the number to be held daily, the best means of pressurizing penitents—there was considerable diversity, determined in part by the revivalist's personal predilections, in part by church milieu and denominational emphasis. Caughey was rarely deflected from using the call to the communion rail. The Palmers, equally wedded to the device, found in Scotland a prejudice against it, and in Glasgow while waiting for the installation of a communion rail, Walter Palmer called on penitents to stand up in the congregation; on other occasions, when the rail was too crowded, he encouraged the spillover to raise their right hands "that we may unite our supplications on your behalf." Hammond, working amongst Scottish churches suspicious of anxious seats, consistently held inquiry meetings immediately after the daily service. Finney's methods varied from place to place: when working with Methodists he used the communion rail; in Manchester and Huntingdonshire he held separate "meetings for anxious inquirers"; in Scotland he challenged the prevailing antipathy toward public decision by encouraging the anxious to stand or raise their hands.[112]

Rather was it in their evangelical message that these revivalists differed. The predominant theology of the revival, *as preached*, was essentially Arminian, and the Americans contributed to that emphasis. Finney and Hammond would have rejected this label, but in practical terms their appeal to sinners was as broad as the Methodists', even if never so crude as the simplistic theology of William Carter and his ilk. Certainly neither of them was as boldly Calvinist as, it seemed, were Charles Spurgeon or Grattan Guinness. Similarly, none of the Americans, not even Mrs. Palmer, with her premillennialist explanation of female preaching as a sign of "the last days," could be designated "visionaries and enthusiasts." A significant gulf divided their views from those of such preachers as the gentleman-evangelist Captain John Trotter, utterly convinced of his infallibility and the proximity of Christ's Second Coming, and of the Welshman Humphrey Jones, who in early 1859 gave a precise date and time when the Holy Spirit would descend in bodily form at Aberystwyth to initiate the millennium.[113] Rather the Americans shared in the broad, unrelenting optimism of more midstream evangelicals such as William Arthur, whose tracts (*The Conversion of All England, May we hope for a Great Revival?*) provide excellent illustrations of the widespread conviction that the Christian world was on the verge of great achievements. "The entire conversion of England and America, within the next fifty years," Arthur wrote, "would not be so great a work for the Christians now existing, as the progress made since a hundred years ago has been for those then existing."[114] However, within this common context emphases differed. Not only were Finney and Hammond set apart from the others in being unable to disguise their Calvinism completely, but Hammond's own theology appears to have emphasized God's love much more than Finney's. In this he stood nearer to Moody and the generation still to reach maturity than to the preachers of the first half of the century.[115] Moreover, Hammond was the only one of the group not to embrace holiness, while the doctrine was much more peripheral to Finney's work than it was to Caughey's and the Palmers'.

In both the British and American revival, sanctification or holiness ("perfectionism" was widely regarded as too extravagant a term) played a much more prominent role than hitherto. The Tuesday meeting, Oberlin perfectionism, and Caughey's earlier campaigns suggest that from the 1830s in America, and from at least the 1840s in Britain, the search had intensified for a higher level of piety than that achieved at conversion. They also suggest the weighty Methodist contribution to the fuller flowering of the doctrine in the 1850s, when a number of highly popular works flooded the transatlantic evangelical market. Other American publications besides Mrs. Palmer's—William Boardman's *Higher Christian Life* and Thomas Upham's *The Life of Faith*—were read extensively in Britain during the revival. Simultaneously Richard Poole, James Milbourn, and other English Methodists sought with considerable success "to revive . . . *the Great Gun of revivalism.*"[116] Many "High-Church" Wesleyans "discountenance[d] the profession of holiness." But the efforts of popular Methodist evangelists and of Caughey and the Palmers, in whose hands the search for holiness was often little more than the pursuit of a sentimental experience, considerably extended the influence of the doctrine.[117]

One historian has suggested that the spread of holiness at this time might be interpreted as a religious equivalent of the secular cult of self-improvement.[118] It may also have been encouraged by more strictly internal church developments, perhaps by the need felt by some church members to set higher standards of piety and Christian living at a time when the criteria for ordinary church membership seemed to be deteriorating, perhaps too by the increasing number of inward-looking characteristics of revivals themselves. Often, as has been seen, the converts in revivals were already church members, and the movement of 1858-63 confirmed this pattern: Hammond's inquirers included "unconverted communicants in the churches"; Finney dealt with "careless professors of religion"; Caughey's and the Palmers' list of "justified" included a considerable percentage of church members.[119] That attention should be given to the holiness and "the higher Christian life" of the churches' membership was simply one more dimension of the displacement of evangelical energies from external to internal activity.

But "re-conversions" cannot account for the huge recorded increases in membership. The major Welsh and English Methodist denominations grew from a total of 444,369 members in 1859 (the lowest total since 1839) to 565,272 in 1863; only in 1866 was the progress reversed. There were, as figure 7 indicates, denominational and regional variations. Welsh Wesleyans registered a phenomenal growth of almost 20 percent in 1859-60; the Irish figure of almost 16 percent was similarly impressive. In England the annual returns of the various Methodist bodies never reached these proportions, but they indicate that all except the New Connexion (whose peak came in the mid-1850s) experienced a sharp upturn in growth rate in 1858 or 1859 and that all except the Wesleyans registered a second upswing in 1862 after the first phase of revival appeared to be over by 1861. The Baptist increase during the two peak revival years of 1859 and 1860 averaged over 10 members per church, and above-average growth continued up to 1862; Congregationalists apparently experienced "a proportionate share" of the general nonconformist increase during this period;[120] General Baptist returns were much less dramatic than most, but they indicate that following the stagnant decade after 1846 there was a 16 percent increase of nearly 3,000 between 1856 and 1864, with the period of most marked growth coming in the two years after 1860.

The background of the Americans' converts suggests that some of these additions had been sucked in from outside evangelicalism. A few had been members of nonevangelical denominations: the Finneys and the Palmers made much of the handful of Quakers, Unitarians, and Roman Catholics they managed to attract. A few genuinely seem to have been from the ranks of the "unchurched": some in Finney's Bolton audiences were described as being "not usually found" in religious meetings; amongst Caughey's Sheffield converts of 1858 were youngsters "from the corners of the streets, who have never been inside a church or chapel."[121] But in the main the pattern described in earlier chapters was repeated: the majority of converts came from within the unregenerate but evangelically minded group of church adherents. Even when the Americans used halls instead of chapels to reach the unchurched, it was largely the churches themselves that contributed the audiences.

Many of these "congregational converts" were closely acquainted with or related to professing Christians. Moral pressures, especially in the family orbit, could be intense. Following the conversion of James Barlow, Finney's Bolton host, in Ireland during the summer of 1859, his wife felt "the want of a Saviour that [she and her husband] might again find sympathy in the same thing." She turned to Finney for help and was converted. The force of example extended further into the household as "Lizzy the servant girl [and] Sarah the cook . . . submitted" later the same day.[122] Perhaps the strongest family pressures of all were those exerted on the young. Certainly all the Americans (and not just Hammond, with his special children's meetings) gave considerable attention to children and adolescents. Precise figures are available for Caughey's converts only. By far the largest proportion, sometimes as many as 50 percent, were under twenty. This was the case in Sheffield's Watery Street Wesleyan Reform and Surrey Street UMFC chapels in 1858. In the latter revival 260 out of 503 converts were between the ages of eight and twenty. Of the 270 professing conversion in Hanover Chapel during Caughey's services in the same city in 1861, 34 were under nine and another 98 under fifteen.[123] Such data, together with other contemporary evidence, point to a revival fed largely from within the evangelical churches and disproportionately from the young and the Sunday schools.

The Americans' relative failure outside the established evangelical network was reflected in the absence from their audiences of the socially outcast. They were all proud of the social mix in their congregations; the claim that "all classes," "high and low, rich and poor" attended their services was a recurrent motif in descriptions of their revivals, as of the revival generally. However, the Palmers' "simple and uneducated" hearers, Caughey's "rude rough men," and Hammond's "poor and illiterate" inquirers generally embraced not vagrants and those on the fringes of society, but the "respectable," or at least regularly employed, working class. Miners, blacksmiths, and sailors were converted in the Palmers' northeastern revival; Caughey dealt happily with iron- and steelworkers and factory operatives in Sheffield; Mrs. Finney coped with "shop girls," "factory women," and "poor mothers"; her husband made an impression on Huntingdonshire shepherds and farm laborers, and millworkers in the industrial north.[124] Though these revivalists' audiences "generaly consisted of working people, the majority of whom were female," as in the case of Finney's Bolton congregations, they also had a considerable middle-class leavening. These particular Bolton services of Finney's achieved the conversion of some influential mill owners and schoolteachers; the Palmers boasted the attendance of brewers, master butchers,

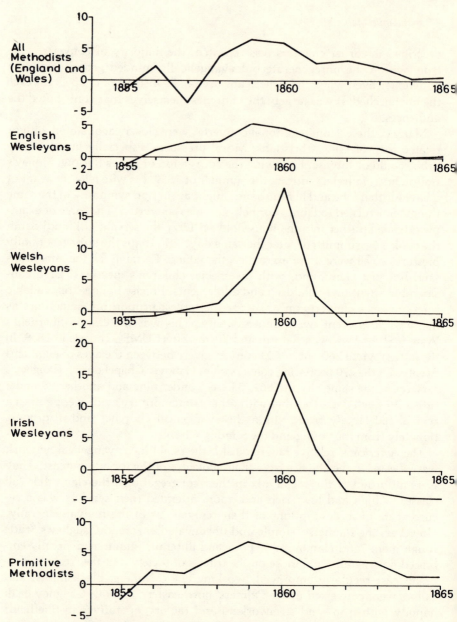

Figure 7. Selected British Nonconformist Growth Rates, 1855-65. Baptist growth rates represent the net increase in membership per church per annum; all other growth rates represent the annual net gain or loss in membership expressed as a percentage of total membership in the previous year.

SOURCES: Gilbert, "Growth and Decline," pp. 104, 106; *Minutes of Several Conversations between Methodist Preachers . . . at their . . . Annual Conference, 1855-65.*

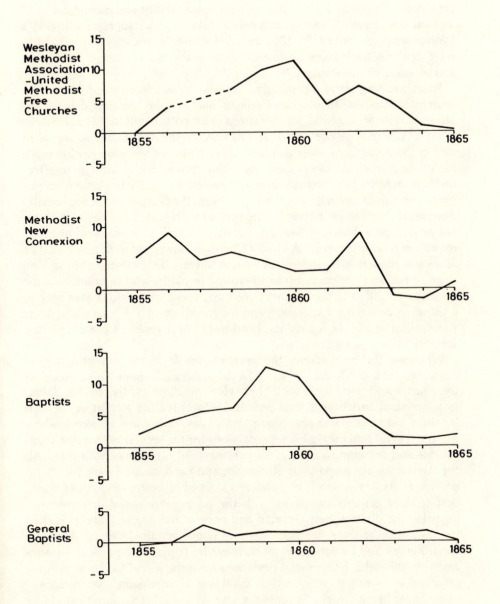

FIGURE 7 (continued)

physicians, "ladies and gentlemen of high respectability and mental culture," and on one much-treasured occasion a duke's granddaughter; Caughey's Wolverhampton converts in 1862 included a town councillor; in the Lanarkshire coal region Hammond preached to "men and women of education and superior circumstances."[125]

From one perspective this mingling of social classes represented the socially prominent imposing their code of religion and morality on their dependents. James Barlow arranged nightly meetings in his cotton mill for his operatives, many of whom were converted, and he was not the only manufacturer with whom the Americans were acquainted who exerted pressure on his work force; the conversion of sea captains in Sunderland had a contagious effect on their crews; while domestic servants were a group particularly susceptible to pressures from their employers.[126] From the perspective of the socially dependent themselves, however, the revival represented not social control, but an occasion, however fleeting, for social equality. It was said of Hammond's revival in Annan: "A kindly Christian sympathy took possession of all hearts rendering the people oblivious to class distinctions, and causing them to realize their common brotherhood in nature and in grace." At the communion rail or in the inquirers' meeting, social distinctions gave way to a common concern for salvation and for the winning of Christ's kingdom: this was, after all, the logical implication of the revivalist's preaching "the equality of . . . salvation to all."[127]

Whatever the perspective, the practical result of the intermingling of classes tended to be the end of "social feuds" and the advent of "social peace" in the churches.[128] Sometimes social behavior was significantly altered. Salvation, spiritual enrichment, and practical efforts for the advent of the millennium were the major preoccupations of revivalists and church leaders, but the revival had inevitable repercussions for the secular activity of evangelicals and sometimes, at its most pervasive, of nonevangelicals, too. All the Americans preached total abstinence and on occasions were successful enough to incur the wrath of publicans starved of customers. All of them, despite their genuine sympathy with the poor, were social quietists who regarded the division between rich and poor as ineradicable and preached the restitution to their rightful owners of goods acquired through fraud or theft; Finney and Caughey, as on their earlier trips, were particularly successful in this field. Other social deviations from the sound Christian norm— prostitution, swearing, wife-beating, gambling, theatre-going, for instance— came under harsh attack. At times the tone of a whole community could be dramatically changed, albeit temporarily. At the height of the revival in Sunderland and North Shields there were no criminal cases to bring before the assize courts, and theatres and taverns were apparently closed; the Palmers later boasted very similar effects of revival in Macclesfield and Cardiff.[129] The Americans' activities indicate that the drama and power of revival could endow the chapel with even greater social prestige, throw nonbelievers in a community onto the defensive, and briefly force community behavior into a mold of which evangelicals approved.

The religious excitement, rapid rate of church growth, and moderating effect on community behavior that accompanied the peak of revival could not last, of course. By the time the Palmers left Britain in the autumn of 1863 (when only Caughey remained to wave the American revivalist flag) the high point of revival lay in the past (figure 7). Wesleyanism in Ireland and Wales, which had experienced the most explosive growth, now saw a "reaction" far more marked than in England. After 1861 Welsh Wesleyans suffered decreases in membership in every year until 1866, Irish Wesleyans every year until 1868 (and not until the mid-1870s were their 1861 totals actually bettered). In England from 1864 to 1866 not one of the major Methodist denominations could average an annual growth rate of over 1 percent; Baptists' average additions per church from 1863 to 1866 slumped to the low levels of the early 1850s; General Baptists' membership went into a three-year decline after 1864.[130] New admissions were just keeping pace with deaths and lapses in membership. The revival had been based largely on the unconverted in church attendance. Now that the Sunday schools and the adherents had been thoroughly worked over by revivalists hungry for an immediate success, the numbers of the untapped but sympathetic unconverted were severely depleted. Revivalists continued to operate throughout the decade, but the revival itself—in statistical terms—was over.

Conclusion

British and American evangelicals constituted a lively transatlantic community. If American evangelicals were socially and ecclesiastically more powerful than the British, if that power gave them a greater confidence, if that confidence was translated at times into a seemingly boundless optimism for the future of America as God's chosen country, and if the foundation of these attitudes was a revivalism more deeply rooted and far-flung than anything Britain could offer, British and American evangelicals nevertheless saw themselves as branches of the same closely knit family. The contagious element in revivalism, seen so clearly locally, operated at a transatlantic level, too. In the late 1820s and early 1830s, in the late 1830s and early 1840s, and again in the late 1850s, both British and American evangelical churches experienced a significantly quickened rate of growth.

In such a context the American new-measure developments were bound to make an impression in Britain. The emotionalism, postrevival disorder and reaction, theological heterodoxy, and the association of many of the affected churches with slavery discouraged some British churches from employing novel means. But many found the sight of voluntarist churches thriving on systematic revivalism too exciting to ignore. With discretion they appropriated some American usages—protracted meetings, itinerating evangelists, the public call for commitment—and made room in their pulpits for the occasional American preacher.

The most successful of these were primarily urban revivalists. Earlier in the century the major American impact had been made by Lorenzo Dow, temperamentally closer to the frontier exhorter than to more respectable eastern and urban itinerants. Dow had helped in the British appropriation of the camp meeting, essentially a rural and semi-rural instrument of evangelism. But later, as Britons increasingly fretted over the religious state of urban society, Americans worked to good effect in cities and large towns, particularly in northern England. Charles Finney, his reputation made amongst the small towns of western New York, turned his attention in his later career to urban work and experienced his most worthwhile British achievements in city churches. Bred and based in New York City, Walter and Phoebe Palmer performed effectively in an urban context. Caughey, by far the most successful of American revivalists in Britain during the period, was also the one most consistently found in well-populated areas, particularly the manufacturing centers of the industrial north. Interestingly, the established American revivalist with least British success was Asahel Nettleton. If this was largely because by 1831 he lacked the necessary physical strength, it is also relevant that he was ill-at-ease outside the network of small towns in New England and New York State.

To a large extent these revivalists had to be able to show that their brand of revival was untainted by the religious and social disorder of those of an earlier generation. The Kentucky Revival and British Methodist revivals at the turn of the century had thrived on a seemingly unrestrained emotionalism distasteful to the wider evangelical world. The Americans of the next generation, purveyors of a more sophisticated urban revivalism whose rougher edges were constantly being polished, had lost much of this frontier "enthusiasm." Their well-planned meetings ended well before midnight and rarely showed any emotionalism to which British evangelicals might take exception. So much had the situation altered that in 1859 it was the Irish and not the American revival that caused concern. Moreover, none of the later American group was as ostentatiously republican as the headstrong Dow, nor were their indoor movements challenging to the social order in the same way as were the outdoor assemblies, late-night meetings, and itinerant preaching in the troubled years of the late eighteenth and early nineteenth centuries. The criticisms of British society made by these later Americans rarely extended beyond uncomplimentary references to the union of church and state and to the extent of intemperance; they never encouraged social disruption. What residual distrust there was grew out of the American revivalists' reputation for generating church schism. The Scottish splits of the 1840s and Caughey's contribution to the Methodist disruption of 1849 indicated that revivals could still be as divisive as in Dow's day. Even in 1859-60, when the Americans were unwilling to challenge prevailing denominational policy, the case of the Booths suggested the continuing potency of revivalism as a disruptive force.

By 1865 the improved reputation of American revivalists and their statistical success at a time when British evangelicals were finding it increasingly difficult to achieve growth at the rate of the first few decades of the century guaranteed them a continuing role in British evangelical life. The British movement of 1859-60 has been regarded in this study as the climax of the developments of a generation or so; yet in cultivating interdenominationalism, itinerant lay evangelism, and the doctrine of holiness, it marked the prelude to a new era, one in which the American dimension was more clearly represented than ever. The Keswick Holiness Meetings, established in the mid-1870s, traced their origins to Oberlin and American Methodist advocates of the "second blessing" and not simply to British perfectionist streams; indeed the Americans Asa Mahan (who spent his declining years in England as editor of *The Divine Life*) and Hannah and Robert Pearsall Smith were prominent in establishing this middle-class Higher Life Movement.[1] Sympathetic to Keswick, and in Britain at the time of its organization, were Dwight L. Moody and his singing half, Ira D. Sankey. Their British activity needs no recapitulation here,[2] but their interdenominationalism, use of halls and theatres rather than churches, and emphasis on lay activity were simply better-organized versions of characteristics that had been apparent in British revivals for twenty years or more. Moody benefited from the increasing tolerance shown to American revivalists. When members of the aristocracy regularly turned up at Moody's evening meetings in the London Royal Opera House, when he was seen as the healer of a generation's bitterness in Scottish churches, and when Lord Shaftesbury regarded him as a means of elevating the enfranchised masses, it was clear that an enormous revolution had taken place in the status of American revivalists since the days when Irish magistrates had sought to clap Lorenzo Dow into prison.

Notes

Preface

1. Henry F. May, "The Recovery of American Religious History," *American Historical Review* 70 (1964):79-92.
2. Perry Miller, *The Life of the Mind in America: From the Revolution to the Civil War* (New York, 1965), pp. 6-7.
3. John Kent's helpful "American Revivalism and England in the Nineteenth Century," *Past and Present Conference Papers, 1966,* is the only serious, if brief, attempt to deal with this important subject.
4. P. A. M. Taylor, *Expectations Westward: The Mormons and the Emigration of Their British Converts in the Nineteenth Century* (London, 1965); Louis Billington, "The Millerite Adventists in Great Britain, 1840-50," *Journal of American Studies* 1 (1967):191-212; idem, "The Churches of Christ in Britain: A Study in Nineteenth-Century Sectarianism," *Journal of Religious History* 8 (1974):21-48.

Chapter 1

1. *Christian Advocate and Journal* (hereafter cited as *Christian Advocate*), 23 September 1826.
2. F. Wayland, *The Moral Dignity of the Missionary Enterprise*, 6th ed. (Edinburgh, 1826), p. 29.
3. John Keep, *Narrative of the origin and progress of the Congregational Church in Homer, Cortland County, N.Y. . . .* (New York, 1833), p. 13.
4. Charles G. Finney, *Lectures on Revivals of Religion*, ed. William G. McLoughlin (Cambridge, Mass., 1960), pp. viii-ix.
5. See particularly William G. McLoughlin, *Modern Revivalism: Charles Grandison Finney to Billy Graham* (New York, 1959); Bernard W. Weisberger, *They Gathered at the River: The Story of the Great Revivalists and Their Impact upon Religion in America* (Boston, 1958); Timothy L. Smith, *Revivalism and Social Reform in Mid-Nineteenth-Century America* (New York, 1957); Whitney R. Cross, *The Burned-over District: The Social and Intellectual History of Enthusiastic Religion in Western New York, 1800-1850* (Ithaca, N.Y., 1950).

6. Frank Thistlethwaite, *America and the Atlantic Community: Anglo-American Aspects, 1790-1850* (New York, 1963); C. I. Foster, *An Errand of Mercy: The Evangelical United Front, 1790-1837* (Chapel Hill, 1960); Brian Harrison, *Drink and the Victorians: The Temperance Question in England, 1815-1872* (London, 1971), pp. 101-4; Betty Fladeland, *Men and Brothers: Anglo-American Antislavery Cooperation* (Urbana, Ill., 1972).

7. Weisberger, *They Gathered at the River*, pp. 20-50; John P. Boles, *The Great Revival, 1787-1805* (Lexington, Ky., 1972), passim; Charles A. Johnson, *The Frontier Camp Meeting* (Dallas, 1955), pp. 33-41; Catharine C. Cleveland, *The Great Revival in the West, 1797-1805* (Chicago, 1916), pp. 87-125.

8. S. B. Halliday and D. S. Gregory, *The Church in America and Its Baptisms of Fire . . .* (New York, 1896), pp. 396-401; Joshua Bradley, *Accounts of Religious Revivals in many parts of the United States from 1815 to 1818 . . .* (Albany, N.Y., 1819), passim.

9. R. Smith, *Recollections of Nettleton, and the Great Revival of 1820* (Albany, N.Y., 1848), p. 24.

10. Bennet Tyler, *Memoir of the Life and Character of Rev. Asahel Nettleton, D.D.,* 5th ed. (Boston, 1855), pp. 13-24, 30, 99-100; Francis Wayland and H. L. Wayland, *A Memoir of the Life and Labors of Francis Wayland, D.D., LL.D.,* 2 vols. (New York, 1867), 1:108-11.

11. Smith, *Recollections*, pp. 15-16, 28-40; Tyler, *Nettleton*, pp. 45-54.

12. For Finney (1792-1875), see especially McLoughlin, *Modern Revivalism*, pp. 11-121 and passim; Charles G. Finney, *Memoirs* (New York, 1876); Cross, *Burned-over District*, pp. 151-69.

13. Finney, *Memoirs*, pp. 234-324; Charles C. Cole, "The New Lebanon Convention," *New York History* 31 (October 1950):385-97.

14. Joel Parker to Finney, 4 April 1831, F-OC. For Lorenzo Dow, the eccentric Methodist itinerant, see chapter 4.

15. The *Lectures* treated revivalism as a science. Revivals could be produced by employing prescribed means in obedience to discoverable divine laws, as the titles of certain lectures suggest: "How to Promote a Revival," "Means to Be Used with Sinners," "Measures to Promote Revivals." Finney, *Lectures on Revivals*, pp. vii-lii.

16. Sidney E. Mead, *Nathaniel William Taylor, 1786-1858: A Connecticut Liberal* (Chicago, 1942).

17. Samuel Merwin et al. to Finney, 12 April 1831; Taylor to Finney, 11 June 1832, F-OC.

18. George M. Marsden, *The Evangelical Mind and the New School Presbyterian Experience* (New Haven, 1970), pp. 31-103, 250-51.

19. For a good example, see Keep, *Congregational Church in Homer*.

20. Gamaliel S. Olds, *Review of a Narrative, by Rev. John Keep* (Syracuse, 1833), p. 3; *Biblical Repertory and Theological Review* 7 (1835):660; "An Eye Witness," *A Portrait of what are called "New Measures" . . .* (Troy, N.Y., 1835); John W. Nevin, *The Anxious Bench*, 2d ed. (Chambersburg, Pa., 1844); Edward D. Griffin, *A Letter to the Rev. Ansel D. Eddy, . . . on . . . the late revivals of religion in the Presbytery of Geneva* (Williamstown, Mass., 1832), pp. 5-7.

21. Perry Miller, *The New England Mind: The Seventeenth Century* (New York, 1939), pp. 280-99.

22. "Philalethes," *The Importance of Revivals as exhibited in the late Convention at New Lebanon . . .* (Ithaca, N.Y., 1827). p. 5.

23. F. Denison, ed., *The Evangelist: or Life and Labors of Rev. Jabez S. Swan . . .* (Waterford, Conn., 1873), pp. 28-29, 69-107, 181; Jacob Knapp, *Autobiography* (New York, 1868), pp. 28, 36-44, 72-73, 122-23; Wayland and Wayland, *Francis Wayland*, 1:106-11, 182-83, 289-91, 338-39.

24. McLoughlin in *Modern Revivalism* and Weisberger in *They Gathered at the River* both recognize Finney's debts to frontier revivalism but overestimate his agency in adapting it to urban and eastern environments and in creating a "modern revivalism."

25. *Biblical Repertory and Theological Review* 7 (1835):610.

26. Charles C. Goss, *Statistical History of the First Century of American Methodism . . .* (New York, 1866), p. 110.

27. George Peck, *The Life and Times of George Peck, D.D.* (New York, 1874), pp. 22-23; Gilbert Haven and Russell Thomas, *Father Taylor, The Sailor Preacher . . .* (Boston, 1872), pp. 73-75; Tobias Spicer, *Autobiography of Rev. Tobias Spicer . . .* Boston, 1851), p. 33.

28. William B. Sprague, *Annals of the American Pulpit . . .* , vol. 7, *The Methodists* (New York, 1860), p. 272; D. W. Clark, *Life and Times of Rev. Elijah Hedding, D.D. . . .* (New York, 1855), p. 129.

29. A. G. Meacham, *A Compendious History of the Rise and Progress of the Methodist Church . . .* (Hallowell, Upper Canada, 1832), pp. 424-25; George Coles, *My First Seven Years in America*, ed. D. P. Kidder (New York, 1852), p. 70.

30. Samuel A. Seaman, *Annals of New York Methodism . . .* (New York, 1892), p. 496; Nathan Bangs, *A History of the Methodist Episcopal Church*, 4 vols. (New York, 1840-41), 1:47-71, 3:303-4; *Methodist Quarterly Review* 37 (1877):494-95. Methodist membership rapidly caught up with that of urban Presbyterians, even in cities where the latter were strong. In 1831 Methodist totals in New York City and Philadelphia stood at 5,021 and 5,229 respectively; the three presbyteries of New York embraced over 7,300 communicants, the presbytery of Philadelphia over 7,100. In both cities the gap was narrower than these figures suggest, since Presbyterian returns included churches outside the two cities' boundaries while the Methodists' did not. *American Quarterly Register* 3 (1831):209, 212; *Minutes of the Annual Conferences of the Methodist Episcopal Church* [hereafter cited as *Minutes of MEC*] (1831).

31. Seaman, *Annals of N.Y. Methodism*, p. 175; *Wesleyan-Methodist Magazine* 25 (1802): 422-23; 33 (1810):84-85; W. McDonald, *History of Methodism in Providence, Rhode Island . . .* (Boston, 1868), pp. 58-63. See also N. Bangs, *History*, passim, and the pages of the New York *Methodist Magazine*, 1-8 (1818-25).

32. Abel Stevens, *Life and Times of Nathan Bangs, D.D.* (New York, 1863), p. 183.

33. Seaman, *Annals of N.Y. Methodism*, pp. 170-71; N. Bangs, *History*, 3:375.

34. *Wesleyan-Methodist Magazine* 26(1803):373; *Christian Advocate*, 14 March 1828.

35. *Methodist Magazine* 3(1820):160.

36. According to N. Bangs, *History*, 4:52-53, the New England Methodist John Lord introduced four days' meetings in September 1827, and the Calvinists soon followed his example.

37. *Christian Advocate*, 26 March 1830, 31 August 1842; Halliday and Gregory,

Church in America, pp. 596-97; James Mudge, *History of the New England Conference of the Methodist Episcopal Church, 1796-1810* (Boston, 1910), pp. 385-86.

38. *Christian Advocate,* 25 September 1829.

39. Goss, *Statistical History,* p. 110; Herman C. Weber, *Presbyterian Statistics through One Hundred Years, 1826-1926* (Philadelphia, 1927), p. 44.

40. *Christian Advocate,* 25 June 1830. Methodists themselves were scarcely innocent. See John Bangs, *Autobiography of Rev. John Bangs of the New-York Annual Conference . . .* (New York, 1846), p. 121.

41. Spicer, *Autobiography,* pp. 101-2.

42. *Christian Advocate,* 12 October 1827.

43. Margaret Bayard Smith to Jane Kirkpatrick, 12 October 1822, in Gaillard Hunt, ed., *The First Forty Years of Washington Society: Portrayed by the Family Letters of Mrs. Samuel Harrison Smith (Margaret Bayard) . . .* (New York, 1906), p. 159.

44. Zephaniah Platt to Finney, 10 March 1828, in McLoughlin, *Modern Revivalism,* p. 51.

45. Helen Platt to Lydia Finney, 23 April 1827, F-OC.

46. Finney, *Memoirs,* pp. 4-5, 90-91, 136-37, 288-89; *Christian Advocate,* 25 January, 21 March 1828.

47. For this claim, see Gilbert H. Barnes, *The Antislavery Impulse* (New York, 1933), p. 7.

48. Finney, *Memoirs,* p. 307.

49. *Christian Advocate,* 24 February 1853; William C. Conant, *Narratives of Remarkable Conversions and Revival Incidents . . .* (New York, 1858), pp. 424-25; *Oberlin Evangelist,* 29 April 1857. Smith, *Revivalism and Social Reform,* pp. 45-62, outlines by denomination the acceptance of new-measure revivalism between 1842 and 1857.

50. *Monthly Miscellany of Religion and Letters* 3 (1840):236; Robert Baird, *Religion in America . . .* (New York, 1844), pp. 214-16; Walter C. Palmer, *Life and Letters of Leonidas L. Hamline, D.D. . . .* (New York, 1866), p. 349; *New York Observer,* 13 March 1856; James F. Findlay, *Dwight L. Moody: American Evangelist, 1837-1899* (Chicago, 1969), pp. 262-63; Wayland and Wayland, *Francis Wayland,* 2:177-78.

51. I use "urban" in this discussion to refer in the main to places that had a population of 10,000 or more. Historians have given relatively little attention to the place of revivalism in the religious life of the cities in the early and middle decades of the nineteenth century. This is largely the result of the powerful influence of the work of William Warren Sweet, which applies Frederick Jackson Turner's frontier thesis to the history of religion in the national period. See especially Sweet's *Religion on the American Frontier, 1783-1840,* 4 vols. (New York and Chicago, 1931-46), and *Revivalism in America: Its Origin, Growth and Influence* (New York, 1944), which generally ignores urban and eastern revivalism in this period. Cf. Smith, *Revivalism and Social Reform,* p. 15, which recognizes that during the 25 years before the Civil War "revival fervor emerged from the frontier to dominate the urban religious scene."

52. Edwin Scott Gaustad, *The Great Awakening in New England* (New York, 1957), pp. 25-28; Conant, *Remarkable Conversions,* pp. 36-38; Bradley, *Religious Revivals,* passim.

53. *Christian Advocate*, 22 April 1831.

54. James Patterson to Finney, 14 December 1827, F-OC. In 1800 there were only 6 cities in the whole country with a population of over 10,000. The figure reached 23 by 1830, and—after the great urban leap of the 1840s—62 by 1850; in 1860 there were 92. U.S. Bureau of the Census, *Historical Statistics of the United States, Colonial Times to 1957* (Washington, D.C., 1960), p. 14.

55. Henry C. Fish, *Primitive Piety Revived, or The Aggressive Power of the Christian Church* (Boston, 1855), p. 240.

56. "The Annual Report of the Methodist Episcopal Church Sunday School Union" for 1857 in Addie Grace Wardle, *History of the Sunday School Movement in the Methodist Episcopal Church* (New York, 1918), p. 108; *Christian Advocate*, 15 June 1827; Richard Wheatley, *The Life and Letters of Mrs. Phoebe Palmer* (New York, 1876), p. 169; McLoughlin, *Modern Revivalism*, pp. 149-52.

57. Samuel Gregg, *The History of Methodism within the bounds of the Erie Annual Conference of the Methodist Episcopal Church* (New York, 1873), pp. 40-41, 47-49.

58. Seaman, *Annals of N.Y. Methodism*, pp. 327, 402-3; *Christian Advocate*, 16 December 1826.

59. David O. Mears, *Life of Edward Norris Kirk, D.D.* (Boston, 1877), pp. 90-91; *Revivalist* (1838), pp. 246-47.

60. Carroll S. Rosenberg, *Religion and the Rise of the American City: The New York City Mission Movement, 1812-1870* (Ithaca, N.Y., 1971), p. 187, shows how in New York this emphasis came to change as a result of the depression of 1837-43 and of continued city growth; the evangelism of city missions came to be overshadowed by a "more melioristic, pragmatic mood."

61. Halliday and Gregory, *Church in America*, pp. 205-10.

62. Conant, *Remarkable Conversions*, pp. 380-82.

63. Albert Barnes, "Revivals of Religion in Cities and Large Towns," *American National Preacher* 15 (1841):69.

64. McLoughlin, *Modern Revivalism*, p. 79.

65. Baker, doctrinally an Old-School man, worked as an itinerant evangelist in the south and west; Barnes's Methodist family background and Princeton training fused into a New-School Presbyterianism and urgent evangelism; Beecher, son of Lyman Beecher, held Presbyterian and Congregational pastorates in Indianapolis and then Brooklyn, in both of which he stimulated evangelical activity. See the entries in Allen Johnson and Dumas Malone, eds., *Dictionary of American Biography* (New York, 1928-36), hereafter cited as *DAB*.

66. Knapp, *Autobiography*, p. 107; Stephen Parks, *Troy Conference Miscellany* . . . (Albany, N.Y., 1854), pp. 91-92.

67. B. F. Tefft, *Methodism Successful, and the internal causes of its success* (New York, 1860), pp. 154-55, 195-96; Sprague, *Annals of the Pulpit*, 7: 837-41; W. H. Norris to G. Peck, 3 April 1848; L. A. Eddy to G. Peck, 4 March 1847, P-SU; Maffitt to ?, 9 September 1841, SNEC-BU; C. C. North to J. B. Wakeley, 30 August 1872; Maffitt to G. Coles, n.d., MC-DU; Heman Bangs, *The Autobiography and Journal of Rev. Heman Bangs* . . . (New York, 1872), pp. 233-34; Grover C. Loud, *Evangelized America* (New York, 1928), pp. 210-13.

68. Knapp, *Autobiography*, pp. 122, 135, 137.

69. Mears, *Kirk*, pp. 165, 334.

70. George C. Baker, *An Introduction to the History of Early New England Methodism, 1789-1839* (Durham, N.C., 1941), p. 20; *Christian Advocate*, 3 June 1858.

71. Knapp, *Autobiography*, p. 130.

72. Barnes, "Revivals of Religion," p. 2; *New York Evangelist*, 26 January 1833.

73. Orville Dewey, *Letters of an English Traveller to his Friend in England, on the "Revivals of Religion" in America* (Boston, 1828), p. 117. Beecher and Nettleton feared that the western revivalists were stimulating a tide of uncontrollable democracy. McLoughlin, *Modern Revivalism*, pp. 35-36.

74. Barnes, "Revivals of Religion," p. 38.

75. Cross, *Burned-over District*, p. 155; Finney, *Lectures on Revivals*, p. 276.

76. Stephen Allen and W. H. Pilsbury, *History of Methodism in Maine, 1793-1886* (Augusta, Me., 1887), pp. 241-42.

77. *Christian Advocate*, 27 February 1829, 25 June 1830; Conant, *Remarkable Conversions*, pp. 359-60; Barnes, "Revivals of Religion," pp. 53-54.

78. Barnes, "Revivals of Religion," pp. 51-52; Rosenberg, *New York City Mission Movement*, pp. 32-52, 240-42.

79. Denison, *Swan*, pp. 203-4; *Wesleyan-Methodist Magazine* 36 (1813): 157-58; A. Kent to A. Stevens, 1 March 1847, MC-DU.

80. Tyler, *Nettleton*, pp. 74-76; *Christian Advocate*, 14 May 1830.

81. Calvin Colton, *History and Character of American Revivals of Religion*, 2d ed. (London, 1832), pp. 61-62.

82. Heman Humphrey, *Revival Sketches and Manual* (New York, 1859), pp. 242-58.

83. Barnes, "Revivals of Religion," pp. 14-15, 66-67.

84. Conant, *Remarkable Conversions*, p. 364; Seaman, *Annals of N.Y. Methodism*, p. 310.

85. Shepherd Knapp, *A History of the Brick Presbyterian Church in the City of New York* (New York, 1909), pp. 253-54.

86. *Christian Advocate*, 10 March, 31 March, 2 June 1827, 16 September 1840, 8 April 1858; Barnes, "Revivals of Religion," p. 31.

87. Barnes, "Revivals of Religion," p. 58.

88. Finney, *Memoirs*, pp. 293-98, 437; Cross, *Burned-over District*, pp. 6, 56, 70-73.

89. Mudge, *New England Conference*, pp. 220-21; Baird, *Religion in America*, p. 182; Thomas C. Cochran and William Miller, *The Age of Enterprise: A Social History of Industrial America*, rev. ed. (New York, 1961), p. 20.

90. Conant, *Remarkable Conversions*, pp. 380, 411.

91. A. Green to W. Kidd, 11 November 1799; F. Garrettson to R. Reece, 8 December 1825, MC-DU.

92. *Wesleyan-Methodist Magazine* 37 (1814):315-17; Marsden to W. McKendree, 20 May 1812, 4 May 1814; Marsden to the New York Conference, 1 June 1812, 8 May 1814, MC-DU.

93. Coles, *First Seven Years*, pp. 229-30; Coles to G. Cubitt, 21 February 1845, MC-DU; T. B. Sargent to G. Peck, 2 April 1855, P-SU.

94. George G. Smith, *The History of Methodism in Georgia and Florida, from 1785 to 1865* (Macon, Ga., 1877), p. 288.

95. See, for example, T. Rankin to W. Watters, 28 July 1796, B-DC; H. M. Johnson to G. Peck, 23 June 1841, P-SU; J. B. Wakeley to W. M. Thornton, 10 May 1864, MC-DU.

96. *Minutes of the New Jersey Annual Conference of the Methodist Episcopal Church* (1905), pp. 131-33; Smith, *Methodism in Georgia*, p. 419.

97. Statistics are available from 1815. The last year in which British North America attracted more British immigrants than did the United States was 1835. *Thirty-third General Report of the Emigration Commissioners*, Parliamentary papers, 1873, vol. 18.

98. George Coles, *My Youthful Days . . .* , ed. D. P. Kidder (New York, 1852), pp. 199-211; *Minutes of MEC* (1884), p. 94; (1893), p. 122.

99. *Minutes of MEC* (1842), pp. 355-56; (1852), pp. 42-43; 1872, p. 79; (1876), p. 73; (1879), p. 79: (1880), pp. 36-37; (1888), p. 89; (1889), p. 375; (1892), p. 412; (1899), pp. 454-55; (1900), p. 449; *Minutes of the Annual Conferences of the Methodist Episcopal Church, South* [hereafter cited as *Minutes of MECS*] (1887), pp. 86-88; (1894), pp. 15-17; Coles, *Youthful Days*, p. 247.

100. *Minutes of MEC* (1876), p. 74; (1877), pp. 48-49; (1894), p. 116.

101. Ibid. (1841), pp. 248-49; (1859), pp. 150-51; (1865), p. 235; (1884), p. 324; *Minutes of MECS* (1872), p. 717; (1895), pp. 55-57; W. Copeland to J. Emory, 17 August 1820, MC-DU; Journal of the New York Conference (MEC), NYC-NYPL.

102. *Minutes of MEC* (1842), pp. 355-56; (1846), pp. 7-8; (1848), p. 245; (1850), p. 454; (1859), p. 297; (1869), pp. 33-34; (1878), p. 22; (1893), p. 103; J. C. Tackaberry Journal, 1:3-15, MC-DU.

103. *Minutes of MEC* (1850), p. 444; (1873), p. 90; (1892), pp. 112-13; (1895), pp. 115-16; (1896), p. 433.

104. Ibid. (1862), pp. 5-6; (1870), p. 235; (1871), p. 57; (1872), p. 113; (1875), p. 128; (1879), pp. 78-79; (1880), p. 80; (1881), p. 325; (1882), pp. 73, 81-82; (1884), pp. 93-94; (1892), pp. 411-12; (1893), pp. 102-3; (1896), p. 433; (1899), p. 440.

105. Ibid. (1849), p. 406; (1855), pp. 539-40; (1864), p. 90; (1869), p. 180; (1875), p. 114; (1876), p. 74; (1877), p. 42; (1878), pp. 43-44; (1879), pp. 58-59; (1884), pp. 93-94; (1888), p. 344; (1889), p. 375; (1891), p. 392; (1892), p. 406; (1893), pp. 102-4; (1896), p. 433; (1900), p. 438; *Minutes of MECS* (1856-57), p. 674; (1874), p. 80.

106. James Dixon, *Methodism in America . . .* (London, 1849), p. 24; *Methodist Quarterly Review* 27 (1867: 267-71; Peck, *George Peck*, p. 214; T. Coke to F. Asbury, 10 August 1787; D. P. Kidder to E. Osborn, 5 and 22 March 1862; S. Dando to G. Coles, 23 October 1824; J. Hollingsworth to G. Coles, 20 March 1833; J. McLintock to S. A. Purdy, 5 July 1832, MC-DU.

107. *Minutes of MEC* (1798), pp. 79-80; (1810), p. 181; (1862), pp. 5-6; (1870), pp. 174, 226; (1884), p. 325; (1888), p. 87; *Minutes of MECS* (1870), p. 450.

108. John Holland, *Memoirs of the Life and Ministry of the Rev. John Summerfield, A.M.*, 6th ed. (New York, 1845), passim; *Methodist Quarterly Review* 37 (1877):484-85.

109. Finney to Weld, 21 July 1836, in Gilbert H. Barnes and Dwight L. Dumond, eds., *Letters of Theodore Dwight Weld, Angelina Grimké Weld and Sarah Grimke, 1822-1844*, 2 vols. (New York, 1944), 1:318-20. Ronald G. Walters, *The Antislavery Appeal: American Abolitionism after 1830* (Baltimore, 1976), pp. 37-53, offers a thoughtful examination of the relationship between evangelicalism and reform.

110. Frederick Douglass, *Narrative of the Life of Frederick Douglass, An American Slave . . .* , ed. Benjamin Quarles (Cambridge, Mass., 1960), pp. 155-60.

111. R. Emory to J. McLintock, 22 August 1846; R. Pilter to G. Coles, 8 May 1845; G. Scott to T. E. Bond, 3 February 1845: J. Stanley to G. Coles, 7 February 1842, MC-DU; Dixon, *Methodism in America*, p. 60.

112. *Minutes of MEC* (1862), pp. 73-74; (1876), p. 74; (1877), p. 104; (1878), p. 60; (1879), pp. 99-100; (1887), p. 91; (1888), pp. 84-85; Douglass, *Life*, pp. 84-85; Autobiographical Statement of D. Wise, SNEC-BU.

113. R. Pilter to G. Coles, 19 February 1844, MC-DU. The British Conference refused to enter into official relations with the MECS.

114. Of the 493 ministers whose deaths are recorded in *Minutes of MECS* between 1845 and 1865, only 12 (2.4%) were clearly British-born. The comparable figure for the MEC was 77 (7.4%) out of 1,039.

115. *Minutes of MEC* (1883), p. 91.

116. J. Stanley to G. Coles, 7 February 1842, MC-DU.

117. In addition to *Minutes of MEC* and *Minutes of MECS*, I have relied on the following section in Weber, *Presbyterian Statistics*, and Samuel W. Dike, "A Study of New England Revivals," *American Journal of Sociology* 15 (1909):361-78.

118. Seaman, *Annals of N.Y. Methodism*, p. 273; Wakeley to G. Peck, 22 January 1846, P-SU.

119. Figures in parentheses indicate the year of greatest growth/decline.

120. T. Morrell to N. Reed, 16 May 1792, MC-DU; N. Bangs, *History*, 1:344-56; Smith, *Methodism in Georgia*, p. 69.

121. N. Bangs, *History*, 2:21-24, 292. This paragraph and the following three draw particularly on ibid., vols. 2, 3, and 4; Meacham, *Compendious History*; Smith, *Methodism in Georgia*; Clark, *Hedding*; D. Kilburn's record of itinerancy, MC-DU.

122. N. Bangs, *History*, 2:361.

123. Clark, *Hedding*, p. 423.

124. Ibid., p. 487.

125. Cochran and Miller, *Age of Enterprise*, p. 27; George Brown, *Recollections of Itinerant Life . . . ,* 3d ed. (Cincinnati, 1866), pp. 269-70; John D. Lang, *Religion and Education in America . . .* (London, 1840), p. 320.

126. When the millennium had not arrived, the new date of 22 October 1844 was set. This proved to be the movement's final climax. For Millerism, see Cross, *Burned-over District*, pp. 287-321.

127. McLoughlin, *Modern Revivalism*, pp. 9-10.

128. Old-School Presbyterians, benefiting perhaps from their more cautious approach during the previous wave of revivals, continued to grow modestly in the mid-1840s. Weber, *Presbyterian Statistics*, p. 44.

129. Parks, *Troy Conference*, pp. 65-66.

130. *Christian Advocate*, 5 January 1848.

131. H. Bangs, *Autobiography*, p. 275.

132. Emory S. Bucke et al., eds., *The History of American Methodism*, 3 vols. (Nashville, 1964), 2:1-192; T. J. Thompson to T. E. Bond, 30 October 1846; O. P. Twiford to T. E. Bond, 24 November 1846; E. J. Poulson to T. E. Bond, 24 November 1846, B-DC.

133. *Oberlin Evangelist*, 16 January 1861; *Methodist Quarterly Review* 23 (1863): 452-53.

134. Cross, *Burned-over District*, pp. 268-69; Gilbert C. Fite and Jim E. Reese, *An*

Economic History of the United States, 2d ed. (Boston, 1965), p. 134; Douglas C. North, *The Economic Growth of the United States, 1790-1860* (Englewood Cliffs, N.J., 1961), p. 53.

135. Smith, *Methodism in Georgia*, p. 339; George Peck, *National Evils and Their Remedy . . .* (New York, 1841), pp. 24-25.

136. Peck, *George Peck*, pp. 161-62.

137. N. Bangs, *History*, 2:354-55; 3:29-32, 76, 95-99, 175-78, 431-34.

138. See, for example, *Christian Advocate*, 26 July 1843.

Chapter 2

1. *Congregational Magazine* 10 (1827):392-94.

2. See, for example, John Rippon's *Baptist Annual Register*, 4 vols. (1790-1802), and the early volumes of the *Baptist Magazine*, *Congregational Magazine*, and *Evangelical Magazine*.

3. *Congregational Magazine* 18 (1835):604.

4. William W. Patton, *A Filial Tribute to the Memory of Rev. William Patton, D.D.* (Washington, D.C., 1880), pp. 12-13, 17-18; R. W. Dale, ed., *The Life and Letters of John Angell James . . .* , 2d ed. (London, 1861), pp. 219-20, 242, 246; William B. Sprague, *Letters from Europe, in 1828 . . .* (New York, 1828), pp. 68-135; William Orme, *Discourses on the Blasphemy against the Holy Spirit . . .* (London, 1828), pp. 274-75.

5. W. R. Ward, *Religion and Society in England, 1790-1850* (London, 1972), pp. 1-104; Alan D. Gilbert, "The Growth and Decline of Nonconformity in England and Wales . . . before 1850 . . ." (D.Phil. thesis, Oxford University, 1973), pp. 150-315.

6. William T. Owen, "The Life and Thought of Dr. Edward Williams, with special reference to his influence on Welsh and English Nonconformity" (Ph.D. thesis, University of London, 1960), pp. 122-241; Olin. C. Robison, "Particular Baptists in England, 1760-1820" (D. Phil. thesis, Oxford University, 1963), passim; J. W. Morris, *Memoirs of the Life and Writings of the Rev. Andrew Fuller* (London, 1815), pp. 262-72.

7. *Congregational Magazine* 13 (1830):225-31; Henry F. Burder, *Memoir of the Rev. George Burder* (London, 1833), pp. 220-23; *Congregational Year Book* (1849), p. 132; *Baptist Magazine* 33 (1841):273-74. Between 1790 and 1838 Congregational membership increased from 26,000 to 127,000, and Baptist from 20,000 to 100,000. Gilbert, "Growth and Decline," p. 45.

8. *Congregational Magazine* 11 (1828):500.

9. Ibid., n.s. 5 (1841):569-75; 15 (1831):201-2. In contrast, additions of 50 to 100 over a period of months were common in Nettleton's Congregational revivals in New England.

10. John Sibree and M. Caston, *Independency in Warwickshire* (London, 1855), passim.

11. Henry Allon, *Memoir of the Rev. James Sherman . . .* , 2d ed. (London, 1863), pp. 99-100, 142-49, 172-87; James to W. Patton, 2 February 1828, in Dale, *James*, p. 244.

12. See, for example, Henry F. Burder, *Pastoral Discourses on Revivals in Religion . . .* (London, 1829); Joseph Fletcher, *On the Prosperity of Christian Churches,*

and the Revival of Religion . . . (London, 1829); John Angell James, *A Pastoral Letter on the Subject of Revivals in Religion* . . . (London, 1829); John Howard Hinton, *The Means of a Religious Revival* . . . (London, 1829).

13. Orme, *Discourses*, pp. 141, 258-59, 265; *Congregational Magazine* 11 (1828): 614: *Evangelical Magazine*, n.s. 6 (1828):529.

14. *Baptist Magazine* 21 (1829):80; *Baptist Annual Register*, 1(1790-93):60.

15. John H. Hinton, *The Work of the Holy Spirit in Conversion* . . . (London, 1830), pp. xviii, xxii-xxiv, 81, and passim.

16. *Baptist Magazine* 22 (1830):279-84, 318-23; 23(1831):3-8.

17. Ibid., 21(1829):190-92.

18. *Evangelical Magazine*, n.s. 7 (1829), 242-46.

19. *Congressional Magazine* 13 (1830):127.

20. Dale, *James*, pp. 245, 262-64; Ernest R. Sandeen, *The Roots of Fundamentalism: British and American Millenarianism, 1800-1930* (Chicago, 1970), p. 20; J. F. C. Harrison, *Robert Owen and the Owenites in Britain and America* (London, 1969), pp. 96-97.

21. Thomas W. Jenkyn, *On the Union of the Holy Spirit and the Church in the Conversion of the World* (London, 1837), pp. 187-212; Burder, *Pastoral Discourses*, pp. 16, 28-30; Fletcher, *Revival of Religion*, pp. vi-ix.

22. James to W. Patton, 13 December 1828, 12 April 1829, in Dale, *James*, pp. 248, 261.

23. James to W. Patton, 30 November 1833, and James to W. Sprague, 10 July 1834, in Dale, *James*, pp. 268-69, 345; *New York Observer*, 19 April 1834. Americans engaged in tit-for-tat moralizing: they criticized the weak-kneed, compromising approach to temperance of British evangelicals and their reluctance to move from anti-spirits to total abstinence. See, for example, John Codman, *A Narrative of a Visit to England* (Boston, 1836), pp. 116-19.

24. In 1832 the Baptist minister Joseph Belcher began to edit the "unsectarian" *Revivalist*, a vehicle for American news that later called itself an "Anglo-American Magazine."

25. *Congregational Magazine* 14(1831):787-89; 16(1833):374-76; 18(1835):327, 380-85; 19(1836):461-72; *DAB*, s.v. "Cox, Samuel Hanson" and "McIlvaine, Charles Pettit."

26. Phelps to Finney, 29 August 1833, F-OC.

27. Wardlaw to Nettleton, 18 July 1831; Bolton to Nettleton, 4 August 1831; R. Wilson to Nettleton, 18 May 1832, N-HS; Journal of Lewis Tappan, 17 July 1843, T-LC; Allon, *Sherman*, pp. 277-78; Sherry P. May, "Asahel Nettleton: Nineteenth-Century American Revivalist," (Ph.D. thesis, Drew University, 1969), pp. 124-27.

28. James H. Hotchkin, *A History of the Purchase and Settlement of Western New York* . . . (New York, 1848), p. 132; Calvin Colton, *Thoughts on the Religious State of the Country (America)* . . . (London, 1837), pp. 2-3; idem, *American Revivals*, p. 106. Nettleton, worried about anxious seats, was not wholly pleased with the book. A. Dickinson to Nettleton, 26 March and 12 April 1832, N-HS.

29. Frances Trollope, *Domestic Manners of the Americans*, ed. Donald Smalley (New York, 1960), pp. 74-81 and passim.

30. *Congregational Magazine* 16 (1833):423-30.

31. *New York Observer*, 13 December 1834.

32. Andrew Reed and James Matheson, *A Narrative of the Visit to the American Churches by the Deputation from the Congregational Union of England and Wales*, 2 vols. (London, 1835), 1:374-86, 2:8-52, 74, 273, and passim.

33. Owen Chadwick, *The Victorian Church*, 2 vols. (London, 1966, 1970), 1:60-95; *New York Observer*, 15 June 1833.

34. Dale, *James*, p. 266; *Congregational Magazine* 17(1834):235-41; John Hinton, *The History and Topography of the United States*, 2 vols. (London, 1832), 2:370-80. William Hull, *Ecclesiastical Establishments not Inconsistent with Christianity . . .* (London, 1834), pp. 48-52.

35. Reed and Matheson, *Narrative*, 2:132-52; F. A. Cox and J. Hoby, *The Baptists in America . . .* (New York, 1836), pp. v, 28-29.

36. *Congregational Magazine*, n.s. 2(1838):393-402, 665-78; n.s. 3(1839):677; n.s. 7(1843):132-36; James Matheson, *Our Country; or, The Spiritual Destitution of England Considered . . .* (London, 1839), pp. 23-31, 58-59.

37. *Congregational Magazine*, n.s. 3(1839):677-86; H. U. Faulkner, *Chartism and the Churches* (New York, 1916), p. 17; Chadwick, *Victorian Church*, 1:333-36.

38. Rostow's social tension chart, based on fluctuations in the trade cycle and wheat prices, suggests that 1837-42 were years of high social tension. W. W. Rostow, *British Economy in the Nineteenth Century* (Oxford, 1948), p. 125.

39. Faulkner, *Chartism and the Churches*, pp. 96-101; Andrew Reed, *The Advancement of Religion the Claim of the Times* (London, 1843), pp. 207-8, 267-68, 288-300; John Harris, *Christian Patriotism; a sermon . . .* (London, 1842), p. 5 and passim.

40. Gilbert, "Growth and Decline," pp. 317-416.

41. Francis A. Cox, *Suggestions designed to promote the Revival and Extension of Religion . . .* , 5th ed. (London, 1836), passim; Richard S. Storrs, *Memoir of the Rev. Samuel Green* (Boston, 1836), p. 105; *Baptist Magazine* 18(1836):74; Codman, *Visit to England*, pp. 76-77, 174-75.

42. In the late 1820s the Congregationalist John Morison launched a periodical, *The Monthly Bible Class-Book, upon the American Plan. . . .*

43. Reed, *Advancement of Religion*, p. 254; Cox, *Suggestions*, p. 11.

44. *Revivalist* (1839), pp. 349-50; *Baptist Magazine* 28 (1836):414; J. Anthony to J. Blackburn, 6 December 1841, B-WL (5, L52/6/22).

45. Cox, *Suggestions*, p. 18; *Baptist Magazine* 29(1837):365-66; 30(1838):93. For the character of the Welsh example, see chapter 3; for Methodist stimulus to Calvinist enterprise, see Richard Carwardine, "Methodism, the New Dissent and American Revivalism," *Journal of the United Reformed Church History Society* 2 (Oct. 1978).

46. *Baptist Magazine* 27 (1835):28-29; 29(1837):365; 33(1841):322-23; "An Affectionate Appeal to the Churches of Christ," pp. 2-3, 24, in Thomas Pulsford, *Helps for Revival Churches and Christian Instruction Societies . . .* (London, 1846).

47. Dale, *James*, p. 355; A. Perrey, *Narrative of the Services Connected with One Weeks Revival Meetings in Boston . . .* (1834). Five years earlier Boston's Independent minister wrote that he had "just established Meetings amongst my friends combining the leading features of the American plan." T. Haynes to T. Wilson, 17 June 1829, W-WL (382/33).

48. *Revivalist* (1834), pp. 314-16; 1836, p. 105; *Baptist Magazine* 26(1834):433-35.

49. By April 1838 a 7th edition of 2,000 copies was needed. The British edition

carried prefaces by John Angell James, George Payne, and N. S. S. Beman and was annotated and revised by William Patton.

50. Keep to T. Keep, 5 August 1839, K-OC; Keep to G. Smith, 13 November 1839, S-SU.

51. *DAB*, s.v. "Beman, Nathan Sidney Smith" and "Patton, William"; *Congregational Magazine*, n.s. 3(1839):378-79; Weisberger, *They Gathered at the River*, pp. 113-16; James to W. Sprague, 22 July 1839, in Dale, *James*, pp. 355-56.

52. Mears, *Kirk*, pp. 44-45, 63-74, 95, 98.

53. Ibid., pp. 76-78, 153-55, 318, 334; Allon, *Sherman*, pp. 277-78; Keep to L. Keep, 5 November 1839, K-OC.

54. Dale, *James*, p. 355; Allon, *Sherman*, pp. 273-75, 458, and passim; *The Church Awakened: A Report of Special Meetings for the Revival of Religion held in Surrey Chapel, London . . .* (London, 1838).

55. Allon, *Sherman*, pp. 275-79, 331-32; *Evangelical Register* 10(1838):531; D. Tyssil Evans, *The Life and Ministry of the Rev. Caleb Morris* (London, 1902), pp. 213-17; Edward N. Kirk, *Sermons on Different Subjects . . .* , 5th ed. (New York, 1842), pp. 329-35; *Revivalist* (1839), pp. 26-30.

56. *Revivalist* (1839), pp. 26, 62-64, 137; *New York Observer*, 7 February 1835; Andrew Reed, *The Revival of Religion: a narrative of the State of Religion at Wycliffe Chapel during the year 1839*, 5th ed. (London, 1840), p. 18 and passim; E. F. Bodley, *Three Sermons on Revivals of Religion* (London, 1843); *Baptist Magazine* 33 (1841): 157-59.

57. Reed, *Revival of Religion*, p. 23.

58. *Baptist Magazine* 34(1842):82; 36(1844):59.

59. Sherman, unlike Reed, was ready to use the anxious meeting. Allon, *Sherman*, p. 276.

60. *Baptist Magazine* 32 (1840):697-98.

61. Ibid., 28(1836):295; 29(1837):121-22, 500-1; *Congregational Magazine*, n.s. 4(1840):727.

62. Charles Larom, *The Awakening: A memorial of a year of revived religion, in the First Baptist Church, Sheffield* (Sheffield, 1840), p. 7; Reed, *Revival of Religion*, pp. 8-15; *Revivalist* (1839), p. 318; *Baptist Magazine* 33(1841):538; *Congregational Magazine*, n.s. 4(1840):727; *Baptist Reporter*, 6th ser., 2 (1843):135.

63. *Baptist Magazine* 28 (1836):296; 33(1841):538; *Congregational Magazine*, n.s. 4(1840):728; Larom, *Awakening*, pp. 10, 37; Reed, *Revival of Religion*, p. 18.

64. *Congregational Magazine*, n.s. 4(1840):674-75; Gilbert, "Growth and Decline," pp. 126ff, 325ff, 444ff. The proportion of members to adherents, or "hearers"— which in the 1830s might be as few as 1 to 6—increased as the century proceeded. *Congregational Magazine* 18(1835):548-49.

65. *Baptist Magazine* 28 (1836):162; 32(1840):506, 697; Reed, *Revival of Religion*, pp. 28-43; *Baptist Reporter*, 6th ser., 2 (1843): 166, 350; Thomas W. Lacqueur, *Religion and Respectability: Sunday Schools and Working Class Culture, 1780-1850* (London, 1976), pp. 166-69.

66. Gilbert, "Growth and Decline," pp. 104, 106, 114-19; *The Centenary of the Association: The Circular Letter . . . of . . . the Northamptonshire Association* (Northampton, 1865), pp. 18-19.

67. *Evangelical Magazine*, n.s. 10(1832):iv, 399; *Baptist Magazine* 24 (1832):74,

119-20, 263, 446-47; Rostow, *British Economy*, p. 125; E. J. Hobsbawm and George Rudé, *Captain Swing* (London, 1973), pp. 248-51.

68. James to W. Patton, 14 March 1834, in Dale, *James*, pp. 338-39; Gilbert, "Growth and Decline," pp. 418ff.

69. Taylor, *Expectations Westward*, p. 145; Billington, "Millerite Adventists," pp. 191-212. For other strains of millennialism and their Anglo-American character, see Harrison, *Robert Owen*, pp. 92-139.

70. Harrison, *Robert Owen*, p. 102.

71. Gilbert, "Growth and Decline," p. 106; *Christian Witness* 3(1846):64; 4(1847): 486; *Baptist Magazine* 39(1847):65, 511; 40(1848):325-28, 389-92.

72. *Congregational Magazine*, n.s. 4(1840):888-89; Charles Larom, *Townhead: The History of the Baptist Church, assembling in Townhead Street, Sheffield* (Sheffield, 1870), pp. 43-44; Allon, *Sherman*, pp. 279-82, 331-32; *Baptist Record and Biblical Repository* 3 (1846): 72-73, 286-87; *Baptist Reporter*, n.s. 4(1847):210; *Christian Witness* 2(1845):151-60, 483-88.

73. *Baptist Magazine* 30(1838):149-54; 31(1839):263; 33(1841):621-29; James to J. Fletcher, 2 November 1840, in Dale, *James*, pp. 283-84.

74. *Congregational Magazine*, n.s. 6(1842):790-93; n.s. 7(1843):502-3, 857-63, 950-54; n.s. 8(1844):463-64; James to J. Fletcher, 2 November 1840; James to W. Patton, 27 June 1843, in Dale, *James*, pp. 418-21.

Chapter 3

1. C. G. Finney, *Darlithiau ar Adfywiadau crefyddol*, trans. E. Griffiths (Swansea, 1839); *Christian Witness* 7 (1850):315; Thomas Rees, *History of Protestant Nonconformity in Wales . . .* , 2d ed. (London, 1883), pp. 429-39; Rees to Finney, 19 April 1850, F-OC. The annual membership returns of the Wesleyans indicate a growth from 16,053 in 1838 to 19,287 in 1841; their numbers then dropped steadily until 1848. Gilbert, "Growth and Decline," p. 54.

2. *New York Observer*, 7 March 1835; David Williams, *A History of Modern Wales* (London, 1950), p. 166.

3. *Christian Witness* 1(1844):950; Kenneth O. Morgan, *Wales in British Politics, 1868-1922* (Cardiff, 1963), pp. 11-18.

4. T. Rees, *Nonconformity in Wales*, pp. 429-31; E. T. Davies, *Religion in the Industrial Revolution in South Wales* (Cardiff, 1965), pp. 55-57.

5. D. M. Evans, *Christmas Evans: a Memoir . . .* (London, 1863), pp. 133-46, 163-73, 211-17; James R. Jones, "Remarks on the Characteristics of Welsh Preaching," in William Rees, *Memoirs of the late Rev. W. Williams, of Wern* (London, 1846), pp. 157-86.

6. William Jones, *Prize Essay on the Character of the Welsh as a Nation in the Present Age* (London, 1841), p. 49; *Baptist Magazine* 29(1837):260; E. Morgan, *A Memoir of the Reverend John Elias* (London, 1844), pp. 167-68; Owen Jones, *Some of the Great Preachers of Wales* (London, 1885), pp. 250-51.

7. Davies, *Religion in the Industrial Revolution*, p. 75.

8. James Kendall, *Rambles of an Evangelist* (London, 1853), pp. 41-43; Evans, *Evans*, pp. 2-26, 203-09; *Artegall: or remarks on the . . . Inquiry into the State of Education in Wales* (London, 1848), p. 30.

9. Jones, *Prize Essay*, pp. 67-68; *New York Observer*, 7 March 1835; Jones, *Great Preachers*, 252-59.

10. *Christian Witness* 1(1844):951; W. Rees, *Williams*, pp. 118-19; Evans, *Evans*, pp. 133-43.

11. Alan Conway, ed., *The Welsh in America: Letters from the Immigrants* (Cardiff, 1961), pp. 3-13, 51-93.

12. B. W. Chidlaw, *The Story of My Life* (Philadelphia, 1890), pp. 14-89.

13. R. Tudur Jones, *Hanes Annibynwyr Cymru* (Swansea, 1966), p. 216; Chidlaw, *Story of My Life*, p. 75; Michael Jones et al. to Finney, 27 February 1840, F-OC.

14. Chidlaw, *Story of My Life*, pp. 94-100; *Baptist Magazine* 29(1837):260.

15. Chidlaw, *Story of My Life*, pp. 100-10; Jones, *Hanes*, pp. 200-1.

16. Jones, *Great Preachers*, p. 486; W. Rees, *Williams*, pp. 80-81.

17. David Young, *The Origin and History of Methodism in Wales and the Borders* (London, 1893), pp. 706-16.

18. Williams, *Modern Wales*, pp. 173-75, 251; Morgan, *Wales in British Politics*, p. 14; David Williams, *The Rebecca Riots: A Study in Agrarian Discontent* (Cardiff, 1955), pp. 122-36; idem, "Chartism in Wales," in *Chartist Studies*, ed. Asa Briggs (London, 1959); Davies, *Religion in the Industrial Revolution*, pp. 76-87; W. Rees, *Williams*, pp. 19-24.

19. Jones, *Great Preachers*, pp. 382-84; Jones, *Prize Essay*, pp. 40-41.

20. Owen, "Edward Williams," pp. 268-69; for Roberts (1767-1834), see *Dictionary of Welsh Biography*.

21. Michael Jones et al. to Finney, 27 February 1840, F-OC.

22. Griffiths to Finney, 13 July 1840, F-OC.

23. Ibid.; Evan Davies, *Revivals in Wales . . .* (London, 1859), p. 21.

24. *Y Tyst A'r Dydd*, 10 September 1875; T. Rees, *Nonconformity in Wales*, pp. 429-30.

25. Islay Burns, *The Pastor of Kilsyth; or, Memorials of the Life and Times of the Rev. W. H. Burns, D.D.* (London, 1860), pp. 98-102; W. Burns, "Kilsyth, 1839," in *Narratives of Revivals of Religion in Scotland, Ireland and Wales* (Glasgow, 1839), pp. 1-2; *Congregational Magazine* 13(1830):515-16.

26. *Revivalist* (1832), pp. 119-25, 141-42; John Campbell, *Memoirs of David Nasmith . . .* (London, 1844), p. 220; Nettleton to W. Sprague, 16 March 1833, N-HS.

27. Campbell, *Nasmith*, pp. 76-77, 207-74, 454-57.

28. *Christian News*, 19 August 1865.

29. R. H. Campbell, *Scotland since 1707: The Rise of an Industrial Society* (Oxford, 1965), pp. 108-10, 121-24, 152; Alexander Wilson, *The Chartist Movement in Scotland* (Manchester, 1970), pp. 1-19; Patrick Fairbairn, "Hindrances to a Revival of Religion," in W. M. H. [William Maxwell Hetherington?], ed., *Lectures on the Revival of Religion, by ministers of the Church of Scotland* (Glasgow, 1840), pp. 365-69; Burns, "Kilsyth, 1839," pp. 6-7; William Adamson, *The Life of the Rev. Fergus Ferguson* (London, 1900), pp. 29-32; Alexander Cumming, *Memorials of the Ministry of the Rev. Alexander Cumming . . .* (Edinburgh, 1881), pp. 171ff; *New York Observer*, 9 January 1841; Marjory Bonar, *Reminiscences of Andrew A. Bonar, D.D.* (London, 1895), pp. 83ff; William Adamson, *The Life of the Rev. James Morison, D.D.* (London, 1898), pp. 109-10, 251-52.

30. Thomas Brown, *Annals of the Disruption* . . . (Edinburgh, 1884), p. 450. As in England, some ministers who in more stable times might have been wary of revival efforts were disposed to see revivals as the best answer to economic disaster and heightened social tension. W. M. H., "Preface" to *Lectures on the Revival of Religion,* pp. xxi-xxii; Robert Buchanan, "Introductory Essay" to James Robe, *Narrative of the Revival of Religion at Kilsyth, Cambuslang, and other places in 1742* (Glasgow, 1840), pp. vii-xii.

31. *Christian News,* 2 September 1865.

32. J. R. Fleming, *A History of the Church in Scotland* (Edinburgh, 1927), p. 16. Finney can be placed in a line of descent from those on both sides of the Atlantic who sought to reconcile orthodox Calvinism with the rational ideals of the Enlightenment, particularly John Witherspoon and other American college presidents who put the teachings of the Scottish Common Sense school to this use.

33. *Christian News,* 5 August, 14 October 1865; Ninian Wight, *Memoir of the Rev. Henry Wight* (Edinburgh, 1862), pp. 20-95; Helen Kirk, *Memoirs of Rev. John Kirk, D.D.* (Edinburgh, 1888), pp. 138ff.

34. Burns, "Kilsyth, 1839," passim; *New York Observer,* 25 January 1840.

35. Adamson, *Morison,* pp. 36-244.

36. Kirk, *Kirk,* pp. 36-199; John Kirk, *The Way of Life Made Plain* . . (Glasgow, 1844), passim; Adamson, *Ferguson,* pp. 26-45.

37. Kirk, *Kirk,* pp. 13, 155, 172-74, 187, 275ff; Adamson, *Ferguson,* p. 28; Wight, *Wight,* p. 5; J. H. S. Burleigh, *A Church History of Scotland* (London, 1960), p. 316.

38. Adamson, *Morison,* p. 258; Fergus Ferguson, Jr., *A History of the Evangelical Union* . . . (Glasgow, 1876), passim; idem, "Morisonianism," in *The Cyclopaedia of Religious Denominations.* . . . *Written by members of the respective bodies* (Glasgow, 1853), pp. 248-52.

39. Ferguson, *Evangelical Union,* pp. 273-349; Dale, *James,* pp. 418-21; Adamson, *Ferguson,* pp. 53-59.

40. Burleigh, *Church History,* pp. 334-69; Burns, *Burns,* pp. 181-82; Cumming, *Cumming,* pp. 21-22; Brown, *Annals of the Disruption,* passim.

41. Adamson, *Morison,* pp. 236-41, 436-38; Ferguson, *Evangelical Union,* pp. 353-57; idem, "Morisonianism," p. 254.

42. Ferguson, "Morisonianism," p. 255; Adamson, *Morison,* pp. 232-65; Kirk, *Kirk,* pp. 214-319.

43. *New York Observer,* 25 January 1840; *Congregational Magazine,* n.s. 3(1839): 613-28; n.s. 8 (1844):504-7; Tim Jeal, *Livingstone* (London, 1973), pp. 12-13; Sherlock Bristol, *The Pioneer Preacher* (New York, 1898), pp. 320-25.

Chapter 4

1. Harold Begbie, *Life of William Booth, the Founder of the Salvation Army,* 2 vols. (London, 1920), 1:9, 61-62.

2. Robert Emory, *The Life of the Rev. John Emory, D.D.* . . . (New York, 1841), pp. 84-131; A. Clarke to Emory, 20 August 1820, MC-DU.

3. See, for example, *Wesleyan-Methodist Magazine,* 3d ser., 8 (1829):341-43; Wilbur Fisk, *Travels in Europe* . . . , 4th ed. (New York, 1838); John P. Durbin,

Observations in Europe . . . , 2 vols. (New York, 1844), 2:44ff; Horace M. Du Bose, *Life of Joshua Soule* (Nashville, 1911), pp. 196, 200-7; Spicer, *Autobiography*, pp. 142-91; J. Trippett to G. Peck, 23 November 1842, P-SU; W. W. Lake to G. Coles, 29 January 1842; J. C. Tackaberry, "Short Sketch of my voyage across the Atlantic," MC-DU.

4. J. Hawtrey to J. Emory, 4 August 1820; A. Clarke to J. Emory et al., 6 February 1832, MC-DU.

5. Fisk, *Travels*, pp. 581-82, 598-99.

6. *Christian Advocate*, 4 November 1826, 27 January, 10 March, 16 November 1827; *Wesleyan-Methodist Magazine*, 3d ser., 6(1827):400-4, 470-71, 699; 3d ser., 7(1828):626-27, 695-99, 844; 3d ser., 8(1829):338, 343, 611-12, 691-92, 3d ser., 9(1830):20.

7. Durbin, *Observations*, p. 106; Fisk, *Travels*, p. 602.

8. For Dow's life (1777-1834) and character, see in particular Lorenzo Dow, *The Dealings of God, Man, and the Devil; as exemplified in the Life, Experience and Travels of Lorenzo Dow . . .* (New York, 1854); Charles C. Sellers, *Lorenzo Dow: The Bearer of the Word* (New York, 1928); *Christian Advocate*, 3 January 1861.

9. Dow, *Dealings*, pp. 34-54; L. Dow to H. Dow, 2 April 1800, MC-BPL.

10. Dow, *Dealings*, pp. 114-38, 163-64.

11. Ward, *Religion and Society in England*, pp. 75-83.

12. Dow, *Dealings*, p. 123. Dow also worked amongst the "Second Division," the Kilhamites, or Methodist New Connexion, "democratic reformers" who had separated from the Wesleyans in the 1790s; he was critical of their fault-finding attitude to the parent connection. Ibid., p. 133.

13. Ibid., pp. 124, 137. In 1806 various of these disconnected societies united on a federal basis as Independent Methodists. W. J. Townsend, H. B. Workman, and G. Eayrs, *A New History of Methodism*, 2 vols. (London, 1909), 1:559.

14. *Wesleyan-Methodist Magazine* 25 (1802):217-18, 262-64, 422-26, 521-23; 26(1803):82-93, 125-35, 181-84, 268-85, 326-33; 27(1804):135-38, 233-34; 28(1805): 573-74; 29(1806):94-95, 188-91; 30(1807):255; *Primitive Methodist Magazine* 1(1819): 149-50; H. B. Kendall, *The Origin and History of the Primitive Methodist Church*, 2 vols. (London, 1909), 1:31-135; John T. Wilkinson, *Hugh Bourne, 1772-1852* (London, 1952), pp. 29-91.

15. Dow, *Dealings*, pp. 170-74; *Primitive Methodist Magazine* 12 (1830):25-26, 80-85, 122-30, 236-42, 359-60, 434-36; 14(1832):113-15; 21(1839):iii, 15, 31-34, 153-55, 272-73, 300-2, 317, 350-51. For Hugh Bourne's "mission" in 1844-45 to the weak Primitive Methodist societies in the northeastern United States and Canada, see Wilkinson, *Bourne*, pp. 161-68.

16. *Christian Advocate*, 29 June 1827, 7 January 1846, 5 March 1891; Joseph Hillman, *The History of Methodism in Troy, N.Y.* (Troy, N.Y., 1888), p. 75; James Caughey, *Earnest Christianity Illustrated . . . with a Brief Sketch of Mr. Caughey's Life, by John Unwin, Sheffield* (London, 1857), p. 7.

17. Benjamin Gregory, *Sidelights on the Conflicts of Methodism, 1827-1852* (London, 1898), pp. 368-69; Joseph Dyson, "James Caughey: A Great American Evangelist," in Newspaper Cuttings, Sheffield City Library; Daniel Wise's "Preface" to James Caughey, *Methodism in Earnest . . .* ed. Daniel Wise (Boston, 1850), pp. v-vi.

18. James Caughey, *Letters on Various Subjects*, 5 vols. (London, 1844-47), 1:6-9, 15; Wise's "Preface" to Caughey, *Methodism in Earnest*, p. viii.

19. Thomas F. Gordon, *Gazetteer of the State of New York* . . . (Philadelphia, 1836); *Minutes of MEC* (1832-40); John Carroll, *Case and his Cotemporaries . . . constituting a Biographical History of Methodism in Canada . . .* , 4 vols. (Toronto, 1867-74), 3:488-93; *The Pittsfield Methodist*, March 1890.

20. Caughey, *Letters*, 1:16-87, 94, 110; *A Brief Memoir of the Labours . . . of the Rev. James Caughey . . . by "A Wesleyan Methodist"* (London, 1847), pp. 5-7, 40, 68-69.

21. Caughey, *Letters*, 1:159, 186, 203; 2:67.

22. Ibid., 1: 229-39; 2:82, 92-100, 115, 146-50; John H. James, *The Work of God Acknowledged and Reviewed: . . . a sermon preached in Brunswick and Great Homer-Street Wesleyan Chapels, Liverpool, in reference to the recent revival of religion* (Liverpool, 1843).

23. Caughey, *Letters*, 5:164.

24. E. R. Wickham, *Church and People in an Industrial City* (London, 1957), pp. 20, 22, 46-84.

25. Fisk, *Travels*, p. 682.

26. James Dixon, *Memoir of the late Rev. William Edward Miller, Wesleyan Minister* (London, 1842), pp. 29-32; Thomas Harris, *A Memoir of the Rev. William Bramwell* (London, 1846), pp. 34-58; *Agency and Progress of Wesleyan-Methodism as exemplified by statistical details, and considered with reference to its facilities for Promoting and Sustaining a General Revival of Religion throughout the Country* (London, 1845), pp. 11-12 and table 2; *Wesleyan-Methodist Magazine*, 3d ser., 7(1828):145-48; 3d ser., 13(1834):378-81.

27. *Agency and Progress*, table 2.

28. *The Wesleyan Revivalist, by a Local Preacher in the Wesleyan Connexion* (Castle Donington, 1840), pp. 45-46; Wickham, *Church and People*, pp. 97-106; Caughey, *Letters*, 5: 128-30.

29. E. P. Thompson, *The Making of the English Working Class*, rev. ed. (London, 1968), pp. 427-30, 917-23; Robert F. Wearmouth, *Methodism and the Working-class Movements of England, 1800-1850* (London, 1937), pp. 133-34; Richard W. Dixon, *The Life of James Dixon, D.D.* . . . (London, 1874), pp. 206ff, 478.

30. Robert Currie, *Methodism Divided: A Study in the Sociology of Ecumenicalism* (London, 1968), p. 95.

31. Caughey to ?, 12 April 1847, MC-MCA; Caughey, *Letters*, 4:263-68.

32. Caughey, *Letters*, 1:211; Caughey to ?, 16 December 1845, MC-MCA; *Minutes of MEC* (1891), p. 104. Caughey died in his 81st year.

33. *Christian Advocate*, 7 January 1846; Begbie, *Booth*, 1:9-14, 175; Dyson, "James Caughey"; Kendall, *Rambles*, pp. 107-10; James Caughey, *Report of a Farewell Sermon, delivered in the Methodist New Connexion Chapel, Parliament St., Nottingham* . . . (Nottingham, 1847), p. 2; *Sheffield Iris*, 22 August 1844; Caughey, *Earnest Christianity*, p. 154.

34. *Christian Advocate*, 5 March 1891; James Caughey, *A Voice from America; or, Four Sermons preached by the Rev. J. Caughey . . .* , 2d ed. (Manchester, 1847), pp. 5-14.

35. James Caughey, *Revival Miscellanies . . .* (London, n.d.), pp. 408-9.

36. Caughey, *Letters*, 4:301-6; Harrison, *Drink and the Victorians*, pp. 179-81; Joseph Barker, *The Life of Joseph Barker*, ed. J. T. Barker (London, 1880), pp. 201ff; *Sheffield Daily Telegraph*, 12 September 1924.

37. Caughey, *Letters*, 1:175-76; 2:222-23; 4:78-81, 264-66, 307-8; *Sheffield Iris*, 22 August 1844. At times there were 70 or 80 at the communion rail.

38. *Penitent Benches* (Nottingham, n.d.), p. 4; *Wesleyan-Methodist Magazine*, 3d ser. 6(1827):402; Richard Treffry, Jr., *Memoirs of the Life, Character and Labours of the Rev. John Smith . . .*, 2d ed. (London, 1833), pp. 270-76, 287; idem, *Memoirs of Mr. John Edwards Trezise . . .* (London, 1837), pp. 84-85; *Agency and Progress*, pp. 19-20 and appendix B. Even amongst the Primitive Methodists, more receptive than most to innovations in revivals, the "mourners' ring" (in which members encircled penitents) was far more common than the "penitents' form" in the 1830s; only in the 1840s did the latter become commonplace. See the *Primitive Methodist Magazine* for this period.

39. *Penitent Benches*, passim.

40. Caughey, *Letters*, 4:197-211, 267-68; 5:101-5; James Caughey, *Parting Sermon . . . delivered in Sans Street Chapel Sunderland . . .* (Sunderland, 1846), p. 8 and passim.

41. Roland Wilson, *Carver Street Methodist Church, Sheffield, 1805-1955* (Sheffield, 1955), pp. 6-7; Caughey, *Letters*, 4:268, 299-300; 5:121, 160-63; Dyson, "James Caughey"; *Sheffield Iris*, 22 August 1844.

42. Gregory, *Sidelights*, p. 368; Caughey, *Letters*, 4:264; 5:5; *Sheffield Daily Telegraph*, 12 September 1924; Albert T. Bradwell, *Autobiography of a Converted Infidel . . .* (Sheffield, 1844), pp. 6-8.

43. Bradwell, *Autobiography of an Infidel*, passim.

44. *Christian Advocate*, 30 April 1845; Caughey, *Voice from America*, p. 13; Caughey, *Letters*, 5:134.

45. James Dixon, *Methodism in its Origin, Economy, and Present Position . . .* (London, 1843), pp. 163-66.

46. Caughey, *Letters*, 2:59, 99, 233-38; Caughey, *Voice from America*, pp. 9-10, 14-22, 37; John H. James, *Dr. Campbell and the Wesleyans . . .* (London, 1847), pp. 7-11; Dixon, *Dixon*, pp. 271, 483.

47. *Brief Memoir*, p. 11.

48. Caughey, *Letters*, 5:90, 97-99; Caughey, *Earnest Christianity*, pp. 290-94, 364-70; *Brief Memoir*, p. 20; *Morning Chronicle*, 15 and 16 April 1846.

49. Caughey, *Letters*, 2:100; 4:114-29; J. Kendall to J. Bunting, 5 January 1846, in W. R. Ward, *Early Victorian Methodism: The Correspondence of Jabez Bunting, 1830-1858* (London, 1976), pp. 338-39; *Sheffield Mercury*, 10 July 1847. The huge decline in Wesleyan membership in Birmingham in the 5th year after Caughey's departure was a direct consequence of schism, not of backsliding by the revivalist's converts.

50. Caughey, *Earnest Christianity*, pp. 358-61; Caughey, *Letters*, 4:114; Gregory, *Sidelights*, p. 427; W. B. Carter, *The Case Tested . . .* (London, 1847), p. 9.

51. William Carvosso, *A Memoir . . .*, ed. B. Carvosso (London, 1836), p. 51; Caughey, *Letters*, 2:121-24, 196-97; 3:155-56, 183-84, 240; 4:133-35; Gregory, *Sidelights*, p. 345; W. H. Harvard to J. Bunting, 11 November 1839, in Ward, *Early Victorian Methodism*, p. 236.

52. Ward, *Religion and Society in England*, p. 287.

53. *Brief Memoir*, pp. 11, 16. The difference should not be overstressed. The spontaneity of earlier revivals had not lain in a complete absence of prior effort. Bramwell entered every circuit with the aim of "getting up a revival." C. W. Andrews, *William Bramwell, Revivalist* (London, n.d.), p. 47.

54. *Brief Memoir*, pp. 8, 21, 63, 69-70; Carter, *Case Tested*, pp. 34-35.

55. Gregory, *Sidelights*, pp. 344-45, 368-69, 390-91, 400; *Sheffield Mercury*, 23 January 1847; *Brief Memoir*, pp. 17-18; *A Review of the Whole Case, or What Has Conference Done in reference to the Rev. James Caughey* . . . (Sheffield, 1847), p. 5.

56. Gregory, *Sidelights*, pp. 72-74, 400-3, 496; *Protest in favor of the Rev. James Caughey* (Sheffield, n.d.), p. 2; *Brief Memoir*, p. 21; Thomas P. Bunting, *The Life of Jabez Bunting, D.D.*, 2 vols. (London, 1859, 1887), 1:272-76, 436-37; Ward, *Religion and Society in England*, pp. 81, 97-99, 161-62; J. C. Leppington to J. Bunting, 25 May 1846, in Ward, *Early Victorian Methodism*, pp. 339-40.

57. *Review of the Whole Case*, pp. 5-13; *Brief Memoir*, p. 23; *Sheffield Mercury*, 23 January 1847. The regulation of 1807, directed against Dow and prohibiting Conference from employing American ministers unless they were properly accredited, could not be applied. Caughey's papers had been examined by the Manchester Conference of 1841. *Protest in favor of Caughey*, p. 5; *A Dialogue on the "Whole Case" of the Rev. James Caughey, by a Wesleyan Leader* (Sheffield, n.d.), p. 11.

58. Caughey, *Letters*, 4:91; *Brief Memoir*, pp. 29-32.

59. Caughey, *Letters*, 4:v-xxiii; Caughey, *Earnest Christianity*, pp. 348-51; Joseph Beaumont, *The Life of the Rev. Joseph Beaumont, M.D.* (London, 1856), pp. 80-81, 187, 259, 288, 292; *Brief Memoir*, pp. 22-26; Gregory, *Sidelights*, p. 400; *Review of the Whole Case*, p. 16.

60. *Review of the Whole Case*, pp. 7-8, 16-17; *Brief Memoir*, pp. 53-60, 64; Gregory, *Sidelights*, pp. 400-401; *Sheffield Mercury*, 22 and 29 August 1846, 16 January 1847.

61. *Brief Memoir*, pp. 21, 46-47, 72-76; *Sheffield Mercury*, 23 January, 20 March, 10 July 1847; Caughey to ?, 18 January 1847; Caughey to ?, 12 April 1847, MC-MCA; Caughey, *Farewell Sermon*, pp. 18-19.

62. *Sheffield Mercury*, 9 January 1847; Carter, *Case Tested*, pp. 26-29; *Brief Memoir*, p. 32; W. Vevers to J. Bunting, 11 March 1847 in Ward, *Early Victorian Methodism*, p. 348.

63. *Sheffield Mercury*, 10 July 1847. Caughey was firmly antislavery, but he was inevitably compromised (at least until the MEC schism of 1844) by the extent of slaveholding in his denomination. Robert Johnson and Richard Allen, *Four Letters to the Reverend James Caughey* . . . (Dublin, 1841).

64. J. B. Melson, *Farewell Address to the Rev. James Caughey* . . . (Birmingham, 1847), p. 3; *Brief Memoir*, pp. 18, 77-78, 81; Caughey, *Letters*, 4: x, xxii-xxiii.

65. *Protest in favor of Caughey*, p. 5; *Brief Memoir*, pp. 30, 56-60; *Review of the Whole Case*, pp. 3, 7, 17; Gregory, *Sidelights*, p. 357; John Kent, *Jabez Bunting: The Last Wesleyan* (London, 1955); idem, "The Clash Between Radicalism and Conservatism in Methodism; 1815-1848" (Ph.D. thesis, Cambridge University, 1950).

66. Caughey was "a hero of the Fly Sheets." Kent, "The Clash in Methodism," pp. 233-50, 291; Currie, *Methodism Divided*, p. 71; Ward, *Religion and Society in*

England, pp. 261, 263-64; Thomas Jackson, *The Life of the Rev. Robert Newton, D.D.* (London, 1855), p. 295; Caughey, *Letters,* 3:236-45; Gregory, *Sidelights,* p. 413; *Protest in favor of Caughey,* p. 10; *A Faithful Verbatim Report of The "Fly Sheets" . . . By a Wesleyan Minister, who is not yet expelled* (London, 1849), pp. 65-69, 72; *Sheffield Daily Telegraph,* 1 June 1927; Joseph Dyson, "United Methodist Free Churches: History of the Movement in Sheffield," in Newspaper Cuttings, Sheffield City Library.

67. Dixon, *Miller,* pp. 184-85; *Christian Advocate,* 1 May 1827.

Chapter 5

1. Robert S. Fletcher, *A History of Oberlin College,* 2 vols. (Oberlin, Ohio, 1943), 1:3-203; Finney, *Memoirs,* passim; McLoughlin, *Modern Revivalism,* pp. 81-83.

2. Mears, *Kirk,* pp. 189-201; Lyman Beecher, *The Autobiography of Lyman Beecher,* ed. Barbara Cross, 2 vols. (Cambridge, Mass., 1961), 2:390-93; Emerson Andrews, *Living Life; or, Autobiography . . . ,* 3d ed. (Boston, 1881), pp. 24-46, 57-98; Wayland and Wayland, *Francis Wayland,* 1:165-67, 406-7, 425, 2:7-42.

3. Fletcher, *Oberlin,* 1:456-71, 2:903; letters of Keep to his wife and son, 1839 and 1840, K-OC.

4. Lewis Tappan Journal, 1843, T-LC.

5. Tappan to W. Albright, 29 January 1844, T-LC; McLoughlin, *Modern Revivalism,* pp. 108-12; unidentified newspaper cutting sent by A. M. Potter to Finney, 25 January 1859, F-OC; *Congregational Magazine,* n.s. 5 (1841):175.

6. Brown to Finney, 13 February 1849; Roe to Finney, November 1849, F-OC; Brian Harrison, *Dictionary of British Temperance Biography* (Sheffield, 1973), p. 16; Henry Bell, *A Jubilee Memorial of the Union Chapel, Houghton, Huntingdon* (Cambridge, 1890), pp. 1-9, 20-24.

7. Brown to Finney, 3 June 1849, April 1850; Roe to Finney, November 1849; J. E. Simmons to Finney, 12 February 1850; E. A. Finney to H. Bissell, 25 December 1849; J. Harcourt to Finney, 21 February 1851, F-OC; *Baptist Reporter,* n.s. 7 (1850): 126; Bell, *Union Chapel,* pp. 22, 32, 41.

8. Roe to Finney, November 1849, May and June 1850, 20 February, 3 March 1851, F-OC; Arthur S. Langley, *Birmingham Baptists* (London, 1930), pp. 122-24.

9. Dale, *James,* passim. Two hundred thousand copies of *The Anxious Inquirer* were issued between 1834 and 1839; it was widely read in America.

10. James to Finney, 26 and 29 January 1850; ? to James, 26 January 1850; E. A. Finney to H. Bissell, 25 December 1849, F-OC; Finney, *Memoirs,* pp. 390-94.

11. *Biblical Repertory and Princeton Review* 19(1847):237-77.

12. James to Finney, n.d. ("Friday"), n.d. ("Monday morning"), 28 and 29 January, 27 February 1850; E. A. Finney to H. Bissell, 22 April 185C, F-OC; Dale, *James,* pp. 544-46.

13. Finney, *Memoirs,* pp. 392-95; Henry Baker, *Historical Memoranda relating to . . . Ebenezer Chapel, Steelhouse Lane, Birmingham . . .* (Birmingham, 1903), pp. 53-54, 58, 139; E. A. Finney to H. Bissell, 22 April 1850, F-OC; *Baptist Reporter,* n.s. 7(1850):32, 224, 272, 496; *Birmingham Mercury,* 8 December 1849, 19 January 1850.

14. E. A. Finney to A. Atkinson and J. R. Finney, 1 April 1850; Redford to Finney,

6 December 1850, 29 January, 4 February 1851; J. Campbell to Finney, 22 November 1850, F-OC; George Redford, *The Great Change: a Treatise on Conversion* (London, 1843), p. 59 and passim; C. G. Finney, *Lectures on Systematic Theology . . .* , edited and revised, with an introduction by George Redford (London, 1851).

15. *Baptist Magazine* 40 (1848):391; J. Campbell, "Rev. Professor Finney . . . ," handbill, 1 May 1850; R. Joseland to Finney, 8 May 1850; E. A. Finney to H. Bissell, 13 May 1850; Crowe to Finney, 4 March 1851; Redford to Finney, 18 March 1851, F-OC.

16. B. Stocks to Finney, 14 March 1850; Parsons to Finney, 8, 16, and 20 April 1850, F-OC; Edwin P. Hood, ed., *The Earnest Minister: a Record of the Life . . . of the Rev. Benjamin Parsons, of Ebley, Gloucestershire* (London, 1856), passim.

17. Campbell to Finney, 1 May 1850, F-OC.

18. See chapter 2.

19. *Christian Witness* 6(1849):513-15; 7(1850):545-46; 8(1851):1-5; 10(1853):209-11, 255-63; David E. Ford, *Alarm in Zion . . .* (London, 1848), pp. 41-44; Dale, *James*, pp. 542-43; *British Banner*, 1 September 1852.

20. Dale, *James*, pp. 544-46; Willis B. Glover, *Evangelical Nonconformists and Higher Criticism in the Nineteenth Century* (London, 1954), pp. 11ff; Chadwick, *Victorian Church*, 1:527ff, 558ff.

21. Robert Ferguson and A. Morton Brown, *Life and Labours of John Campbell, D.D.* (London, 1868), pp. 25-46, 148, and passim.

22. Campbell to Finney, 28 March 1850, F-OC.

23. Campbell to Finney, 3 and 16 April, 10 October, 13 and 20 November 1850, 18 August 1851; E. A. Finney to H. Bissell, 22 April 1850; H. W. Beecher to Finney, 30 August 1850, F-OC; *Congregational Year Book* (1850), pp. 1, 15, 26-27; *Christian Witness* 3 (1846):135; 7(1850): 271-73, 298, 302.

24. J. Ewing Ritchie, *The London Pulpit*, 2d ed. (London, 1858), pp. 91-101; Charles G. Finney, "Memoirs," pp. 851-52, F-OC.

25. Allon to Finney, 10 November 1849; Mahan to Finney, 25 January 1850, F-OC; Asa Mahan, *Autobiography: Intellectual, Moral, and Spiritual* (London, 1882), pp. 135-39; *Oberlin Evangelist*, 2 January 1850. Mahan (1799-1889) had fully participated in the great revivals of the 1820s and 1830s in America. He had been in Europe since July 1849 advocating peace, temperance, antislavery, and revivalism.

26. For the profound influence of Finney's writings on the founder of the YMCA, see Clyde Binfield, *George Williams and the Y.M.C.A.: A Study in Victorian Social Attitudes* (London, 1973), pp. 17-18.

27. John Campbell, *Valedictory Services and Farewell Sermon of Professor Finney . . .* (London, 1851), p. 12; Campbell to Finney, 6 and 16 April, 29 November 1850; C. Roe to Finney, November 1849, F-OC; *Christian Witness* 7 (1850):474; Finney, *Memoirs*, p. 401.

28. Campbell to Finney, 1 November 1850, F-OC.

29. Campbell, *Valedictory Services*, pp. 5-10; John R. Dix, *Pen Pictures of Popular English Preachers* (London, 1851), pp. 207-8; *Christian Witness* 7(1850):474-75, 546-47; R. W. Dale, *Nine Lectures on Preaching . . .* (London, 1877), pp. 146-47. Cf. Finney to T. Rees, 27 January 1859, R-NLWA: "I must . . . lay the foundations deeper in the convictions, and build up a more permanent structure, than I could do by a few appeals addressed to the feelings. . . . I must reason with the people."

30. Charles G. Finney, *Repentance* . . . (London, 1851); idem, *A Fourth Voice from America; or, two sermons preached by the Rev. C. G. Finney . . . at Borough Road Chapel* . . . (London, 1849).

31. *Christian News*, 18 and 25 July 1850.

32. James E. Johnson, "Charles G. Finney and Oberlin Perfectionism," *Journal of Presbyterian History* 46(1968):42-57, 128-37.

33. Dale, *James*, pp. 531-32; *Evangelical Magazine* 29 (1851):578-83; *Christian Witness* 9(1852):135.

34. *Oberlin Evangelist*, 18 June 1845. Lamb had been considerably influenced by Caughey; he and most of his congregation were in 1848 forced to leave their chapel because of "changes in [his] religious views." James G. Miall, *Congregationalism in Yorkshire* (London, 1868), p. 377; *The Way of Holiness* 17 (December 1925).

35. Mahan, *Autobiography*, pp. 174, 289-96; *Oberlin Evangelist*, 7 November 1849; Mahan to Finney, 5 and 25 January 1850, F-OC.

36. John Hall, ed., *Forty Years' Familiar Letters of James W. Alexander, D.D.*, 2 vols. (New York, 1860), 2:124; Redford to Finney, 6 December 1850, F-OC; Alfred V. Churchill, "Midwestern," *Northwest Ohio Quarterly* 23(1951):167-68.

37. E. A. Finney to H. Bissell, 22 April, 16 August 1850; Campbell, "Rev. Professor Finney . . . ," handbill, 1 May 1850; J. A. James to Finney, n.d. ("Saturday"), F-OC; Finney, *Memoirs*, pp. 401-14.

38. Campbell kept the fires burning during Finney's absence by securing the help of Rev. Ebenezer Cornwall, friend of the Evangelical Union and admirer of Finney. Cornwall to Finney, 16 August, 1850, F-OC.

39. *Leeds Times*, 29 December 1849.

40. Finney, "Memoirs," p. 862, F-OC. The Tabernacle had a capacity of about 3,000.

41. Campbell to Finney, 22 October 1850, 18 August 1851; E. A. Finney to H. Bissell, 16 August 1850, F-OC; Ferguson and Brown, *Campbell*, pp. 430-31; Campbell, *Valedictory Services*, pp. 12-14; *Wesleyan Times*, 5 August 1850.

42. Finney, *Memoirs*, p. 411; Chadwick, *Victorian Church*, 1:440-55; Daniel Wilson, *A Revival of Spiritual Religion* . . . (London, 1851), passim; B. Philpot, *On Religious Revivals* . . . (London, 1851), p. 9.

43. Ritchie, *London Pulpit*, p. 93.

44. Richard Hofstadter, *Anti-intellectualism in American Life* (New York, 1963), pp. 55-116.

45. Cranbrook to Finney, 16 August 1850; Moore to Finney, 30 April, 15 October 1850, 4 March 1851, F-OC.

46. *Christian Witness* 5 (1848):556-68; E. A. Finney to H. Bissell, 16 August 1850; P. Brown to E. A. Finney, 25 January 1850, F-OC.

47. Finney, *Memoirs*, pp. 409, 413; Finney, "Memoirs," p. 865, F-OC; C. G. Finney to J. Finney, 5 December 1850; Campbell and church officers to Finney, 2 April 1851, F-OC; *British Banner*, 30 October 1850.

48. Campbell to Finney, 22 October 1850; 18 August, 10 November 1851; J. Moody to Finney, 27 October 1852; Brown to Finney, 9 November 1853, F-OC.

49. J. Stevenson to Finney, 27 May 1850; R. Simpson to Finney, 8 and 14 March 1851, F-OC.

50. *Christian Witness* 7(1850):314, 357-64, 473-76; Redford to Finney, 3 December 1850; J. Moody to Finney, 27 October 1852, F-OC; Ferguson and Brown, *Campbell*, pp. 421-23; *Evangelical Magazine*, n.s. 29(1851): 717-21.

51. Finney, *Memoirs*, p. 406; Keep to Finney, A. Mahan, and H. Cowles, 19 August 1839, C-OC.

52. L. Tappan to Finney, 17 August 1832, F-OC; *The English Pulpit; collection of sermons by the most eminent divines of England* (New York, 1849), pp. 4-5. For the movement from a prevailing sacerdotal view of the ministry in America to one in which the minister's basic obligation was to bring the sinner to a decision, see Sidney E. Mead, "The Rise of the Evangelical Conception of the Ministry in America: 1607-1850," in H. Richard Neibuhr and Daniel D. Williams, eds., *The Ministry in Historical Perspectives* (New York, 1956), pp. 208-49.

53. *New York Observer*, 26 April 1834; Dale, *James*, pp. 311-12; *Christian Witness* 10 (1853):255ff.

54. John Campbell, *Letters to the Independent Churches of Great Britain . . .* (London, 1856), pp. 27-31; J. A. James, "The Conversion of the Soul the Great End of the Ministry," in J. A. James et al., *The Chester Conference . . .* (London, 1853), pp. 46-47; Reed and Matheson, *Narrative*, 2:200; J. Leavitt to Nettleton, 3 September 1832, N-HS.

55. Campbell, *Valedictory Services*, pp. 12-14. The public nature of commitment demanded by the revivalist grated on delicate sensibilities. "Generally speaking, the modes of admission into churches in England are easier on the feelings of the candidates . . . than in churches of the same name in America," reported Calvin Colton. *New York Observer*, 7 February 1835; Campbell to Finney, 3 April 1850, F-OC.

56. Reed and Matheson, *Narrative*, 1:374ff. No British pastor could match the record of someone like Joel Hawes, no new-measure fanatic, who experienced a series of ten revivals in 44 years in his Hartford church. Edward A. Lawrence, *The Life of Rev. Joel Hawes, D.D. . . .* (Hartford, 1871), pp. 110-14, 134-35.

57. Quoted in Baird, *Religion in America*, p. 207. The significance of Goodrich's academic position should not be overlooked. During the Second Great Awakening the seminaries and colleges of higher education, dominated by the Congregational and Presbyterian denominations, repeatedly experienced revivals in a way that would have been regarded as fanatical by British universities. Halliday and Gregory, *Church in America*, pp. 216-25; *Evangelical Magazine*, n.s. 11 (1833):68-71.

58. Peter G. Mode, "Revivalism as a Phase of Frontier Life," *The Journal of Religion* 1(1921):337-54.

59. America was arguably a country which, compared with Britain, lacked sufficiently authoritative institutions to impose restraints on behavior. Andrew Reed's criticism of the American approach to temperance had a more general application: "[The Americans] have only one fault—they know not when to stop." Reed and Matheson, *Narrative*, 2:164.

60. Wayland and Wayland, *Francis Wayland*, 2:10.

61. *Christian Advocate*, 9 November 1842, 4 November 1846; *New York Observer*, 19 and 26 April 1834; A. Phelps to Finney, 29 August 1833, F-OC.

62. *Baptist Magazine* 34(1842):82.

63. Robert Currie, "A Micro-Theory of Methodist Growth," *Proceedings of the*

Wesley Historical Society, 361(1967):65-73; Alan Everitt, "Nonconformity in Rural Parishes," *Agricultural History Review* 18(1970):178-99.

64. *Wesleyan-Methodist Magazine*, 3d ser., 2(1823):473-74; *Baptist Magazine* 34(1842):543-44; 35(1843):505; 36(1844):226-27; 39(1847):406.

65. Dale, *James*, p. 423.

66. *Evangelical Magazine*, n.s. 6 (1828):488. Francis Cox attributed the success of inquiry meetings in America to the fact that "intercourse with each other . . . is unchecked by artificial distinctions of pride or rank." Cox, *Suggestions*, p. 9.

67. Dixon, *Methodism in America*, pp. 142, 149; Coles, *First Seven Years*, pp. 108-11; N. Bangs, *History*, 3:187-88.

68. Durbin, *Observations*, p. 77; Frederick J. Jobson, *America, and American Methodism* (New York, 1857), p. 233. The receptions afforded to visiting delegates reflected the comparative status of Methodists in the two countries. No American Methodist in Britain was ever feted like Robert Newton, who preached to both houses of Congress and had an audience with President Martin Van Buren. Newton himself noted "the immense sway [of American Methodists] over public opinion." Jackson, *Newton*, pp. 200-5, 212.

69. Finney, *Memoirs*, p. 400; G. Redford to Finney, 3 December 1850, F-OC.

Chapter 6

1. *New York Observer*, 26 August 1858; Humphrey, *Revival Sketches*, pp. 298-99.

2. Samuel Coley, *The Life of the Rev. Thos. Collins*, 2d ed. (London, 1869), p. 442.

3. *Southern Christian Advocate*, 8 January 1857.

4. There is no definitive study of the revival of 1857-58. The most helpful treatment is provided by Smith, *Revivalism and Social Reform*, pp. 63-79. McLoughlin, *Modern Revivalism*, pp. 163-64, is too brief and underestimates the extent of the revival. See also Russell E. Francis, "Pentecost, 1858: A Study in Religious Revivalism" (Ph.D. thesis, University of Pennsylvania, 1948), and Carl L. Spicer, "The Great Awakening of 1857 and 1859" (Ph.D. thesis, Ohio State University, 1935). For the unprecedented lay participation in the revival see Conant, *Remarkable Conversions*, pp. 365, 416: "The people are the preacher"; "Democracy under CHRIST" was "in beautiful harmony with the nature of modern American experience."

5. Weber, *Presbyterian Statistics*, pp. 18, 44; J. Edwin Orr, *The Second Evangelical Awakening in Britain* (London, 1948), p. 36; *Minutes of MEC* (1858); P. A. Peterson, *Handbook of Southern Methodism* (Richmond, Va., 1883), p. 115.

6. *Christian Advocate*, 19 June, 30 October 1856, 15 January 1857; James W. Alexander, *The American Sunday-School and Its Adjuncts* (Philadelphia, 1856), pp. 70, 327; Spicer, "Great Awakening," p. 57; *New York Observer*, 11 September 1856; Wardle, *Sunday School Movement*, p. 89.

7. *New York Observer*, 3 June 1858. There were extensive revivals in schools and colleges in 1857-58.

8. David O. Mears, *An Autobiography, 1842-93* (Boston, 1920), pp. 12-14; *Christian Advocate*, 17 January, 5 June 1856; *Southern Christian Advocate*, 24 September 10 December 1857; Alexander, *American Sunday-School*, p. 327.

9. *Minutes of MEC* (1857, 1858).

10. *Christian Advocate*, 14 January, 11 February, 4, 11, and 25 March, 22 April 1858.

11. *New York Observer*, 27 May 1858.

12. Ibid., 25 March, 1 April, 1 July 1858; *Oberlin Evangelist*, 24 March 1858; Humphrey, *Revival Sketches*, pp. 278-79; *Christian Advocate*, 18 March 1858, 28 July 1859.

13. Wayland and Wayland, *Francis Wayland*, 2:213.

14. James W. Alexander et al., *The Man of Business Considered in his Various Relations* (New York, 1857); Fish, *Primitive Piety Revived*, especially pp. 34-64; William Arthur, *The Duty of Giving Away a Stated Proportion of our Income* (Philadelphia, 1857); idem, *The Successful Merchant* (London, 1852), which went into numerous American editions in the 1850s; *Gold and the Gospel* (New York, 1855).

15. *New York Observer*, 19 March, 29 October, 24 December 1857, 29 July 1858; *Christian Advocate*, 2 July, 15 October, 12 November 1857; Alexander, "The Merchant's Clerk Cheered and Counselled" in Alexander et al., *Man of Business*, p. 20; *Southern Christian Advocate*, 24 December 1857.

16. A. J. Patterson, *A Discourse on The Revival . . .* (Portsmouth, N.H., 1858), p. 8; Conant, *Remarkable Conversions*, p. 357.

17. *Christian Advocate*, 15 October 1857, 21 January 1858; *Southern Christian Advocate*, 15 October, 5 November 1857; Spicer, "Great Awakening," pp. 102-3.

18. *New York Observer*, 11 June 1857; *Christian Advocate*, 10 July, 7 and 21 August, 6 November 1856, 22 January, 10 September 1857.

19. Bucke et al., eds., *History of American Methodism*, 2:196-99; Clifford S. Griffin, "The Abolitionists and the Benevolent Societies, 1831-1861," *Journal of Negro History* 44(1959):195-216.

20. *Christian Advocate*, 26 June 1856, 7 January, 4 February 1858; *New York Observer*, 3 and 24 June, 1 July, 5 August 1858; *Southern Christian Advocate*, 13 May 1858.

21. Spicer, "Great Awakening," pp. 87-89, 132, 210-11; *Oberlin Evangelist*, 17 March 1858.

22. *Christian Advocate*, 30 October 1856; Ronald P. Formisano, *The Birth of Mass Political Parties: Michigan, 1827-1861* (Princeton, 1971).

23. *Christian Advocate*, 9 and 30 October 1856, 2 April 1857; *New York Observer*, 31 January, 13 November 1856, 2 July 1857.

24. *Christian Advocate*, 2 and 16 October 1856; *New York Observer*, 30 October 1856; Russell E. Francis, "The Religious Revival of 1858 in Philadelphia," *Pennsylvania Magazine of History and Biography* 70(1946):57.

25. *Christian Advocate*, 5 February 1857.

26. Ibid., 6 and 13 November, 11 December 1856, 5 February 1857, 20 December 1860; *Southern Christian Advocate*, 23 October 1856.

27. Francis, "Religious Revival of 1858," p. 64; *New York Observer*, 6 May 1858; William L. Van Deburg, "William Lloyd Garrison and the 'Pro-Slavery Priesthood': The Changing Beliefs of an Evangelical Reformer, 1830-1840," *Journal of the American Academy of Religion* 43(1975):235n; *Christian Advocate*, 4 February 1858.

28. Spicer, "Great Awakening," appendix B; *New York Observer*, 15 April, 26 August 1858.

29. *Southern Christian Advocate*, 15 January, 21 May, 27 August, 3 and 10 September, 8 October 1857; Finney, *Memoirs*, p. 444.

30. *Southern Christian Advocate*, 10 September 1857, 17 March 1859. The highest southern growth rates were recorded in the following conferences: Missouri (8.53), Georgia (8.75), Alabama (9.23), Virginia (11.64), Arkansas (13.61), East Texas (13.85), St. Louis (15.65), West Virginia (20.37), and Texas (21.41).

31. *New York Observer*, 10 January 1856.

32. *Brownson's Quarterly Review* 15(1858):289-322; *Christian Advocate*, 3 and 31 January, 7 February 1856; 8 January, 18 June, 27 August 1857; 4 February 1858.

33. *Christian Advocate*, 15 May 1856, 2 April, 5 November 1857.

34. Ibid., 22 April 1858; *Southern Christian Advocate*, 17 June, 15 July, 14 October 1858; *New York Observer*, 5 August 1858.

35. Smith, *Revivalism and Social Reform*, pp. 154-62.

36. *Southern Christian Advocate*, 25 March, 26 August 1858.

37. *Christian Advocate*, 10 February, 28 April, 28 July 1859.

38. See, for example, the *Cincinnati Gazette*, 26 and 29 March 1858, 13 October 1860.

39. Cf. Roy F. Nichols, *The Disruption of American Democracy*, 2d ed. (New York, 1962), pp. 139, 142-43.

40. K. S. Inglis, "Patterns of Religious Worship in 1851," *Journal of Ecclesiastical History* 11(1960):74-86; E. H. Weeks to Finney, 26 May 1853, OC-OC.

41. *Christian Advocate*, 18 January 1855; see also the pages of the *Revivalist*, a Lincolnshire-based magazine of evangelical zealots.

42. Horton Davies, *Worship and Theology in England*, 4 vols. (London, 1961-62), 4:333-34.

43. *Christian Advocate*, 19 November 1854, 6 and 27 September 1855; B. E. Hardman, "The Evangelical Party in the Church of England, 1855-1865" (Ph.D. thesis, Cambridge University, 1964), pp. 230ff.

44. *Congregational Year Book* (1858), pp. 30-42.

45. *Freeman*, 6 January 1858; B. R. Mitchell and Phyllis Deane, *Abstract of British Historical Statistics* (Cambridge, 1962), pp. 64, 283, 343, 410; *Revivalist* (1858), pp. 30-39, 57-63, 76-78; Benjamin Gregory, *The Life of Frederick James Jobson, D.D.* (London, 1884), pp. 46-47.

46. *Revivalist* (1862), pp. 68-70.

47. W. Patton, *Suffering with Christ the True Spirit of a Revival* (London, 1859), pp. 3-4; Isabella L. Bishop, *The Aspects of Religion in the United States of America* (London, 1859).

48. See, for example, John G. Lorimer, *The Recent Great Awakening in America* . . . (Glasgow, 1859); Octavius Winslow, "Is the Spirit of the Lord Straitened?" . . . (London, 1858); J. A. James, *On the Revival of Religion* (London, 1859); B. Evans, *The American Revivals* . . . (London, 1859); Samuel I. Prime, *The Power of Prayer* . . . (London, 1859); Committee of the Y.M.C.A. of Philadelphia, *The Work of God in Philadelphia in 1858* (London, 1859), with an introduction by Henry Groves, a Briton who witnessed the revival.

49. *Freeman*, 16 March, 27 April, 20 July 1859; William Carus, ed., *Memorials of the Right Reverend Charles Pettit McIlvaine* . . . ,2d ed. (London, 1882), pp. 176-202.

50. Evans, *American Revivals*, pp. 4-5; Winslow, "*Spirit of the Lord*," pp. 84-85.

51. *New York Observer*, 7 October 1858, 13 January 1859; G. B. Cheever et al., *An Accurate and Detailed Account of the Extraordinary Revival of Religion in America and Ireland* . . . (London, 1859), p. 23; A Canadian, *The American Revival and Individual Agency* . . . (London, 1859), pp. 13-15.

52. Evans, *American Revivals*, passim.

53. *New York Observer*, 7 October 1858, 11 August, 6 October 1859; Robert Braithwaite, *The Life and Letters of Rev. William Pennefather, B.A.*, 2d ed. (London, 1879), pp. 297-98, 314-17, 338; Findlay, *Moody*, pp. 149-50.

54. A. R. Scott, "The Ulster Revival of 1859" (Ph.D. thesis, Trinity College [Dublin], 1962), pp. 57, 65-100, 112, 119-200; Cheever et al., *Extraordinary Revival*, pp. ii-iv; *Christian Remembrancer*, 39(1860):364-416; Robinson Scott, *The American Revival* . . . (Dublin, 1860), pp. iii-iv, 52-60.

55. Scott, "Ulster Revival," pp. 168, 170, 197, 223; Theodore L. Cuyler, *Recollections of a Long Life* . . . (London, 1902), p. 86; *Christian Advocate*, 14 November 1861, 18 September 1863; *The Revival*, 27 August 1859.

56. Scott, "Ulster Revival," pp. 121-24, 257-83.

57. *The Great Revival* . . . (Nottingham, 1859), pp. 5-9.

58. *Christian News* for 1859; Hamilton MacGill, *On the Present Revival of Religion in Scotland* . . . (London, 1860).

59. *The Revival* for 1859-60. Twenty years later Catherine Booth reflected, "We had united prayer-meetings all over [England] to pray for [revival], and it did not come." *The War Cry*, 23 December 1880.

60. Davies, *Revivals in Wales*, p. 89.

61. John Venn, *The Revival in Wales* . . . (London, 1860), pp. 2-5.

62. Eifion Evans, *When He Is Come: An Account of the 1858-60 Revival in Wales* (Bala, 1959), pp. 28-85; *Christian Advocate*, 18 February 1858; Davies, *Revivals in Wales*, pp. 2-12; T. R. Roberts, *Eminent Welshmen* . . . (Cardiff, 1908), p. 349.

63. Gilbert suggests that the revival was closely connected with the great wave of evictions of tenants by Anglican landlords in 1859. "Growth and Decline," p. 262.

64. Coley, *Collins*, p. 441.

65. William Taylor, *William Taylor of California* . . . , rev. ed. (London, 1897), pp. 150, 157-61; *Christian Advocate*, 18 December 1862.

66. *Christian Advocate*, 1 and 15 January, 19 February, 12 and 19 March, 27 August 1857.

67. Ibid., 25 June, 23 July, 20 and 27 August, 3 September 1857; *Revivalist* (1857), pp. 72, 137-38, 187.

68. *Revivalist* (1856), pp. 46-47; (1857), pp. 185-91; (1858), pp. 10-11, 32-33, 57-63, 76-78, 89-92, 129-31, 145-60.

69. Ibid. (1859), pp. 16, 24-32, 75, 91-92, 125, 140-43; *United Methodist Free Churches Magazine* 2(1859):280-83; *Wesleyan Times*, 18 July 1859; *Messenger of Life*, 1(1859):173.

70. For Caughey's later itinerancies, see *Revivalist* (1860-67).

71. *British Banner*, 20 March 1856; Brown to Finney, 16 June 1856; Finney to Brown, 1 October 1857, F-OC; cf. G. Cockle to Finney, 25 August 1858, G-T; Finney, *Memoirs*, pp. 442-48; Elizabeth A. Finney, "A [Manuscript] Journal Kept . . . during a Visit to England in 1859-1860 . . . ," pp. 1-15, Oberlin College Library, Oberlin, Ohio.

72. E. A. Finney, "Journal," pp. 16-18, 30; Finney, *Memoirs*, pp. 448-49; M. Robinson to Finney, 4 February 1859: J. Campbell to Finney, 5 January 1859, F-OC.

73. Finney, *Memoirs*, pp. 450-52; *British Standard*, 11 March, 1, 8, 15, and 29 April 1859. In 1856 Campbell had criticized *The Rivulet*, a collection of hymns written by T. T. Lynch, for anti-evangelicalism. The ensuing furor shook the Congregational Union.

74. Redford to Finney, 25 May 1858, 25 January 1859, F-OC.

75. E. A. Finney, "Journal," pp. 19ff; *Wesleyan Times*, 6 August 1860.

76. Finney, *Memoirs*, pp. 455-58; Kirk to Finney, 10 May and 29 July 1859; Ferguson, Jr., to Finney, 1 July 1859, F-OC.

77. E. A. Finney, "Journal," pp. 28, 40-41; *St. Ives, Ely, Bedford, Peterborough, and Lynn Gazette*, 26 February 1859; Finney, *Memoirs*, p. 454; *United Methodist Free Churches Magazine* 2(1859):516, 618; *Freeman*, 26 October 1859.

78. *Bolton Chronicle*, 31 December 1859; Finney, *Memoirs*, pp. 458-68; *Oberlin Evangelist*, 29 February, 11 April, 23 May 1860.

79. *Oberlin Evangelist*, 15 August 1860; Finney, *Memoirs*, pp. 468-70.

80. *Oberlin Evangelist*, 12 September 1860.

81. George Hughes, *The Beloved Physician, Walter C. Palmer, M.D.* . . . (New York, 1884); Wheatley, *Mrs. Palmer*, pp. 196-97, 238-57, and passim.

82. Abel Stevens, *Life and Times of Nathan Bangs, D.D.* (New York, 1863), p. 368. Much of the flavor of this connection can be sampled in the correspondence of the Palmers for the 1840s and 1850s. See PC-NYPL.

83. Wheatley, *Mrs. Palmer*, pp. v, 219-27; Hughes, *Palmer*, pp. 164-88.

84. Orr, *Second Evangelical Awakening*, pp. 14-15.

85. Wheatley, *Mrs. Palmer*, pp. 249, 336-37, 348; Weeks to Finney, 26 May 1853, OC-OC; Phoebe Palmer, *Faith and Its Effects* . . . (London, 1856); idem, *The Way of Holiness* . . . (London, 1856); idem, *Present to My Christian Friend* . . . (London, 1857); idem, *Incidental Illustrations of the Economy of Salvation* . . . (London, n.d.).

86. Wheatley, *Mrs. Palmer*, pp. 349-50; Young to P. Palmer, 17 August 1859, MS-DU.

87. Wheatley, *Mrs. Palmer*, pp. 353-54, 366-67; Phoebe Palmer, *Four Years in the Old World* . . . (New York, 1866), pp. 93-268; *Wesleyan-Methodist Magazine*, 5th ser., 6(1860):738-41.

88. *Christian Advocate*, 1 November 1860, 26 June 1862.

89. *Revivalist* (1859), pp. 171-75; William Bunton, "A Visit to Dr. Palmer's Revival Meetings at the Wesleyan Chapel (Banbury), 1860," ed. B. S. Trinder, *Cake and Cockhorse: The Magazine of the Banbury Historical Society* 8 (1966):75-77.

90. *Christian Advocate*, 9 October 1862; *Minutes of Several Conversations between the Methodist Ministers . . . at their . . . annual conference . . . 1862* (London, 1862), pp. 326-27.

91. *Christian Advocate*, 13 November 1862, 23 July 1863.

92. Begbie, *Booth*, 1:154-322.

93. *Minutes made at the forty-third Annual Conference of the Primitive Methodist Connexion* (London, 1862), p. 28.

94. *Minutes of the sixty-fifth Annual Conference of the Methodist New Connexion* (Manchester, 1861), p. 50.

95. *Revivalist* (1863), p. 123.

96. Ibid., pp. 122-23; Palmer, *Four Years*, p. 556; *Christian Advocate*, 4 April 1861.

97. P. C. Headley, ed., *The Harvest Work of the Holy Spirit. Illustrated in the Evangelistic Labors of Rev. Edward Payson Hammond* (Boston, 1863), pp. 22, 37-61.

98. Ibid., pp. 177-78; McLoughlin, *Modern Revivalism*, pp. 155-58; *DAB*, s.v. "Hammond, Edward Payson."

99. Caughey had conducted a "brief campaign" at Phoebe Palmer's behest in Norfolk Street Church, New York City, in 1849-50. Wheatley, *Mrs. Palmer*, pp. 191-92; Caughey to W. and P. Palmer, 4 March 1850; Caughey to P. Palmer, 13 September 1851; J. S. Mitchell to W. and P. Palmer, 3 June 1850, PC-NYPL.

100. *Christian Advocate*, 2 and 23 March 1854, 19 July 1860.

101. Olive Anderson, "Women Preachers in Mid-Victorian Britain: Some Reflections on Feminism, Popular Religion and Social Change," *Historical Journal* 12(1969): 467-84.

102. P. J. Jarbo, *A Letter to Mrs. Palmer, in reference to Women Speaking in Public* (North Shields, 1859), pp. 1-2; A. A. Rees, *Reasons for Not Co-operating in the Alleged "Sunderland Revivals"* (Sunderland, 1859), pp. 6-14; Robert Young, *North of England Revivals: Prophesying of Women* (Newcastle-on-Tyne, 1859); Catherine Booth, *Female Teaching . . .* 2d ed. (London, 1861).

103. Phoebe Palmer, *Promise of the Father . . .* (Boston, 1859), pp. 1-2, 13. Much exercised by her shortcomings "as an experimental Christian," Mrs. Palmer sent a copy to Queen Victoria.

104. *Oberlin Evangelist*, 11 April 1860; *Christian News*, 15 October 1859, 2 January 1864; E. A. Finney, "Journal," passim.

105. *Revivalist* (1860), p. 45.

106. Hughes, *Palmer*, pp. 71-72; Headley, *Harvest Work*, pp. 62, 195; E. A. Finney, "Journal," pp. 52, 59; *Revivalist* (1858), pp. 145-60.

107. Palmer, *Four Years*, p. 105; Headley, *Harvest Work*, pp. 100-17; *Revivalist* (1859), p. 125; Minutes of Trinity Church, Huntingdon [in the keeping of the church], insertion between 21 April and 2 August 1859; E. A. Finney, "Journal," p. 55.

108. Begbie, *Booth*, 1:322, 364-404; William Carter, *The Power of God . . .* (London, 1863), p. 78.

109. *Christian Advocate*, 21 July 1859; Finney, "Memoirs," p. 1022, F-OC.

110. *Christian News*, 8 September 1860; E. A. Finney, "Journal," pp. 51-57; J. Kirk to Finney, 19 July 1859, F-OC; Alexander Morison, *Finney versus Morison . . .* (Glasgow, 1859).

111. Wheatley, *Mrs. Palmer*, p. 362.

112. *Revivalist* (1860), pp. 2, 41, 43.

113. *Christian Advocate*, 23 February 1860; Evans, *When He Is Come*, p. 50.

114. William Arthur, *The Conversion of All England* (London, 1859), p. 13.

115. Headley, *Harvest Work*, pp. 164-67.

116. *Revivalist* (1857), pp. 73, 121.

117. Wheatley, *Mrs. Palmer*, pp. 369-70. Mrs. Palmer was criticized (with some justice) for deviating from the orthodox Wesleyan doctrine of sanctification; she seemed to say that to experience holiness the individual had simply to *believe* that he had achieved it, that failure to achieve holiness could nullify regeneration, and that public testimony was necessary to maintain a sanctified state. *Christian Advocate*, 3 and 10 January, 21 and 28 February 1856; H. Mattison to G. Peck, 9 January 1852,

P-SU; John Leland Peters, *Christian Perfection and American Methodism* (New York, 1956), pp. 112-13. She was wholly orthodox, however, in seeing holiness as instantaneously achieved and as forfeitable and in denying that it meant complete sinlessness. Palmer, *Way of Holiness*, pp. 37, 46-47, and passim.

118. Anderson, "Women Preachers in Mid-Victorian Britain," p. 447.

119. Headley, *Harvest Work*, p. 92; *Christian News*, 24 September 1859; *Revivalist* (1859), pp. 16, 75.

120. *Congregational Year Book* (1861), pp. 11, 332.

121. E. A. Finney, "Journal," pp. 46, 61; *Oberlin Evangelist*, 11 April, 15 August 1860; *Revivalist* (1858), p. 89; (1859), p. 173; (1863), pp. 91, 122.

122. E. A. Finney, "Journal," pp. 60-62.

123. *Revivalist* (1861), p. 182; Surrey Street Chapel (UMFC), Sheffield, Register of church members, 1858-94, May and June 1858, NR-SCL.

124. *Revivalist* (1858), pp. 90, 130; (1859), pp. 174, 187-88; (1864), p. 71; *Christian Advocate*, 12 January 1860; E. A. Finney, "Journal," pp. 52, 57, 59, 72; *St. Ives . . . Gazette*, 26 February 1859; Headley, *Harvest Work*, p. 95.

125. *Bolton Chronicle*, 3 March 1860; Finney, *Memoirs*, p. 467; E. A. Finney, "Journal," pp. 36, 70-71; *Revivalist* (1859), pp. 172, 174; (1860), p. 7; (1862), p. 92; Wheatley, *Mrs. Palmer*, pp. 379, 395; Headley, *Harvest Work*, pp. 94-95.

126. Finney, *Memoirs*, pp. 463-64; *Christian Advocate*, 12 January 1860, 23 July 1863.

127. Headley, *Harvest Work*, p. 103; *Revivalist* (1858), p. 130.

128. *Revivalist* (1859), p. 174.

129. *Revivalist* (1861), p. 141; Wheatley, *Mrs. Palmer*, pp. 355-57; *Christian Advocate*, 24 April 1862.

130. Gilbert, "Growth and Decline," pp. 49, 54, 104, 106.

Conclusion

1. Walter B. Sloan, *These Sixty Years: The Story of the Keswick Convention* (London, n.d.), pp. 9ff.

2. Findlay, *Moody*, pp. 149-91.

Bibliography

A short bibliography cannot hope to be truly representative of the rich mine of printed primary material on evangelicalism. What follows is intended to help in the use of the notes and to list some of the more rewarding works. Several hundred other items that contribute to an understanding of transatlantic revivalism may be found in the bibliography to my "American Religious Revivalism in Great Britain, c. 1826-c. 1863" (D. Phil. thesis, Oxford University, 1974), copies of which are deposited in the Bodleian Library, Oxford, and in Rose Memorial Library, Drew University, Madison, New Jersey.

I. Newspapers and Periodicals

Baptist Annual Register (London)
Baptist Magazine (London)
Baptist Reporter and Missionary Intelligencer (London)
Biblical Repertory and Theological Review, from 1837 *Biblical Repertory and Princeton Review* (Princeton)
Bolton Chronicle
British Banner (London)
British Standard (London)
Christian Advocate and Journal (New York)
Christian News (Glasgow)
Christian Witness (London)
Congregational Magazine (London)
Evangelical Magazine and Missionary Chronicle (London)
Freeman (London)
Messenger of Life (London)
Methodist Magazine (New York)
Methodist Quarterly Review (New York)
Monthly Miscellany of Religion and Letters (Boston)
New York Evangelist

New York Observer
Oberlin Evangelist
Primitive Methodist Magazine (Leicester, Bemersley, London)
Revival (London)
Revivalist (London, 1832-44)
Revivalist (London, Louth, Hull, 1853-64)
Sheffield Iris
Sheffield Mercury and Hallamshire Advertiser
Southern Christian Advocate (Charleston, S.C.)
United Methodist Free Churches Magazine (London)
Wesleyan-Methodist Magazine (London)
Wesleyan Times (London)

II. Autobiographies, Biographies, Memoirs, etc. (Primary and
    Secondary Works)

Adamson, William. The Life of the Rev. Fergus Ferguson. London, 1900.
____. The Life of the Rev. James Morison, D.D. London, 1898.
Allon, Henry. Memoir of the Rev. James Sherman; including an unfinished Auto-
    biography. 2d ed. London, 1863.
Bangs, Heman. The Autobiography and Journal of Rev. Heman Bangs. . . . New
    York, 1872.
Beecher, Lyman. The Autobiography of Lyman Beecher. Edited by Barbara Cross.
    Cambridge, Mass., 1961.
Begbie, Harold. Life of William Booth, The Founder of the Salvation Army. 2 vols.
    London, 1920.
Binfield, Clyde. George Williams and the Y.M.C.A.: A Study in Victorian Social
    Attitudes. London, 1973.
Bradwell, Albert T. Autobiography of a Converted Infidel: being a Record of His
    Experience from childhood to his conversion under the ministry of the Rev.
    J. Caughey at Sheffield, and including a History of his Infidel Opinions. Shef-
    field, 1844.
Campbell, John. Memoirs of David Nasmith: his labours and travels in Great Britain,
    France, The United States, and Canada. London, 1844.
Chidlaw, B. W. The Story of My Life. Philadelphia, 1890.
Clark, D. W. Life and Times of Rev. Elijah Hedding, D.D. New York, 1855.
Coles, George. My Youthful Days. Edited by D. P. Kidder. New York, 1852.
____. My First Seven Years in America. Edited by D. P. Kidder. New York, 1852.
Cumming, Alexander. Memorials of the Ministry of the Rev. Alexander Cumming,
    late of Victoria Free Church, Glasgow. Edinburgh, 1881.
Dale, R. W., ed. The Life and Letters of John Angell James: including an unfinished
    autobiography. 2d ed. London, 1861.
Denison, F., ed. The Evangelist: or Life and Labors of Rev. Jabez S. Swan. Water-
    ford, Conn., 1873.
Dixon, James. Memoir of the late Rev. William Edward Miller, Wesleyan Minister.
    London, 1842.
Dixon, Richard W. The Life of James Dixon, D.D., Wesleyan Minister. London, 1874.

Dow, Lorenzo. *The Dealings of God, Man, and the Devil; as exemplified in the Life, Experience and Travels of Lorenzo Dow.* . . . New York, 1854.

Evans, D. M. *Christmas Evans: a Memoir.* . . . London, 1863.

Ferguson, Robert, and Brown, A. Morton. *Life and Labours of John Campbell, D.D.* London, 1868.

Finney, Charles G. *Memoirs.* New York, 1876.

Headley, P. C. *The Harvest Work of the Holy Spirit. Illustrated in the Evangelistic Labors of Rev. Edward Payson Hammond.* Boston, 1863.

Holland, John. *Memoirs of the Life and Ministry of the Rev. John Summerfield, A.M.* 6th ed. New York, 1845.

Hughes, George. *The Beloved Physician, Walter C. Palmer, M.D., and His Sunlit Journey to the Celestial City.* New York, 1884.

Jackson, Thomas. *The Life of the Rev. Robert Newton, D.D.* London, 1855.

Kirk, Helen. *Memoirs of Rev. John Kirk, D.D.* Edinburgh, 1888.

Knapp, Jacob. *Autobiography.* New York, 1868.

Mahan, Asa. *Autobiography: Intellectual, Moral, and Spiritual.* London, 1882.

Mears, David O. *Life of Edward Norris Kirk, D.D.* Boston, 1877.

Peck, George. *The Life and Times of George Peck, D.D.* New York, 1874.

Rees, William. *Memoirs of the late Rev. W. Williams, of Wern.* Translated by James Rhys Jones. London, 1846.

Spicer, Tobias. *Autobiography of Rev. Tobias Spicer: containing incidents and observations; also some account of his visit to England.* Boston, 1851.

Stevens, Abel. *Life and Times of Nathan Bangs, D.D.* New York, 1863.

Tyler, Bennet. *Memoir of the Life and Character of Rev. Asahel Nettleton, D.D.* 5th ed. Boston, 1855.

Wayland, Francis, and Wayland, H. L. *A Memoir of the Life and Labors of Francis Wayland, D.D., LL.D.* 2 vols. New York, 1867.

Wheatley, Richard. *The Life and Letters of Mrs. Phoebe Palmer.* New York, 1876.

Wight, Ninian. *Memoir of the Rev. Henry Wight.* Edinburgh, 1862.

Wilkinson, John T. *Hugh Bourne, 1772-1852.* London, 1952.

III. Contemporary Works

Baird, Robert. *Religion in America; or, an account of the origin, progress, relation to the State, and present condition of the evangelical churches in the United States.* New York, 1844.

Bangs, Nathan. *A History of the Methodist Episcopal Church.* 4 vols. New York, 1840-41.

Barnes, Albert. "Revivals of Religion in Cities and Large Towns." *American National Preacher* 15(1841):1-72.

Booth, Catherine. *Female Teaching: or the Rev. A. A. Rees versus Mrs. Palmer, being a reply to the pamphlet by the above gentleman on the Sunderland Revival.* 2d ed. London, 1861.

Brief Memoir of the Labours and a Vindication of the Character and Call of the Rev. James Caughey, Including a Critical Examination of the resolution of the Wesleyan Conference, and of the President's declaration prohibitory of his labours, by "A Wesleyan Methodist," A. London, 1847.

Bunton, William. "A Visit to Dr. Palmer's Revival Meetings at the Wesleyan Chapel (Banbury), 1860." Edited by B. S. Trinder. *Cake and Cockhorse: The Magazine of the Banbury Historical Society* 8(1966):75-77.

Burns, W. "Kilsyth, 1839." *Narratives of Revivals of Religion in Scotland, Ireland and Wales*. Glasgow, 1839.

Campbell, John. *Valedictory Services and Farewell Sermon of Professor Finney . . . with critical observations on his preaching.* London, 1851.

Carter, W. B. *The Case Tested: being an Inquiry into the Character and Labours of the Rev. James Caughey*. London, 1847.

Caughey, James. *Earnest Christianity Illustrated; or, Selections from the Journal of the Rev. James Caughey . . . with a Brief Sketch of Mr. Caughey's Life, by John Unwin, Sheffield*. London, 1857.

_____. *Letters on Various Subjects*. 5 vols. London, 1844-47.

_____. *Methodism in Earnest: being the History of a Great Revival in Great Britain*. Edited by Daniel Wise. Boston, 1850.

_____. *Parting Sermon of the Rev. James Caughey . . . delivered in Sans Street Chapel, Sunderland on Friday evening Sept. 4, 1846*. Sunderland, 1846.

_____. *Report of a Farewell Sermon, delivered in the Methodist New Connexion Chapel, Parliament St., Nottingham by the Rev. James Caughey, of America, on the 12 May 1847*. Nottingham, 1847.

_____. *Revival Miscellanies; containing Twelve Revival Sermons, and thoughts on Entire Sanctification*. London, n.d.

_____. *A Voice from America; or, Four Sermons preached by the Rev. J. Caughey, the Great American Revivalist*. 2d ed. Manchester, 1847.

Codman, John. *A Narrative of a Visit to England*. Boston, 1836.

Colton, Calvin. *History and Character of American Revivals of Religion*. 2d ed. London, 1832.

Conant, William C. *Narratives of Remarkable Conversions and Revival Incidents: including . . . an account of the rise and progress of the Great Awakening of 1857-8*. New York, 1858.

Cox, Francis A. *Suggestions designed to promote the Revival and Extension of Religion, founded on observations made during a journey in the The United States of America in the Spring and Summer of 1835*. 5th ed. London, 1836.

Davies, Evan. *Revivals in Wales: Facts and Correspondence supplied by pastors of the Welsh Churches*. London, 1859.

Dialogue on the "Whole Case" of the Rev. James Caughey, by a Wesleyan Leader, A. Sheffield, n.d.

Dixon, James. *Methodism in America: with the Personal Narrative of the Author, during a Tour through a Part of the United States and Canada*. London, 1849.

Durbin, John P. *Observations in Europe, principally in France and Great Britain*. 2 vols. New York, 1844.

Finney, Charles G. *A Fourth Voice from America; or, two sermons preached by the Rev. C. G. Finney . . . at Borough Road Chapel, London, Nov. 22 and 23, 1849*. London, 1849.

_____. *Lectures on Revivals of Religion*. Edited by William G. McLoughlin, Jr. Cambridge, Mass., 1960.

_____. *Lectures on Systematic Theology, embracing Moral Government, the Atonement, Moral and Physical Depravity*. Edited by George Redford. London, 1851.

_____. *Repentance: its Nature, Grounds, Necessity, and Infinite Importance.* London, 1851.

Fish, Henry C. *Primitive Piety Revived, or The Aggressive Power of the Christian Church.* Boston, 1855.

Gregory, Benjamin. *Sidelights on the Conflicts of Methodism, 1827-1852.* London, 1898.

Halliday, S. B., and Gregory, D. S. *The Church in America and Its Baptisms of Fire: Being an Account of the Progress of Religion in America, in the Eighteenth and Nineteenth Centuries, as seen in the Great Revivals in the Christian Church.* New York, 1896.

Humphrey, Heman. *Revival Sketches and Manual.* New York, 1859.

Jarbo, P. J. *A Letter to Mrs. Palmer, in reference to Women Speaking in Public.* North Shields, 1859.

Kendall, James. *Rambles of an Evangelist.* London, 1853.

McArthur, Alexander. *Finney versus Morison: or, Oberlin Strictures on Morisonian Faith.* Glasgow, 1859.

Melson, J. B. *Farewell Address to the Rev. James Caughey, delivered at the Town Hall, Birmingham, July 14th 1847.* Birmingham, 1847.

Palmer, Phoebe. *Faith and Its Effects: or, Fragments from my Portfolio.* London, 1856.

_____. *Four Years in the Old World; comprising the Travels, Incidents, and Evangelistic Labors of Dr. and Mrs. Palmer in England, Ireland, Scotland, and Wales.* New York, 1866.

_____. *Incidental Illustrations of the Economy of Salvation. Its Doctrines and Duties.* London, n.d.

_____. *Present to My Christian Friend on Entire Devotion to God.* London, 1857.

_____. *Promise of the Father; or, A Neglected Specialty of the Last Days.* Boston, 1859.

_____. *The Way of Holiness, with Notes by the Way: being a Narrative of Religious Experience resulting from a determination to be a Bible Christian.* London, 1856.

Protest in favor of The Rev. James Caughey. Sheffield, n.d.

Reed, Andrew, and Matheson, James. *A Narrative of the Visit to the American Churches by the Deputation from the Congregational Union of England and Wales.* 2 vols. London, 1835.

Review of the Whole Case, or What Has Conference Done in reference to The Rev. James Caughey, and why was it done?, A. Sheffield, 1847.

Ward, W. R. *Early Victorian Methodism: The Correspondence of Jabez Bunting, 1830-1858.* London, 1976.

IV. Secondary Works: Books, Articles, and Theses

Boles, John P. *The Great Revival, 1787-1805.* Lexington, Ky., 1972.

Bucke, Emory S., et al., eds. *The History of American Methodism.* 3 vols. Nashville, 1964.

Chadwick, Owen. *The Victorian Church.* 2 vols. London, 1966, 1970.

Cleveland, Catharine C. *The Great Revival in the West, 1797-1805.* Chicago, 1916.

Cross, Whitney R. *The Burned-over District: The Social and Intellectual History of Enthusiastic Religion in Western New York, 1800-1850.* Ithaca, N.Y., 1950.

Currie, Robert. *Methodism Divided: A Study in the Sociology of Ecumenicalism.* London, 1968.

Davies, E. T. *Religion in the Industrial Revolution in South Wales.* Cardiff, 1965.

Dike, Samuel W. "A Study of New England Revivals." *American Journal of Sociology* 15 (1909):361-78.

Findlay, James F., Jr. *Dwight L. Moody: American Evangelist, 1837-1899.* Chicago, 1969.

Fletcher, Robert S. *A History of Oberlin College.* 2 vols. Oberlin, Ohio, 1943.

Gilbert, Alan D. "The Growth and Decline of Nonconformity in England and Wales, with special reference to the period before 1850." D.Phil. thesis, Oxford University, 1973.

Harrison, Brian. *Drink and the Victorians: The Temperance Question in England, 1815-1872.* London, 1971.

Kendall, H. B. *The Origin and History of the Primitive Methodist Church.* 2 vols. London, 1909.

Kent, John. "American Revivalism and England in the Nineteenth Century." *Past and Present Conference Papers, 1966.*

McLoughlin, William G., Jr. *Modern Revivalism: Charles Grandison Finney to Billy Graham.* New York, 1959.

Mead, Sidney E. *Nathaniel William Taylor, 1786-1858: A Connecticut Liberal.* Chicago, 1942.

Miller, Perry. *The Life of the Mind in America: From the Revolution to the Civil War.* New York, 1965.

Owen, William T. "The Life and Thought of Dr. Edward Williams, with special reference to his influence on Welsh and English Nonconformity." Ph.D. thesis, University of London, 1960.

Smith, Timothy L. *Revivalism and Social Reform in Mid-Nineteenth-Century America.* New York, 1957.

Thistlethwaite, Frank. *America and the Atlantic Community: Anglo-American Aspects, 1790-1850.* New York, 1963.

Thompson, E. P. *The Making of the English Working Class.* Rev. ed. London, 1968.

Ward, W. R. *Religion and Society in England, 1790-1850.* London, 1972.

Wardle, Addie G. *History of the Sunday School Movement in the Methodist Episcopal Church.* New York, 1918.

Weber, Herman C. *Presbyterian Statistics through One Hundred Years, 1826-1926.* Philadelphia, 1927.

Weisberger, Bernard W. *They Gathered at the River: The Story of the Great Revivalists and Their Impact on Religion in America.* Boston, 1958.

Wickham, E. R. *Church and People in an Industrial City.* London, 1957.

Index

Abolition. *See* Antislavery sentiment of
  evangelicals
Adams, John Quincy, 42
Adherents, unconverted, 26, 78, 80, 89, 193,
  197, 212
Advertising in revivalism, 22, 76, 78, 117,
  142, 145, 150, 188
Aitken, Robert, 38, 116, 124, 169
Alexander, James W., 17, 144
Allen, Hugh, 146
Allen, Richard, 55
Allon, Henry, 142
Altar, call to the, 13, 15-16, 18, 22, 120. *See
  also* Anxious seat
American Bible Society, 165
American Home Missionary Society, 165
American Sunday School Union, 19, 69
American Systematic Beneficence Society,
  163
American Tract Society, 20, 165
Andrews, Emerson, 135, 170
Anglicans. *See* Church of England
Anti-Catholicism: in America, 18, 24-25, 29,
  66, 104, 164, 168; in Britain, 29, 69-70, 128,
  140, 145, 173, 192
Antinomianism. *See* Strict Calvinism
Anti-Slavery Convention (1843), 135
Antislavery sentiment of evangelicals: in
  America, 42-44, 51, 98, 135-36, 164-65,
  167, 188, 219, 221; in Britain, 32, 42-44,
  66, 103, 135-36, 140, 171, 173. *See also*
  Slavery issue
Anti-State Church Association, 136
Anxious Inquirer, The (James), 137, 185
Anxious meeting. *See* Inquiry meetings

Anxious seat, 8-9, 13, 16-18, 68, 79, 144, 148,
  171, 174, 190, 210. *See also* Altar, call to
  the; Communion rail, call to the; Penitents'
  bench
Arminianism, 8, 10, 60, 103, 190
Armstrong, William, 34, 39
Arthur, William, 191
Asbury, Francis, 11, 29, 32
Associations, 87
Atherton, William, 111, 128-30, 133

Backsliders, 26, 51, 80, 83, 148. *See also*
  Revival converts
Bainbridge, Thomas, 44
Baird, Robert, 17, 135
Baker, Daniel, 21, 204
Bamford, Mr. (lay evangelist), 187
Band Room Methodists, 106
Bangs, Heman, 53
Bangs, Nathan, 12, 182
Baptist Church (America): growing respect-
  ability of, 23; and itinerant evangelists, 21;
  and revivals, 9-10, 54, 150, 160; schism of,
  53, 55, 164; and slavery, 53, 66, 164
Baptist Church (Britain), 60; and America,
  62, 68; and Finney, 138-39; and itinerancy,
  77, 87; patterns of growth and church
  membership of, 61, 80-83, 192, 195, 197,
  209; and revivals, 61-63, 71-73, 76-80, 82,
  94, 148, 169, 171; theology of, 61, 92. *See
  also* Calvinist Dissenters
Baptist Home Missionary Society (BHMS),
  72-73, 83, 137, 139, 153
Barlow, James, 179, 189, 193, 196
Barnes, Albert, 8, 18, 21, 23, 83, 97

Barnes, William, 77
Beatty, Robert, 39
Beaumont, Joseph, 111, 130, 133
Beecher, Edward, 8
Beecher, Henry Ward, 21, 163
Beecher, Lyman, 6, 8, 134-35, 205-6
Belcher, Joseph, 210
Beman, Nathaniel Sidney Smith, 73-74
Benevolent Empire, 24
Benson, Joseph, 40
Bible class, 72, 80, 94, 160
Bible societies, 20
Biblical Repertory and Princeton Review, 138
Birney, James, 43
Blackstock, Moses, 38
Boardman, Richard, 29
Boardman, William, 191
Bolton, Robert, 67
Bonar, Andrew, 99
Bonar, Horatio, 99
Book Concern of Methodist Episcopal Church, 40
Booth, Catherine, 187, 189, 199, 227
Booth, William, 102, 170, 184-85, 187, 189, 199
Bosner, Michael, 172
Bottomley, Thomas, 37
Bourne, Hugh, 106-7, 216
Bowers, Abraham, 39
Bradwell, Albert, 124
Bramwell, William, 40, 115-16, 120, 124, 127-29, 219
Breckinridge, Robert, 66
Brett, Pliny, 55
Brine, John, 61
Bristed, John, 69
British Banner, 141
British Standard, 176
Broadhead, John, 43
Brown, George, 51
Brown, Potto, 136-37, 141-42, 147, 176-77, 189
Buchanan, James, 167
Buckley, John, 34
Bunting, Jabez, 128-29, 133
Burch, Thomas, 38
Burchard, Jedediah, 8
Burder, George, 61
"Burned-over District" (Western New York), 5, 54, 59, 61, 109, 134

Burns, W. C., 99
Burns, William, 95-97, 99
Bushnell, Horace, 19

Calhoun, John C., 42
Calvinism, 104, 191, 215. *See also* Moderate Calvinism; Strict Calvinism
Calvinist Dissenters (England and Wales): in America, 44; and Church of England, 69, 82, 146; and Finney, 85, 92-94, 135-49, 154-55, 176-77, 179; patterns of growth of, 80-83; and revivals, 59-80, 83-86, 127, 136-55, 176-77, 179; and role of women, 188; and slavery, 66, 136; and visiting Americans, 135; in Wales, 85-94. *See also* individual churches such as Baptist Church (Britain); Congregational Church (Britain)
Calvinistic Methodists (Wales), 86-87, 91-92, 174
Calvinists (America): and Methodists, 13-17; and new-measure revivalism, 4-10, 28, 52. *See also* individual churches such as Congregational Church (America); Presbyterian Church (America)
Cambridge, Alice, 106
Campbell, John, 140-42, 145, 147-48, 150, 176-77, 228
Camp-Meeting Methodists, 107
Camp meetings: in America, 4, 11, 13-15, 18, 20, 59, 87, 110, 151, 182; in Britain, 106-7, 117, 172, 198
Capers, William, 102
Carlyle, Thomas, 141
Carter, William, 187, 189, 191
Castlereagh, Lord, 104
Catholic Church. *See* Roman Catholic Church
Caughey, James: and British denominationalism, 190; critics of, 109, 126-33; early career of, 107, 109; and entire sanctification, 121, 144, 191; and Finney, 144, 179, 186; first visit of, to Britain (1841-47), 102, 109-33, 138, 141; and impact of campaigns on church membership, 111-15; later visits of, to Britain (1857-66), 175-76, 186, 188-92, 193, 195-97; political attitudes of, 116-17; portraits of, 108, 122, 132; preaching style of, 118-19, 143; revival converts of, 110-11, 117, 120-21, 123-26, 175-76, 192, 193, 196; revival message of, 118-21, 190-91; revival methods of, 110, 117-20, 127-28, 145, 184, 190; and slavery issue,

131, 188, 219; and urban revivalism, 102, 183, 199; and Wesleyan Methodist Conference, 128-33, 175, 184, 219; work of, in Canada and U.S., 110, 175; mentioned, 21, 134, 139, 148, 174, 177, 183, 185, 187

Causes of revivals. *See* Revivals

Chalmers, Thomas, 98

Charles, David, 173

Chartism, 70-71, 92, 116-17, 125

Chidlaw, Benjamin, 90-91, 94

Children in revivals, 19, 56, 150, 186, 193. *See also* Sunday schools

Cholera revivals: in America (1832), 51, 54; in Britain (1832-33 and 1849), 73, 82, 86, 88-89, 119

Christian Advocate and Journal, 40

Christian News, 100

Christian Revivalists, 106

Christian Witness, 141

Church for Theatre Converts, 189

Church growth and decline. *See* Church membership, statistical patterns of

Church membership, statistical patterns of: in America, 45-56, 159-62, 169, 198, 208; in Britain, 56, 69, 80-83, 85-86, 111-17, 192, 194-95, 197, 198, 209, 213, 218; compared in city and country (America), 27-28, 203. *See also* individual denominations

Church of England: anti-evangelicalism of, 70, 89, 136, 139, 152-54; attitude of American evangelicals to, 29, 152; and conflict with Dissenters, 69, 82; evangelical members of, support revivals, 145-46, 152, 169-70; and Methodists, 103; weakness of, 60, 86, 115; mentioned, 37, 116. *See also* Tractarianism

Church of Scotland, 94, 99

Church rates, 69, 92, 140

Church schism, 73-74; checks revivals, 50, 53, 55, 80; as product of revivals, 9, 23, 97-99, 106-7, 133, 199; stimulates revivals, 86, 99, 164-65. *See also* Methodist Episcopal Church; Methodists (British); Old-School Presbyterian Church; Presbyterian Church (America)

City missions, 24, 39, 95, 97

Clapham sect, 152

Clarke, Adam, 40

Clowes, William, 107

Codman, John, 66

Coke, Thomas, 29, 40, 104

Cokesbury College, 40

Coles, George, 32, 34, 40, 44

Colton, Calvin, 66-68, 85, 149, 152

Communion rail, call to the, 120, 183-84, 190, 196. *See also* Anxious seat

Congregational Church (America): and Methodists, 14-17, 151; and revivals, 5-6, 8, 13-17, 23, 150, 166, 223; and Sunday school converts, 160

Congregational Church (Britain): and America, 62, 68, 74; and Church of England, 154; and Evangelical Union, 100; and Finney, 92-93, 138-42, 144-48, 176-79, 190; and Hammond, 185-86; itinerancy in, 87; and millennialism, 65; patterns of growth and church membership of, 61-62, 80-83, 192, 209; and revivals, 71-80, 85, 90-91, 94, 148, 153, 169; and social class, 24, 82, 149. *See also* Calvinist Dissenters

Congregational Union, 66, 141-42, 147-49, 170, 228

Conversion, theology of, 6, 8-9, 14, 63-64, 98, 138, 152. *See also* Arminianism; Moderate Calvinism; Strict Calvinism; individual revivalists

Conversion of All England, The (Arthur), 191

Converts. *See* Revival converts

Cooke, John, 172

Cookman, George, 37, 43

Cooper, Ezekiel, 12

Cooper, John, 34

Corn Laws, 83, 98, 140

Cornwall, Ebenezer, 222

Countess of Huntingdon's Connexion, 76, 140

Cox, Francis, 68-69, 72, 78, 224

Cox, Samuel H., 66, 135

Cranbrook, James, 146

Craps, John, 77

Crime and revivals, 147, 168, 173, 196. *See also* Revivals and the transformation of society

Cross, Whitney, 54

Crowe, William, 139

Cumming, Alexander, 99

Cunningham, William, 100

Cutler, Benjamin, 17

Cuyler, Theodore L., 172

Dale, R. W., 143

Davenport, James, 5

Davenport, Zachariah, 34
Davidson, James, 38
Davies, John, 39
Dawes, William, 135
Day Star, 100
Days of fasting and prayer, 4, 50, 146, 148
Deism, 25, 50, 61, 140
De Vinne, Daniel, 44
Dickens, John, 40
Dickinson, Anstin, 149
Dissenters' Chapels Act, 83
Divine Life, The (Mahan), 200
Dixon, James, 117, 125, 133, 154
Domestic Manners of the Americans
    (Trollope), 67
Douglass, Frederick, 43
Dow, Lorenzo, 6, 16, 111, 125, 134-35;
    in Britain, 102, 104, 106-7, 116, 127, 129,
    184, 198-200, 216, 219; portrait of, 105
Dunn, Samuel, 133
Durbin, John Price, 102-3, 154
Dutch Reformed Church, 165
Dwight, Timothy, 5-6, 97-98

Eardley, Sir Culling, 152
Economic context of revivals: in America, 20,
    50-56, 162-64, 169; in Britain, 82-83, 94,
    96, 116-17, 170, 214-15. *See also* Revivals
Edwards, Jonathan, 59, 100, 150
Egalitarian aspect of revivals, 3-4, 23, 196
Ekin, George, 39
Elias, John, 87, 90-92
Elliott, Charles, 39-40
Embury, Philip, 29
Emerson, Ralph Waldo, 141
Emigrants from Britain, 33-39, 44, 89-90,
    109-10, 139, 172
Emory, John, 37, 102
Emotionalism in revivals: in America, 4, 8,
    12, 16, 23-24, 67, 74, 93-94, 149-50, 173,
    198-99; in Britain, 62, 64-65, 77, 79, 88,
    103, 120, 126, 144, 149-51, 172-74, 184-85,
    199
Entire sanctification, 39-40, 111, 121, 123,
    143-44, 182-83, 185-86, 190-91, 199-200,
    229. *See also* Caughey, James; Palmer,
    Phoebe; Perfectionism
Episcopalians. *See* Protestant Episcopal
    Church
Evangelical Alliance, 43, 135

Evangelical Calvinists (England and Wales).
    See Calvinist Dissenters (England and
    Wales)
Evangelical Calvinists (Ireland), 171
Evangelical Calvinists (Scotland), 95-101,
    189. *See also* individual churches such as
    Church of Scotland; Free Church (of Scot-
    land); United Secession Church
Evangelical Magazine, 148
Evangelical Revival of the eighteenth century
    (Britain), 60, 150
Evangelical Union, 100, 221; and Finney,
    101, 148, 177, 190
Evangelical unity. *See* Interdenomination-
    alism in revivals
Evangelists. *See* Itinerant evangelism;
    individual evangelists such as Caughey,
    James; Finney, Charles Grandison
Evans, Benjamin, 171
Evans, Christmas, 92
Everett, James, 127, 133, 175
Everett, Lewis, 93
Everett, Robert, 59, 90, 93
Excitement in revivals. *See* Emotionalism in
    revivals
Expectation of revivals, 4, 49-50, 56, 78-79,
    89, 116-17, 151
Extradenominationalism, 189

Factory Education Bill, 83
Faith and Its Effects (Palmer), 182
Farrar, Abraham, 111
Female preaching, 187-88, 191. *See also*
    Palmer, Phoebe
Ferguson, Fergus, Jr., 98-99, 177
Ferguson, Fergus, Sr., 98-99, 177
Field preaching. *See* Camp meetings; Outdoor
    preaching
Finney, Charles Grandison: and British
    denominationalism, 154-55, 179, 190; chal-
    lenge of, to traditional Calvinism in
    America, 5-6, 8-10, 16-17, 28, 95, 148-49,
    215; and Caughey, 144, 179, 186; first
    British visit of (1849-51), 134-48, 150, 152,
    154-55, 223; influence in Britain of writings
    of, 83-85, 89-94, 97-98, 100, 102, 171, 222;
    and Methodists, 16, 177, 179; and Oberlin,
    134; perfectionism of, 135, 143-44, 191;
    portraits of, 7, 178; pulpit style of, 16, 22,
    94, 142-43, 179, 184; revival converts
    of, 17, 136-39, 145-47, 177, 179, 192, 193,

196; revival message of, 138, 143, 190-91; revival methods of, 6, 8, 10, 16, 24, 144-45, 148, 190; second British visit of (1858-60), 101, 176-77, 179, 186, 188-92, 193, 196-97; suspicion of, in Britain, 83-84, 93-94, 137-38, 141, 143-44, 147-48, 176-77; and urban revivalism, 6, 10, 18, 21-22, 25-27, 177, 198-99; views of, on slavery and social reform, 43, 134-36, 145, 167, 188; mentioned, 13, 74, 78, 102, 174. *See also Lectures on Revivals of Religion; Lectures on Systematic Theology; Memoirs*

Finney, Elizabeth Atkinson, 134, 144, 176, 179, 188, 193

"Finney's Revival" (Wales), 84, 86, 93-94, 174

First Great Awakening (America), 5, 18, 150, 159

Fish, Henry Clay, 18

Fisk, Wilbur, 102-3, 115

Five Points House of Industry, 24

Fletcher, John, 40

Fletcher, Joseph, 65

Fly Sheets (Everett), 133

Forlong, Gordon, 186

Formisano, Ronald P., 165

"Four days' meetings," 73, 90, 203. *See also* Protracted meetings

Fox, Henry, 38

Free Church (of Scotland), 99-101, 186

Free Church College, 185

Free Church movements, 24

Free Gospellers, 106

Free Methodists. *See* United Methodist Free Churches

French, Charles, 38

Frontier revivalism, 4, 6, 14, 18, 56, 65, 87-89, 151, 198-99

Fuller, Andrew, 61

Fullerism, 61

Gadsbyites, 61

Gallaway, James, 78-79

Galwad ddifrifol ar Ymofynwr am y Gwirionedd (Roberts), 92-93

Garrettson, Freeborn, 29

Garrison, William Lloyd, 43, 166

General Baptists: growth rates of, 192, 195, 197

George III, 32, 104, 106

German higher criticism, 140-41

Gibson, William, 172

Gilbert, Alan, 71, 80

Gill, John, 61

Glasgow Theological Academy, 84, 99

Gold, George, 43

Goodman, Neville, 175

Goodrich, Chauncey A., 151, 223

Gothard, William, 39

Graham, Charles, 104

Grant, Hay McDowell, 187

Graves, J., 172

Great Change, The (Redford), 139

Greeley, Horace, 170

Green, Ashbel, 29

Green, Samuel, 67, 72

Greenbury, David, 129-30

Griffin, John, 62

Griffiths, Daniel, 148

Griffiths, James, 93

Griffiths, Samuel, 174

Growth rates. *See* Church membership, statistical patterns of

Guinness, Henry Grattan, 187, 191

Guthrie, John, 99-100

Half-Way Covenant, 150

Halliday, Samuel, 20

Hamline, Leonidas, 182

Hammett, William, 50

Hammond, Edward Payson, 171, 185-92, 193, 196-97

Hannah, John, 110

Harcourt, John, 136-37, 177

Harris, John (Congregationalist), 83

Harris, John (Methodist), 38

Harris, Joseph, 92

Harris, Thomas, 127

Harrison, J. F. C., 82

Harrison, William H., 22

Hawes, Joel, 67, 223

Henry, Thomas Charlton, 62

Hewitt, John, 38

Hewitt, Nathaniel, 67

High Calvinism. *See* Strict Calvinism

Higher Christian Life (Boardman), 191

Higher criticism, 140-41

Higher Life Movement, 200

Hill, Rowland, 76

Hinton, John Howard, 63-64, 72, 84

History and Character of American Revivals (Colton), 67, 82

Hitchcock, George, 142, 147-48, 176
Hobsbawm, Eric, 82
Hoby, James, 68-69
Holdich, Joseph, 34
Holiness. See Entire sanctification; Perfectionism
Hollis, George, 38
Hopkinsian Calvinism. See Strict Calvinism
Hosmer, William, 164
House-to-house visiting, 4, 24-25, 79
Howell, Morgan, 93
Hughes, George, 33
Hull, William, 69
Humphrey, Heman, 25, 66, 159
Hunt, Aaron, 13
Hymns, 15, 93, 120, 171. See also Singing
"Hyper-Calvinism." See Strict Calvinism

Immigrants in America: evangelical, 33-39, 44, 90, 109, 137, 139, 182; missions to, 20; Roman Catholic, 18, 24, 168
Independents. See Congregational Church (Britain)
Infidelity, 6, 18, 25, 29, 50, 61, 66, 69-70, 104, 124, 140, 160, 164
Inquiry meetings: in America, 5, 8, 225; in England, 64, 76-77, 79-80, 144-45, 171, 212; in Scotland, 97, 186, 190, 196; in Wales, 87, 90-91
Inskip, John, 21
Interdenominational competition, 14-17, 51, 80, 126
Interdenominationalism in revivals: in America, 15, 160, 162, 165, 182; in Britain, 78-79, 82, 99-100, 102, 136, 171-72, 179, 188-90, 199-200. See also Union prayer meetings
Irving, Edward, 65
Itinerant evangelism (America): in cities, 18, 21-23; criticized, 52-53; in eastern Calvinist churches, 5; in 1857-58 revival, 174; on frontier, 4, 18, 151; of Methodists, 11, 13-14, 32-39; in new measures, 8-9, 17, 68, and passim. See also individual evangelists such as Finney, Charles Grandison; Knapp, Jacob; Nettleton, Asahel
Itinerant evangelism (Britain): in English Calvinist Dissent, 61, 72-73, 77, 137, 148, 153; in English Methodism, 105-7, 109-13, 115-16, 153, 184, and passim; in revival of 1859-63, 186-87; in Scotland, 100; in

Wales, 87-88. See also individual evangelists such as Caughey, James; Dow, Lorenzo; Finney, Charles Grandison; Pulsford, Thomas

Jackson, Andrew, 69
James, John Angell: and disestablishment, 69; and Finney, 83-84, 137-38, 141, 177; and instantaneous conversion, 149; and revivals, 62, 64, 66, 73; welcomes visiting Americans, 59, 67, 185; mentioned, 82, 139, 143
James, John H., 111
Jenkyn, Thomas, 65, 84
Jobson, Frederick, 154, 170
Jones, Humphrey Rowland, 173-74, 191
Jones, John (Llanllyfni), 90
Jones, John (Talsarn), 93
Jones, Michael, 93

Keep, John, 73, 76, 135, 149
Kentucky Revival, 4, 173, 199
Keswick Holiness Meetings, 200
Kirk, Edward Norris, 21-25, 73-76, 78, 97, 135, 142; portrait, 75
Kirk, John, 97-100, 177, 179
Knapp, Jacob, 9, 21-23, 25

Ladies' prayer meetings, 179, 188
Lamb, William, 144, 222
Lancet, 173
Lane Theological Seminary, 134
Lapsed churchgoers. See Backsliders
Lay evangelism, 187, 189, 199. See also individual evangelists such as Hammond, Edward Payson; Palmer, Phoebe; Weaver, Richard
Lay participation in revivalism: in America, 8, 19-20, 25, 39, 160; in Britain, 71-72, 79, 88, 95, 133, 143, 145, 148, 154-55, 171-72. See also individuals such as Barlow, James; Brown, Potto
Leavitt, Joshua, 6, 95
Lectures on Revivals of Religion (Finney), 6, 202; in Britain, 73, 135, 148; in England, 83-84, 107, 136, 141; in Scotland, 97-98; in Wales, 85, 89-94
Lectures on Revivals of Religion (Sprague), 67, 139
Lectures on Systematic Theology (Finney), 138-39, 143, 145, 148

Lee, Jesse, 12
Leeds Temperance Society, 145
Letters (Caughey), 175
Life of Faith, The (Upham), 191
Life of William Carvosso, 40
Livesey, William, 37, 44
Livingstone, Charles, 100
Lord, William, 110
Lorimer, James C., 99
Lutherans, 23
Lynch, T.T., 228

McClelland, James, 44
McClintock, John, 175
McClure, William, 172
McCurdy, David, 38
McIlvaine, Charles Pettit, 66, 170
McKendree, William, 32
McLoughlin, William G., 52
McMullen, Alexander, 34
McNeile, Hugh, 169
Maffit, John Newland, 21-22, 25, 33
Magic Methodists, 106
Mahan, Asa, 134, 142, 144, 200, 221
Mariners' chapels, 20
Marsden, Joshua, 32
Marsh, Joseph, 34
Maternal associations, 71-72, 95
Mather, James, 37
Matheson, James, 68
Mattison, Hiram, 164
May We Hope for a Great Revival? (Arthur), 191
"Means." *See* Moderate Calvinism; New measures
Mears, David O., 160
Melson, J.B., 131
Memoir of David Stoner, 40
Memoirs (Finney), 16, 154
Methodist Episcopal Church, South (MECS), contribution to, 29-44; and British Wesleyan Methodist Conference, 32, 102-3; as church of common people, 11, 16, 23, 54; compared with British Methodists, 125, 154; free seating of, 24; growing refinement of revivalism of, 24; growing status and respectability of, 23, 40, 42, 225; holiness in, 186; influence on Calvinists of, 10, 14-17, 154; and itinerant evangelists, 21-22; and Millerite Adventists, 109; missions of, 20, 39; in New England, 151; and new-measure revivalism, 10-17; organization of, 14; patterns of growth and church membership of, 10, 15, 28, 30-31, 45-54, 158-60, 203; reasons for rapid growth of, 10-11; schism in, 55, 164-65, 219; and slavery, 43-44, 51, 53, 66, 163-64, 219; Sunday schools of, 19; theology of conversion of, 14; in urban areas, 11-28, 30-31, 182; mentioned, 111, 129
Methodist Episcopal Church, South (MECS), 44-48, 53-54, 159-61, 167, 208
Methodist New Connexion, 80, 131, 184-85, 216; growth rates of, 192, 195, 197
Methodist New Connexion Conference, 184
Methodist Protestant Church, 51, 55
Methodist Revival of eighteenth century (Wales), 86
Methodists (America). *See* Methodist Episcopal Church; Methodist Episcopal Church, South
Methodists (Britain), 42; and American slavery, 43-44; church membership and combined growth rates of, 46-48, 56, 80-81, 192, 194; contributions of, to American Methodism, 32-44, 168; evangelical message of, 99, 191; and female ranting, 187; and Finney, 139, 145; influence of, on Calvinist evangelicals, 60, 73, 144, 154; revival methods of, 79, 186; and revivals, 65, 103, 115-16, 150-51, 172; schisms of, 80; status of, 154, 224. *See also* Methodist New Connexion; Primitive Methodist Church (Britain); United Methodist Free Churches; Wesleyan Methodist Church (Britain)
Methods of revivalism. *See* Anxious seat; New measures; Protracted meetings
Miall, Edward, 71
Milbourn, James Codd, 187, 191
Millennialism, 11, 18, 29, 42, 54, 59, 65, 146, 167-69, 191, 196, 213
Miller, John C., 169
Miller, William (Adventist), 52
Miller, William (Wesleyan Methodist), 115, 117, 124
Millerite Adventist movement, 52-54, 82, 109
Millet, Deborah, 10
Millson, J., 144
Milner, Isaac, 37
Minutes of the Annual Conferences of the Methodist Episcopal Church, 32

Mobbing of revivalists, 23, 25, 72, 104
Moderate Calvinism: in America, 3-6, 9-10,
    149; in England, 60-61, 63-64, 78, 83-84; in
    Scotland, 96-100; in Wales, 91-93. *See also*
    Calvinism; New Divinity; Strict Calvinism
Moody, Dwight L., 17, 74, 102, 119, 152,
    172, 184, 200
Moore, John, 146
Moral and social reform. *See* Antislavery
    sentiment of evangicals; Crime and revivals;
    Revivals and the transformation of society;
    Temperance
Morgan, David, 174
Morison, James, 98-100, 177
Morison, John, 141
Morison, Robert, 99
Morisonians. *See* Evangelical Union
Mormons, 82
Morning Chronicle, 126
Morris, Caleb, 76
Morris, Thomas, 107
Mourners' bench. *See* Anxious seat
Mourners' ring, 218

Nash, David, 39
Nasmith, David, 95
Nelson, John, 116
Nettleton, Asahel: in America, 5-9, 25, 78,
    135, 207, 209-10; in Britain, 67, 95, 199
New Dissent. *See* individual churches such as
    Baptist Church (Britain); Calvinist Dis-
    senters; Congregational Church (Britain)
New Divinity, 3, 6, 10; English response to,
    63-64, 83-84. *See also* Moderate Calvinism
New Lebanon Convention, 6, 9, 188
New measures: adopted by British evangelical
    Calvinists, 71-80, 137; and American
    Methodism, 10-17; British views of, 68, 83-
    84, 148; described, 3, 8, 68; modification
    and growing acceptance of, in America,
    17-18; opposed by strict Calvinists in
    America, 8-9. *See also* Anxious seat; Finney,
    Charles Grandison; Protracted meetings
New-School Presbyterian Church, 8, 55, 73-
    74, 97, 160, 164
Newton, Robert, 37, 129-30, 133, 224
"New Views." *See* Moderate Calvinism
New York Evangelist, 95
New York Tribune, 170
Nonconformists. *See* Calvinist Dissenters
North, Brownlow, 187
Noyes, John Humphrey, 143

Oberlin Collegiate Institute, 101, 134-36, 138,
    142-45, 147, 176, 179, 200
Oberlin Evangelist, 17
Oberlin perfectionism. *See* Perfectionism
Odgers, Joseph, 38
O'Kelly, James, 50, 55
Old Dissent, 60
Old-School Presbyterian Church: growth of,
    60, 208; opposes Finney and new measures,
    6, 138, 151; in revival of 1857-58, 160, 165;
    and schism, 55. *See also* Presbyterian
    Church (America)
Oneida Community, 143
Osborn, Elbert, 40
Osborn, George, 129, 133
Ouseley, Gideon, 38, 104, 110-11
Outdoor preaching: in America, 4; and
    Caughey, 128; in England, 62, 72, 78, 125,
    153, 189; in Ireland, 111; in Scotland, 95,
    97, 99; in Wales, 87
Owen, Abraham, 34, 39
Owen, Robert, 70

Paine, Thomas, 50
Palmer, Phoebe: career of, 182; message of,
    190-91, 229; methods of, 183-84, 190;
    portrait of, 180; publications of, 182, 188;
    revival converts of, 183, 185-86, 192, 193,
    196; and slavery, 188; and urban reviv-
    alism, 199; visit to Britain (1859-63), 172,
    182-92, 193, 196-197; and women's rights,
    188; mentioned, 19
Palmer, Walter C.: portrait of, 181. *See also*
    Palmer, Phoebe
Parker, Joel, 18
Parker, Theodore, 141
Parsons, Benjamin, 140
Particular Baptists. *See* Baptist Church
    (Britain)
Pastoral revivals, 4, 21, 62
Patterns of revival. *See* Church membership,
    statistical patterns of; individual denomin-
    ations
Patterson, Adoniram, 163
Patterson, James, 18
Patton, William, 59, 73-74, 95, 170
Payment of revivalists, 22, 128, 136, 188-89
Payne, George, 83
Peace movement, 135, 221
Pease, Louis, 24
Peck, George, 55, 102, 164
Peck, Mrs. George, 10

Penitents' bench, 120, 127, 218. *See also* Anxious seat

Pennefather, William, 172

Perfectionism, 16, 135, 143-44, 168. *See also* Entire sanctification

Perry, John, 39

Phelps, Anson, 66

Pilmoor, Joseph, 29

Plymouth Brethren, 171

Poole, Richard, 175, 179, 191

Popery. *See* Anti-Catholicism; Roman Catholic Church

Power of Prayer (Prime), 170

Prayer meetings: in America, 4, 5, 8, 20, 24, 168; in England, 61, 63, 71, 78-79, 120, 127, 146, 173, 188; in Scotland, 95, 97, 173; in Ulster, 172; in Wales, 87, 93. *See also* Union prayer meetings

Preaching style. *See* Revival preaching style

"Presbygationalists," 5

Presbyterian Church (America): and college revivals, 223; free pews in, 24; on frontier, 4, 87-88; and new-measure revivalism, 6, 8, 13-17, 21, 24, 150; patterns of growth and church membership of, 15, 51-52, 203; schism of, 13, 55, 73, 163; and slavery, 66. *See also* New-School Presbyterian Church; Old-School Presbyterian Church

Presbyterians (Ireland), 44, 172

Presbyterians (Scotland), 44, 94, 189-90. *See also* Church of Scotland; Free Church (of Scotland); United Secession Church

Prescott, Walter, 39

Prime, Samuel I., 170

Primitive Methodist Church (America), 216

Primitive Methodist Church (Britain), 102, 107, 124, 131, 169, 171, 185, 187; growth rates of, 192, 194, 197

Promise of the Father (Palmer), 188

Proselytism, 80, 126. *See also* Interdenominational competition

Protestant Episcopal Church, 15, 24, 42, 160

Protestant Society for the Protection of Religious Liberty, 153

Protracted meetings: in America, 8-9, 14, 18, 20-21, 63, 68, 74, 159, 168; in Britain, 198; in Canada, 110; in England, 73-74, 76-80, 107, 111, 127, 142, 148; in Scotland, 97, 100. *See also* "Four days' meetings"; Special services

Psychology of revivals. *See* Expectation of revivals

Pulsford, Thomas, 73, 77-79, 83, 136

Puseyism, 70, 84, 128, 140

Quaker Methodists, 106

Quakers (America), 24

Quakers (Britain), 135, 139, 171, 192

Radcliffe, Reginald, 187, 190

Raffles, Thomas, 67

Ranters, 118, 142. *See also* Primitive Methodist Church (Britain)

Ravenscroft, S., 34

Raynor, James, 39

"Reaction" after revivals, 22, 50, 179. *See also* Church membership, statistical patterns of

Redemptorists, 168

Redford, Benjamin, 37

Redford, George, 67, 73, 138-39, 141, 144, 176

Reece, Richard, 120, 133

Reed, Andrew, 68, 72, 77, 79, 142, 149, 212, 223

Reed, Mrs. Andrew, 72

Rees, Thomas, 85-86

Reformed Methodism (Britain), 124, 131, 169, 175-76. *See also* Methodists (Britain); United Methodist Free Churches

Reformed Methodists (America), 55

Relief Church, 100

Religious census of 1851, 145, 169

Religious Worship Act, 169

Republican Methodists, 50, 55

Restitution of goods in revivals, 119, 147, 196

Revival converts: age and sex of, 22, 27, 80, 124, 149, 160, 162-64, 186, 193; "backslide," 8-9, 49-50, 68, 83, 125-26, 148; in Caughey's campaigns, 110-11, 117, 120-21, 123-26, 175-76, 192, 193, 196; in Finney's campaigns, 17, 136-39, 145-47, 177, 179, 192, 193, 196; in Palmers' campaigns, 183, 185-86, 192, 193, 196; psychological and social pressures on, 25-26, 54-55, 80, 118-19, 153-54, 160, 163-64, 193, 196; social class and occupations of, 16-17, 26-27, 51-52, 76-78, 96, 123-24, 136, 146-47, 193, 196; statistics of, 76-77, 110, 120-21, 123-26, 137-38, 147, 173, 176-77, 179, 183, 185-86, 192-95, 209; from Sunday schools, 53, 80, 124, 149, 159, 161, 193; from within evangelicalism, 26, 80, 117, 124-26, 145, 192, 193

Revival of 1857-58 in America, 20, 24, 27, 53, 159-69; reported in Britain, 170-74
Revival of 1859-60 in Britain, 169-97, 199
Revival preaching style: aimed at specific groups and individuals, 79, 118-19; in American Methodism, 14, 16; in Britain and America compared, 149; in English Calvinist Dissent, 79, 149; of evangelical Anglicans, 146; in new-measure revivalism, 8, 22; simplicity and directness of, 8, 16, 93, 118-19, 146, 149; in Wales, 86-87, 93. *See also* individuals such as Caughey, James; Finney, Charles Grandison; Palmer, Poebe
Revivalists. *See* Itinerant evangelism; individual evangelists such as Caughey, James; Dow, Lorenzo; Finney, Charles Grandison
Revivalists (of Leeds), 106
Revivals: alleged anti-intellectualism of, 146; allegedly stimulated by social tension, 82; as alleged stimulus to social disruption, 23; and antislavery excitement, 51; and attitudes toward slavery, 42-44; constraints on, in Britain, 147-54; growing refinement of, 23-24, 199; impact of war on, 50, 53-56; and politics (America), 21, 25, 53, 55-56, 165-67, 169; and politics (Britain), 79, 82-83, 91-92, 97-98, 116-17; precipitants of, 49-56, 82-83, and passim; and sectional animosities in America, 165-67, 169; showmanship in, 22; in small towns, 25-27, 89, 150; and social cohesion, 25-27, 89; and social pressures to conform, 13, 25-27, 153-54, 196-97; as stimulus to social harmony, 71, 82-83, 116-17, 119, 164-67, 196, 215; a winter phenomenon, 121, 167. *See also* Economic context of revivals; Egalitarian aspect of revivals; Emotionalism in revivals; New measures; Protracted meetings; Special Services
Revivals and epidemic disease, 54, 88, 119. *See also* Cholera revivals
Revivals and the transformation of society, 3, 18, 26, 79-80, 168-69, 173, 196-97. *See also* Crime and revivals; Millennialism
Revivals in America: Albany, N.Y., 12, 74; Atlanta, Ga., 168; Auburn, N.Y., 17; Baltimore, 12, 18, 162; Boston, 6, 12, 18, 22, 25, 134, 162, 176; Bridgeton, N.J., 162; Bristol, R.I., 14, 25; Brooklyn, 164; Buffalo,

N.Y., 17; Burlington, N.J., 162; Charleston, S.C., 12; Chicago, 162; Cincinnati, 162; Colleges, 223-24; Connecticut, 5; De Kalb, N.Y., 16; Georgia, 15; Hartford, Ct., 134, 223; Ithaca, N.Y., 55; Kansas, 166; Lowell, Mass., 27; Massachusetts, 5; Morrisville, Pa., 162; Mystic, Ct., 25; Newark, N.J., 12, 175; New England, 18, 50, 209; New Haven, Ct., 12, 18; New Orleans, 22; New York City, 6, 12, 15, 18, 20, 24, 26, 45, 59, 74, 134, 162, 168, 175-76, 229; New York Mills, 25; New York State, 5; Northampton, Mass., 68; Philadelphia, Pa., 6, 12, 18, 162, 175; Pittsfield, Mass., 25, 110; Providence, R.I., 12, 134; Remsen, N.Y., 174; Rochester, N.Y., 16, 17, 24, 26-27, 134; Salisbury, Ct., 25; Scranton, Pa., 164; Steuben, N.Y., 174; Steubenville, Ohio, 162; Trenton, N.J., 45; Washington, D.C., 12, 15. *See also* First Great Awakening (America); Second Great Awakening
Revivals in Canada: Hamilton, 182; Montreal, 110
Revivals in England: Andover, 62; Barnet, 172; Bath, 62; Birmingham, 76, 111, 113-14, 137-39, 185; Black Country, 169; Bolton, 177-78, 189, 192, 193, 196; Boston, Lincs., 73; Bradford, Yorks., 170; Bristol, 62, 176; Carlisle, 183; Chesterfield, 111; Congleton, 106; Cornwall, 103, 169, 184-85; Cumberland, 100; Exeter, 176; Guernsey, 184; Hanley, 175; Haworth, 78-79; Hertfordshire, 78; Houghton, Hunts., 136-37, 177; Huddersfield, 111, 113-14; Hull, 111-12, 114; Huntingdon, 177, 188-89; Lancashire, 82; Leeds, 111-12, 114, 125-26; Leicester, 176; Lincoln, 111; Lincolnshire, 176; Liverpool, 111-12, 114, 125; London, 76-79, 140-49, 169, 176-78, 182, 189; Louth, 175; Macclesfield, 196; Manchester, 175, 179, 185-86, 188-90; Newcastle-on-Tyne, 183, 189; North Shields, 183, 196; Northumberland, 100; Norwich, 62; Nottingham, 111, 176, 185; Portsea, 62; Reading, 62; Rochford, Essex, 77; St. Ives, Cornwall, 170; St. Ives, Hunts., 177; Scarborough, 171; Sheffield, 78-79, 111-12, 114-26, 170, 175, 192-93; Stockport, 78; Sunderland, 111, 183, 196; Walsall, 176, 185; West Bromwich, 79; Wolverhampton, 185, 196; Worcester, 139; York, 111, 113-14; York-

shire, 82. *See also* Evangelical Revival of eighteenth century

Revivals in Ireland: Ahoghill, 172-73; Bandon, 110; Belfast, 182; Dublin, 110. *See also* Ulster Revival of 1859

Revivals in Scotland, 65, 96-97, 103, 173, 182; Aberdeen, 96, 177, 189; Annan, 189, 199; Cambuslang, 94; Dundee, 96; Edinburgh, 177-78, 188, 190; Glasgow, 97, 177, 183, 190; Greenock, 95; Kilmarnock, 96; Kilsyth, 94, 96-97; Kirk o'Shotts, 94; Lanarkshire, 96, 196; Lawers, 94; Moulin, 94; Musselburgh, 185-86; Perth, 96; Shotts, 96

Revivals in Wales, 85-86, 93-94, 174, 185; Cardiff, 189, 196; Cardiganshire, 174; Llanuwchllyn, 91; Merionethshire, 91; Merthyr Tydfil, 88. *See also* "Finney's Revival" (Wales); Welsh Revival of 1859

Rivulet affair, 176, 227

Roberts, John, 92-93

Roberts, Robert R., 110

Roberts, Samuel, 92

Roby, William, 61

Roe, Charles Hill, 72, 76-77, 136-37, 177

Roman Catholic Church, 37, 70, 104, 128, 168, 173. *See also* Anti-Catholicism

Routledge, William, 39

Rudé, George, 82

Rusk, James, 37

Rutherford, Alexander, 99-100

Ryle, John C., 169

Sabbatarianism, 140, 159

Salvation Army, 102, 189

Sanctification. *See* Entire sanctification; Perfectionism

Sankey, Ira D., 172, 184, 200

Saunders, Moses, 79

Schism. *See* Church schism

Scott, John, 129

Scott, Orange, 43

Scott, Robinson, 172

Scottish Congregational Union, 99

Scripture Doctrine of Christian Perfection (Mahan), 144

Second Great Awakening, 3-4, 18, 45, 50, 52, 55-56, 151, 223

Secular press and revivals, 23, 27, 126, 159, 170, 188

Seren Gomer, 92

Shaftesbury, seventh earl of, 152, 169, 200

Sharman, Abraham, 124, 133

Sharman, John, 133

Sherman, James, 67, 72, 76, 83, 141-42, 144, 212

Shipherd, John Jay, 134

Showmanship in revivals, 22

Sigston, James, 129

Sim, George, 34

Simpson, Matthew, 175

Singing, 22, 87, 107, 183. *See also* Hymns

Skinner, Thomas Harvey, 18

Slavery issue: and American evangelicals, 42-44, 51, 53, 66, 131, 135-36, 145, 164-65, 167, 198; and influence on revivals, 51, 53, 165-67, 169. *See also* Antislavery sentiment of evangelicals

Smith, Hannah Pearsall, 200

Smith, Robert Pearsall, 200

Sneath, Richard, 13

Social class in revivals. *See* Revival converts

Social harmony stimulated by revivals. *See* Revivals

Socialism, 70, 126, 160, 164, 167

Social morality of revivals. *See* Crime and revivals; Revivals and the transformation of society; Slavery issue

"Society" meetings, 87

Soule, Joshua, 102

Sparkes, Thomas, 39

Special services, 76-77, 127, 136-47, 176, 182-85, 189. *See also* Protracted Meetings; Revivals in England

Spicer, Tobias, 10, 15

Sprague, William Buell, 59, 67-68, 100, 138

Spring, Gardiner, 26, 66

Spurgeon, Charles Haddon, 169, 174, 191

Stead, Henry, 39

Stevens, Abel, 165

Stevenson, George, 34

Stevenson, John, 76

Stillwellites, 55

Stokes, Charles, 39

Stow, Baron, 170

Stowell, Hugh, 169

Strauss, David Friedrich, 140-41

Strawbridge, Robert, 29

Strict Calvinism: in America, 4-6, 9-10, 13-14, 17; in England, 60-61, 78, 148-49; in Scotland, 94, 96; in Wales, 91-92

Stuart, Moses, 83, 97

Summerfield, John, 37, 42; portrait of, 41
Summersides, William, 107
Sumner, John Bird, 170
Sunday schools, 61, 153, 182; and revivals
    (America), 19, 26, 39, 72, 160, 162; and
    revivals (Britain), 72, 80, 89, 94-95, 146-
    47, 193, 197
Swan, Jabez, 9, 21-22, 25

Taber, Gideon, 154
Tackaberry, John, 38
Tappan, Arthur, 95, 134-35
Tappan, Lewis, 6, 67, 134-35
Taylor, Dan, 61
Taylor, Nathaniel W., 6
Taylor, William, 174
Temperance, 4; in America, 18, 21, 26-27, 44,
    168, 182, 223; in Britain, 67, 196, 210, 221;
    in England, 79-80, 119-20, 135-36, 140,
    145; in Scotland, 95-96, 98, 100; in Wales,
    90, 94
Tent services, 72, 78, 136
Theatres, preaching in, 6, 21, 169, 189, 200
Theology of revivals. *See* Arminianism; Con-
    version, theology of; Moderate Calvinism;
    Strict Calvinism
Thompson, Edward, 117
Thompson, Thomas, 39
Tract distribution, 20, 61, 71, 79, 95, 146
Tractarianism, 70, 84, 128, 140
Treffry, Richard, Sr., 116
Tregelles, Samuel, 176
Trollope, Frances, 67, 69
Trotter, John, 191
Tuesday meeting, 182, 191. *See also* Union
    prayer meetings
Turner, Frederick Jackson, 151

Ulster Revival of 1859, 159, 172-74, 177
Union chapels, 136, 138, 142
Union of Presbyterian Synods, 172
Union prayer meetings, 82, 160, 162, 171,
    174, 189, 227. *See also* Interdenomination-
    alism in revivals
Unitarians (America), 6, 17, 25, 160
Unitarians (Britain), 146, 192
United Methodist Free Churches, 171, 185,
    187; and Caughey, 175-76, 195; and Finney,
    177; growth rates of, 192, 195, 197
United Secession Church, 97-100
Universalists, 25, 160

Unwin, John, 131, 133, 175
Upham, Thomas, 191
Urban revivalism, 198-99; adjustments in,
    from 1820s in America, 18-28, 204; and
    American Methodism, 12-13, 15. *See also*
    Caughey, James; Finney, Charles Grandison;
    Palmer, Phoebe; Revivals in America;
    Revivals in England

Vagrant Act, 153
Van Buren, Martin, 224
Vasey, Thomas, 29
Village preaching, 61-62
Visit to the American Churches (Reed and
    Matheson), 97
Voluntary system in America, 3, 37, 56, 68-
    69, 152, 154, 171, 198

Wakeley, Joseph, 45
Walters, Thomas, 34
Ward, Pelatiah, 54
Wardlaw, William, 67
Watkins, Ruth, 107
Watson, Thomas, 38
Waugh, Thomas, 110
Way of Holiness, The (Palmer), 182
Way of Salvation, The (Morison), 98
Wayland, Francis, 3, 9, 17, 135, 151-52
Weaver, Richard, 184, 187, 189
Weeks, Edward, 144, 182
Weld, Theodore, 42
Wells, Algernon, 70
Welsh Revival of 1859, 159, 173-74
Welsh Temperance Society, 90
Wesley, John, 29, 37, 40, 120, 125
Wesley Banner and Revival Record, The, 133
Wesleyan Methodist Association, 131, 192,
    195, 197
Wesleyan Methodist Church (America), 43
Wesleyan Methodist Church (Britain): and
    Caughey, 110-33, 175, 219; and Dow, 104-
    7, 219; and entire sanctification, 121; and
    evangelists, 184-85; and Finney, 179; in
    Ireland, 172, 192, 194, 197; and Palmers,
    182-85; patterns of growth and church
    membership of, 111-17, 192, 194, 197, 213,
    219; receives American delegates, 37, 102-
    3; and respectability, 42, 117, 125; and re-
    vivals, 103-7, 126-27, 169, 171, 174; schism
    in, 115, 131, 133, 199; in Sheffield, 124; and
    slavery, 103; and temperance, 119-20; in

Wales, 91, 174, 192, 194, 197. *See also* Methodists (Britain)

Wesleyan Methodist Conference (Britain): and Caughey, 110-11, 128-33, 175, 219; and Dow, 104, 107, 219; and female preaching, 187; and Palmers, 184-85; relations of, with American Methodists, 37, 208

Wesleyan Methodist Magazine, 106

West, Francis, 127

Western Christian Advocate, 40

Whatcoat, Richard, 29

Wheeler, William, 37

Whitefield, George, 18, 102

Wight, Henry, 98

Williams, Edward, 60-61, 92

Williams, George, 142, 147-48, 176

Williams, Robert, 29

Williams, William (Llandeilo), 91

Williams, William (Wern), 90

Williamson, Richard, 39

Wilson, John, 40

Wilson, William, 67

Winchester, Lewis, 62

Wise, Daniel, 43, 164

Witherspoon, John, 215

Women in revivals, 8, 13-15, 19, 143. *See also* Female preaching; Finney, Elizabeth Atkinson; Ladies' prayer meetings; Maternal associations; Palmer, Phoebe; Revival converts

Women's rights, 188

Work of the Holy Spirit, The (Hinton), 63

World's Anti-slavery Convention, 135

World's Temperance Convention, 135

Worrell, Henry, 182

Yale Seminary, 5-6, 151

Young, Robert, 149, 183, 187

Young Men's Christian Association, 27, 165, 171

ABOUT THE AUTHOR

Richard Carwardine is a lecturer in American history at the University of Sheffield, England. He specializes in nineteenth-century popular religion and in social and reform movements in Britain and America, and has had an article published in the *Journal of American History*.